W9-BRC-449

DICTIONARY OF PROJECT MANAGEMENT TERMS

THIRD EDITION

J. LeRoy Ward, PMP, PgMP

Published by

ESI International
901 North Glebe Road, Suite 200
Arlington, Virginia 22203

© 2008 by ESI International

All rights reserved. No part of this publication may be reproduced,
stored in a retrieval system, or transmitted, in any form or by
any means, electronic, mechanical, photocopying, recording, or
otherwise, without the prior written permission of
ESI International.

First Edition 1997
Second Edition 2000
Third Edition 2008

Printed in the United States of America

ISBN 978-1-890367-45-9

"CAPM" is a certification mark of the Project Management
Institute, Inc., which is registered in the United States and other
nations.

"OPM3" is a certification mark of the Project Management
Institute, Inc., which is registered in the United States and other
nations.

"PgMP" is a certification mark of the Project Management
Institute, Inc., which is registered in the United States and other
nations.

"PMBOK" is a trademark of the Project Management Institute,
Inc., which is registered in the United States and other nations.

"PMI" is a service and trademark of the Project Management
Institute, Inc., which is registered in the United States and other
nations.

"PMI-RMP" is a service mark of the Project Management
Institute, Inc., which is registered in the United States and other
nations.

"PMI-SP" is a service mark of the Project Management Institute, Inc., which is registered in the United States and other
nations.

"PMP" is a certification mark of the Project Management
Institute, Inc., which is registered in the United States and other
nations.

To Patty—

Thanks for letting me "commandeer" the kitchen table with all my materials for more than six months while working on this third edition. If nothing else, we certainly learned how to expertly eat our dinners balanced on our laps as we watched the evening news!

Acclaim for *Dictionary of Project Management Terms:*

"I have known LeRoy Ward for over 15 years, and he never ceases to amaze me. His depth and breadth of knowledge in the world of project management are truly unequalled. This new book sets a new standard in reference material for those attempting to learn project speak. Anyone working in the project management arena who does not possess this masterfully constructed, easy-to-use compendium of terms and terminology will see their ability to communicate and understand their peers severely impacted. This is a MUST have!"

— Lee R. Lambert, PMP, CEO, Lambert Consulting Group.
Dublin, Ohio

"LeRoy Ward's book contains an exhaustive collection of terms and definitions that are indispensable to the working vocabulary of today's project management professionals. This work, offering the global project management community the latest jargon that project managers use every day, presents clear, concise meanings, often with detailed examples. This dictionary is an indispensable reference for the industry practitioner!"

— Prabir K. Bagchi, PhD, Senior Associate Dean and
Professor of Operations and Supply Chain Management,
School of Business, The George Washington University.
Washington, DC

"With the increased need for global project management expertise, guides like the Dictionary of Project Management Terms *by LeRoy Ward are a must-have for the industry practitioner. No project manager should be without it!"*

— Ricardo Viana Vargas, MSc, IPMA-B, PMP, President,
Macrosolutions and Member of the Project Management
Institute (PMI®) Board of Directors.
Belo Horizonte, Brazil

"LeRoy Ward brings his expertise over many years in project management to create the definitive list of PM terms. The Dictionary of Project Management Terms *is a valuable addition to any project manager's library but especially so for those studying for the PMP® exam. This is the most comprehensive list available and is invaluable for any project manager as a reference tool."*

— Ron Kempf, PMP, MBA, Principle, RDK Associates and former Director of PM Competency Development, HP Services. Commerce, Michigan

"This book is one of the rare examples of a successful marriage of quantity and quality. No wonder that, along with the PMBOK® Guide, *it is one of the two most popular, most recognized, and most useful books among project management professionals in Poland. And no wonder that it became the basis for creating and promoting a common project management terminology, which is one of the most crucial aspects of communication in the PM environment."*

— Piotr Maciejczyk, Chairman, Management Training and Development Center. Warsaw, Poland

"My warmest regards for Mr. Ward's dedication and contribution of this excellent book. Project management is now a global language in any business field. I am sure that this book will be a great solution for every level of project manager to promote a better understanding among their teams and clients."

— Akira Sugino, President, Fuji Xerox Learning Institute. Tokyo, Japan

"Effective communication is at the heart of project management, and a common language is essential for effective communication. This edition of the Dictionary of Project Management Terms *is an accurate, authoritative, and accessible resource that defines our common language. It belongs on the desk of every project manager."*

— Scott Williams, Chief Learning Officer, Nexient Learning. Toronto, Canada

Contents

Preface

In the more than 11 years since the first edition of this work—originally titled *Project Management Terms: A Working Glossary*—was published, the discipline of project management not only has undergone an evolution but also has witnessed a revolution! Bold statement, I know, but let's look at the facts. As we go to press, there are more than 44,000 books about project management on Amazon.com, more than 25,000 project management jobs listed on MonsterIndia.com, roughly 20 million licensed users of Microsoft® Project, a quarter of a million PMP®*s (and an equal number of PMI®**members), and, get this, more than 103,000,000 hits on Google! And the growth continues unabated. I daresay there exist few other disciplines that have seen such rapid growth in such a relatively short period of time.

But let's look beyond the numbers and see where the quiet revolution is occurring. More than 10 years ago, Dr. Victor Hartmann, then Head of Global Drug Development for Novartis Pharmaceuticals (Basel, Switzerland), and one of our clients, remarked to me: "I want our project managers to be the CEOs of their projects." And who could blame him? According to the Tufts Center for the Study of Drug Development, the average drug costs $800 million and takes 11 years to develop. Someone responsible for that kind of project should indeed have the skills of a CEO. Since then, I have heard many other executives make similar proclamations. In other words, they want their project and program managers to be business leaders. Accordingly, with this distinct trend in mind, I have taken the liberty of adding a number of general business, financial, investment, and accounting terms that someone who is, indeed, the CEO of their projects should know.

---

*"PMP" is a certification mark of the Project Management Institute, Inc., which is registered in the United States and other nations.

**"PMI" is a service and trademark of the Project Management Institute, Inc., which is registered in the United States and other nations.

Another key development in project management is the impressive work that the U.S. government is doing to develop world-class project and program managers to successfully execute large, complex initiatives in the fields of information technology, defense, health care, construction, infrastructure development, research and development, and a host of other mission-critical areas. As a whole, the U.S. government has developed a comprehensive list of project and program manager competencies, has constructed curriculum paths for various categories of projects and applications, has established career paths and internal certifications for their project and program managers, and has required federal agencies seeking funds for major projects to assign highly competent project managers to lead the effort. In recognition of the tremendous advancement the U.S. government has made in the field, I have added terms that many of its project and program managers will find useful in their work, as may many others as well.

Finally, in my global travels I have witnessed an evolving international business culture populated by professionals who tend to read the same business books and listen to the same keynote speakers, who are educated outside their home countries, and who feel just as comfortable in a boardroom in Tokyo as one in Bangalore. I have heard such idiomatic expressions as "a no-brainer" spoken by a Singaporean project manager as well as a Swedish program manager. I have heard similar kinds of expressions wherever I travel. And, I often find that project and program managers around the world like to know what the latest expressions are, no matter where they originate. Toward that end, I included some of the more widely used idiomatic expressions that one might hear in a team meeting regardless of where one is practicing project management.

All together then, this third edition contains almost twice as many terms as the second edition. In the process of compiling this work, I have made an honest attempt to reach far and wide to gather relevant, practical, useful terms for those of us in the field. I have purposely gone outside my own borders and made a sincere attempt to create an international work that any project or program manager anywhere will find helpful. With the kind assistance of my colleagues at ESI International I have also redesigned the book to fit easily into your purse, bag, backpack, or briefcase with a soft cover that folds easily while reading, all to make it easier to find the information you need.

If, after several years of use, your version is torn, tattered, dog-eared, marked up, and covered with coffee stains, then, and only then, will I have considered my effort a success.

I hope you find it a useful, valuable reference.

Oak Hill, Virginia
August 2008

About the Author

J. LeRoy Ward, Executive Vice President, is responsible for ESI International's worldwide product offerings and international partnerships. Complementing a 17-year career with four U.S. federal agencies, Mr. Ward has delivered project management programs to clients around the world.

Mr. Ward has authored numerous articles and publications: *PMP®Exam: Practice Test and Study Guide;* with Ginger Levin, *PMP®Exam Challenge!* and *PgMP^{SM*} Exam: Practice Test and Study Guide;* with Carl Pritchard, *The Portable PMP® Prep: Conversations on Passing the PMP®Exam*, a nine-disc CD audio set; and with multiple authors, *ProjectFRAMEWORK®: A Project Management Maturity Model.* A dynamic and popular speaker, Mr. Ward frequently presents on program and project management and related topics at professional association meetings and conferences worldwide.

Mr. Ward holds bachelor of science and master of science degrees from Southern Connecticut State University and a master of science degree in technology management *with distinction* from American University. He is a member of numerous professional associations, including the International Project Management Association, the American Society of Training and Development, and the Project Management Institute (PMI®). He is certified by PMI® as a Project Management Professional (PMP® No. 431) and a Program Management Professional (PgMP^{SM}), one of the first to earn the designation.

---

*"PgMP" is a certification mark of the Project Management Institute, Inc., which is registered in the United States and other nations.

About ESI International

ESI International delivers continuous learning programs that help technical and specialized professionals to better manage their programs, projects, contracts, requirements, and vendor relationships. Our high-quality training and professional services include more than 100 cross-functional courses as well as assessments and coaching services. Along with our academic partner, The George Washington University, ESI awards industry-recognized certificates, including Associate's Certificates in Project Management and Contract Management; Master's Certificates in Program Management, Project Management, Project Management with a Concentration in IT Project Management, and Government Contracting; an Advanced Master's Certificate in Project Management; and Professional Certificates in Business Analysis and Business Skills.

Our extensive global infrastructure, proven operational excellence, and results-oriented philosophy allow our corporate and government clients to develop their employees' skills, consistently implement strategic plans, and increase the effectiveness of their internal systems and processes. Since 1981, ESI has served more than 950,000 professionals and 1,000 clients worldwide.

Call us or visit our Web site at www.esi-intl.com for more information about ESI's products and services.

Americas: (888) ESI-8884 or +1 (703) 558-3000
EMEA: +44 (0)20 7017 7100
Asia Pacific: +65 6505 2040
India: +91 80 41141344

Acknowledgments

The late Michael Bloomfield, one of the great blues and rock guitar virtuosos of the 1960s and 1970s, and founder of one of the best bands on earth (my humble opinion), The Electric Flag, once remarked that there's music all around us, in every sound we hear. And, to me, a large part of that music is the language we speak. In my 32 years in project management my travels have taken me around the world many times over. I've been exposed to literally hundreds of different languages and dialects. It never ceases to amaze me how the human race has divided itself up into so many ways to communicate, and yet, in business, the world has converged on one: English. Why? It's simple: If everyone can speak the same language, it's just a lot easier to understand one another.

The language of project management is no different. That's why, more than 11 years ago, I made a humble attempt to offer the industry a consistent lexicon drawing from a wide variety of sources and adding many on my own. The response has been overwhelming. Today, more than 200,000 copies of this dictionary are in circulation and used daily by project managers around the world. And, many very kind people approach me all the time at conferences and other industry events thanking me for my efforts.

However, it is my turn to thank my coworkers, colleagues, and friends who have helped make this third edition possible.

First and foremost, I must recognize and sincerely thank **Myron Taylor, Editor-in-Chief,** and **Mary Saxton, Senior Editor,** for their incredible dedication, commitment, and just plain hard work to make this edition a reality. Myron project managed the effort superbly, coordinating all the various aspects of book production including editing, graphic arts, font selection and formatting, page layouts, and printing. With the project in his hands, I never had to worry about the schedule. Mary and I have now worked together on several publications, and one could not find a more accomplished professional. She assiduously reads and rereads every word to ensure it conveys the message and intent accurately and clearly. Her attention to detail is legendary, noteworthy, and certainly required when tackling my writing! I am indebted to her more than she knows for improving upon my work and making it easier to digest and understand.

I would also like to thank **Ginger Levin (Chairperson)** and the members of the Technical Advisory Board, including **Raed Haddad, Nancy Nee, Renee Speitel,** and **Paul Travers.** These individuals not only are accomplished project managers in their own right but also have honed their craft working in, or consulting for, many of the world's largest corporations implementing comprehensive project, program, and portfolio management practices on a global basis for literally thousands of people. Their perspective on project management is indeed global, and you, the reader, are the beneficiary of their collective experience. Their studious review of and commentary on the terms included here ensure that we have not created a publication for its own sake, but for the explicit use of practitioners in the field.

I am especially pleased to thank **Angela Costanzo, Graphic Designer,** for her very professional cover design. For this third edition, I wanted something completely different from the first two editions. Angela created many samples from which to choose, and her creative flair and expertise are evident in the book you now hold in your hands. Thanks also to **Erin Ward, Research Assistant** (and my daughter!) for the many hours she spent one summer trolling through many Web sites and source documents checking and rechecking my selections. This can be arduous and detailed work, but is is necessary for a book such as this and she did it superbly.

Finally, I want to thank **Mike Burns, Head of Document Design,** for transforming the final manuscript into a publication-ready document, expertly formatted for final publication. Formatting a book like this takes patience, skill, and a keen eye, and Mike has all of these.

My thanks to you all!

Technical Advisory Board

Ginger Levin, PMP, PgMP, D.P.A.
Chairperson
Independent Consultant
Lighthouse Point, Florida

Raed S. Haddad, MS, MSCE
Senior Vice President
Global Delivery Services
ESI International
Arlington, Virginia

Nancy Y. Nee, MS, PMP
Executive Director
Business Analysis Programs
ESI International
Arlington, Virginia

Renee Speitel
Principal
R&R Speitel Associates
Former Vice President, Worldwide Engagement PMO
HP Services
Marlborough, Massachusetts

Paul Travers, PMP
First Vice President
Global Infrastructure Solutions Program Management
Merrill Lynch
Hopewell, New Jersey

Introduction

Whether you're looking for definitions of terms, phrases, or acronyms, you'll find them all arranged alphabetically in this indispensable reference. Each entry is succinctly defined and cross-referenced, providing important insight into some aspect of project management.

Four types of references assist you in using this dictionary to its fullest extent:

See references following acronyms direct you to the complete spelling and definition of the entry. You can find the definition of scores of acronyms, such as ACWP (actual cost of work performed) and PDCA (plan-do-check-act cycle).

See references following terms or phrases direct you to the more widely used terms or phrases and their full definitions. For example, if you look up responsibility matrix, you will be directed to responsibility assignment matrix for the full definition.

See also references following terms or phrases direct you to other entries that provide additional or comparative information. For example, when you look up the word acceptance, you'll find that it is one way of dealing with the consequences of a risk. But you'll also find a reference to the other three ways of dealing with the consequences of a risk: avoidance, mitigation, and transfer. That means if you remember just one of the ways to deal with risk, this dictionary will lead you to the others!

And finally, the *Also called* references following entries denote terms that are often used interchangeably, such as analogous estimating and top-down estimating.

For those of you studying for the PMP® or PgMP℠ certification exams, you will find this dictionary an excellent study aid.

AACE

See Association for the Advancement of Cost Engineering.

ABBA CHART

Graph (named for Wayne Abba) that is composed of four different indicators showing trends in historic and projected efficiency to date.

ABC

See activity-based costing.

ABC/M

See ABC method.

ABC METHOD (ABC/M)

Inventory-management technique that categorizes items in terms of importance. More emphasis is placed on the higher-cost items (A) than on the lower-cost (B) with little time focused on those categorized as (C).

ABILENE PARADOX

Groupthink as described by management expert Jerry B. Harvey in his 1988 book *The Abilene Paradox and Other Meditations on Management* as well as in a short video. *See also* groupthink.

ABM

See activity-based management.

ABOUT FACE

To change direction.

ABOVEBOARD

Open and honest.

ACCEPTABLE QUALITY LEVEL (AQL)

Maximum number of nonconforming items that can be included in an acceptable lot, usually expressed as a percentage. *See also* lot.

ACCEPTANCE

(1) Risk response strategy that prepares for and deals with the consequences of a risk, either actively (for example, by developing a contingency plan to execute if the risk event occurs) or passively (for example, by accepting a lower profit if some activities run over budget). *See also* avoidance, mitigation, *and* transfer.

(2) In U.S. government contract law, also referred to as acceptance of offer. In contract law, the act of accepting an offer (that is, awarding a contract based on an offer under a request for proposals).

(3) In U.S. government contract law, also referred to as acceptance of work. The act of an authorized representative of the government by which the government, for itself or as agent of another, assumes ownership of existing identified supplies tendered or approves specific services rendered as partial or complete performance of the contract.

ACCEPTANCE CRITERIA

Requirements that a project or system must demonstrably meet before customers accept delivery.

ACCEPTANCE PERIOD

Number of calendar days available to a buyer for awarding a contract from the date specified in the solicitation for receipt of offers.

ACCEPTANCE REVIEW

Process by which a buyer or end user determines that the item, product, or service presented for acceptance complies with its specification.

ACCEPTANCE SAMPLING

Statistical procedure used in quality control that involves testing a batch of products to determine whether the proportion of units having a particular attribute exceeds a given percentage. Sampling involves three determinations: batch size, sample size, and the maximum number of defects that will be allowed before rejecting the entire batch.

ACCEPTANCE TEST PROCEDURE

Step-by-step set of instructions for the preparation and operation of the acceptance test and the evaluation of the acceptance test results.

ACCEPTANCE TESTING

Applying performance and capability measurements to project deliverables to ensure that they meet specifications and requirements and satisfy the customer.

ACCEPTANCE TIME

Definite period of time that one party to a negotiation has to accept an offer by another party. Instead of forcing a quick decision, this tactic can be used to give the other negotiator more time to grasp a solution or ideas.

ACCOUNTABILITY

(1) Total responsibility of an individual for the satisfactory completion of a specific assignment.

(2) State of assuming liability for something of value, either through a contract or because of one's position of responsibility.

ACCOUNTABILITY MATRIX

See responsibility assignment matrix.

ACCOUNTING PERIOD

Set period of time, usually one month, in which project costs and revenues are posted for information and analysis.

ACCOUNTS PAYABLE

List of debts owed based on the purchase of services, inventory, supplies, and so on.

ACCOUNTS RECEIVABLE

List of monies due on current accounts based on the sale of products or services.

ACCREDITATION

Formal recognition granted by a regulatory board to an organization identifying it as being qualified to perform ISO 9000 quality system assessments of other organizations.

ACCRUAL ACCOUNTING

Method of accounting whereby revenue is recognized when it is realized and expenses are recognized when incurred, without regard to time of receipt or payment of cash.

ACCRUED BENEFIT COST METHOD

Actuarial cost method under which units of benefit (for example, a pension benefit) are assigned to each cost accounting period and are valued as they accrue, based on the services performed by each employee in the period involved. The measure of normal cost under this method for each cost accounting period is the present value of the units of benefit deemed to be credited to employees for service in that period. The measure of the actuarial liability at a plan's inception date is the present value of the units of benefit credited to employees for service prior to that date.

ACCRUED COSTS

Accumulated actual costs recognized over a specific time period.

ACCRUED REVENUE

Accumulated revenue recognized over a specific time period.

ACCUMULATING COSTS

Collecting cost data in an organized manner, such as through a system of accounts.

ACH

See automated clearing house.

ACID TEST

Most rigorous and severe form of testing for reliability, maintainability, and other criteria. Term is derived from the fact that gold resists acids that corrode other metals; the "acid test" was used to identify metals purporting to be gold.

ACQUISITION

(1) Obtaining supplies or services by and for the use of an organization through a purchase or lease, regardless of whether the supplies or services are already in existence or must be created, developed, demonstrated, or evaluated.

(2) One company taking a controlling interest in another company.

ACQUISITION CONTROL

System for acquiring project equipment, material, and services in a uniform and orderly fashion and for managing that acquisition process.

ACQUISITION METHODS

Ways in which goods or services are acquired from contractors, such as by sealed bid, competitive negotiation, and sole- or single-source award.

ACQUISITION PLAN

Document that addresses all technical, business, management, and other significant considerations that will control an acquisition.

ACQUISITION PROCESS

Process of acquiring goods or services for new or existing work.

ACQUISITION STREAMLINING

Term used in the U.S. federal government to describe any effort that results in more efficient and effective use of resources to design and develop or produce quality systems. This includes ensuring that only necessary and cost-effective requirements are included, at the most appropriate time in the acquisition cycle, in solicitations and resulting contracts for the design, development, and production of new systems or for modifications to existing systems.

ACTION ITEM

Task, activity, or piece of work that has been identified as needing to be done, typically as a result of a discussion or meeting, and assigned to a specific individual for accomplishment.

ACTION PLAN

Detailed document describing project tasks that need to be done, when, and by whom.

ACTIVE LISTENING

Paying close attention to what is said, asking the other party to describe carefully and clearly what is meant, paraphrasing what the party speaking has communicated, and requesting that ideas be repeated to clarify any ambiguity or uncertainty.

ACTIVE REPAIR TIME

Portion of downtime during which one or more technicians are working on the system to effect a repair. This time includes preparation time, fault location time, fault correction time, and final checkout time for the system.

ACTIVITY

Element of work that is required by the project, uses resources, and takes time to complete. Activities have expected durations, costs, and resource requirements and may be subdivided into tasks. *See also* task.

ACTIVITY-BASED COSTING (ABC)

Methodology that assigns costs to products or services based on the resources they consume. It assigns functional costs, both direct and indirect, to the activities of an organization and then traces those activities to the product or service that caused the activities to be performed. ABC shows how effectively resources are being used and how all relevant activities contribute to the cost of a product or service.

ACTIVITY-BASED MANAGEMENT (ABM)

Approach to management that uses detailed economic analyses of important business activities to improve strategic and operational decisions. Attempts to increase the accuracy of cost information by more precisely allocating overhead and other indirect costs to products, projects, or customer segments. To successfully implement ABM, overhead and other indirect costs must be tracked by activity, which can then be traced to products, projects, or customers.

ACTIVITY CODE

Unique identifier of a task or an activity that is a work package or forms part of a work package in a work breakdown structure (WBS). Used to help in identifying and gathering costs attributed to the accomplishment of the work. *See also* work breakdown structure.

ACTIVITY DEFINITION

Identification of specific activities that must be performed to produce the project deliverables. Typically, the activities are identified using the WBS, statements of work (SOWs), historical documentation, time and resource constraints, and basic assumptions affecting the project. *Also called* activity description. *See also* statement of work.

ACTIVITY DESCRIPTION

See activity definition.

ACTIVITY DURATION

Best estimate of the time (hours, days, weeks, months, or sometimes years) needed to accomplish the work involved in an activity, considering the nature of the work and the resources required for it.

ACTIVITY DURATION ESTIMATING

Estimating the number of work periods needed to complete individual activities.

ACTIVITY LIST

Enumeration of all the activities to be performed on a project. Organized as an extension to the WBS to ensure that all activities that are part of the project scope (and only those activities) are listed. Includes descriptions of each activity to ensure that project team members understand all the work that must be accomplished.

ACTIVITY-ON-ARC

See precedence diagramming method.

ACTIVITY-ON-ARROW (AOA)

See arrow diagramming method.

ACTIVITY-ON-NODE (AON)

See precedence diagramming method.

ACTIVITY SEQUENCING

Process of identifying dependencies between and among project activities to determine when each activity can start based on network logic. Proper sequencing helps to develop a realistic and achievable schedule.

ACT OF GOD

Event that is so violent, catastrophic, and unforeseen that it could not have been prevented. Such an act makes performance of a contract obligation impossible and the contractor is excused from late delivery. Many contracts today do not have act of God clauses because the parties may practice a religion that has many gods (as in India, for example, where Hinduism is the dominant religion) or because a country's government may have a policy of rejecting religion completely so that officially there is no God (as in many Communist countries). Thus, the term used would be act of Nature.

ACTOR

Any identifiable person or group that handles or interacts with the work. May be an actual person, a role played by a person, a job function, or an organizational unit. An automated system can also be an actor.

ACTUAL CASH VALUE

Cost of replacing damaged property with other property of like kind and quality in the physical condition of the property immediately before the damage.

ACTUAL COST

(1) Amount a buyer pays to a seller for a product or service. It may be, but need not be, the same as market, insurable, or retail value.

(2) Cost a seller actually incurs to produce a product or provide a service, as distinguished from forecast final cost.

ACTUAL COST OF WORK PERFORMED (ACWP)

Total costs (direct and indirect) incurred in accomplishing work during a given time period. *See also* earned value.

ACTUAL DAMAGES

Losses directly related to a breach or tortuous act that can readily be proved to have been sustained and for which the injured party should be compensated.

ACTUAL FINISH DATE

Point in time when work ended on an activity. In some cases, the activity may be considered "finished" when work is "substantially complete."

ACTUAL INCURRED RATES

Rates that reflect actual expenditures as they have been recorded in the organization's accounting system.

ACTUAL START DATE

Point in time when work started on an activity.

ACTUARIAL ASSUMPTION

Prediction of future conditions affecting pension costs, such as the mortality rate, employee turnover, compensation levels, pension fund earnings, and changes in values of pension fund assets).

ACTUARIAL COST METHOD

Technique that uses actuarial assumptions to measure the present value of future pension benefits and pension fund administrative expenses, and that assigns the cost of such benefits and expenses to cost accounting periods.

ACV

See at-completion variance.

ACWP

See actual cost of work performed.

ADAPTABILITY

In software development, the ease with which software satisfies differing system constraints and user needs.

ADAPTIVE ACTION

In agile project management, a term used in lieu of "corrective action" indicating that the future cannot be known and, therefore, when problems and issues are encountered, it is better for the team to quickly adapt to changing conditions than to try to correct something that was not known, nor could have been known, at the outset.

ADAPTIVE MAINTENANCE

In information technology, maintenance performed to change a system in order to keep it usable in a changed environment.

ADEQUATE DISCLOSURE

Information in footnotes and financial statements that provides a full and clear picture of a firm's financial status.

ADEQUATE EVIDENCE

Information sufficient to support the reasonable belief that a particular act or omission has occurred.

ADEQUATE PRICE COMPETITION

In U.S. federal contracting, a situation in which two or more responsible offerors, competing independently, submit priced offers that satisfy the government's expressed requirement and—

(a) The award will be made to the offeror whose proposal represents the best value where price is a substantial factor in source selection; and

(b) There is no finding that the price of the otherwise successful offeror is unreasonable. Any finding that the price is unreasonable must be supported by a statement of the facts and approved at a level above the contracting officer.

ADJOURNING

See Tuckman's Model of Team Development (Stage 5).

ADM

See arrow diagramming method.

ADMINISTRATIVE CLOSURE

Activities associated with generating, gathering, and disseminating information to formalize acceptance of the product or service of the project by the sponsor, client, or customer for a specific project phase or at project completion.

ADMINISTRATIVE EXPENSE

Expense that cannot be easily associated with a specific function or project but contributes in some way to the project or general business operations.

ADR

See alternative dispute resolution.

AD VALOREM

Latin for "according to value" and referring to a way of assessing duties or taxes on goods or property. Referred to in many countries as "ad valorem taxes." For example, in certain localities in the U.S. the property tax is based on the value of the property and not on its size.

ADVANCE PAYMENT

(1) Advance of money made by the buyer to the contractor before, in anticipation of, and applicable to performance under a contract.

(2) In U.S. federal procurement, advances of money by the government to a prime contractor before, in anticipation of, and for the purpose of complete performance under one or more contracts. Such advances are expected to be liquidated from payments due to the contractor incident to performance of the contracts. Because they are not measured by performance, they differ from partial, progress, or other payments based on the performance or partial performance of a contract. Advance payments may be made to prime contractors for the purpose of making advances to subcontractors.

ADVANCE PAYMENT BOND

Bond that secures fulfillment of the contractor's obligations under an advance payment provision.

ADVERTORIALS

Advertisements that are cleverly written to resemble editorials and appear in print media. They provide more information on the product or service being described than a regular advertisement would.

AFFILIATES

Associated business organizations or individuals if, directly or indirectly, (1) either one controls or can control the other or (2) a third party controls or can control both.

AFFINITY DIAGRAM

Tool used to gather a large amount of ideas, opinions, or issues from a group of participants in a short period of time. Participants then organize the information according to the natural relationships that exist within the information. For example, when identifying project risks each team member will write individual risk events on sticky notes (one risk per sticky note). The team members will then place the risk events into groupings of like items until there is consensus. This process takes place in complete silence. After final groupings are established, the participants name each grouping of risk events.

AGENCY

(1) In U.S. contract law, a legal relationship in which an agent acts under the direction of a principal for the principal's benefit.

(2) Any executive department, military department, defense agency, government corporation, government-controlled corporation, or independent establishment in the executive branch of the U.S. government (including the Executive Office of the President) or any independent regulatory agency.

AGENT

Person who acts under the direction of a principal for the principal's benefit in a legal relationship known as agency.

AGILE METHODS

(1) Any one of a number of named and unnamed nontraditional approaches, methods, and techniques used to develop software systems that meet user requirements typically by including users early and often in the development process and using iterations and prototypes as deliverables rather than formal documentation so the user can actually experience the system in reality rather than relying on written words or symbols to describe it. *See also* extreme programming, scrum, crystal methods, feature driven development, lean development, dynamic systems development method, *and* agile modeling.

(2) In project management, the approaches, methods, and techniques used to manage a project whose product or service is produced using agile methods. *See also* agile project management.

AGILE MODELING

One of a variety of agile software development methods proposed by Scott Ambler based on the values, principles, and practices that focus on modeling and documentation of software. Agile modeling recognizes that modeling is a critical activity for project success and addresses how to model in an effective and agile manner.

AGILE PROJECT MANAGEMENT

Value-driven approach to managing a project that combines elements of traditional project management with a wide variety of tools, techniques, methods, approaches, and perspective to better and more efficiently deliver products and services to users. Agile project management has six principles and five phases. The six principles are—

- Deliver customer value
- Employ interactive, feature-based delivery
- Champion technical excellence
- Encourage exploration
- Build adaptive (self-organizing, self-disciplined) teams
- Simplify

The five phases are—

- Envision: determining the product vision, scope, and community and how the team will work together

- Speculate: developing a feature-based release, milestone, and iteration plan to deliver the product vision

- Explore: delivering developed, tested features in a short time frame to gain feedback from the users

- Adapt: reviewing the delivered results and making modifications based on user feedback

- Close: officially concluding the project and conducting lessons learned

Adherents of agile project management assert that it is more than a narrow set of methods; rather, it is a cultural phenomenon whose tenets are more based on chaos theory than didactic project management techniques.

AGILE (SOFTWARE DEVELOPMENT) MANIFESTO

Declaration by adherents to agile software development methods such as extreme programming, scrum, dynamic systems development method, adaptive software development, crystal, feature driven development, pragmatic programming, and others to the need for an alternative to documentation-driven, heavyweight software development processes. The manifesto reads, in part:

"We are uncovering better ways of developing software by doing it and helping others do it. Through this work we have come to value—

Individuals and interaction over process and tools,

Working software over comprehensive documentation,

Customer collaboration over contract negotiation,

Responding to change over following a plan."

AGREEMENT

Mutual assent between two or more competent parties, usually reduced to writing in a contract.

AGREE TO DISAGREE

Set aside an irreconcilable difference to maintain a civil dialogue and move on to other matters.

A GUIDE TO THE PROJECT MANAGEMENT BODY OF KNOWLEDGE

See PMBOK®*Guide.

AHP

See Analytic Hierarchy Process.

AIQ

See average incoming quality.

---

*"PMBOK" is a certification mark of the Project Management Institute, Inc., which is registered in the United States and other nations.

ALLOCABLE COST

Cost assignable or chargeable to one or more cost objectives as defined or agreed upon by the contractual parties.

ALLOCATED BASELINE

Baseline in which each function and subfunction of the product is allocated a set of performance and design requirements. These requirements are stated in sufficient detail for allocation to hardware, software, procedural data, facilities, and personnel.

ALLOWABLE COST

Cost that can be recovered for the performance of a contract.

ALLOWANCE FOR BAD DEBTS

Recording a subtraction from accounts receivable to allow for those accounts that will not be paid.

ALPHA TEST

First test of a new product, concept, or idea to find and eliminate any design defects or flaws. Alpha tests usually are done internally or with a select set of clients and rarely with the general public. *See also* beta test.

ALTERNATIVE DISPUTE RESOLUTION (ADR)

Any one of a number of approaches or procedures to resolving controversy, disagreements, and disputes without resorting to litigation. Such approaches or procedures may include, but are not limited to, the following:

• Binding arbitration—The presentation of a dispute to an impartial or neutral individual (arbitrator) or panel (arbitration panel) for issuance of a binding decision, which usually is not reviewable by the courts.

• Conciliation—Building a positive relationship between the parties to a dispute. A third party or conciliator (who may or may not be totally neutral to the interests of the parties) may be used by the parties to help establish communication, clarify misperceptions, deal with strong emotions, and build the trust necessary for cooperative problem-solving.

• Cooperative problem-solving—It does not use the services of a third party and typically takes place when the concerned parties agree to resolve a question or issue of mutual concern.

• Dispute panels—One or more neutral or impartial individuals in a panel who are available to the parties as a means to clarify misperceptions, fill in information gaps, or resolve differences over data or facts. The panel reviews conflicting data or facts and suggests ways for the parties to reconcile their differences.

• Facilitation—The use of techniques to improve the flow of information in a meeting between parties to a dispute. The term "facilitator" is often used interchangeably with the term "mediator," but a facilitator typically does not become as involved in the substantive issues as does a mediator.

• Fact-finding—The use of an impartial expert (or group) selected by the parties, an agency, or an individual with the authority to appoint a fact finder to determine what the facts are in a dispute. The rationale behind the efficacy of fact-finding is the expectation that the opinion of a trusted and impartial neutral will carry weight with the parties.

• Interest-based problem-solving—A technique that creates effective solutions while improving the relationship between the parties. The process separates the person from the problem, explores all interests to define issues clearly, brainstorms possibilities and opportunities, and uses some mutually agreed-upon standard to reach a solution.

• Mediated arbitration—A variation of the arbitration procedure in which an impartial or neutral third party is authorized by the disputing parties to mediate their dispute until they reach an impasse. If an impasse is reached, the third party is authorized by the parties to issue a binding opinion on the cause of the impasse or the remaining issue(s) in dispute.

• Mediation—The intervention into a dispute or negotiation of an acceptable, impartial, and neutral third party who has no decision-making authority. The objective of this intervention is to assist the parties in voluntarily reaching an acceptable resolution of issues in dispute.

• Minitrials—A structured settlement process in which each side to a dispute presents abbreviated summaries of its case before the major decision makers for the parties who have authority to settle the dispute. The process generally follows more relaxed rules than might be found in court or other proceedings.

• Nonbinding arbitration—*See* arbitration.

• Ombudsmen—Individuals who rely on a number of techniques to resolve disputes including counseling, mediating, conciliating, and fact-finding. Usually, when an ombudsman receives a complaint, he or she interviews parties, reviews files, and makes recommendations to the disputants. Typically, ombudsmen do not impose solutions; they persuade the parties involved to accept their recommendations.

• Partnering—Association formed to improve a variety of working relationships, primarily between a buyer and a seller, by seeking to prevent disputes before they occur. The method relies on an agreement in principle to share the risks involved in completing a project and to establish and promote a nurturing environment. (Partnering is different from partnership, which is a legal relationship that exists between two or more parties. *See also* partnership.)

• Settlement conference—A pretrial conference conducted by a settlement judge or referee and attended by representatives for the opposing parties (and sometimes attended by the parties themselves) to reach a mutually acceptable settlement of the matter in dispute. The method is used in the U.S. judicial system and is a common practice in some jurisdictions.

ALTERNATIVES
Different means available to attain objectives.

ALTERNATIVES ANALYSIS
Process of breaking down a complex situation to generate different solutions and approaches and evaluate the impact of trade-offs to attain objectives.

ALTERNATIVES IDENTIFICATION
Technique used to generate different approaches to completing the project.

AMBIGUITY
Contract language that can be understood to have more than one reasonable meaning.

AMBIGUOUS JURISDICTIONS
Potentially confusing situation in which two or more parties hold related responsibility for project work, and their work boundaries and role definitions are unclear.

AMENDMENT
(1) Written, agreed-upon change to a legal document, usually a contract.

(2) Alteration to a solicitation.

AMERICAN NATIONAL STANDARDS INSTITUTE (ANSI)
Voluntary organization that helps to set standards and also represents the United States in the International Organization for Standardization (ISO).

AMORTIZATION
Accounting procedure that incrementally accounts for the cost or revenue value of a limited-life or intangible asset through periodic adjustments to income.

AMOUNT AT STAKE
Extent of positive or adverse consequences that could occur to the project if a specific risk, or series of risks, occurs. The potential value (positive or negative) associated with a risk. *See also* project risk.

ANALOGOUS ESTIMATING
Using the actual duration or cost of a previous, similar activity as the basis for estimating the duration or cost of a present or future activity; a form of expert judgment. *Also called* top-down estimating.

ANALYSIS
(1) Study and examination of something complex by separating it into more simple components. Typically includes discovering the parts of the item being studied, how they fit together, and why they are arranged in a particular way.

(2) Study of variances for cause, impact, corrective action, and results.

ANALYTIC APPROACH

Process of breaking a problem into its constituent parts to better understand and thereby solve the problem.

ANALYTIC HIERARCHY PROCESS (AHP)

Approach to complex decision making developed by Thomas Saaty. It helps identify and weight selection criteria, analyzing the data collected for the criteria in order to expedite the decision-making process.

ANGEL INVESTOR

Venture capitalist who invests in new, high-risk companies with innovative ideas that do not attract the larger, more professionally managed venture capital firms.

ANNUAL BASIS

Statistical technique in which financial numbers for a period of less than 12 months are adjusted to an annual figure. To be accurate, seasonal variations must be taken into account.

ANNUALIZE

See annual basis.

ANNUAL PERCENTAGE RATE

Cost of credit that consumers will pay over a 12-month period, expressed as a simple annual percentage.

ANNUAL PERFORMANCE BOND

Single bond furnished by a bidder, in lieu of separate bonds. In U.S. federal contracting it is furnished by a contractor, in lieu of separate performance bonds, to secure fulfillment of the contractor's obligations under contracts requiring bonds entered into during a specific government fiscal year.

ANNUAL RECEIPTS

Annual average gross revenue of an organization.

ANNUAL REPORT

Formal financial statement containing a descriptive narrative of business operations for the year just ended. Issued by corporations for their shareholders, employees, and other interested parties. In the U.S., its regulatory version, required by the Securities and Exchange Commission for publicly traded companies, is "Form 10-K."

ANNUITY

In finance, a series of fixed or variable payments, usually over a fixed number of years or for the lifetime of a person (in which case it would be called a life-contingent annuity or simply a life annuity).

ANSI

See American National Standards Institute.

ANTICIPATORY BREACH

Breaking a contract before the actual time of required performance, wherein one party informs the other of its intentions not to fulfill its obligations.

AOA

See activity-on-arrow.

AON

See activity-on-node.

AOQ

See average outgoing quality.

APM BODY OF KNOWLEDGE

Publication developed by the Association for Project Management (APM) in the United Kingdom that is divided into seven sections and contains 52 knowledge areas or topics that, when taken as a whole, describe "good practice" in project management. It is used by the APM, in part, in its certification program, which assesses an individual's competence in managing a project.

APPARENT LOW BIDDER

Prospective contractor who has submitted the lowest compliant bid for all or part of a project as described in a set of bid or tender documents.

APPLICATION

Act of putting to use new techniques or applying existing techniques to a project.

APPLICATION AREA

Category of projects with common elements not present in all projects; usually defined in terms of either the product of the project (that is, by similar technologies or industry sectors) or the type of customer (for example, internal versus external or government versus commercial).

APPLICATION MODEL

Model used to graphically and textually represent the required data and processes within the scope of the application development project.

APPLICATION PROTOTYPING

Developing requirements dynamically, usually through an iterative process, rather than specifying all requirements at the outset of the project. Allows the customer to play an active role in defining the requirements as the project is being executed. *See also* rapid prototyping.

APPLICATION SOFTWARE

Software program that carries out a task, or sequence of tasks (for example, a database manager, spreadsheet, graphics program, or word processor). *See also* system software.

APPLIED DIRECT COST

Amount of money that is incurred during a given time period and is associated with the consumption of labor, material, and other direct resources, regardless of the date of commitment or date of payment.

APPLIED RATES

Rates used by internal management for budgeting and reporting for the current accounting period. Applied rates do not need to match the negotiated bidding rates; a conservative project manager or organization often sets them slightly above the bidding rates.

APPORTIONED COST ACCOUNT

Cost account with a direct performance relationship to some other discrete activity, called the reference base. For example, assembly inspection normally has a direct relationship to assembly hours such that for every 200 hours of assembly, 25 hours of assembly inspection are required.

APPORTIONED EFFORT

Effort related to some other discrete or measurable effort, usually as a constant percent of the other effort but by itself not measurable as a work package, such as quality assurance or quality control.

APPRAISAL VALUE

Opinion of an asset's fair market value, based on an appraiser's knowledge, experience, and analysis of the asset class.

APPROACH

Overall method by which project objectives, including methodologies, life cycles, responsibilities, and other associated strategies, tactics, practices, and procedures, will be realized.

APPROVED BIDDERS LIST

List of contractors that have been prequalified for the purpose of submitting competitive bids or tenders.

APPROVED CHANGE

Change to the project scope, schedule, or budget that has been approved by a higher authority.

AQL

See acceptable quality level.

ARBITER

Person appointed by a court, but who is not a judicial official, to decide a controversy according to the law. Unlike an arbitrator, an arbiter needs the court's confirmation of his or her decision for it to be final.

ARBITRATION

Formal system to deal with grievances and administer corrective justice as part of collective bargaining agreements. May be binding or nonbinding.

ARBITRATOR

Impartial person who resolves a dispute or disagreement between two or more parties. In binding arbitration, the parties must accept the decision of the arbitrator.

ARC

Line connecting two nodes.

ARROW

In ADM, graphic presentation of an activity. The tail of the arrow represents the start of the activity; the head of the arrow represents the finish. Unless a time scale is used, the length of the arrow stem has no relation to the duration of the activity.

ARROW DIAGRAMMING METHOD (ADM)

Network diagramming technique in which activities are represented by arrows. The tail of the arrow represents the start of the activity; the head of the arrow represents the finish of the activity. The length of the arrow does not represent the expected duration of the activity. Activities are connected at points called nodes (usually drawn as circles) to illustrate the sequence in which the activities are expected to be performed. *Also called* activity-on-arrow.

ASAP (AS SOON AS POSSIBLE)

Doing something as quickly as is humanly possible; with great urgency. The acronym itself is said as a word.

AS-BUILT DESIGN

Documentation that depicts and describes the configuration of the item or product as it was actually and finally designed, including all changes and modifications to the original accepted design.

AS-BUILT DRAWINGS

See as-built design.

AS-BUILT SCHEDULE

Final project schedule showing actual start, duration, and finish dates. *Also called* as-performed schedule.

ASEAN (ASSOCIATION OF SOUTHEAST ASIAN NATIONS)

Trading block of 10 countries in Southeast Asia. Originally formed as an anticommunist military alliance, it is now focused on developing a free-trade agreement among member nations. Current members include Brunei Darussalam, Cambodia, Indonesia, Lao PDR, Malaysia, Myanmar, Philippines, Singapore, Thailand, and Vietnam.

AS-IS STATE

Typically, a graphical representation of a work or business process in an organization that is the current way things are done. *See also* TO-BE state.

AS-OF DATE

See data date.

AS-PERFORMED SCHEDULE

See as-built schedule.

ASSET

Any item, tangible or intangible, owned by an individual or corporation that could be converted into cash. Examples include accounts receivable, temporary investments, notes receivable, or nonmonetary property.

ASSIGNMENT OF CLAIMS

In U.S. federal procurement, the transfer or making over by the contractor to a bank, trust company, or other financing institution, as security for a loan to the contractor, of its right to be paid by the government for contract performance.

ASSIGNMENT OF CONTRACT

Transfer of the rights and obligations under a contract to another party.

ASSOCIATION FOR THE ADVANCEMENT OF COST ENGINEERING (AACE)

Professional organization that advances the science and art of cost engineering.

ASSUMPTION

Factor that is considered to be true, real, or certain and is often used as a basis for decision making.

ASX

See Australian Securities Exchange.

AT-COMPLETION VARIANCE (ACV)

Difference between the budget at completion (BAC) and the estimate at completion (EAC).

AT LOGGERHEADS

To be in dispute with another person regarding an issue.

ATTORNEY-IN-FACT

Agent, independent agent, underwriter, or any other company or individual holding a power of attorney granted by a surety. *See also* power of attorney.

ATTRIBUTE

Characteristic or property that is appraised in terms of whether it does or does not exist (for example, heads or tails on a coin) with respect to a given requirement.

ATTRIBUTE SAMPLING

Statistical technique used to determine the quality, and therefore the acceptance, of an item by inspecting samples of the larger population. An attribute may be a qualitative or quantitative characteristic of an item that is either met or not met according to the specifications.

ATTRITION

Reduction in numbers of employees, usually as a result of resignation, retirement, or death.

AUDIT

(1) Formal examination of a project's accounts or financial situation.

(2) Methodical examination of the project, either in whole or in part, usually conducted according to a preestablished schedule, to assess overall progress performance.

(3) In U.S. federal procurement, (a) a review of an offeror's or contractor's books and financial records to evaluate reporting accuracy, financial risk, or cost reasonableness that is transmitted to the contracting officer or another government

official; (b) a document prepared by an auditor submitting information and advice to the requesting agency or official related to the auditor's—

• Analysis of the contractor's financial and accounting records or other related data as to the acceptability of the contractor's incurred and estimated costs

• Review of the financial and accounting aspects of the contractor's cost-control systems; and

• Other analysis or review that required access to the contractor's financial and accounting records supporting proposed and incurred costs.

AUDIT TRAIL

Record of documentation describing actions taken, decisions made, and funds expended and earned on a project. Used to reconstruct the project after the fact for lessons learned and other purposes.

AUDITABILITY

Capability of a project or portion of a project to undergo formal investigation of records relating to financial status or progress performance.

AUDITOR

Person who conducts an audit.

AUSTRALIAN QUALITY AWARD

Award honoring the quality practices of Australian organizations. Based on a model certified by the Australian Quality Council, an organization recognized by the Australian government as the preeminent authority on quality management. Seven categories of criteria are used by the Council to determine the award winners: leadership; strategy, policy, and planning; information and analysis; people; customer focus; quality of process, product, and service; and organizational performance.

AUSTRALIAN SECURITIES EXCHANGE (ASX)

Primary stock exchange of Australia, which began as separate state-based exchanges as early as 1861 and currently operates in an all-electronic format. The major market index is the S&P/

ASX 200, which is made up of the top 200 shares in the ASX and has supplanted the All Ordinaries index, which runs parallel to the S&P/ASX 200.

AUTHORITARIAN MANAGEMENT STYLE

Management approach in which the project manager tells team members what is expected of them, provides specific guidance on what should be done, makes his or her role within the team understood, schedules work, and directs team members to follow standard rules and regulations.

AUTHORITY

(1) Power or influence, either granted to or developed by individuals, that leads to others doing what those individuals direct.

(2) Formal conferment of such influence through an instrument such as a project charter.

AUTHORIZE

Give final approval; a person who can authorize something is vested with authority to give final endorsement, which requires no further approval.

AUTHORIZED UNPRICED WORK

Customer-authorized additions or deletions to the project scope (as described in the statement of work) that are being worked on by the project team prior to their being negotiated.

AUTHORIZED WORK

Effort that has been approved by higher authority and may or may not be expressed in specific terms.

AUTOCRATIC MANAGEMENT STYLE

Management approach in which the project manager makes all the decisions and exercises tight control over the project team. This style usually is characterized by communication from the project manager downward to the team and not vice versa.

AUTOMATED CLEARING HOUSE (ACH)

Secure, private electronic payment transfer system that connects all U.S. financial institutions by way of the Federal Reserve Board or other ACH operators. Types of fund transfers that are carried out through this network include direct paycheck deposits and debit card purchases.

AVAILABILITY

Degree to which a system (or system component) is operational and accessible when required for use.

AVERAGE INCOMING QUALITY (AIQ)

Average quality level going into the inspection point.

AVERAGE OUTGOING QUALITY (AOQ)

Average quality level leaving the inspection point after acceptance and rejection of a number of lots. If rejected lots are not checked 100 percent and defective units removed or replaced with good units, the AOQ will be the same as the AIQ.

AVERAGE-SAMPLE-SIZE CURVE

Plotted curve showing the average sample size that can be expected to occur under various sampling plans for a given quality process. *See also* sample size.

AVOIDANCE

Risk response strategy that eliminates the threat of a specific risk event, usually by eliminating its potential cause. The project management team can never eliminate all risk, but certain risk events often can be eliminated. *See also* acceptance, mitigation, *and* transfer.

AWARD

Notification by an organization that it will contract with another party. Usually is made by acceptance of an offer or tender that has been made by a contractor or seller.

AWARD FEE

Payment that the contractor receives above the base fee in a cost-plus-award fee (CPAF) contract. Total amount of fee available to be awarded is set forth in the original contract and should be an amount that is sufficient to provide motivation for excellence in such areas as quality, timeliness, technical ingenuity, and cost-effective management.

AWARD LETTER

Document notifying the winning contractor of the buyer's acceptance of its offer or proposal.

AXE TO GRIND

Personal interest or hidden agenda that an individual will advance. In many cases, other team members know about this and will say of the individual something like "he has an axe to grind" as a result of his past experience with the sales department.

B

B2B

See business-to-business.

B2C

See business-to-consumer.

BA

See business analyst.

BAC

See budget at completion.

BACKCHARGE

Cost of corrective action taken by the buyer that is chargeable to the contractor under the terms of the contract.

BACKDATING

Dating any agreement, contract, letter, document, or other important documentation earlier than the date drawn or the date of signing.

BACKFITTING

Addition of new type equipment to the configuration of operating systems or the installation of equipment in production systems that have been delivered without such equipment. *Also called* retrofit.

BACKLOG

Known work input that is beyond the workload capability of an organization or segment of an organization for any given period of time.

BACK TO SQUARE ONE

Back to the beginning. Start over again.

BACK TO THE DRAWING BOARD

Develop a new design (or solution) typically after the first one failed or did not completely measure up to expectations.

BACK UP

(1) In software, to copy software files onto a different medium that can be sorted separately from the original files and used to restore the original files, if needed.

(2) The act of creating these files (backup).

(3) The set of copied files (backup).

BACKWARD PASS

Calculation of late finish and late start dates for uncompleted portions of all network activities. Determined by working backward through the network logic from the project's end date. *See also* network analysis *and* forward pass.

BAD DEBT

Actual or estimated losses arising from uncollectible accounts receivable due from customers and other claims, and any directly associated costs (for example, collection costs and legal costs).

BAD SMELLS

In extreme programming (XP), it refers to early warning signals.

BAFO

See best and final offer.

BALANCE SHEET

Financial statement that sets forth an organization's assets, liabilities, and net worth.

BALANCED MATRIX

Form of project organization in which the project manager's authority over project resources is roughly equal to that of the organization's functional managers.

BALANCED SCORECARD

Approach used to measure business performance. Developed by Robert Kaplan and David Norton, it includes not only financial performance but also other elements such as customer value, internal business process, innovation, and employee performance. It is implemented by translating the organization's vision and strategy statements into a comprehensive and quantifiable set of objectives and performance measures, by obtaining organization-wide acceptance of the measures, by creating appropriate reward systems, and by collecting and analyzing performance results as they relate to the measures.

BALLPARK ESTIMATE

Very rough estimate (usually cost estimate), but with some knowledge and confidence, and within an accepted level of variance, as in somewhere in the ballpark.

BANKRUPTCY

State of being unable to pay the debts of a company due to a lack of cash. Under U.S. law, in a Chapter 7 bankruptcy the company goes out of business, liquidates its assets, and pays off creditors (for pennies on the dollar) under the direction of a court-appointed trustee. In Chapter 11 bankruptcy the company remains in operation and tries to reorganize its management and operations in order to become a viable business once again.

BAR CHART

See Gantt chart.

BARGAINING

Persuasion, alteration of assumptions and positions, and give-and-take that may apply to price, schedule, technical requirements, type of contract, or other terms of a proposed contract.

BARGAINING POWER

Measure of influence one party has over the other party in a negotiation. It comes in many forms and is never totally one-sided, because both parties have bargaining strengths and weaknesses. It must be perceived by at least one party to have an effect on negotiations. In fact, the power need not be real as long as it is perceived.

BARRISTER

Legal practitioner in England who acts much like a U.S. trial lawyer. However, a solicitor prepares the case for the barrister to litigate.

BASE FEE

Fixed dollar amount established at the beginning of a cost-plus-award-fee contract as the minimum amount of profit the contractor will receive, regardless of performance quality.

BASELINE

(1) Original plan (for a project, work package, or activity), plus or minus any approved changes. May be used with a modifier (for example, cost baseline, schedule baseline, performance measurement baseline).

(2) Nominal plan with which deviations will be compared.

BASELINE FINISH DATE

Original planned finish date for a project, work package, or activity, plus or minus any approved changes.

BASELINE PROJECT PLAN

See project plan.

BASELINE START DATE

Original planned start date for a project, work package, or activity, plus or minus any approved changes.

BASELINING

Process whereby all managers concerned collectively agree on the specific description of the program, requirements, and funding and make a commitment to manage the project or program along those guidelines.

BASE PAY RATE

Amount of money paid to an employee on an hourly basis for regular or overtime work.

BASIC AGREEMENT

(1) In U.S. federal procurement, a written instrument of understanding, negotiated between an agency or contracting activity and a contractor, that—

• Contains contract clauses applying to future contracts between the parties during its term; and

• Contemplates separate future contracts that will incorporate by reference or attachment the required and applicable clauses agreed upon in the basic agreement.

(2) A basic agreement is not a contract.

BASIC ORDERING AGREEMENT (BOA)

Instrument of understanding (not a contract) executed between a procuring activity and a contractor that sets forth negotiated contract clauses that will be applicable to future procurements entered into between the parties during the term of the agreement. It includes as specific a description as possible of the supplies or services and a description of the method for determining pricing, issuing, and delivery of future orders.

BASIC RESEARCH

Research directed toward the increase of knowledge in science. The primary aim of basic research is a fuller knowledge or understanding of the subject under study, rather than any practical application thereof.

BASIS OF ESTIMATE

Justification for developing and arriving at a specific cost or time estimate, whether it be a single point estimate or a range estimate.

BASIS POINT

0.01% in yield. For example, in increasing from 5.00% to 5.05%, the yield increases by five basis points.

BATCH

See lot.

BCR

See benefit-cost ratio.

BCWP

See budgeted cost of work performed.

BCWS

See budgeted cost of work scheduled.

BEAT ABOUT THE BUSH

Fail to come to the point. Prevaricate.

BEHIND THE EIGHT BALL

Being in a disadvantaged position.

BENCHMARK

(1) Measured point of reference used to make comparisons.

(2) Test or tests conducted on computer hardware, software, or telecommunications equipment to determine that the configuration performs according to vendor-published performance specifications and satisfies certain functional requirements that are unable to be measured in terms of performance or design criteria.

BENCHMARKING

(1) Comparing project practices with those of similar projects to provide a standard by which to measure performance.

(2) Comparing organizational practices, procedures, and processes with those of other organizations, whether in the same industry or not, to provide a standard by which to measure performance.

(3) Conducting a test or tests on computer hardware, software, or telecommunications equipment to determine whether it meets certain requirements.

BENEFIT

Gain to be accrued from the successful completion of a project. Benefits are compared with costs to ensure the selection of the most advantageous project or the most effective approach to complete a project.

BENEFIT-COST ANALYSIS

Process of estimating tangible and intangible costs (outlays) and benefits (returns) of various project alternatives and using financial measures, such as return on investment or payback period, to evaluate the relative desirability of the alternatives. *See also* cost-benefit analysis.

BENEFIT-COST RATIO (BCR)

Financial measurement method used in project selection, it is one tool that often is used in a benefit-cost analysis. Requires that benefits, as well as costs, be quantified. Calculated by using the following formula: B / C. A BCR greater than one indicates that the value of the project's benefits are greater than its costs. For example, if we estimate benefits of $4 and costs of $2 (4 / 2), we will calculate a BCR of 2, or 2:1 indicating $2 of benefit for each dollar of cost. BCR does not provide profitability information, nor does it indicate magnitude of cost or benefit.

BENEFIT MEASUREMENT METHODS

Comparative approaches, scoring models, benefit contributions, or economic models used for evaluating the positive aspects of projects.

BENEFITS MANAGEMENT

Any action taken to define, create, maximize, ensure, and sustain the benefits provided by a program.

BENEFITS MANAGEMENT STRATEGY

Detailed description and definition of how the program team will identify, deliver, and realize the program's expected benefits.

BENEFITS MANAGER

In program management, the individual assigned the single responsibility of ensuring that the identified benefits are achieved to the greatest degree possible.

BENEFITS PROFILE

Definition of the benefit identified as being desired by the program and its associated metrics for knowing when the benefit was realized.

BENEFITS REALIZATION PLAN

Scheme or plan of action that describes in detail how the benefits defined early in the program will be realized and attained throughout the life cycle of the program.

BENEFITS REGISTER

In program management, a record of the benefits to be achieved as a result of initiating the work effort. Benefits typically are described in business terms and are managed by the benefits manager to ensure the benefits are achieved to the greatest degree possible.

BENEFITS REVIEW

Meeting, usually conducted after a major program benefit or group of benefits has been realized, to assess the overall progress of the benefits strategy and results as compared with the benefits profile. Such meetings serve as a forum to publicize success and to inform stakeholders of the benefits delivery progress, as well as to identify future potential benefits.

BEST AND FINAL OFFER (BAFO)

(1) Final offer by a contractor to perform the work after incorporating negotiated and agreed-upon changes in the bid or tender documents and any other changes to the prospective contractor's cost or technical proposal.

(2) Offer or tender submitted in a competitive negotiated procurement after written or oral discussions have been conducted.

BEST-CASE SCENARIO

(1) In decision-tree analysis, the project's budget/cost baseline minus the sum of all positive impacts at 100 percent, OR the project's profit baseline plus the sum of all positive impacts at 100 percent—not the expected value of all the positive impacts, but all the positive impacts themselves.

(2) Best possible project outcome given the circumstances.

BEST EFFORTS

Contractual obligation to attempt to meet a goal, which requires contractors to use their best efforts to perform the work within the estimated contract cost and schedule.

BEST VALUE

Most advantageous trade-off between price and performance. Best value is determined through a process that compares strengths, weaknesses, risk, price, and performance, in accordance with selection criteria, to select the most advantageous value to the buyer.

BETA DISTRIBUTION

Continuous probability distribution used to model events that take place within a range between a minimum and maximum value; used extensively in project management to describe the time to complete a task. *See also* Program Evaluation and Review Technique.

BETA TEST

Test of a product in its intended external environment, with the results used for their intended application. *See also* alpha test.

BEYOND A REASONABLE DOUBT

Legal standard needed to be met in a criminal trial in the U.S. to declare guilt of the defendant. When deciding if the fact at issue is true or not, there is overwhelming and convincing evidence that it is true, compared with the evidence purporting that it is not.

BIA

See business impact analysis.

BIASED SAMPLE

Sample that is neither truly representative nor random as a result of poor sampling procedures.

BID

(1) Offer to perform the work described in a set of bid or tender documents at a specified cost.

(2) Procurement or tender document generally used when the source selection decision will be determined based primarily on price. *See also* proposal *and* quotation.

BID BOND

Legal instrument, obtained by the seller and required by the buyer, that ensures the work will be performed even if the seller cannot complete the work. The company from whom the bid is obtained is legally liable for the performance of the contract and is called the guarantor.

BID COST CONSIDERATIONS

Consideration of the contractor's approach, reasonableness of cost, cost realism, forecast of economic factors affecting cost, and cost risks used in the cost proposal.

BIDDER

One who submits a bid.

BIDDERS CONFERENCE

Meeting with prospective contractors prior to preparation of bids and proposals. Ensures that all prospective contractors have a clear and common understanding of the procurement or tender. *Also called* contractors conference, vendors conference, *or* prebid conference.

BIDDERS LIST

List of suppliers judged capable by the buyer's organization from which bids, proposals, or quotations may be solicited. The list is developed and maintained by the buyer's organization. Verification of the suppliers' capability typically involves review of financial status and past performance, as well as on-site review of facilities and personnel.

BIDDING TIME

(1) Time allowed prospective contractors to prepare and submit their bids.

(2) Time between issuing the solicitation and opening the bids.

BID GUARANTEE

Form of security to ensure that the prospective contractor:
(1) will not withdraw a bid within the period specified for acceptance; and (2) will execute a written contract and furnish required bonds, including any necessary coinsurance or reinsurance agreements during the time specified in the bid.

BID LIST

List of contractors invited to submit bids for goods or services as specified.

BID/NO BID

Decision point for management to either approve or disapprove the preparation of a proposal in response to a request for proposal, tender, invitation to bid, request for quotation, or any other vehicle by which a buyer solicits responses from a prospective seller.

BID OPENING

Public opening of bids submitted in a sealed bid procurement.

BID PROTEST

Process by which an unsuccessful contractor may seek a remedy for possibly unjust contract awards.

BID RESPONSE

Communication, positive or negative, from prospective contractors in response to the invitation to bid.

BID SAMPLE

Sample to be furnished by a contractor to show the characteristics of its product offered in a bid.

BILATERAL CONTRACT

Contract in which parties exchange promises to perform reciprocal obligations in the future. Contrasted with unilateral contracts, in which one party makes a promise in exchange for the performance of another party.

BILLABLE

Costs and/or expenses that are covered under a contractual agreement between two entities and may be billed to the buyer.

BILLING CYCLE

Interval between when invoices are sent to clients, normally one month but can be shorter or longer depending on specific agreements.

BILL OF LADING

Document used to show receipt of goods for shipment issued by an organization in the business of transporting or forwarding goods (including airbills).

BILL OF MATERIALS (BOM)

(1) Set of physical elements required to complete a project.

(2) Hierarchical view of the physical assemblies, subassemblies, and components needed to fabricate a manufacturing product.

(3) Descriptive and quantitative list of materials, supplies, parts, and components required to produce a designated complete end item of material, assembly, or subassembly.

BILL OF QUANTITIES

Project costing calculation completed before using a WBS and based on a per-component or per-project cost. Used widely in the construction industry.

BINDING ARBITRATION

Arbitration in which parties are legally bound to the decision of the arbitrator. *See also* arbitration.

BITE THE BULLET

To accept reality, no matter how harsh, and move forward with fortitude.

BLACK BELT

Designation given to a leader of a Six Sigma team who is responsible for implementing process-improvement projects to increase customer satisfaction levels and business productivity. Black Belts are highly knowledgeable and skilled in the use of the Six Sigma methodology and tools, having typically completed four to six weeks of specific Six Sigma training. Additionally, they have demonstrated mastery of the subject matter through application on a real project and the passing of a stringent examination. *See also* Green Belt *and* Master Black Belt.

BLACK BOX

System, component, or object with known inputs, known outputs, a known input-output relationship, and unknown or irrelevant contents. The user sees what goes in and what comes out, but does not know what happens to the data as they are being processed.

BLACK BOX TESTING

See functional testing.

BLACK NOISE

Nonrandom sources of variation (special cause).

BLOCK DIAGRAM

Graphic representation of a system or subsystems linked to illustrate the relationships between components/subsystems. Often used to depict process or workflow.

BLUE-RIBBON COMMITTEE

Group of experts who rigorously examine evidence, documents, and testimony to certify that a high-risk project has been properly planned, that risks have been quantified or otherwise adequately addressed, and that the probability of success is sufficient for the project to be funded or launched.

BOA

See basic ordering agreement.

BODY LANGUAGE

Nonverbal communication, often unintended, from one party to another. Consists of facial expressions, physical stance and gestures, and any other physical expression that either complements or contradicts the spoken word. Body language often helps parties to a discussion better understand the real meaning of the spoken word.

BOGEY

Standard of performance set up as a mark to be attained. A negotiator using the bogey tactic blames the negotiation position on a standard set by a third party or a situation beyond the negotiator's control (for example, management policy). Any reason might be used as long as it is beyond the negotiator's control.

BOILERPLATE

Standard and essential contract terminology and clauses that are not subject to frequent change. Use of the term can be dangerous because it may lull contract parties into thinking they need not read the clauses, assuming no changes from previous contracts, or assuming the data are not significant.

BOM

See bill of materials.

BONA FIDE

(1) Genuine.

(2) Made honestly and in good faith.

BONA FIDE EMPLOYEE

In U.S. federal procurement, a person, employed by a contractor and subject to the contractor's supervision and control as to time, place, and manner of performance, who neither exerts nor proposes to exert improper influence to solicit or obtain government contracts nor holds out as being able to obtain any government contract or contracts through improper influence.

BOND

Written instrument executed by an offeror or contractor (the principal) and a second party (the surety or sureties) to ensure fulfillment of the principal's obligations to a third party identified in the bond. Reimbursement of any loss sustained by the obligee if the principal's obligations are not met is ensured to the extent stipulated in the bond.

BONDING COSTS

Costs arising when the buyer or the contract requires assurance against financial loss to itself or others by reason of the act or default of the contractor.

BONE UP ON

Study hard and become familiar with a topic.

BONUS

Extra compensation paid to an employee or contractor, usually for superior performance.

BOOK VALUE

Difference between a company's total assets and its intangible assets and liabilities. A company's book value may be higher or lower than its market value.

BOOM

See business object-oriented modeling.

BOOTSTRAP

To help a company or project start from scratch with an infusion of capital, resources, or other needed items.

BORROWED RELATING STYLE

Style of relating in which the behavior, as such, does not enhance feelings of self-worth, but is personally acceptable because it is a tool used in pursuit of a desired goal. For example, a deeply nurturing individual uses a borrowed relating style when disciplining an employee. Administering the discipline may do nothing for the individual's sense of self-worth, but being of help to the employee does a great deal for their sense of self-worth. In a borrowed relating style, one's behavior is chosen from outside the Motivational Value System™ but is still supportive of one's underlying purpose, which hasn't changed.

BOTH-WIN

See win-win.

BOTTLENECK

Process constraint that determines the capacity or capability of a system and restricts the rate, volume, or flow of a process.

BOTTOM LINE

Net income after taxes. In general, it is an expression as to the end results of something, for example, the net worth of a corporation on a balance sheet, sales generated from a marketing campaign, or the final decision on most any subject. (Often said: "Give me the bottom line.")

BOTTOM-LINE GROWTH

Growth in profits.

BOTTOM-UP BUDGET

See bottom-up estimate.

BOTTOM-UP ESTIMATE

Cost or budget estimate derived by first estimating the cost of the project's elemental tasks at the lower levels of the WBS and then aggregating those estimates at successively higher levels of the WBS. The project manager typically includes indirect costs, general and administrative expenses, profit, and any reserves when calculating the total project cost estimate. *See also* definitive estimate.

BOVESPA

São Paulo Stock Exchange (In Portuguese: Bolsa de Valores de São Paulo). The largest stock exchange in Latin America, which is linked to all Brazilian stock exchanges, including Rio de Janeiro's Boverj, where only government bonds are traded. The benchmark indicator of Bovespa is the 50-stock Índice Bovespa.

BPO

See business process outsourcing.

BRACKETING

Technique used to group or class issues or solutions that are linked together. Negotiators can use this technique to identify issues that are critical to a mutually satisfactory result.

BRAINSTORMING

Problem-solving technique that can be used for planning purposes, risk identification, improvement efforts, and other project-related endeavors. Participants are invited to share their ideas in a group setting, where no disapproving verbal or nonverbal behaviors are permitted. The technique is designed to generate a large number of ideas by helping people to think creatively and allowing them to participate fully, without feeling inhibited or criticized by others.

BRANCHES

Possible scenarios resulting from choices or events; shown on a decision tree as a set of lines connected to a decision (box or node) or an event (circle).

BRAND

Symbol, name, term, design, graphic, illustration, or any other feature or type of symbology that identifies a seller's goods or services as being distinct from those of other sellers in the marketplace. Can identify one item, several items, or a family of items. Trademark is the legal term for brand.

BRAND EQUITY

Attractiveness and familiarity with a brand image in the marketplace. High brand equity enables the owner of the brand to charge premium prices.

BRASSBOARD CONFIGURATION

Experimental device (or group of devices) used to determine feasibility and to develop technical and operational data. It normally is a model sufficiently hardened for use outside of laboratory environments to demonstrate the technical and operational principles of immediate interest. It may resemble the end item but is not intended for use as the end item.

BRD

See business requirements document.

BREACH

Failure to perform a contractual obligation. *See also* material breach.

BREACH OF CONTRACT

(1) Failure, without legal excuse, to perform any promise that forms any part of a contract. Applies to both express promises in a contract and implied promises that are inherent in the transaction.

(2) Unequivocal, distinct, and absolute refusal to perform under the contract.

BREADBOARD CONFIGURATION

(1) Technique used in proof-of-concept modeling that represents how a product will work but not how a product will look.

(2) In the U.S. Department of Defense, an experimental device (or group of devices) used to determine feasibility and to develop technical data. It normally will be configured for laboratory use only to demonstrate the technical principles of immediate interest. It may not resemble the end item and is not intended for use as the projected end item.

BREAKDOWN

Identification of the smallest activities or tasks in a project for estimating, monitoring, and controlling purposes.

BREAK-EVEN CHART

Graphic representation of the relationship between total value earned and total costs for various levels of production, plotted on a time or volume scale.

BREAK-EVEN POINT

(1) In business enterprises, the point at which revenues from sales exactly equal total incurred cost, for example:

Revenues = Variable Costs + Fixed Costs.

(2) In decision making such as make versus buy, lease versus buy, and so forth, it is the point of indifference, meaning that level of activity where either method results in exactly the same cost. These types of break-even decisions often involve making assumptions about levels of activity such as number of units needed.

BRICKBAT

In U.S. military, a top-priority program.

BRIDGE FINANCING

Short-term financing used by start-up companies to pay for operating expenses during negotiations for a second-stage round of venture capital investment.

BRITISH STANDARD (BS) 6079-1:2002. GUIDE TO PROJECT MANAGEMENT

Standard issued by the British Standards Institute (BSI) providing guidance on the planning and execution of projects and the application of project management techniques. The standard has broad relevance to projects in many industries and the public sector, both in the United Kingdom and abroad. This standard primarily aims to provide guidance for relative newcomers to project management and to act as a helpful reference for more experienced practitioners and those who interact with project management teams.

BROOKS'S LAW

The complexity and communications cost of a project rise with the square of the number of developers such that the number of communications channels increases geometrically while the work expands only linearly. Expressed as $n^2 - n \ / \ n$ where n equals the number of developers. The "law" does not suggest a ban on adding people to a project but calls for proper division of labor to reduce the chaotic effect of having too many communications channels. Advanced by and named after Dr. Fred Brooks, father of the IBM Operating System 360, and popularized in his now-classic work *The Mythical Man-Month*.

BUCK STOPS HERE, THE

Responsibility is not passed beyond this point, typically the person in ultimate authority.

BUDGET

Quantitative expression of management's plans to perform specified work. Used to present management's intentions and objectives to all levels of the organization, monitor implementation of the plans, and provide a quantitative basis for measuring and rewarding individual and unit performance.

BUDGET AT COMPLETION (BAC)

Sum of approved cost estimates (including any overhead allocation) for all activities in a project. *See also* earned value.

BUDGET COSTS

(1) Translation of the work estimate into hourly rates, quantity units of production, and so forth. Used for comparison with actual costs to determine variances, evaluate performance, and alert those responsible to implement corrective action as needed.

(2) Assigned expenditure plan for specified cost elements.

BUDGET DECREMENT

Amount of a reduction in available funds for an activity.

BUDGETED COST OF WORK PERFORMED (BCWP)

Sum of approved cost estimates (including any overhead allocation) for activities (or portions of activities) completed during a given period. *See also* earned value.

BUDGETED COST OF WORK SCHEDULED (BCWS)

Sum of approved cost estimates (including any overhead allocation) for activities (or portions of activities) scheduled to be performed during a given period. *Also called* performance measurement baseline *or* planned value. *See also* earned value.

BUDGET ESTIMATE

Estimate of the funds needed to obtain project approval, which includes a combination of fixed and unit prices for labor, material, equipment, and other direct and indirect costs.

BUDGETING

Process of translating resource requirements into a funding profile, typically over a time frame.

BUDGET UPDATE

Change to an approved cost baseline, generally revised only in response to scope changes.

BUDGET YEAR(S) (BY)

In U.S. Department of Defense (DOD) funding, the fiscal year(s) (FY) for which funding is requested in the budget submission. As a result of the 1986 National Defense Authorization Act (NDAA), DOD submits a request for two years of funding (two BYs) when the first year covered by the budget request is an even-numbered year (for example, the FY2000 President's Budget (PB) requested DOD funds for FY2000 and FY2001). When the budget request occurs in an odd-numbered year, DOD requests funds only for that year (for example, the FY2001 PB requested DOD funds only for FY2001). Even though DOD is required to request funds for two years in even-year budget submissions, Congress appropriates money only for the first FY.

BUG

Problem in a computer software program prohibiting it from executing successfully. The term is derived from an actual event in the early days of computing when a bug (a moth) flew into the inside of a Mark II Computer and got stuck in a relay, thereby impeding its operation. Grace Hopper (deceased), who went on to become a rear admiral in the U.S. Navy, and one of the most prominent computer scientists of her area, is alleged to have remarked "they're debugging" the system when her colleagues found and removed the moth. The remains of the moth can be found in the group's logbook at the Smithsonian Institution's National Museum of American History in Washington, D.C.

BUILD

Operational version of a software product incorporating a specified subset of the complete system functionality. *See also* version.

BULK MATERIAL

(1) Material bought in lots; generally, no specific item is distinguishable from any other in the lot.

(2) Items that may be purchased from a standard catalog description and are bought in quantity to be distributed as needed.

BURDEN

See indirect cost.

BURDEN RATE

See indirect cost rate.

BUREAUCRATIC AUTHORITY

Influence derived from an individual's knowing the organization's rules, regulations, and procedures and the ways to use them to obtain desired results in an expedient and expeditious manner.

BURN RATE

Rate at which funds are expended on a project (for example, total dollars per day or total dollars per week). Usually quoted based on labor hours only, but may include materials as well.

BURN-IN

Operation of an item under stress to stabilize its characteristics.

BURNOUT

Exhaustion of a person working too hard and for too many hours under enormous stress.

BUSINESS AGREEMENT

Commitment to perform a task or series of tasks to accomplish objectives leading to a deliverable or completion of a project.

BUSINESS ANALYSIS

Set of tasks, knowledge, and techniques associated with eliciting, validating, structuring, and documenting requirements based on business needs in order to solve a business problem.

BUSINESS ANALYST (BA)

Individual within an organization who serves as a liaison between the organizational stakeholders, end users, and technical solution development team; provides decision support for risk for the client acceptor; and acts as a requirements manager. The BA is responsible for the elicitation and documentation of requirements in the most appropriate format for the technical solution development team, scaling the approach and documentation to match the relative risk of the endeavor.

BUSINESS BENEFITS MANAGER

See benefits manager.

BUSINESS CASE

See project business case.

BUSINESS CYCLE

Recurrent periods during which a nation's economy moves into and out of recession and recovery.

BUSINESS IMPACT ANALYSIS (BIA)

Formal analysis of the effect on the business if a specific process fails or loses efficiency. It also will identify the minimum performance level of a given process that an organization requires to continue operating.

BUSINESS INTELLIGENCE

Data, information and knowledge about the market one serves, competitors in that market, and how to market to a given audience. Also refers to the information technology used to gather, store, access, and analyze those data with the goal of making better decisions to generate revenue.

BUSINESS OBJECT-ORIENTED MODELING (BOOM)

Modeling technique used to deal with the complexity of a system by breaking it down into smaller units, called objects, where each object embodies the behavior and data of one part of the system. BOOM provides detailed processes for making the initial business case for a project and determining business requirements.

BUSINESS PLAN

Description of a business, typically over a five-year period, that should include: product(s) and/or service(s) offered; market conditions; competitor analysis; key personnel required; financing needs; risk factors; and expected revenues and earnings.

BUSINESS PROCESS MODEL

Deconstruction and graphical depiction of a specific business process or functional area within an organization. The model shows how each functional area breaks down into processes, each process breaks down into subprocesses, and each subprocess breaks down into activities.

BUSINESS PROCESS OUTSOURCING (BPO)

Specific form of outsourcing in which an organization contracts out to a third party the management, operations, and optimization of a business function such as accounts payable, purchasing, claims processing, or human resources based on a set of predetermined performance metrics. *See also* outsourcing *and* contracting out.

BUSINESS PROCESS REENGINEERING

See reengineering.

BUSINESS RELATIONSHIP MANAGER

Individual who acts as a liaison between a business unit and the information technology (IT) organization. The position can be placed in either organizational unit but is found most commonly in the IT organization. The purpose of the position is to facilitate the activities of the IT organization with the business to ensure the needs of the business are being met.

BUSINESS REQUIREMENTS DOCUMENT (BRD)

Elaboration of the regulatory, business, user, and system requirements, created by the business analyst and handed off to the systems analyst. The BRD provides insights into the current and future states of the organization, includes detailed profiles of user communities, and provides a baseline for requirements management.

BUSINESS RISK

Risk—with its inherent potential for either profit or loss—that is associated with any particular endeavor.

BUSINESS RULES

Obligations concerning actions, process, and procedures that define, and possibly constrain, some aspect of the business. Business rules govern the way a business initiates actions and responds to situations under various conditions.

BUSINESS TECHNOLOGIST

Individual who has mastered the skills of both business strategy and technology and can work comfortably within either sphere in an organization but is best used on a project team to facilitate discussions between the technology professionals in the organization and the business users who are the ultimate users of the systems created.

BUSINESS-TO-BUSINESS (B2B)

Type of commercial transaction and process where a business entity is marketing, selling, and delivering its products and services to other businesses as opposed to individual consumers.

BUSINESS-TO-CONSUMER (B2C)

Type of commercial transaction and process where a business entity is marketing, selling, and delivering its products to individual consumers as opposed to other businesses.

BUYING IN

Submitting or tendering an offer below anticipated costs, with the expectation of increasing the contract amount after award, for example, through unnecessary or excessively priced contract modifications.

BY

See budget year(s).

BY THE BOOK

Acting in a very rigid manner according to preestablished rules, regulations, and procedures. Often used in a pejorative sense, as in "she does everything by the book." Shows a complete lack of flexibility and creativity.

C

CA

See chartered accountant.

CAC 40

Benchmark French stock market index representing a capitalization-weighted measure of the 40 most significant values among the 100 highest market caps on Euronext Paris. The English translation of CAC means continuous assisted quotation.

CAD

See computer-aided design.

CAGR

See compound annual growth rate.

CALENDAR

Tool used to identify project workdays in developing a project plan. Can be altered so that weekends, holidays, weather days, religious festivals, and so on are not included as project workdays.

CALENDAR RANGE

Span of the calendar from the calendar start date, or unit number one, through the last calendar unit to be performed.

CALENDAR START DATE
First calendar unit of the working calendar.

CALENDAR UNIT
Smallest unit of time used in scheduling the project, generally expressed as hours, days, or weeks, but also can be in shifts or even minutes. Used primarily in specific project management software packages.

CALIBRATION
Comparison of an item against a known standard.

CALL A SPADE A SPADE
To tell it like it is; to be brutally honest.

CALL CENTER
Organization that handles inbound and/or outbound communications with customers.

CANADIAN QUALITY AWARD
Originally introduced in 1984 as the Canada Awards for Excellence, the award was revised to reflect the conceptual structure of the U.S. government's Malcolm Baldrige National Quality Award and released in 1989. The National Quality Institute of Canada, which administers the award, uses it to recognize Canadian organizations that successfully practice continuous quality improvement. The award relies on The Roadmap to Excellence guide, which identifies the following 10 steps to continuous improvement: support the quality principles; reward the quality criteria; take quality tests; develop an improvement plan; spread the quality message; enact the improvement program; monitor the improvement plan; retest for quality; maintain gains; and continuous improvement.

CAP
See change acceleration process.

CAPABILITY
In quality management the ability of a product, process, practicing person, or organization to perform its specified purpose based on tested, qualified, or historical performance, and to achieve measurable results that satisfy established requirements or specifications.

CAPABILITY MATURITY MODEL

Model used to describe the relative maturity of an organization, or subset of an organization, with respect to processes such as software engineering, product development, people development, systems integration, and project management, among others. Usually consists of five maturity levels that have been described as end-state conditions. The current practice of an organization is compared with the model, from which a determination is made as to which of the five levels the organization's practices represent. This information is then used to guide the organization into establishing action plans to advance to the next level. The first and perhaps best known capability maturity model was developed by the Software Engineering Institute for software engineering processes. It remains, to this day, the gold standard of maturity models. In project management, ESI® has developed ProjectFRAMEWORK®, a maturity model for project management processes, and many competitor companies have proprietary models as well.

CAPABILITY MATURITY MODEL® INTEGRATION (CMMI®)

Five-level process improvement and assessment model developed by the Software Engineering Institute that incorporates systems engineering, software development, integrated product and process development, and supplier sourcing maturity models into an integrated framework. It is supplanting the Software Capability Maturity Model®.

CAPABILITY VALIDATION

Technical verification of the ability of a proposed automated data processing system configuration, replacement component, or software to satisfy functional requirements.

CAPACITY

(1) Total of all human and material resources and financial assets available to a project, program, or initiative typically contained in an organization's portfolio.

(2) Measure of the amount of input a system can process and/or the amount of work a system can perform; for example, number of users, number of reports to be generated.

CAPACITY ANALYSIS

Analysis most frequently employed in a machine or process area to project capacity for additional business.

CAPACITY PLANNING

Forward-looking activity in which an organization attempts to identify the amount of work it can produce in a given time frame based on the resources and skill sets it has available to do the work. If the work exceeds the capacity of the organization, then either the additional work will not get done or the organization can increase its capacity either internally or through contracting in order to accomplish it.

CAPITAL

In finance, money and any other property of an organization used in transacting its business.

CAPITAL ASSET

Physical property of an organization that generally has a long, useful life, such as equipment, vehicles, or buildings.

CAPITAL BUDGET

Estimated amount of money planned to be expended for capital assets in a given fiscal period.

CAPITAL EXPENDITURE (CAPX)

Money paid for improvements that will have a life of more than one year (long-term assets).

CAPITALIZATION

Treatment of expenditures as assets rather than current expenses. Under general accounting practices in certain countries, contractors are required to capitalize costs of tangible assets when they exceed predetermined amounts.

CAPITAL PLANNING AND INVESTMENT CONTROL (CPIC)

A decision-making process in U.S. federal agencies for ensuring that information technology investments integrate strategic planning, budgeting, procurement, and the management of information technology in support of agency missions and business needs. The term comes from the Clinger-Cohen Act of 1996 and is generally used in relationship to information technology management issues.

CAPITAL PROGRAMMING

In the U.S. federal government, an integrated process within an agency for planning, budgeting, procurement, and management of the agency's portfolio of capital assets to achieve its strategic goals and objectives with the lowest life-cycle cost and least risk.

CAPITAL PROPERTY

Plant, equipment, and other facilities subject to depreciation.

CAPM®*

See Certified Associate in Project Management.

CAPX

See capital expenditure.

CAREER PATH PLANNING

Process of integrating an individual's career planning and development into the organization's personnel plans, with the objective of satisfying the organization's requirements and the individual's career goals.

CARTE BLANCHE

Unrestricted power to act at one's own discretion; unconditional authority.

CASE TOOLS

See computer-aided software engineering tools.

CASH COWS

Products or services that produce a large amount of revenue or margin because they have a large market share.

CASH FLOW

Amounts, sources, and uses of cash in an organization.

---

*"CAPM" is a certification mark of the Project Management Institute, Inc., which is registered in the United States and other nations.

CASH-FLOW ANALYSIS

Establishment of the source and application of funds by time period and the accumulated total cash flow for the project to measure actual versus budgeted costs. Needed for determining the project's funding requirements at the lowest carrying charges and used to measure progress of the project.

CASH-FLOW STATEMENT

Report that measures the flow of cash into and out of a business, most commonly on a monthly basis. One of four financial statements found in the annual report, it categorizes a company's cash receipts and disbursements for a given fiscal year by three major activities: operations, investments, and financing.

CATEGORIZATION SCHEME

Predetermined description used to group potential projects or programs into categories for further decision making.

CATEGORY OF MATERIAL

Particular type of goods, acquired or produced by a contractor, that consists of identical or interchangeable units and is intended to be sold, consumed, or used during project performance.

CAUSAL ANALYSIS

Process used to analyze the possible causal associations among a set of variables.

CAUSE-AND-EFFECT DIAGRAM

See Ishikawa diagram.

CBR

See concurrent budget resolution.

CCA

See Clinger-Cohen Act.

CCB

See change control board.

CDR

See Critical Design Review.

CDRL

See Contract Data Requirements List.

CELLULAR PROCESSING

Technique used to design, group, and manage production operations as self-contained flexible cells capable of start-to-finish actions in processing a group of items.

CENTER OF EXCELLENCE

See project management office.

CENTER OF EXPERTISE

See project management office.

CENTRALIZED CONTRACTING

Single function responsible for the entire contracting process. Person in charge of this function is accountable to management for the proper performance of contracting activities.

CER

See cost estimating relationship.

CERTIFICATE OF COMPETENCY (COC)

Document issued by the U.S. Small Business Administration stating that the holder is responsible (with respect to all elements of responsibility, including, but not limited to, capability, competency, capacity, credit, integrity, perseverance, tenacity, and limitations on subcontracting) for the purpose of receiving and performing a specific government contract.

CERTIFICATE OF CONFORMANCE

In U.S. federal procurement, a certificate signed by a contractor representative stating that the supplies or services required by the contract have been furnished in accordance with all applicable contract requirements. The certificate further states that the supplies or services are of the quality specified and conform in all respects to the contract requirements, including specifications, drawings, preservation, packaging, packing, marking requirements, and physical item identification (part number), and are in the quantity shown on the certificate or on an attached acceptance document.

CERTIFICATE OF OCCUPANCY

Document by a local government agency signifying that a building or dwelling conforms to local building code regulations.

CERTIFICATE OF PROGRAM COMPLETION

Document, signed by the key stakeholders, indicating their acceptance of the products or services delivered by the program and that the program has been completed.

CERTIFICATION

(1) Assessment by an independent, accredited third party to confirm a quality system's conformance to the ISO 9000 or other series of standards.

(2) Signed representation that certain facts are accurate.

CERTIFIED ASSOCIATE IN PROJECT MANAGEMENT (CAPM®)

(1) Professional certification awarded by the Project Management Institute to individuals who have met the established minimum requirements in knowledge, skills, experience, and application in the discipline of project management. Requires less knowledge, fewer skills, and less experience than the Project Management Professional (PMP®) certification.

(2) Individual holding such certification.

CFR

See Code of Federal Regulations.

CHAEBOLS

Major Korean business conglomerates.

CHAKU CHAKU

Japanese term for "load load," an efficient method of production in which all machines needed to make a part or assemblies are physically situated in the correct sequence of manufacturing very close together, thereby eliminating or greatly reducing the time required to move materials from one machine to the next. Typically, each machine performs a different stage of production, such as turning, drilling, cleaning, testing, or sandblasting.

CHAMPION

(1) Person who spearheads an idea or action and promotes it throughout the organization.

(2) Person with significant influence who takes personal responsibility (although usually not for day-to-day management) for the successful completion of a project for the organization.

CHANCE

Possibility of an indicated outcome in an uncertain situation. *See also* probability.

CHANGE

(1) Increase or decrease in any project characteristics—time, cost, or technical requirements.

(2) Deviation from agreed-upon specifications, definition, functionality, or plans; alternative approach to project work accomplishments.

(3) Alteration in a contract as permitted by a contract clause.

(4) Alteration, modification, elimination, or introduction of a method of producing work results or achievements in an organization.

CHANGE ACCELERATION PROCESS (CAP)

Set of critical tools that facilitates an organization's plan for achieving path-breaking improvements in organizational change initiatives. The need for CAP can well be understood using a simple law of mechanics, $Vg = Ug + Ag * Tg$. Where Vg = group velocity, Ug = initial group velocity, Ag = group acceleration, and Tg = group time. The final velocity (Vg) with which the organization or the group achieves its change initiative objectives depends on its initial velocity or enthusiasm for change and the positive acceleration with which the participants move forward together.

CHANGE AGENT

(1) In quality management, a person who is responsible for and leads a change initiative project or business-wide initiative by defining, researching, planning, and building business support and carefully selecting volunteers to be part of a change team.

(2) Any individual who undertakes a responsibility whose end goal is the delivery of a product or service that changes the way an organization works. Project managers are thought by many to be change agents because they deliver change to an organization in the form of new systems, products, processes, or a combination of all three that will forever change the way work is accomplished.

CHANGE CONTROL

(1) Process of monitoring and dealing with changes to the schedule, cost, or scope of a project, or its overall objectives. May be considered a subset of configuration management.

(2) Defined process and procedure for change management during the project life cycle.

CHANGE CONTROL BOARD (CCB)

Formally constituted group of stakeholders responsible for approving or rejecting changes to the project baselines. *Also called* configuration control board.

CHANGE CONTROL DOCUMENTS

Formal documents used in the configuration management process to track, control, and manage the change of configuration items over the project's life cycle.

CHANGE CONTROL PROCEDURE

Process for initiating changes to the project baseline configuration; analyzing the impact of changes to project cost, schedule, and scope; approving or disapproving changes; and updating project or product specifications and baselines.

CHANGE CONTROL SYSTEM

Collection of formal, documented procedures that defines the steps by which official project documents may be changed.

CHANGE EQUILIBRIUM

Balance of forces in the organization that either drives or acts as obstacles to change.

CHANGE MANAGEMENT

(1) *See* configuration control.

(2) Process used to introduce and implement a new system or set of procedures (the "change") in an organization so that the users or beneficiaries of the change assimilate it into their everyday work life. Training is an important part of the change. Change management is basically a process of acculturation.

CHANGE MANAGEMENT PLAN

(1) Premeditated, documented approach to implementing configuration control.

(2) Approach used to assimilate a new system or set of procedures in an organization.

CHANGE ORDER

(1) Written directive issued by the buyer requiring the contractor to make changes according to the provisions of the contract document.

(2) In U.S. federal procurement, a written order, signed by the contracting officer, directing the contractor to make a change that the changes clause authorizes the contracting officer to order without the contractor's consent.

CHANGE REGISTER

Record of the changes that need to be, or have been, implemented on a project or program.

CHANGE REQUEST

(1) Request for modification to the terms of a contract or to the description of the product or service to be provided.

(2) Formal written statement asking to make a modification to a deliverable.

CHANGED CONDITIONS

Change in the contract environment, physical or otherwise, from what was contemplated at the time of bid, causing the seller to seek additional monies or time from the buyer to complete the contract requirement. Most often seen in construction projects.

CHARISMATIC AUTHORITY

Influence derived from an individual's personality. People do what is asked of them because they like the asker.

CHARTER

See project charter.

CHARTERED ACCOUNTANT (CA)

British accountant who is a member of the Institute of Chartered Accountants.

CHART OF ACCOUNTS

Numbering system used to identify and monitor project costs by category (for example, labor, supplies, or materials). Usually, based on the corporate chart of accounts of the performing organization. *See also* code of accounts.

CHECKLIST

Structured tool, usually industry or activity specific, used to direct that a set of required steps be performed.

CHECK SHEET

One of the seven tools of quality. A simple tracking tool for compiling data from historical sources, or observations as they happen, so that patterns and trends can be detected and shown.

CHINESE WALL

Imaginary wall or barrier between departments within a service company constructed in an effort to avoid a conflict of interest. For example, if a firm performs both consulting and auditing, such a wall is constructed so that the consulting department does not know the results of the audit, which it could use as a sales opportunity.

CHUNKING

Process, often used in systems or software development, of delivering pieces of the system to the user to gain immediate benefit, rather than waiting to develop and deliver the entire system at one time. Chunking typically improves the speed of delivery, which often results in improved customer satisfaction.

CHUNKS

Basic building blocks of product architecture.

CHURN

(1) Number or percentage of one-time visitors to Web sites who are not converted into loyal customers.

(2) Number or percentage of loyal customers who abandon a relationship with an online retailer.

CLAIM

Written demand or assertion by one of the contracting parties seeking the payment of money, a change in interpretation of contract terms, or other relief arising under or relating to the contract.

CLARIFICATION

Communication with a potential contractor on a competitively negotiated procurement for the purpose of eliminating minor irregularities, informalities, or apparent clerical mistakes in a proposal.

CLASSIFICATION OF RISKS

Process used to allocate responsibility for risks and identify causes and potential control mechanisms.

CLASSIFIED INFORMATION

(1) Any information or material, regardless of its physical form or characteristics, that is owned by, produced by or for, or under the control of the United States government, and determined pursuant to Executive Order 12356 of April 2, 1982, or prior orders, to require protection against unauthorized disclosure, and is so designated.

(2) Any information deemed sensitive and proprietary by its owner such that it requires protection against unauthorized disclosure.

CLAUSE

Term or condition used in contracts or in both solicitations and contracts, and applying after contract award or both before and after award.

CLEARANCE NUMBER

Number of successively inspected units that must be found free of defects before a certain action to change the inspection procedure can be taken.

CLIENT

Customer, principal, owner, promoter, buyer, or end user of the product or service created by the project.

CLIENT QUALITY SERVICES

Creation of a mutual feedback system between buyer and seller to define expectations, opportunities, and anticipated needs.

CLINGER-COHEN ACT (CCA)

Public law of the U.S. government. Initially, Division D and Division E of the 1996 National Defense Authorization Act (NDAA). Division D of the Authorization Act was the Federal Acquisition Reform Act (FARA) and Division E was the Information Technology Management Reform Act (ITMRA). Both divisions of the act made significant changes to defense acquisition policy. The provisions of this act have been incorporated in Title 40 and Title 44 of the U.S. Code.

CLOSE, BUT NO CIGAR

To fall short of a successful outcome, getting nothing for the effort.

CLOSED-ENDED QUESTIONS

Questions that limit responses to predetermined categories, for example, multiple-choice and yes/no questions. Not suggested when gathering requirements for a system or obtaining a broad range of information from the person to whom the questions are asked.

CLOSEOUT PHASE

Fourth phase in the generic project life cycle, in which all outstanding contractual or other administrative issues are completed and documented in preparation for turning over the product or service to the customer.

CLOSING PROCESSES

Activities associated with formal acceptance of a phase, project, or program and bringing it to an orderly end. *See also* project/program management process groups.

CMMI®

See Capability Maturity Model® Integration.

CO

See contracting officer.

COBIT

See Control Objectives for Information and Related Technology.

COC

See certificate of competency.

COCO

See contractor owned, contractor operated.

COCOMO

See constructive cost model.

COCK-AND-BULL STORY

Unbelievable tale; falsehood.

CODE OF ACCOUNTS

Numbering system used to uniquely identify each element of the work breakdown structure. *See also* chart of accounts.

CODE OF ETHICS

Written statement of principles addressing the behavior of the individuals employed in an organization.

CODE OF FEDERAL REGULATIONS (CFR)

Codification of the general and permanent rules published in the Federal Register by the executive departments and agencies of the U.S. federal government. It is divided into 50 titles, with each volume being updated once each year and issued quarterly.

COEFFICIENT OF DETERMINATION

Measure of the strength of the association between the independent and dependent variables. Coefficient values can range from zero to one. A value of zero indicates that there is no relationship between the independent and dependent variables. A value of one indicates that there is a perfect relationship. The closer the coefficient is to one, the better the regression line fits the data set. For example, a coefficient value of .90 indicates that 90 percent of the variation in the dependent variable has been explained by its relationship with the independent variable.

COEFFICIENT OF VARIATION

Measure of relative dispersion between two samples when sample means are not equal.

COERCIVE AUTHORITY

Influence predicated on fear. People do what is asked of them because they fear the consequences if they do not.

COGS

See cost of goods sold.

COLA

See cost of living adjustment.

COLD CALLING

Making unsolicited calls to prospective customers. The word "cold" means that the person making the call does not know the person who is being called.

COLLABORATION SOFTWARE

Generic term used to describe any electronic and automated application that facilitates communication, trust, and teamwork among a group of people, usually a project team, who work on common tasks or objectives and who are not physically colocated. Examples include such common applications as e-mail and bulletin boards as well as more sophisticated examples such as electronic (that is, Web) conferences and meetings, Webcasts, electronic whiteboards, and instant messaging. Although many of these applications are Internet-based, they do not have to be to fit the definition.

COLLABORATIVE NEGOTIATION

Negotiation style in which both parties work to achieve mutually satisfactory terms and conditions leading to benefits for both sides. *Also called* win-win *or* principled negotiation.

COLLECTIVE BARGAINING

Method whereby representatives of employees (unions) and employers negotiate the conditions of employment, normally resulting in a written contract setting forth the wages, hours, and other conditions to be observed for a stipulated period (for example, three years). The term also applies to union-management dealings during the term of the agreement.

COLLECTIVE BARGAINING AGREEMENT

Contractual agreement with unions or other employee groups.

COLOCATION

Placement of project team members in the same physical location to enhance their ability to perform as a team.

COMBATIVE MANAGEMENT STYLE

Management approach in which the project manager displays an eagerness to fight or be disagreeable over any given situation.

COMMAND FAILURE

Failure of a system because of incorrect commands or signals from the operator or from other components.

COMMERCIAL OFF-THE-SHELF (COTS)

Item, software application, or service available in the commercial market.

COMMISSIONING

(1) Process of substantiating the capability of the project to function as designed.

(2) Activity on a project that encompasses the on-site validation and refinement of the hardware deliverables.

COMMITMENT

(1) Agreement to consign or reserve the necessary resources to fulfill a requirement, until an expenditure occurs.

(2) State of being personally bound to something because of a delegation process or assignment and acceptance.

(3) Approved schedule or budget allowances where time, funding, and resources are formally allocated to an effort.

COMMITTEE OF SPONSORING ORGANIZATIONS OF THE TREADWAY COMMISSION (COSO)

Nonprofit commission that established a common definition of, and created a framework for, evaluating the effectiveness of internal controls in 1992. Used primarily by privately owned companies and nonprofit organizations, the COSO framework views internal controls as consisting of the following five interrelated components: control environment, risk assessment, control activities, information and communication, and monitoring.

COMMODITY

Tangible good or product.

COMMON CARRIER

In the U.S.—

(1) A person or company holding itself out to the general public to provide transportation for compensation. (FAR 47.001)

(2) A person or company holding itself out to the general public to provide telecommunications.

COMMON CAUSE VARIATION

Underlying reasons for the natural variation in a product or the delivery of a service resulting in minor deviations from the specifications or control limits. *See also* special cause variation.

COMMON LAW

Unwritten body of law based on general custom in England and later applied in the United States. It is based on judicial precedent rather than legislative enactment.

COMMUNICATING

Exchanging information.

COMMUNICATION

Effective transfer of information from one party to another; exchanging information between individuals through a common system of symbols, signs, or behavior. Communication comprises four elements: the communicator or sender of a message; the message itself; the medium of the message; and the receiver of the message.

COMMUNICATION BARRIER

Impediment to effective communication. Barriers may be physical, environmental, cultural, temporal, psychological, emotional, linguistic, or from any other source that diminishes the transmission and receipt of a message.

COMMUNICATION BLOCKER

Negative reaction or response to a comment, suggestion, idea, or recommendation that has the effect of diminishing and impeding the communication exchange between the sender and recipient of a message. The sender typically holds the opinion that the recipient summarily dismissed the message content without giving it the level of consideration necessary.

COMMUNICATION CHANNEL

Means of communication used to transmit a message. Three communication channels exist in the project environment: (1) formal—communication within the organization's formal communication structure used to transmit policies, goals, and directives; (2) informal—communication outside the organization's formal communication structure; and (3) unofficial—interpersonal communication within the organization's social structure.

COMMUNICATION MANAGEMENT PLAN

Document that describes the methods for gathering, distributing, and storing various types of information; provides a production schedule showing when each type of information will be produced; details methods for accessing information between scheduled communications; and incorporates procedures for updating and refining the communication plan. Generally, a part of the overall project plan.

COMMUNICATION MODEL

Communication process involving four parts: (1) a communicator or sender—the originator of the message; (2) a message—that which is to be conveyed (thoughts, feelings, or ideas); (3) a medium—the vehicle or method used to convey the message; and (4) a recipient—the person to whom the message is sent.

COMMUNICATION PLANNING

Process used to identify the general or specific information needs of the project stakeholders, the frequency with which the information is presented to them, and the form the communication will take. Also includes general communication such as press releases, articles, and public presentations.

COMMUNICATION REQUIREMENTS

Total information needs of project stakeholders. Information necessary for determining project communication requirements includes (1) project organization and stakeholder responsibility relationships; (2) disciplines, departments, and specialties involved in the project; (3) number of individuals involved in the project and their locations; and (4) external information needs (such as communicating with the media).

COMMUNICATION SKILLS

Methods, techniques, procedures, processes, and actions employed by the sender to ensure that the information transmitted is clear and complete and that it has been properly understood.

COMMUNICATION TECHNOLOGY

Methods used to transfer information among project elements.

COMPARABILITY

Condition that exists when an offered price can be compared with some other price for analysis. Exists when all price-related differences have been identified and accounted for so that the prices being compared are based on relatively equal assumptions.

COMPARABILITY ANALYSIS

Examination of two or more systems and their relationships to discover similarities or differences.

COMPARATIVE RISK RANKING (CRR)

Method to help a group of individuals determine the most important risks facing a project when they cannot agree on what those are when faced with a list of risks that same group identified. CRR uses a multivoting approach combined with pairwise comparison. *See also* pairwise comparison.

COMPATIBILITY

Ability of two or more items or components of equipment or material to exist or function in the same system or environment without mutual interference.

COMPENSABLE DELAY

Delay incurred by a contractor in contract performance for which the buyer must give compensation.

COMPENSATION

Wages, salaries, honoraria, commissions, professional fees, and any other form of remuneration provided directly or indirectly for services rendered. Compensation is provided indirectly if it is paid to an entity other than the individual, specifically in exchange for services provided by the individual.

COMPENSATION AND EVALUATION

Measurement of an individual's performance (evaluation) and the financial payment provided as a reward for that performance (compensation).

COMPENSATORY TIME

Time off granted to an employee at the discretion of the employer for overtime work or other noteworthy deed. *Also called* comp time.

COMPETENCY

Critical skill, or in some cases personality characteristic, required of an individual to complete an activity or project, or otherwise required for a certain position. The ability to think strategically is considered by some to be a critical competency for a person who will be the project manager of a large and complex project.

COMPETITION

Effort of prospective suppliers of products or services to independently secure the business of the buyer by proposing the most attractive contract terms or by offering the highest-quality service or product. Competition in relation to U.S. government activities usually is categorized in three ways: (1) public versus private, in which public-sector organizations compete with the private sector to conduct public-sector business; (2) public versus public, in which public-sector organizations compete among themselves to conduct public-sector business; and (3) private versus private, in which private-sector organizations compete among themselves to conduct public-sector business.

COMPETITIVE ADVANTAGE

Advantage of one competitor over another.

COMPETITIVE BENCHMARKING

Measuring products, services, and processes against those of other organizations engaged in the same business. *See also* benchmarking.

COMPETITIVE NEGOTIATION

(1) Method of acquisition that allows flexible procedures, permits bargaining, and provides an opportunity for prospective contractors to revise their offers before contract award.

(2) Negotiation style in which each party works to achieve terms and conditions offering maximum benefit for themselves. In a competitive negotiation, the parties see themselves as opponents in a win-lose game.

COMPETITIVE PROPOSALS

Procedure used by the U.S. government in negotiated procurement that (1) is initiated by a request for proposals (RFP), which sets out the requirements and the criteria to evaluate offers; (2) includes review of submitted proposals for conformance to requirements or specifications, price, and other factors; (3) usually provides for discussion or negotiation with those prospective contractors found to be within the competitive range; and (4) concludes with the award of a contract to the prospective contractor whose offer is most advantageous considering price and other factors included in the solicitation.

COMPETITIVE RANGE

In U.S. federal procurement, all of the most highly rated proposals based on the ratings of each proposal against all evaluation criteria, unless the range is further reduced for purposes of efficiency.

COMPLETED ACTIVITY

Activity with an actual finish date and no remaining duration.

COMPLEXITY ESTIMATE

Numerical prediction of the probable number of related factors that cause projects to be viewed as complex.

COMPLIANCE

(1) Adhering to any standards, procedures, or processes established as necessary for operational effectiveness.

(2) Meeting all technical, contractual, and price/cost requirements of a request for proposal.

COMPOUND ANNUAL GROWTH RATE (CAGR)

Year-over-year growth rate applied to an investment or other part of a company's activities over a multiple-year period. The formula for calculating CAGR is (Current Value / Base Value).

COMPOUND INTEREST

Interest earned on principal plus interest earned in a preceding period.

COMP TIME

See compensatory time.

COMPROMISING

See conflict resolution.

COMPUTER-AIDED DESIGN (CAD)

Computer system and related software with sophisticated graphics capability that are used to design machinery, buildings, local area networks, computer chips, and the like.

COMPUTER-AIDED SOFTWARE ENGINEERING (CASE) TOOLS

Set of computer programs designed to improve and automate the software development process.

COMPUTER PROGRAM

Series of instructions or statements, in a form acceptable to a computer, that are designed to cause the computer to execute an operation or operations.

COMPUTER RESOURCES

Computer equipment, programs, documentation, services, facilities, and personnel available for a given purpose.

COMPUTER SOFTWARE

Programs, procedures, rules, or routines specifically designed to make use of and extend the capabilities of computer equipment.

COMPUTER SOFTWARE CONFIGURATION ITEM (CSCI)

Under some software development standards, an aggregation of software that is designated for configuration management and treated as a single entity in the configuration management process.

COMPUTER SOFTWARE DOCUMENTATION (CSD)

Technical data (TD) information, including computer listings and printouts, that documents the requirements, design, or details of computer software, explains the capabilities and limitations of the software, or provides operation instructions for using or supporting computer software during the software's operational life.

COMPUTER SOFTWARE UNIT (CSU)

Under some software standards, the smallest subdivision of a computer software configuration item (CSCI) for the purposes of engineering management. CSUs typically are separately compilable pieces of code.

COMPUTER SYSTEM SECURITY OFFICER

Person who ensures that all computer and telecommunications security (C&TS) activities are undertaken at the user site. Includes security activities for planning; awareness training;

risk management; configuration management; certification and accreditation; compliance assurance; incident reporting; and guidance and procedures.

CONCEPT

(1) Imaginative arrangement of a set of ideas.

(2) Phase in a generic project life cycle.

CONCEPT DEVELOPMENT

Phase in a generic project life cycle where the organization is transforming a range of generated concepts into a vision of the project's end result.

CONCEPT GENERATION

Process by which new concepts, especially for product ideas, are generated within an organization. *Also* called idea generation *or* ideation.

CONCEPT OF OPERATIONS (CONOPS)

High-level requirements document that provides a mechanism for users to describe their expectations of the system. It is used as input to the development of formal testable system and software requirements specifications. The CONOPS has the following characteristics:

• Describes the envisioned system

• Identifies the various classes of users

• Identifies the different modes of operation

• Clarifies vague and conflicting needs among users

• Prioritizes the desired and optional needs of the users

• Supports the decision-making process that determines whether a system should be developed

• Serves as the basis for the functional requirements document (FRD)

CONCEPT PHASE

First of four sequential phases in the generic project life cycle where the idea or notion of a project is first articulated. *Also called* idea phase, economic analysis phase, feasibility phase, *or* prefeasibility phase.

CONCEPT STATEMENT

Verbal, graphical, or pictorial statement of a concept presented to stakeholders to gather their reaction prior to investing money for product or idea development.

CONCEPT TESTING

Presentation of the concept statement to stakeholders to get their reaction to a product or idea concept.

CONCEPTUAL DEVELOPMENT

Process of selecting and documenting the best approach for achieving project objectives.

CONCEPTUAL ESTIMATE

See order-of-magnitude estimate.

CONCEPTUAL SOLUTION

Initial technical approach developed to satisfy project requirements as they are known early in the project.

CONCERN

(1) Problem, expressed because of lack of information about skills, resources, equipment, and facilities, that may turn into a risk if neglected. Often resolved as the infrastructure and facilities requirements are put in place.

(2) Business entity organized for profit.

CONCILIATORY MANAGEMENT STYLE

Management approach in which the project manager is friendly and agreeable and attempts to unite all project parties involved to provide a compatible working team.

CONCURRENT BUDGET RESOLUTION (CBR)

Resolution passed by both Houses of Congress but not requiring the signature of the president, setting forth or revising the congressional budget for the United States government (USG). Scheduled to be adopted by the Congress on or before April 15 of each year (Title 2 U.S.C. §632).

CONCURRENT ENGINEERING

Approach to project staffing that calls for implementers to be involved in the design phase. Originally, use of a design team that included both design and manufacturing engineers, and later expanded to include staff members from quality control, purchasing, and other relevant areas to accelerate project completion. Often confused with fast-tracking.

CONDITIONAL DIAGRAMMING METHOD

Diagramming techniques, such as GERT or system dynamic models, that allow nonsequential activities such as loops or conditional branches.

CONFIDENCE INTERVAL

Probability statement about an interval that is likely to contain the true population mean.

CONFIDENCE LEVEL

Measure of the confidence that a particular interval includes the population mean.

CONFIGURATION

Functional and/or physical collection of hardware and software components as set forth in formal documentation. Also, the requirements, design, and implementation that define a particular version of a system (or system component). *See also* configuration control, configuration item, configuration management, configuration management plan, *and* configuration status accounting.

CONFIGURATION AUDIT

Formal review of a project for the purpose of assessing compliance with the configuration management plan.

CONFIGURATION CONTROL

Process of maintaining the baseline identification and monitoring all changes to that baseline. Prevents unnecessary or marginal changes to the project scope while expediting the approval and implementation of changes that are considered needed or that offer significant project benefits.

CONFIGURATION CONTROL BOARD

See change control board.

CONFIGURATION IDENTIFICATION

Process of establishing and documenting an initial project baseline. Provides a systematic determination of all technical documentation needed to describe the functional and physical characteristics of items designated for configuration management to ensure that these documents are current, approved, and available for use at the needed time.

CONFIGURATION ITEM

(1) Element of a configuration that is subject to configuration management.

(2) Aggregation of hardware and/or software that satisfies an end-use function and is designated by the customer for configuration management; treated as a single entity in the configuration management process. A component of a system requiring control over its development throughout the life cycle of the system.

CONFIGURATION MANAGEMENT

(1) Process used to apply technical and administrative direction to document the functional and physical characteristics of an item or system; control any changes to the characteristics; record and report the changes and their implementation status; and audit the item or system to verify conformance to requirements.

(2) Approach used to control changes to these characteristics and provide information on the status of engineering or contract change actions. Comprises three major areas of effort: configuration identification, configuration status accounting, and configuration control.

CONFIGURATION MANAGEMENT PLAN

Formal document that establishes formal configuration management practices in a systems development/maintenance project. *See also* configuration management.

CONFIGURATION STATUS ACCOUNTING

(1) Process of recording and documenting changes to an approved baseline to maintain a record of the status of the system components. Shows actions required and engineering changes completed.

(2) Identifies all configuration items of the initially approved configuration and then continually tracks authorized changes to the baseline.

CONFLICT

Opposition resulting from incompatible expectations.

CONFLICT MANAGEMENT

Process by which an individual uses managerial techniques to deal with disagreements, both technical and personal in nature, that develop among the individuals working on a project.

CONFLICT RESOLUTION

Process of seeking a solution to a problem. Generally, five methods are available: (1) problem solving or confrontation, where two parties work together toward a solution of the problem; (2) compromising, where both sides agree such that each wins or loses on certain significant issues; (3) forcing, where the project manager uses his or her power to direct the solution, resulting in a type of win-lose agreement where one side gets its way and the other does not; (4) smoothing, where the major points of agreement are given the most attention and differences between the two sides are not highlighted and thus are not resolved; and (5) withdrawing, where one or both sides withdraw from conflict.

CONFLICT SEQUENCE

Method of defending one's Motivational Value System™ to return to one's valued relating style. It is the predictable and sequential deployment of strengths when faced with conflict or opposition. Conflict has three progressively serious stages. In Stage 1 conflict, people focus on themselves, the problem, and the other person. In Stage 2, people limit their focus to themselves and the problem. In Stage 3, people only focus on themselves. Conflict can be resolved at any point during the sequence.

CONFRONTATION

See conflict resolution. *Also called* problem solving.

CONJOINT ANALYSIS

In new product development, a quantitative market research technique that helps to determine how individual consumers make trade-off comparisons between a relatively small number of benefits or features.

CONOPS

See concept of operations.

CONSCIOUS NONVERBAL MESSAGES

Messages intentionally sent by the sender to the recipient through the use of nonverbal actions such as facial expressions, gesticulations, or other physical actions. For example, an individual extending a hug knows that he or she is embracing someone and that action normally is perceived as indicating affection. The receiver of a hug generally realizes that the message is a sign of friendship.

CONSENSUAL MANAGEMENT STYLE

Management approach in which the project manager presents problems to team members for discussion or input and encourages them to make decisions. This approach results in an increase in team member commitment to the group decision but also in the amount of time required to reach that decision.

CONSENSUS BUILDING

Deliberative, decision-making process that includes all participants in making the decision, taking into account and validating each participant's viewpoint and ensuring that everyone has the opportunity to contribute his or her opinion.

CONSENT OF SURETY

Acknowledgment by a surety that its bond given in connection with a contract continues to apply to the contract as modified.

CONSEQUENTIAL DAMAGES

(1) Losses, injuries, or damages that do not flow directly and immediately from the act of a party but instead from some of the consequences or results of that party's act.

(2) Any such damages resulting from a seller's breach of contract, including, for example, (1) any loss resulting from general or particular requirements and needs that the seller at the time of contracting had reason to know of and that could not reasonably be prevented, and (2) any injury to people or property proximately resulting from any breach of warranty.

CONSIDERATION

Inducement to a contract—the cause, motive, price, or impelling influence that leads a party to enter a contract. Generally requires two elements: (1) something must be given that the law regards as sufficient legal value for the purpose, either a benefit to the seller or a detriment to the buyer; and (2) the something (benefit or detriment of legal value) must be dealt with by the parties as the agreed-upon price or exchange for the promise.

CONSTANT DOLLARS

Method of relating dollars from several different fiscal years (FYs) by removing the effects of inflation and showing all dollars at the value they would have in a selected base year (BY). Constant dollar series are derived by dividing current dollar estimates by appropriate price indices, a process generally known as deflating. The result is a time series as it presumably would exist if prices were the same throughout as in the BY—in other words, as if the dollar had constant purchasing power. Any changes in such a series would reflect only changes in the real (physical) volume of output. Constant dollar figures are commonly used for gross domestic product (GDP) and its components.

CONSTANT DOLLAR VALUES

Economic units measured in terms of constant purchasing power. Constant dollar values are not affected by general price inflation.

CONSTRAINED OPTIMIZATION METHODS

See project selection methods.

CONSTRAINT

(1) Restriction that affects the scope of the project, usually with regard to availability, assignment, or use of project cost, schedule, or resources.

(2) Any factor that affects when or how an activity can be scheduled.

(3) Any factor that limits the project team's options and can lead to pressure and resulting frustrations among team members.

CONSTRUCTION MANAGEMENT

Process by which a potential owner of a capital facility engages a professional agent, called a construction manager, to coordinate, communicate, and direct the construction process in terms of scope, quality, time, and cost.

CONSTRUCTIVE CHANGE

Buyer's action or inaction that constitutes an unauthorized modification to the contract requirements.

CONSTRUCTIVE COST MODEL (COCOMO)

Software cost and schedule estimating model originally developed by Barry Boehm. Used for estimating the number of person-months required to develop the most common type of software product and expressed as the number of thousands of delivered source instructions. Three levels of complexity: basic, intermediate, and detailed. Principal difference among the three is the detail and quantity of information required to complete the estimate. Using the detailed version, the estimator must consider, and assign a value to, the impact of 14 specific cost drivers related to the software product to be developed. Model is derived from a study of 63 software projects and is nonproprietary.

CONSULTANT

Technical expert, subject matter expert, or solution specialist hired for a particular aspect of the project.

CONSULTATIVE-AUTOCRATIC MANAGEMENT STYLE

Management approach in which extensive information input is solicited from team members, but the project manager makes all substantive decisions.

CONSUMABLE

Administrative or housekeeping items, general purpose hardware, common tools, or any item not specifically identified as controlled equipage or spare parts.

CONSUMER PRICE INDEX (CPI)

Measure of change over time in the buying power of the dollar, derived by comparing the price of like items during different time periods. Published by the U.S. Bureau of Labor Statistics (BLS).

CONTINGENCY

(1) Provision for any risk elements within the project scope; particularly important when a comparison of estimates and actual data suggests that certain risk events are likely to occur. If an allowance for escalation is included in the contingency, that should be a separate item, calculated to fit expected price-level escalation conditions for the project.

(2) Possible future action that may stem from presently known causes, the cost outcome of which cannot be determined accurately. *See also* reserve *and* contingency plan.

CONTINGENCY ALLOWANCE

See contingency reserve.

CONTINGENCY PLAN

Plan that identifies alternative strategies to be used if specified risk events occur. Examples include a contingency reserve in the budget, alternative schedule activity sequences, and emergency responses to reduce the impacts of risk events.

CONTINGENCY PLANNING

Process of producing a contingency plan. Occurs at the outset of the project and is a continuous process throughout the project life cycle.

CONTINGENCY RESERVE

Quantity of money or time that is intended to reduce the impact of missed cost, schedule, or performance objectives, which can be only partly planned (sometimes called "known unknowns"), and that normally is included in the project's cost and schedule baseline.

CONTINGENCY TESTING

Additional testing required in support of a decision to commit added resources to a program, when significant test objectives have not been met during planned tests.

CONTINUOUS IMPROVEMENT

See continuous process improvement.

CONTINUOUS PROCESS IMPROVEMENT

(1) Process by which organizations continuously improve their processes and procedures to meet or exceed customer requirements.

(2) Means through which an organization creates and sustains a culture of continuous improvement.

CONTRACT

(1) Mutually binding agreement that obligates the seller to provide the specified product or service and obligates the buyer to pay for it.

(2) Legal relationship subject to remedy in a court. Generally, contracts fall into one of three broad categories: fixed-price or lump-sum; cost-reimbursement; and unit-price.

CONTRACT ACTION

Action resulting in a contract, including contract modifications for additional supplies or services, but not including contract modifications that are within the scope and under the terms of the contract, such as contract modifications issued pursuant to the changes clause (if a U.S. government contract), or funding and other administrative changes.

CONTRACT ADMINISTRATION

Management of the relationship with the contractor from contract award to closeout, focused specifically on ensuring that the contractor delivers a product or service in conformance with the contract's requirements.

CONTRACT AUTHORITY

Type of budget authority that permits a U.S. federal agency to incur obligations before appropriations have been passed or in excess of the amount of money in a revolving fund. Contract authority must be funded subsequently by an appropriation so that the commitments entered into can be paid.

CONTRACT AWARD

Acceptance of a final offer, usually by issuing a purchase order or signing a legally binding contract formalizing the terms under which the goods or services are to be supplied.

CONTRACT BUDGET BASE

Value of all negotiated contract costs, plus the estimated cost of authorized unpriced work.

CONTRACT CHANGE CONTROL SYSTEM

Process by which the contract may be modified, including the documentation, tracking systems, dispute resolution procedures, and approval levels necessary for authorizing the change.

CONTRACT CLOSEOUT

(1) Completion and settlement of the contract, including resolution of all outstanding items.

(2) Activities that ensure the contractor has fulfilled all contractual obligations and has released all claims and liens in connection with the work performed.

CONTRACT COST OVERRUN/UNDERRUN

Net change in the contractual amount over or under that contemplated by a contract target price, estimated cost-plus fee (any type of cost-reimbursement contract), or redeterminable price, due to the contractor's actual contract costs being over or under target or anticipated contract costs but not attributable to any other cause of cost growth previously defined.

CONTRACT DATA REQUIREMENTS LIST (CDRL)

U.S. Department of Defense Form 1423 list of contract data requirements that are authorized for a specific acquisition and made a part of the contract.

CONTRACT DATES

Times specified in the contract that define the project schedule, deliverables schedule, milestone schedule, or the dates on which any specific action or event must take place.

CONTRACT DISPUTE

Disagreement between the contracting parties, which may occur during contract execution or at completion, may include misinterpretation of any technical requirements or terms and conditions, and may result from changes not anticipated at the time of contract award.

CONTRACT DOCUMENTS

Set of documents that forms the contract. Includes but is not limited to the contract itself, along with all supporting schedules; requested and approved contract changes; any contractor-developed technical documentation, contractor performance reports, and financial documents such as invoices and payment records; and the results of any contract-related inspections.

CONTRACT ELEMENTS

Provisions that must be evident in order to have a legally binding contract. They include an offer, an acceptance, consideration, execution by competent parties, legality of purpose, and clear terms and conditions.

CONTRACT FINANCIAL CONTROL

Control exercised over contract costs by the buyer or the contractor.

CONTRACT FUNDS STATUS REPORT

In U.S. federal procurement, a document, normally prepared quarterly, that forecasts the funds required to complete the project, displaying them at the price level (cost plus fee).

CONTRACT GUARANTEE

Legally enforceable assurance of performance of a contract by a contractor.

CONTRACTING ACTIVITY

In U.S. federal procurement, an element of an agency designated by the agency head and delegated broad authority regarding acquisition functions.

CONTRACTING OFFICE

In U.S. federal procurement—

(1) An office that awards or executes a contract for supplies or services and performs postaward functions not assigned to a contract administration office.

(2) Any contracting office that the acquisition is transferred to, such as another branch of the agency or another agency's office that is performing a joint acquisition action.

CONTRACTING OFFICER (CO)

(1) In U.S. federal procurement, a person with the authority to enter into, administer, and/or terminate contracts and make related determinations and findings. The term includes certain authorized representatives of the CO acting within the limits of their authority as delegated by the CO. A single CO may be responsible for duties in any or all of these areas. The Federal Acquisition Regulation (FAR) reference to the administrative or termination CO does not require that a duty be performed at a particular office or activity or restrict in any way a CO in the performance of any duty properly assigned.

(2) Does not include any representative of the CO.

CONTRACTING OFFICER'S REPRESENTATIVE (COR)

In U.S. federal procurement, also referred to as contracting officer's technical representative (COTR). A person designated by the contracting officer to assist in the technical monitoring or administration of a contract. Procedures vary from agency to agency, but generally a COR must be designated in writing with a copy furnished to the contractor and the contract administration office. The designation does not include any authority to make any commitments or changes that affect price, quality, quantity, delivery, or other terms and conditions of the contract.

CONTRACTING OFFICER'S TECHNICAL REPRESENTATIVE (COTR)

See contracting officer's representative.

CONTRACTING OUT

(1) Term used in the hiring of private-sector firms or nonprofit organizations to provide goods or services for the U.S. government. With this approach, the government remains the financier, has management and policy control over the type and quality of goods or services provided, and can replace contractors that do not perform well.

(2) Generally, hiring an organization to perform the work that had heretofore been accomplished by internal employees. *See also* outsourcing.

CONTRACT MODIFICATION

Written order authorizing the contractor to make changes according to the provisions of the contract documentation.

CONTRACT NEGOTIATIONS

(1) Any discussion between parties to a prospective contract, or modification to an existing contract, that involves bargaining, clarification, and mutual agreement on the structure and requirements of the contract prior to signing it.

(2) Method used in U.S. federal procurement in which a contract results from a bid that may be changed through bargaining. Involves clarification and mutual agreement on the structure and requirements of the contract prior to signing it.

CONTRACTOR

Person or organization undertaking responsibility for the performance of a contract. *See also* supplier.

CONTRACTOR OWNED, CONTRACTOR OPERATED (COCO)

In U.S. federal procurement, a manufacturing facility owned and operated by a private contractor performing a service, under contract, for the government.

CONTRACTOR PERFORMANCE EVALUATION

Comprehensive review of the contractor's technical performance, cost performance, and work delivery schedule.

CONTRACTOR PERFORMANCE REPORTING

Method requiring periodic accounting and reporting by the contractor on performance under contract to date.

CONTRACTOR QUALIFICATION

Review of experience, past performance, capabilities, resources, and current workloads of potential contractors.

CONTRACTOR TECHNICAL EVALUATION

Comprehensive review of the contractor's technical competency, understanding of the technical requirements, and ability to produce technically acceptable goods or services.

CONTRACTORS CONFERENCE

See bidders conference.

CONTRACT PRICING

Efforts involved in determining a specific pricing arrangement. Includes price analysis; cost analysis; the use of accounting and technical evaluations; and systems-analysis techniques to facilitate negotiation of realistic pricing arrangements.

CONTRACT QUALITY REQUIREMENTS

Technical contract requirements concerning the quality of the product or service and contract clauses prescribing inspection and other quality controls incumbent on the contractor to ensure that the product or service conforms to the technical requirements.

CONTRACT RISK

Risk, from either a buyer's or seller's perspective, that is related to a contract, including the level of risk borne by the buyer or seller as a result of the contract type.

CONTRACT RISK ANALYSIS

Assessment of the probability that certain risk events will occur and of the consequences of such events on attaining the contract objectives.

CONTRACT TARGET COST

Total anticipated value of all the negotiated costs in a contract, excluding fee and authorized unpriced work.

CONTRACT TYPE

Also referred to as type of contract. Categories of contracts that are differentiated according to—

(1) The degree and timing of the responsibility assumed by the contractor for the costs of performance; and

(2) The amount and nature of the profit incentive offered to the contractor for achieving or exceeding specified standards or goals.

CONTRACT WORK BREAKDOWN STRUCTURE (CWBS)

Tool used to describe the total product and work to be done to satisfy a specific contract. Normally prepared by a contractor to reflect the statement of work in a specific contract or request for proposal. Used to define the level of reporting the contractor will provide the buyer. *See also* work breakdown structure.

CONTROL

(1) Process of comparing actual performance with planned performance, analyzing variances, evaluating alternatives, and taking corrective action as needed.

(2) One of the key risk response strategies, calling for reduction of the probability of a risk, reduction of the risk's impact, or deflection of the risk to another party. *Also called* mitigation.

CONTROL ACCOUNT

See cost account.

CONTROL CHART

Graphic display of the results of a process over time and against established control limits. Used to determine whether the process is "in control" or "out of control," thereby requiring adjustment.

CONTROL GATE

Specific point in time during the project life cycle (for example, beginning or end of a major phase, expenditure of a specific amount of money, specific results of a set of tests, and so on) at which key project stakeholders convene to assess performance to date, validate key project assumptions, analyze current and future market conditions, and discuss other factors to determine whether the project should: (1) be terminated, (2) proceed according to its original plan, or (3) proceed based on a revised plan. *Also called* phase exit, stage gate, phase gate, phase gate review, kill point, phase review, *or* phase-end review.

CONTROLLER

Experienced accountant who directs internal accounting processes and procedures, including cost accounting; the chief accountant of a company.

CONTROL LIMITS

Bounds beyond which unacceptable performance is indicated. Two control limits are used in statistical process control—upper control limit and lower control limit—and they are established as three standard deviations from the mean of the sample taken.

CONTROLLING PROCESSES

Actions taken by the project team to ensure that project objectives are met, by monitoring and measuring progress and taking corrective action when needed.

CONTROL OBJECTIVES FOR INFORMATION AND RELATED TECHNOLOGY (COBIT)

Set of best practices for information technology (IT) management created by the Information Systems Audit and Control Association (ISACA) and the IT Governance Institute (ITGI) in 1992. The COBIT framework provides managers, auditors, and IT users with a set of generally accepted measures, indicators, processes, and best practices to help maximize the benefits derived through the use of information technology and develop appropriate IT governance and control in an organization.

CONTROL SYSTEM

See change control system.

CONTROLS

See project management controls.

CONVERGENT THINKING

Technique employed to practice thinking that brings together information focused on solving a problem (especially solving problems that have a single correct solution). It usually is practiced in the early phase of a new product or idea. *See also* divergent thinking.

CONVERSION

Process of moving data, information, and programs from the current system to the new, or target, system. Conversion approaches include direct, parallel, phased, and pilot.

CONVERSION PLAN

Formal document that describes the strategies involved in converting data from an existing system to another hardware or software environment.

COOKING THE BOOKS

Fraudulently misrepresenting the financial condition of a company by providing false or misleading information.

COORDINATION

Orchestration of stakeholder actions and project events to achieve project objectives.

COPQ

See cost of poor quality.

COPYRIGHT

Protection granted to authors and artists prohibiting others from reproducing their works without their permission.

COR

See contracting officer's representative.

CORE COMPETENCY

Particular, identifiable, and special skill that is central to the creation of customer value for an organization. Core competencies are found largely in the employees of an organization but also can be manifested in an organization's procedures and processes. An investment in strengthening core competencies throughout an organization forms a source of sustainable competitive advantages.

CORE PROJECT TEAM

Group comprising three to six functional experts who plan and gather resources for a project. The team, which works for or with a project manager, may or may not be responsible for completing the work of the project, but it is responsible for ensuring that the project is completed successfully.

CORPORATE CULTURE

Organizational rules, rituals, procedures, ethics, values, mores, and general operating principles that all members of the group are expected to practice, if not endorse. All-encompassing and generally differentiates one organization from another. Difficult to change and can be done only with great thought and tenacity on the part of management.

CORRECTION

Elimination of a defect.

CORRECTIVE ACTION

Changes made to bring expected future performance of the project in line with the project plan.

CORRECTIVE MAINTENANCE

Maintenance performed to correct faults in hardware or software.

CORRECTNESS

Degree to which a system or component is free from faults in its specification, design, and implementation.

CORRELATION AND STRATIFICATION

One of the seven tools of quality. The correlation diagram is used to plot a defect level on the vertical axis and the experimental value is plotted on the horizontal axis to determine how one variable correlates to the other. The stratification diagram is used to split data into groups and plot the results on a graph. For example, defects measured against a timeline may not appear to have a pattern; however, when plotted against individual operators of machines that produce the product, it will show a different pattern.

COSO

See Committee of Sponsoring Organizations of the Treadway Commission.

COST

(1) Cash value of project activity; value associated with materials and resources expended to accomplish project objectives.

(2) Sum or equivalent that is expended, paid, or charged for something.

COST ACCOUNT

(1) Management control point at which actual costs can be accumulated and compared with BCWP, or earned value.

(2) Cost category that represents the work assigned to one responsible organizational unit on a CWBS, and thus is a natural control point for cost/schedule planning and control.

COST ACCOUNT MATRIX

Chart or conversion table that relates costs to the functional organizations and WBS elements.

COST ACCOUNTING PRACTICE

Disclosed or established accounting method or technique used to measure cost; determine the amount of cost to be assigned to individual cost accounting periods; and allocate costs, directly and indirectly, to cost objectives.

COST AN ARM AND A LEG

Cost an exorbitant amount of money.

COST ANALYSIS

Process used to develop or assess the reasonableness and validity of estimates and resource requirements by estimating the subelements of cost to produce an item or deliver a service. Includes a statement or report of the assessment and related conclusions.

COST AND PRICE ANALYSIS

Examination, usually by a buyer, of a seller's proposed costs to determine whether they are fair and reasonable. *See also* price analysis and cost analysis.

COST AVOIDANCE

Action taken in the present that will decrease costs in the future. For example, an engineering improvement that increases the mean time between failure (MTBF) and thereby decreases operating support costs can be described as a cost avoidance action. It is possible for the engineering change to incur higher costs in the present; however, if the net total life cycle cost (LCC) is less, it is a cost avoidance action. The amount of the cost avoidance is determined as the difference between two estimated cost patterns: one before the change, the other after the change.

COST-BASED BUDGET

Budget based on the cost of goods and services to be received during a given period, whether paid for or not before the end of the period. Not to be confused with an expenditure-based budget, which is based on the cost paid for goods and services received.

COST BASELINE

Time-phased budget used to measure and monitor cost performance on the project. Developed by summing estimated costs by period and usually displayed in the form of an S-curve. *See also* S-curve.

COST-BENEFIT ANALYSIS

Analytic technique that compares the costs and benefits of investments, programs, or policy actions in order to determine which alternative or alternatives maximize net profits. Net benefits of an alternative are determined by subtracting the present value of costs from the present value of benefits.

COST BREAKDOWN STRUCTURE

System for subdividing a program into hardware elements and subelements, functions and subfunctions, and cost categories to provide for more effective management and control of the program.

COST BUDGETING

Allocating cost estimates to individual project components.

COST CAP

In U.S. DOD application, it is the maximum total dollar amount DOD is willing to commit for acquiring a given capability. A cost cap consists of program acquisition costs only and is maintained in constant dollars. Cost caps are applied to selected baseline programs.

COST CEILING

Number equivalent to the cumulative total of the project's cost target plus contingencies.

COST CENTER

Subdivision of an activity for which identification of costs is desired and through which costs can be controlled through one responsible manager.

COST CHANGE CONTROL SYSTEM

Procedure by which the cost baseline may be changed; includes documentation, tracking systems, and approval levels needed to authorize changes.

COST CONTAINMENT

Process of diligently monitoring all expenditures so as not to exceed a specified budget; generally, any action taken to eliminate cost growth within an organization.

COST CONTRACT

Cost-reimbursement contract in which the contractor receives no fee or profit. May be appropriate for research and development work, particularly with nonprofit educational institutions or other nonprofit organizations, and for facilities contracts.

COST CONTROL

Oversight of changes to the project budget. Includes influencing the factors that cause changes to the cost baseline, determining that the cost baseline has changed, ensuring that the changes are beneficial, and managing actual changes when and as they occur.

COST CONTROLS

Processes and tools used to practice cost control, such as variance analysis, integrated cost and schedule reporting, progress analysis, and corrective action.

COST DRIVER

Any factor that determines how much an activity will cost. There are two main types:

(1) Resource driver: costs associated with the quantity of resources used.

(2) Activity driver: costs incurred by the activities required to complete an activity or task. *See also* ABC method *and* activity-based costing.

COST-EFFECTIVE

Best value or performance for the least cost.

COST-EFFECTIVENESS

Measure of the operational capability added by a system as a function of its life cycle cost (LCC).

COST ESTIMATE

(1) Judgment or opinion regarding the cost of an object, commodity, or service. A cost estimate may constitute a single value or a range of values.

(2) Prediction of the expected monetary cost required to perform an activity or task or acquire an item.

(3) Quantitative assessment of the likely costs of the resources required to complete project activities.

COST ESTIMATING

Process of estimating the cost of the resources needed to complete project activities. May include an economic evaluation, an assessment of project investment cost, and a forecast of future trends and costs.

COST ESTIMATING METHODOLOGIES

Different approaches to developing a cost estimate. Examples include comparison/analogy, parametric, detailed engineering/bottom-up, and extrapolation from actuals.

COST ESTIMATING RELATIONSHIP (CER)

Mathematical relationship that defines cost as a function of one or more noncost parameters, such as performance, operating characteristics, or physical characteristics. For example, $ / square feet or meters.

COST FORECASTING

Process of predicting future trends and costs throughout a project.

COST GROWTH

Term related to the net change of an estimated or actual amount over a previously established base figure. The base must be relatable to a program, project, or contract and be clearly identified, including source, approval authority, specific items included, specific assumptions made, date, and amount.

COST INCURRED

Cost identified through the use of the accrual method of accounting.

COST INPUT

Cost, except for general and administrative expenses, that for contract costing purposes is allocable to the production of goods and services during a cost accounting period.

COST MANAGEMENT

Function required to maintain effective financial control of the project by evaluating, estimating, budgeting, monitoring, analyzing, forecasting, and reporting cost information.

COST MANAGEMENT PLAN

Document that describes how cost variances will be managed (for example, different responses for major and minor variances). May be part of the overall project plan.

COST MODEL

Compilation of cost estimating logic that aggregates cost estimating details into a total cost estimate.

COST OBJECTIVE

Function, organizational subdivision, contract, or other work unit for which cost data are desired and for which provision is made to accumulate and measure the cost of processes, products, jobs, capitalized projects, and the like.

COST OF CAPITAL

Rate of return a corporation or individual could earn if it invested its capital in another investment, venture, or project with equivalent risk.

COST(S) OF CONFORMANCE

Costs associated with addressing quality proactively. There are two types: prevention costs (up-front expenditures to ensure satisfaction of customer requirements) and appraisal costs (costs associated with the evaluation of the product or process to see whether customer requirements are being met).

COST OF GOODS SOLD (COGS)

Figure representing the cost of buying raw material and producing finished goods. Included are precise factors— material and factory labor, for example—as well as factors that are variable, such as factory overhead.

COST OF LIVING ADJUSTMENT (COLA)

Annual addition to the wages and benefits of employees to compensate them for the loss of buying power, mainly due to inflation.

COST-OF-LIVING INDEX

Index that measures differences in the price of goods and services over time; it allows for substitutions to other items as prices change.

COST(S) OF NONCONFORMANCE

Costs associated with addressing quality reactively. There are two types: internal failure costs (costs associated with the failure of the processes to make the products acceptable to the customer before the products leave the control of the organization) and external failure costs (costs associated with the determination by the customer that requirements have not been met).

COST OF POOR QUALITY (COPQ)

Total of costs generated as a result of producing defective products or services, including the cost of fulfilling the gap between the desired and actual quality of a product or service. It also includes the cost of lost opportunity due to the loss of resources used in rectifying the defect, which can include labor cost, rework cost, disposition costs, and material costs that have been added to the unit up to the point of rejection. COPQ does not include detection and prevention cost.

COST OF QUALITY

Costs incurred or expended to ensure quality, including those associated with the cost of conformance and nonconformance.

COST OF SALES

See cost of goods sold.

COST OR PRICING DATA

All facts that, as of the date of price agreement or, if applicable, an earlier date agreed upon between the parties that is as close as practicable to the date of agreement on price, prudent buyers and sellers would reasonably expect to affect price negotiations significantly. Cost or pricing data are data requiring certification. Cost or pricing data are factual, not judgmental, and are verifiable. Although they do not indicate the accuracy of the prospective contractor's judgment about estimated future costs or projections, they do include the data forming the basis for that judgment. Cost or pricing data are more than historical accounting data; they are all the facts that can reasonably be expected to contribute to the soundness of estimates of future costs and to the validity of determinations of costs already incurred. They include such factors as: vendor quotations; nonrecurring costs; information on changes in production methods and in production or purchasing volume; data supporting projections of business prospects and objectives and related operations costs; unit-cost trends such as those associated with labor efficiency; make-or-buy decisions; estimated resources to attain business goals; and information on management decisions that could have a significant bearing on costs. The term is used primarily in U.S. federal procurement.

COST OVERRUN

(1) Amount by which a project's actual costs exceed estimates.

(2) Amount by which a contractor exceeds the estimated cost and/or the final limitation (ceiling) of the contract.

COST PERFORMANCE INDEX (CPI)

Ratio of budgeted costs to actual costs (BCWP / ACWP). Often used to predict the amount of a possible cost overrun or underrun using the following formula: BAC / CPI = EAC. *See also* earned value.

COST PERFORMANCE MEASUREMENT BASELINE

Budget costs and measurable goals (particularly time and quantities) formulated for comparisons, analyses, and forecasts of future costs.

COST PERFORMANCE REPORT (CPR)

Written account of cost and schedule progress and earned value, normally prepared monthly.

COST-PLUS-AWARD-FEE (CPAF) CONTRACT

Cost-reimbursement contract that provides for a fee that consists of (1) a base fee (which may be zero) fixed at inception of the contract and (2) an award fee based on a periodic judgmental evaluation by the procuring authority. Used to provide motivation for performance in areas such as quality, timeliness, technical ingenuity, and cost-effective management during the contract. In cost-type contracts, the performance risk is borne mostly by the buyer, not the seller.

COST-PLUS-FIXED-FEE (CPFF) CONTRACT

Type of contract in which the buyer reimburses the contractor for the contractor's allowable costs (as defined by the contract) plus a fixed amount of profit (fee). The fixed fee does not vary with actual cost but may be adjusted if changes occur in the work to be performed under the contract. In cost-type contracts, the performance risk is borne mostly by the buyer, not the seller.

COST-PLUS-INCENTIVE-FEE (CPIF) CONTRACT

Type of contract in which the buyer reimburses the contractor for the contractor's allowable costs (as defined by the contract) and the seller earns its fee (profit) if it meets defined performance or cost criteria. Specifies a target cost, target fee, minimum fee, maximum fee, and fee adjustment formula. After contract performance, the fee (profit) paid to the contractor is determined according to the formula.

COST-PLUS-PERCENTAGE-OF-COST (CPPC) CONTRACT

Type of contract that provides for reimbursement of allowable cost of services performed plus an agreed-upon percentage of the actual cost as profit. In cost-type contracts, the performance risk is borne mostly by the buyer, not the seller.

COST REALISM

In U.S. federal procurement, the costs in an offeror's proposal that: (1) are realistic for the work to be performed; (2) reflect a clear understanding of the requirements; and (3) are consistent with the various elements of the offeror's technical proposal.

COST REASONABLENESS

In U.S. federal procurement, a cost is reasonable if, in its nature and amount, it does not exceed that which would be incurred by a prudent person in the conduct of competitive business.

COST-REIMBURSEMENT CONTRACT

Contract category that involves payment (reimbursement) to the contractor for its actual costs.

COST RISK

(1) Risk associated with failing to complete tasks within the estimated budget allowances.

(2) Assessment of possible monetary loss or gain from the work to be done on a project.

COST SAVINGS

Difference between the target cost and the actual cost incurred as a result of a specific and identifiable action to reduce costs relative to the target. In U.S. government incentive contracts, it is where the contractor and government share in any difference in cost below the estimated target cost incurred by the contractor to achieve the objective of the contract. It differs from cost avoidance in that a cost target has been set from which the amount of savings can be measured. In cost avoidance, the amount is determined as the difference between two estimated cost patterns.

COST/SCHEDULE CONTROL SYSTEM (C/SCS)

Management system requiring the contractor to establish a WBS for all the work to be performed on the contract and to record performance and costs for each element of that structure. Tracks the contractor's performance at a level of detail that will provide early information if the contractor is not performing on schedule or at the estimated costs.

COST/SCHEDULE CONTROL SYSTEM CRITERIA (C/SCSC)

(1) Performance measurement approach that focuses primarily on earned value.

(2) Criteria that specify the minimum requirements a contractor's management control system must satisfy.

COST/SCHEDULE STATUS REPORT (C/SSR)

Information submitted by U.S. government contractors on contracts that are not of sufficient size to warrant a cost performance report, which generally is required with a funding level of at least $2 million and a contract period longer than 12 months. The C/SSR, which contains a summary form, brief narrative on status, and problem analysis report if thresholds are exceeded, is intended to provide the project manager with a description of the contract's cost and schedule status at a given time.

COST-SHARING CONTRACT

Arrangement under which the contractor bears some of the burden of reasonable, allocable, and allowable contract cost.

COST TARGET

Maximum allowable expenditure for material, labor, outsourcing, overhead, and all other expenses associated with a project or program.

COST-TIME PROFILES

Graphical illustration depicting accumulated cost against accumulated time. Used in conjunction with just-in-time manufacturing, business process reengineering, and total quality management.

COST/TIME SLOPE

Theoretical continuum identifying the incremental unit cost required to reduce activity duration by a specific time period.

COST-TO-COST ACCOUNTING

Method of project accounting that is used to recognize revenue in a cost plus or fixed-price contract to determine percent complete of a specific cost category. To calculate percent complete, the actual costs incurred are divided by the forecasted, budgeted costs for the category. For example, if forecasted costs for outsourced consulting services on a project are $20,000 and actual costs are $10,000, the percent complete is 50%.

COST UNDERRUN

Excess of a project's estimated costs over the actual cost for work that was within the project's scope.

COST VARIANCE (CV)

(1) In earned value, the numerical difference between BCWP and ACWP.

(2) Difference between the estimated and actual costs of an activity.

COTR

See contracting officer's technical representative.

COTS

See commercial off-the-shelf.

COULD COST

Technique designed to achieve the best quality and price for goods purchased, based on what a program could cost if both the buyer and seller eliminate all nonvalue-added work done or required by either party.

COUNTERFEIT COMPETITION

Open and blatant praise by negotiators of the benefits of false alternative choices that are supposedly at least as attractive as successfully completing the current negotiation. Presumably, the alternative would become increasingly attractive if the negotiator was forced to make further concessions during negotiations.

CPAF

See cost-plus-award-fee contract.

CPFF

See cost-plus-fixed-fee contract.

CPI

See Consumer Price Index.
See cost performance index.

CPIC

See capital planning and investment control.

CPIF

See cost-plus-incentive-fee contract.

CPM

See critical path method.

CPN

See critical path network.

CPPC

See cost-plus-percentage-of-cost contract.

CPR

See cost performance report.

CRADLE-TO-GRAVE

Total life cycle of a given system, from concept through development, acquisition, operations phases, and final disposition. *Also called* womb-to-tomb.

CRASH COSTS

Amount of money incurred to accelerate a project by crashing the schedule. *See also* crashing.

CRASHING

Taking action to decrease the total project duration by adding resources (human and material) to the project schedule without altering the sequence of activities. The objective of crashing is to obtain the maximum duration compression for the least cost. *See also* duration compression.

CRAWFORD SLIP PROCESS

Idea-generation and identification technique in which a moderator asks a question to the group, each member writes a response on a slip, and then the slips are posted and read. Often repeated until group consensus is reached

CRITERIA

Objectives, guidelines, procedures, and standards to be used for project development, design, or implementation.

CRITICAL ACTIVITY

Activity on a critical path, commonly determined by using the critical path method.

CRITICAL CHAIN

Title of a book by Eliyahu M. Goldratt, as well as the term used to describe the two constraints affecting any project: the critical path and the scarce resources that need to be managed. To keep the critical chain flowing smoothly, Goldratt advises project managers to use safety buffers to allow extra time for tasks that impinge directly on the critical path.

CRITICAL DEFECT

Defect that judgment and experience indicate is likely to result in hazardous or unsafe conditions for individuals using, maintaining, or depending on the product, or that is likely to prevent performance of the tactical function of the product.

CRITICAL DEFECTIVE

Unit of product that contains one or more critical defects and also may contain major or minor defects.

CRITICAL DESIGN REVIEW (CDR)

In U.S. DOD program management, a multidisciplined technical review to ensure that a system can proceed into fabrication, demonstration, and test, and can meet stated performance requirements within cost, schedule, risk, and other system constraints. Generally, this review assesses the system's final design as captured in product specifications for each configuration item in the system's product baseline, and ensures that each configuration item in the product baseline has been captured in the detailed design documentation. Normally conducted during the System Development and Demonstration (SDD) phase. *See also* product baseline.

CRITICAL ISSUE

(1) Aspect of a system's capability (operational, technical, or other) that must be investigated before the system's overall suitability can be known. Must be addressed before deciding whether to proceed to the next phase of development.

(2) Issue so central to project completion or continued performance that it must be resolved immediately.

CRITICAL ITEM

(1) Subsystem, component, material, or other item whose nonavailability when required could jeopardize completion of project objectives.

(2) Item that could have an adverse impact on cost, schedule, quality, or technical performance.

CRITICALITY ANALYSIS

Procedure by which each potential failure mode is ranked according to the combined influence of severity and probability of occurrence.

CRITICAL PATH

In a project network diagram, the series of activities that determines the earliest completion of the project. Will change as activities are completed ahead of or behind schedule. Although normally calculated for the entire project, may also be determined for a milestone or subproject. Often defined as those activities with float less than or equal to a specified value, often zero. *See also* critical path method.

CRITICAL PATH METHOD (CPM)

Network analysis technique used to predict project duration by analyzing the sequence of activities (path) that has the least amount of scheduling flexibility (the least amount of float). Early dates are calculated by a forward pass using a specified start date. Late dates are calculated by a backward pass starting from a specified completion date (usually the forward pass's calculated early finish date for the project).

CRITICAL PATH NETWORK (CPN)

Project plan consisting of activities and their logical relationships to one another. Output of the critical path method.

CRITICAL RISK

Risk that can jeopardize achievement of a project's cost, time, or performance objectives.

CRITICAL SUCCESS FACTORS

Qualitative and quantitative factors that are key to the successful achievement of a project's objectives. Examples include having the proper mix of expert resources; strong collaboration with key stakeholders; good communications; strong alignment of the project's objectives to corporate strategy; and executive support.

CROSSING THE CHASM

In product development, making the transition to the general market from an early market dominated by selected visionary customers.

CRR

See comparative risk ranking.

CRUNCH

Negotiation tactic designed to take another bite at the other party's position no matter how reasonable it is. The user of this tactic is never satisfied and responds in words such as, "You have to do better than that," or "That is not good enough."

CRYSTAL METHODS

One of a variety of agile software development methods. Developed by Alistair Cockburn in the early 1990s, crystal methods focus on face-to-face interactions that reduce reliance on written documentation, thus improving the likelihood of delivering a system the user needs. Its name represents a gemstone. In Cockburn's scheme, the different types of crystal methods are assigned colors arranged in ascending opacity, with the most agile version being Crystal Clear, followed by Crystal Yellow, Crystal Orange, Crystal Red, and so on.

CSCI

See computer software configuration item.

C/SCS

See cost/schedule control system.

C/SCSC

See cost/schedule control system criteria.

CSD

See computer software documentation.

C/SSR

See cost/schedule status report.

CSU
See computer software unit.

CULTURAL RELEVANCE
Demonstration that evaluation methods, procedures, user manuals, systems documentation, training materials, and/or instruments are appropriate for the cultures to which they are applied (for example, having case studies in project management training materials in multiple languages and "localized" to make them more culturally relevant).

CULTURE
In project management, the combined effect of the values, beliefs, attitudes, traditions, and behaviors of the members of an organization.

CUMULATIVE AVERAGE IMPROVEMENT CURVE
Improvement curve model based on the assumption that as the total volume of units produced doubles, the average cost per unit decreases by some constant percentage.

CUMULATIVE COST CURVE
Graphic display used to show planned and actual expenditures to monitor cost variances. The difference in height between the curves for planned expenditures and actual expenditures represents the monetary value of spending variance at any given time.

CURRENT COSTS
Present market value of a product, asset, or service.

CURRENT FINISH DATE
Current estimate of when an activity will finish.

CURRENT LIABILITIES
Debts incurred by a corporation that are expected to be paid within the following 12 months.

CURRENT START DATE
Current estimate of when an activity will begin.

CURRENT YEAR
Fiscal year (FY) in progress.

CUSTODIAL RECORDS

Written memoranda of any kind, such as requisitions, issue hand receipts, tool checks, and stock record books, used to control items issued from tool cribs, tool rooms, and stockrooms.

CUSTOMER

See client.

CUSTOMER ACCEPTANCE

Documented signoff by the customer that all project deliverables satisfy requirements.

CUSTOMER/CLIENT PERSONNEL

Individuals working for the organization who will assume responsibility for the product produced by the project when it is complete.

CUSTOMER RETENTION

Extending the average length of customer relationships to grow a business's revenue. Given that it costs less to sell products and services to an existing customer than it does to find a new customer, customer retention can reduce the cost of goods sold while increasing loyalty and overall revenue.

CUSTOMER SATISFACTION MEASUREMENT

Process of determining how satisfied a customer is with a business's products or services. Such a process can help determine and identify better ways to anticipate and fulfill customers' requirements. Often performed on an ongoing basis through surveys, interviews, and focus groups.

CUTOFF POINT

Minimum acceptable rate of return a corporation is willing to earn on its investments. Often used as one criterion in project selection. *See also* hurdle rate.

CUTOVER

Process of moving from one system to another. Generally refers to a method in which no parallel use of the two systems occurs, making the cutover process a high-risk event should the target system fail to work properly the first time.

CUT SCORE
Point on a score scale at which scores at or above the point are in a different category or classification than scores below the point (for example, pass versus fail).

CUT TO THE CHASE
Get to the point.

CV
See cost variance.

CWBS
See contract work breakdown structure.

CYBERNETIC CONTROL SYSTEM
Automatic control system containing a negative feedback loop.

CYBERNETICS
Interdisciplinary study of the structure of complex systems, and in particular communications processes. Closely related to control theory and systems theory.

CYBERPHOBIA
Fear of computers. *Also called* technofear.

CYCLE 0
In agile project management, the initial iteration of a project to determine its economic, technical, operational, and political feasibility. Typically includes initial requirements and architectural modeling. Usually lasts no longer than two weeks.

CYCLE TIME
Total amount of time from the beginning to the end of a process as defined by the organization and its customers. It is a common term used in the creation of new products. It can include process time, during which a unit is acted upon to bring it closer to an output, and delay time, during which a unit of work is spent waiting to take the next action.

CYCLE-TIME REDUCTION
Any activity that reduces the time it takes an organization to produce a product or deliver a service by minimizing waiting

time, eliminating activities that do not add value, increasing parallel processes, or speeding up the decision processes within an organization.

D

DAMAGE MODE AND EFFECTS ANALYSIS (DMEA)

Analysis of a system or piece of equipment conducted to determine the extent of damage sustained from hostile weapons and the effect of damage on the continued controlled operation and mission completion capabilities of the system or equipment.

DAMAGES

Pecuniary compensation or indemnity that may be recovered in a judicial or quasi-judicial forum by a party who suffers loss, detriment, or injury through breach of contract by the act, omission, or negligence of another party.

DASHBOARD

Tool used for collecting and reporting information about project and program status. A dashboard provides a quick, and usually graphical, summary of project and program status and performance. Can be used at the project, program, and portfolio levels.

DATA

Documented information, regardless of its form or the medium on which it is recorded.

DATABASE

Collection of logically related data stored together in one or more computerized files; an electronic repository of information accessible via a query language interface.

DATABASE MANAGEMENT SYSTEM

Software system that controls the storing, combining, updating, retrieving, and displaying of data records.

DATA COLLECTION

Gathering and recording of facts, changes, and forecasts for status reporting and future planning.

DATA DATE

Point in time that separates actual (historical) data from future (scheduled) data. *Also called* as-of date.

DATA DICTIONARY

Repository of information about data, such as its meaning, relationships to other data, origin, usage, and format. A data dictionary manages data categories such as aliases, data elements, data records, data structure, data store, data models, data flows, data relationships, processes, functions, dynamics, size, frequency, resource consumption, and other user-defined attributes.

DATA MINING

Sifting through a massive volume of information, usually stored in a database, for research, investigative, marketing, and other business purposes.

DATA MODEL

Model showing data requirements of a business area; often considered synonymous with the entity relationship diagram.

DATA REFINEMENT

Necessary rework or redefinition of logic or data developed during planning to properly input milestones, constraints, priorities, and resources.

DATA WAREHOUSE

Massive database of historical information used for the business intelligence requirements of an organization. It integrates data from the various other systems and databases from which it gets data at regularly scheduled intervals. The place where data mining is done.

DATE OF ACCEPTANCE

Date on which a customer provides final approval of the deliverable item or project.

DAX 30

Deutscher Aktien Index 30 is a blue chip stock market index of the 30 major German companies trading on the Frankfurt Stock Exchange

DAYS PAYABLE OUTSTANDING (DPO)

Estimate of the length of time a company or organization takes to pay its vendors after receiving goods or services. If the firm receives favorable terms from suppliers, it has the net effect of providing the firm with free financing. If terms are reduced and a company is forced to pay at the time of receipt of goods, it reduces financing by the trade and increases the firm's working capital requirements. DPO is calculated: DPO = 365 / Payables Turnover (Payables Turnover = Purchases / Payables).

DAYS SALES OUTSTANDING (DSO)

Financial indicator that shows both the age, in terms of days, of a company's accounts receivable and the average time it takes to turn the receivables into cash. Also known as collection period (period average). It is compared with company and industry averages, as well as company selling terms (for example, Net 30) for determination of acceptability by the company. DSO is calculated: DSO = (Total Receivables / Total Credit Sales in the Period Analyzed) x Number of Days in the Period Analyzed. Note: Only credit sales are to be used. Cash sales are excluded.

D&B

See Dun & Bradstreet.

DBA

See doing business as.

DCF

See discounted cash flow.

DEADBEAT

One who does not pay his or her bills.

DEADHEAD

(1) Act of moving a piece of transportation equipment when it is not carrying a payload (for example, a bus being hauled to another location by a tow truck).

(2) Someone who does not pay a fare to be transported from one location to another (for example, a nonworking flight attendant being transported to another airport to work on a future flight).

DEAD LETTER

Letter that is undeliverable by the postal authority but cannot be returned to the sender.

DEBIT

(1) Any bookkeeping entry in recording a transaction, the effect of which is to decrease a liability, revenue, or capital account or increase an asset or expense account.

(2) Having a balance that represents an asset.

(3) The act of making such an entry.

(4) Debit memo or debit invoice used in dealings with customers or suppliers.

DEBT FINANCING

Raising money through selling bonds, notes, or mortgages, or borrowing directly from financial institutions; such debt must be repaid with interest and usually in installments.

DEBUG

To detect, locate, and correct faults in a computer program. *See also* bug.

DECENTRALIZED CONTRACTING

Contract management structure in which the project manager typically has control over the contracting process for his or her project. Either the project manager or a person working directly for the project manager is responsible for contracting activities.

DECISION

Choice that must be made, typically shown on a decision tree as a node on the left.

DECISION MAKING

Analyzing a problem to identify viable solutions and then making a choice among them.

DECISION SUPPORT SYSTEM

Computer software that aids decision making. Simulation programs, mathematical programming routines, and decision rules may be involved.

DECISION THEORY

Technique used in risk quantification to assist in decision making; it points to the best possible course of action, considering project uncertainties.

DECISION TREE

Diagram that shows key interactions among decisions and associated chance events as they are understood by the decision maker. Branches of the tree represent either decisions or chance events. The diagram provides for the consideration of the probability of each outcome.

DECOMPOSING

See decomposition.

DECOMPOSITION

Subdivision of the major project deliverables into smaller, more manageable components until the deliverables are defined in sufficient detail to support future project activities (planning, executing, controlling, and closing).

DECREMENT

Cost or price reduction.

DEEP POCKETS

Having a seemingly inexhaustible amount of money to pay for a project or program.

DE FACTO AUTHORITY

Influence exercised regardless of formal authority and often derived from such power bases as charisma, expert knowledge, position, or bureaucratic knowledge. May be exercised by the project manager or by project team members. *See also* de jure authority.

DE FACTO STANDARDS

Standards set and accepted by the marketplace but lacking approval by recognized standards organizations.

DEFAULT

Failure to perform a legal or contractual duty, honor a promise, discharge an obligation, or perform according to an agreement.

DEFECT

Nonconformance of a characteristic with specified requirements, or a deficiency in something necessary for an item's intended, proper use.

DEFECTIVE

Unit of product that contains one or more defects.

DEFECTIVE COST OR PRICING DATA

Cost or pricing data subsequently found to have been inaccurate, incomplete, or outdated.

DEFECTS PER HUNDRED UNITS

Number of defects per hundred units of any given quantity of product, determined by multiplying the number of defects by 100 and then dividing by the total number of units of product. Expressed as an equation: Defects per 100 units = (Number of defects x 100) ÷ Number of units.

DEFENSE MATÉRIEL ITEM

In the U.S. military, a system or item usually established as an integral program element (PE) or identified as a project within an aggregated PE.

DEFERRED REVENUE

Revenue associated with an item or service that is initially recorded as a liability but is expected to become an asset in the future.

DEFICIT SPENDING

Excess of government expenditures over government revenue, resulting in a shortfall that must be financed through borrowing.

DEFINED BENEFIT PENSION PLAN

Retirement plan that uses a specific predetermined formula to calculate the amount of an employee's future benefit. The most common type of formula is based on the employee's terminal earnings. Under this formula, benefits are based on a percentage of average earnings during a specified number of years at the end of a worker's career—for example, the highest 5 out of the last 10 years—multiplied by the maximum number of years of credited service under the plan. In recent years, a new type of defined benefit plan, a cash balance plan, has become more prevalent. Under this type of plan, benefits are computed as a percentage of each employee's account balance. Employers specify a contribution—usually based on a percentage of the employee's earnings—and a rate of interest on that contribution that will provide a predetermined amount at retirement, usually in the form of a lump sum. In the private sector, defined benefit plans typically are funded exclusively by employer contributions. In the public sector, defined benefit plans often require employee contributions.

DEFINED CONTRIBUTION PLAN

Retirement plan in which the amount of the employer's annual contribution is specified. Individual accounts are set up for participants, and benefits are based on the amounts credited to these accounts (through employer contributions and, if applicable, employee contributions) plus any investment earnings on the money in the account. Only employer contributions to the account are guaranteed, not the future benefits. In defined contribution plans, future benefits fluctuate on the basis of investment earnings. The most common type of defined contribution plan is a savings and thrift plan. Under this type of plan, the employee contributes a predetermined portion of his or her earnings (usually pretax) to an individual account, all or part of which is matched by the employer.

DEFINITE-QUANTITY CONTRACT

Indefinite-delivery contract that provides for delivery of a definite quantity of specific supplies or services for a fixed period; deliveries or performance will be scheduled at designated locations upon order.

DEFINITIVE ESTIMATE

Detailed estimate that is prepared from well-defined data, specifications, or drawings and is accurate to within −5 percent to +10 percent. Used for bid proposals, bid evaluations, contract changes, legal claims, permits, and government approvals.

DEFLATION

Decreases in the price for identical or similar items that result in a decrease in purchasing power.

DEFLECTION

Transference of all or part of a risk to another party, usually by means of a contract provision, insurance policy, or warranty.

DEGRADATION

Lowering of quality, performance, or status; also a gradual impairment in the ability to perform.

DE JURE AUTHORITY

Influence based on conferment of the "legal" or rightful power to command or act. Usually, the formal authority of a project manager is described in some form of documentation (such as a project charter), which may also describe the roles of other functional managers associated with the project. *See also* de facto authority.

DELAY COST

Cost of delaying the completion of an element of a project or program or the project or program itself. Used to guide decision making by the project team.

DELEGATING

Process of distributing authority from the project manager to another individual working on the project.

DELEGATION OF PROCUREMENT AUTHORITY (DPA)

In U.S. federal procurement, a document, issued by authorized agency personnel (usually the head of the contracting activity), that authorizes an individual to make purchases on behalf of the government. This delegation of procurement authority specifies spending and usage limitations unique to the individual.

DELIVERABLE

Measurable, tangible, verifiable outcome, result, or item that must be produced to complete a project or part of a project. Often used more narrowly in reference to an external deliverable, which is a deliverable that is subject to approval by the project sponsor or customer.

DELPHI TECHNIQUE

Form of participative expert judgment; an iterative, anonymous, interactive technique using survey methods to derive consensus on work estimates, approaches, issues, and any matter of importance requiring that a decision be made.

DELTA

Difference or change between reality and what was expected, for example, a funding delta.

DEMING CYCLE

See plan-do-check-act (PDCA) cycle.

DEMING PRIZE

Award established in Japan in 1950 by the Union of Japanese Scientists and Engineers and named after the father of the worldwide quality movement, W. Edwards Deming. The award honors Japanese and non–Japanese private and public organizations for successfully implementing quality control activities. Evaluation criteria for the award consist of the following 10 equally weighted areas: policies; organization; information; standardization; human resources; quality assurance; maintenance; improvement; effects; and future plans.

DEMOCRATIC MANAGEMENT STYLE

Participative management approach in which the project manager and project team make decisions jointly.

DEMONSTRATION

Verifying compliance with the specifications by witnessing how something works or operates.

DEPENDABILITY TECHNIQUE

Method of analyzing a system's behavior, starting at the design level, to identify improvements resulting in increased reliability.

DEPENDENCY

(1) Logical relationship between and among tasks of a project's WBS, which can be depicted graphically on a network diagram.

(2) Relationship among projects and project-related factors that may affect project success. *See also* logical relationship.

DEPENDENCY NETWORK

Graphic representation of the various project and program outcomes showing how each relates to the others in terms of prerequisites or dependencies. Usually done through a combination of PERT, CPM, and/or precedence networking techniques.

DEPENDENT EVENT

Two or more events in which the occurrence of one event is contingent upon the occurrence of another event.

DEPENDENT TASKS

Tasks that are related such that the beginning or end of one task is contingent upon the beginning or end of another.

DEPLOY

To field a system or equipment by placing it into operational use in a production mode.

DEPLOYMENT PLAN

Plan to provide for the smooth introduction of a system or equipment to the user.

DEPRECIATION

Charge to current operations that systematically and logically distributes the cost of a tangible capital asset less residual value over the asset's estimated useful life.

DERIVED REQUIREMENTS

Requirements that arise from constraints; consideration of issues implied but not explicitly stated in the requirements baseline; factors introduced by the selected architecture; information assurance requirements; and design. Derived requirements are defined through requirements analysis as part of the overall systems engineering process and are part of the allocated baseline.

DESCRIPTIVE RISK ANALYSIS

See descriptive risk assessment.

DESCRIPTIVE RISK ASSESSMENT

Narrative description of a risk event that explains what might happen, why it might happen, and ideas for controlling it. *Also called* descriptive risk analysis.

DESCRIPTIVE STATISTICS

Large variety of methods for summarizing or describing a set of numbers. These methods may involve computational or graphical analysis.

DESIGN

Creation of the description of a product or service, in the form of specifications, drawings, data flow diagrams, or any other methods, to provide detailed information on how to build the product or perform the service.

DESIGN/BUILD

Method of construction contracting that combines the architectural, engineering, and construction services required for a project into a single agreement. Under such an agreement, the buyer contracts with a single entity, so that the contractor providing the end product is responsible for both design and construction.

DESIGN OF EXPERIMENTS

Analytical technique used in quality management to help identify the variables that have the most influence on the outcome of a process or procedure.

DESIGN PARAMETERS

Qualitative, quantitative, physical, and functional value characteristics that are inputs to the design process, for use in design trade-offs, risk analyses, and development of a system that is responsive to system requirements.

DESIGN REVIEW

Formal, documented, comprehensive, and systematic examination of a design to evaluate its ability to meet specified requirements, identify problems, and propose solutions.

DESIGN SPECIFICATION(S)

Precise measurements, tolerances, materials, in-process and finished-product tests, quality control measures, inspection requirements, and other specific information that precisely describes how the work is to be done.

DESIGN SYNTHESIS

Process of translating functional and performance requirements into design solutions to include internal and external interfaces.

DESIGN TO COST

Management concept stipulating that rigorous cost goals are established during the development of a system and that control of costs, acquisition, operations, and support is achieved by practical trade-offs between operational capability, performance, costs, and schedule.

DESK CHECKING

(1) Requirements validation technique in which selected stakeholders individually review requirements documentation against a checklist developed for that purpose.

(2) Technique used by computer programmers to test the logic of programs by executing the statements of the algorithm on a sample data set and recording the results on a piece of paper rather than using the computer to determine if the logic is correct. The technique was used in the early days of computing when processor time was extremely expensive. By performing a desk check, the programmer would be able to identify simple logic errors, saving the processor time for uncovering more complex logic problems.

DETAILED DESIGN

Output of system design. A technical or engineering description of a system that provides individual views of the system components, details on the physical layout of the system, and information on the system's individual applications, subsystems, and hardware components.

DETAILED SCHEDULE

Schedule used to communicate day-to-day activities to the people working on the project.

DETERMINATION AND FINDINGS (D&F)

Special form of written approval by authorized officials required by statute or regulation as a prerequisite to taking certain contracting actions.

DETERMINISTIC ESTIMATE

Predetermined, single-value estimate based on the estimator's opinion of the value that is most appropriate given the situation at hand.

DEVELOPMENT

Process of working out and extending the theoretical, practical, and useful applications of a basic design, idea, or scientific discovery.

DEVELOPMENT METHODOLOGY

Set of mutually supportive and integrated processes and procedures organized into a series of phases constituting the development cycle of a product or service.

DEVELOPMENT PHASE

Phase in a generic project life cycle where the product or service to be delivered by the project or program is produced. *Also called* execution phase *or* implementation phase.

DEVIATION

(1) Departure from established requirements.

(2) Written authorization, granted before manufacture of an item, to depart from a specific performance or design requirement.

DEVIATION PERMIT

See production permit.

D&F

See determination and findings.

DIAGNOSTIC MODELING

Part of scientific method that enforces a regimen of proceeding from the known to the unknown in order to understand and solve a problem. The four steps of diagnostic modeling are: investigation; diagnosis; treatment plan identification and selection; and prognosis.

DIALING FOR DOLLARS

Termed used for cold calling in which marketers, insurance agents, stock brokers, and other salespeople make unsolicited telephone calls to unsuspecting customers in the hopes they will buy their products or services.

DIFFERENTIATION IN ORGANIZATION

Principle of bureaucratic organization that states that an organization should be structured around the environment with which it interacts. For example, if a company deals with petroleum interests, it might form a Petroleum Department, further subdivided by types or sources of petroleum.

DIRECT COST

Cost identified with a specific, final cost objective. Not necessarily limited to items that are incorporated into the end product as labor or material. *See also* indirect cost.

DIRECT ENGINEERING

Engineering effort directly related to specific end products.

DIRECTIVE

Written communication that initiates or prescribes action, conduct, or procedure.

DIRECT LABOR

Labor identified with a specific, final cost objective. For example, manufacturing direct labor includes fabrication, assembly, inspection, and testing for constructing the end product; engineering direct labor includes reliability, quality assurance, testing, and design identified with the end product. Direct labor is incurred for the exclusive benefit of the project.

DIRECT LABOR STANDARDS

Specified output or a time allowance established for a direct labor operation. Established by industrial engineers.

DIRECT MAIL

Form of advertising sent specifically to an individual or to an address.

DIRECT MARKETING

Selling using a promotion delivered individually to the prospective customer, typically through the mail system. A more personal form of advertising, it is used by a wide variety of organizations such as catalog houses, magazine publishers, political campaign organizations, and financial institutions.

DIRECT MATERIALS

Raw materials, purchased parts, interdivisional transfers, and subcontracted items required to manufacture and assemble completed products.

DIRECTOR

(1) Member of a board of directors of an organization.
(2) Anyone who leads or supervises a project or entity.

DIRECT OVERHEAD

Portion of overhead costs that can be directly attributable to a project, such as rent, lighting, and insurance.

DIRECT PROJECT COSTS

Costs directly attributable to a project, including all personnel, goods, or services and their associated costs, but not including indirect project costs such as overhead and general office costs incurred in support of the project.

DISABILITY INSURANCE

Insurance that includes paid sick leave, short-term disability benefits, and long-term disability benefits.

DISALLOWANCE

Refusal to recognize a cost as an allowable cost.

DISBURSEMENTS

In budgetary usage, gross disbursements represent the amount of checks issued, cash, or other payments less refunds received. Net disbursements represent gross disbursements less income collected and credited to the appropriation of the fund account, such as amounts received for goods and services provided.

DISCIPLINE

Area of technical expertise or specialty usually defined by a set of theoretical underpinnings, a body of knowledge, and in some instances, certification or licensing requirements.

DISCOUNTED CASH FLOW (DCF)

Financial technique for calculating the present value of future expected expenditures and revenues using net present value.

DISCOUNT FACTOR

Factor that translates expected benefits or costs in any given future year into present-value terms. The discount factor is equal to $1 / (1 + i)^t$ where i is the interest rate and t is the number of years from the date of initiation for the program or policy until the given future year.

DISCOUNTING

Process of reducing a future amount to a present value.

DISCOUNT RATE

Interest rate used in calculating the present value of future cash flow. *See also* discounted cash flow.

DISCRETE CHOICE EXPERIMENT

Quantitative tool used in market research to predict and model customer buying decisions.

DISCRETE EFFORT

In the context of earned value management, a work package or planning package (or lower-level task/activity) that is related to the completion of a specific end product or service that can be directly planned and measured.

DISCRETE WORK PACKAGE

Short-term, measurable job with definite start and end points that can be used to measure work performance or earned value.

DISCRETIONARY DEPENDENCY

Dependency defined by preference, rather than necessity. *Also called* preferred logic, preferential logic, *or* soft logic.

DISINFLATION

Slowing down of the rate at which prices increase, usually during a recession.

DISPOSAL

Act of getting rid of excess, surplus, scrap, or salvage property under proper authority. Disposal may be accomplished by, but is not limited to, transfer, donation, sale, declaration, abandonment, or destruction.

DISPUTE

(1) Disagreement not settled by mutual consent that could be decided by litigation or arbitration.

(2) Disagreement between the contractor and the buyer regarding the rights of parties under a contract.

DISRUPTIVE MANAGEMENT STYLE

Management approach in which the project manager tends to destroy the unity of the team, be an agitator, and cause disorder on the project.

DISTANCE LEARNING

Method of providing education and training to an individual or group of individuals in which the learner is not in the same room as the provider (teacher, professor, instructor) of the information. Requires the use of one or more of a variety of techniques and media to present the subject matter and can include television, satellite broadcasts, correspondence, e-mail, computer-based training, CD-ROM, videotape, Web-based delivery, or any combination thereof. Distance learning is viewed by many executives as a way to reduce training costs by eliminating the need for employees to travel to a course site, as well as having them complete all or part of the training on their own time.

DISTRESS SALE

Sale of a business or property under distress conditions.

DISTRIBUTION LIST

List of people and/or organizations that have received communications from the sender.

DIVERGENT THINKING

Thinking employed to generate a high volume of interesting, unusual, and creative ideas. *See also* convergent thinking.

DIVISION OF LABOR

Specifically assigning persons to various activities within a project by categories of labor, skill, or expertise.

DMEA

See damage mode and effects analysis.

DOCUMENTATION

Collection of reports, information, records, references, and other project data for distribution and archival purposes.

DOCUMENT CONTROL

System to control and execute project documentation in a uniform and orderly fashion.

DOD COMPONENTS

The Office of the Secretary of Defense (OSD); the Military Departments; the Chairman, Joint Chiefs of Staff (CJCS) and Joint Staff; the Unified Combatant Commands (UCCs); the Defense Agencies; and Department of Defense (DOD) field activities.

DOD DIRECTIVE (DODD) 5000.1, THE DEFENSE ACQUISITION SYSTEM

Principal DOD directive on acquisition, it states policies applicable to all DOD acquisition programs. These policies fall into five major categories: flexibility; responsiveness; innovation; discipline; and streamlined and effective management

DOD INSTRUCTION (DODI) 5000.2, OPERATION OF THE DEFENSE ACQUISITION SYSTEM

Establishes a simplified and flexible management framework for translating mission needs and technology opportunities, based on approved mission needs and requirements, into stable, affordable, and well-managed acquisition programs. Specifically authorizes the program manager and the Milestone Decision Authority (MDA) to use discretion and business judgment to structure a tailored, responsive, and innovative program.

DOG AND PONY SHOW

Informal term used to describe a presentation given to stakeholders using various graphic mechanisms such as PowerPoint® slides, flip charts, projections, charts, and other visual media to inform or otherwise persuade the audience to accept or gain consensus on a particular point of view or influence the buying of an idea or product.

DOING BUSINESS AS (DBA)

See fictitious name.

DOLLARIZATION

(1) Use of U.S. dollars by a country as its own currency (for example, Panama).

(2) Linking of a currency's value to that of the U.S. dollar (for example, Hong Kong).

(3) Use of the U.S. dollar for accounting purposes.

DON'T CHANGE HORSES IN MIDSTREAM

Do not change leaders or one's basic approach during the middle of the project.

DON'T GO THERE

Phrase used to avoid a topic of discussion due to sensitivities of the parties to the conversation.

DOUBLE SAMPLE PLAN

See sample plan, double.

DOW JONES INDUSTRIAL AVERAGE

Unmanaged index that tracks the daily share value of 30 large U.S. companies listed on the New York Stock Exchange. A key benchmark of stock performance.

DOWN EVENT

Event that caused an item to become unavailable to initiate its objective (that is, the transition from uptime to downtime).

DOWN SELECT

Reduce the number of contractors working on a program by eliminating one or more for the next phase.

DPA

See delegation of procurement authority.

DPO

See days payable outstanding.

DRILL DOWN

(1) Act of moving from a summarized view of data into a lower level of detail.

(2) To obtain a greater level of detail and information on any topic or issue by a variety of techniques such as analysis, interviews, questionnaires, and so forth.

DROP-DEAD DATE

Latest possible date by which something must be done; an absolute deadline.

DROP SHIP

Location to which the seller or retailer of a product ships the product directly from the manufacturer to the customer without requiring inventory carrying by the seller or retailer.

DRY BULK CARRIER

Vessel used primarily for the carriage of shipload lots of homogeneous, unmarked, nonliquid cargoes such as grain, coal, cement, and lumber.

DRY CARGO LINER

Vessel used for the carriage of heterogeneous marked cargoes in parcel lots. However, any cargo may be carried in these vessels, including part cargoes of dry bulk items or, when carried in deep tanks, bulk liquids such as petroleum and vegetable oils.

DSDM

See dynamic systems development method.

DSO

See days sales outstanding.

DU

See duration.

DUMMY ACTIVITY

Activity of zero duration that shows a logical relationship in the arrow diagramming method. Used when logical relationships cannot be described completely or correctly with regular activity arrows. Shown graphically as a dashed line headed by an arrow.

DUN

To urgently compel a person or a company to pay its bills.

DUN & BRADSTREET (D&B)

U.S.-based, for-profit agency that furnishes subscribers with marketing statistics and the financial standings and credit ratings of businesses. A subsidiary of Moody's Investors Service.

DURABLE GOODS

Goods that have a useful life of more than three years. Orders for such goods are tracked by the U.S. Department of Commerce on a monthly basis because it indicates the extent to which businesses and manufacturers are willing to invest capital for future needs.

DURATION (DU)

Number of work periods required to complete an activity or other project element. Usually expressed as hours, workdays, or workweeks. Sometimes incorrectly equated with elapsed time. *See also* effort.

DURATION COMPRESSION

Shortening of the schedule without reducing the project scope. Often requires an increase in project cost. *Also called* schedule compression. *See also* crashing *and* fast-tracking.

DYNAMIC SYSTEMS DEVELOPMENT METHOD (DSDM)

One of a variety of agile software development methods, DSDM is a framework developed in the early 1990s that formalizes rapid application development (RAD) practices. DSDM has seven stages:

• Preproject—Establishes that the project is ready to begin, funding is available, and everything is in place to commence a successful project.

• Feasibility study—An analysis undertaken to determine whether DSDM is the right approach for the project.

• Business study—A collaborative effort, using a series of facilitated workshops attended by knowledgeable and empowered staff members who can quickly pool their know-how and gain consensus on the priorities of the development.

• Functional model iteration—Builds on the high-level requirements identified in the business study. The DSDM framework works by building a number of prototypes based on risk and evolves these prototypes into the complete system.

• Design and build iteration—The prototypes from the functional model iteration are completed, combined, and tested, and a working system is delivered to the users.

• Implementation—The system is transitioned into use.

• Postproject—Includes postproject cleanup, as well as ongoing maintenance.

E

EA

See enterprise architecture.

EAC

See estimate at completion.

EARLY ADOPTERS

Any individual or group of individuals, consumers, or clients who are the first to use a new product concept before the general target audience for which it was developed. For new processes, these are stakeholders who recognize the benefit of a new way of doing things and do not need to be given an incentive or directed to use the new process.

EARLY FINISH DATE (EF)

Earliest possible point in time when the uncompleted portions of an activity or a project can end, based on network logic and any schedule constraints. May change as the project progresses or as changes are made to the project plan. Used in the critical path method.

EARLY ON

At the beginning of an evolution; for example, planning early on in system development for adequate support.

EARLY START DATE (ES)

Earliest possible point in time when the uncompleted portions of an activity or a project can begin, based on network logic and any schedule constraints. May change as the project progresses or as changes are made to the project plan. Used in the critical path method.

EARLY WARNING SYSTEM

Project control monitoring and reporting system used to alert the project manager if trouble is about to arise.

EARNED HOURS

Time in standard hours credited to a worker or group of workers as the result of successfully completing a given task or group of tasks; usually calculated by summing the products of applicable standard times multiplied by the completed work units.

EARNED VALUE (EV)

Analysis of a project's schedule and financial progress as compared with the original plan. *See also* actual cost of work performed, budgeted cost of work scheduled, budgeted cost of work performed, budget at completion, cost variance, cost performance index, estimate at completion, estimate to complete, schedule variance, *and* schedule performance index.

EARNED VALUE ANALYSIS
See earned value.

EARNED VALUE MANAGEMENT
Project management planning, monitoring, and control technique that integrates scope, schedule, and resources in such a way as to provide for the objective measurement of project performance and progress. Project performance is measured by comparing the earned value (EV), *also called* budgeted cost of work performed (BCWP), to the project's actual cost, *also called* actual cost of work performed (ACWP). Project progress is measured by comparing EV to the planned value (PV), *also called* budgeted cost of work scheduled (BCWS). When expertly applied, EVM provides an early warning of project performance problems.

EARNED VALUE MANAGEMENT SYSTEM (EVMS)
Industry-developed set of 32 standards adopted for use by the U.S. DOD in 1996 for evaluation of contractor management systems. A listing of the standards is contained in the Defense Acquisition Guidebook. The EVMS replaced the Cost/Schedule Control Systems Criteria (C/SCSC), which contained 35 standards for evaluation of contractor management systems. Contractors with systems formally recognized by DOD as meeting the 35 C/SCSC standards prior to November 1996 are considered compliant with the 32 EVMS standards.

EARNED VALUE TECHNIQUE
Technique, procedure, or approach that uses the earned value method of information collection and reporting for a project or program; used to establish the performance measurement baseline. Can be completed manually or by using information technology. *See also* earned value.

EARNINGS
Corporate profits.

EARNINGS BEFORE INTEREST AND TAXES (EBIT)
Indicator of a company's financial performance, calculated as revenue less expenses excluding taxes and interest.

EARNINGS BEFORE INTEREST, TAXES, DEPRECIATION, AND AMORTIZATION (EBITDA)

Earnings before interest, taxes, depreciation and amortization, but after all product/service, sales, and overhead costs are accounted for. Sometimes referred to as operational cash flow.

EARNINGS REPORT

Statement issued by a company to its shareholders and other interested parties reporting its earnings for the latest period.

EBIT

See earnings before interest and taxes.

EBITDA

See earnings before interest, taxes, depreciation, and amortization.

E-BUSINESS (ELECTRONIC BUSINESS)

Conducting all facets of business on the Internet. Applications include, and go beyond, the types of commercial transactions commonly conducted in e-commerce, such as customer relationship management and partner collaboration. Term is used by certain organizations in their advertising campaigns to generally describe a range of service offerings as they relate to conducting business over the Internet.

E-BUSINESS MODEL

Approach to using the Internet to conduct business or reach out to clients, customers, and stakeholders. The model spells out how a company plans to make money online reaching out to its various clients and customers. Examples of such models include—

• B2B—Business-to-business trade in which companies sell to one another

• B2C—Business-to-consumer trade in which companies sell to individual consumers

• B2G—Business-to-government trade in which companies sell to a government entity

• e-Marketplaces—Sites where buyers and sellers trade their goods online

ECB

See European Central Bank.

E-COMMERCE (ELECTRONIC COMMERCE)

Conducting business transactions between businesses, or between businesses and consumers, usually over the Web or by other automated means. Popular applications of e-commerce include the following online activities: buying products; paying bills; conducting banking activities; and booking airline, car, and hotel reservations.

ECONOMETRICS

Use of computer analysis and financial modeling techniques to describe in mathematical terms the relationship between key economic forces such as labor, capital, interest rates, and government policies.

ECONOMIC ANALYSIS

Systematic approach to selecting the most efficient and cost-effective strategy for satisfying an agency's need. Such an analysis evaluates the relative worth of different technical alternatives, design solutions, and/or acquisition strategies, and provides the means for identifying and documenting the costs and associated benefits of each alternative to determine the most cost-effective solution.

ECONOMIC ANALYSIS PHASE

See concept phase.

ECONOMIC EVALUATION

Process used to establish the value of a project in relation to other standards, benchmarks, project profitability, financing interest rates, and acceptance.

ECONOMIC LIFE

Period of time over which the benefits to be gained from a system may reasonably be expected.

ECONOMIC LOT SIZE

Number of units of manufactured items or materials that can be purchased within the lowest unit cost range.

ECONOMIC ORDER QUANTITY (EOQ)

Most economical quantity of parts or items to order at one time, considering the applicable procurement and inventory costs.

ECONOMIC VALUE ADDED (EVA)

Nonconventional accounting practice that measures an operation's real profitability. EVA is simply after-tax operating profit, a widely used measure, minus the total annual cost of capital, which no conventional measure includes. EVA is a registered trademark of Stern Stewart & Co., its developer.

ECONOMY OF SCALE

Reduction in the unit cost of an end product resulting from the production of additional units.

EDI

See electronic data interchange.

EEO

See equal employment opportunity.

EF

See early finish date.

EFFECTIVE INTEREST

True value of the interest rate computed using the compound interest rate for a one-year period.

EFFECTIVENESS

Extent to which the goals of the project or system are attained, or the degree to which a project can be elected to achieve a set of specific requirements. Also, an output of cost-effectiveness analysis.

EFFECTIVE TEAM

Group of people who work with one another in a positive way to accomplish shared objectives.

EFFICIENCY FACTOR

Ratio of standard performance time to actual performance, usually expressed as a percentage.

EFFORT

Number of labor units required to complete an activity or other project element. May be expressed as staff hours, days, or weeks. Should not be confused with duration.

EFFORT REMAINING

Number of work periods remaining in order to complete a task, activity, or project.

EFQM

See European Foundation for Quality Management Excellence Model.

EFT

See electronic funds transfer.

EGOLESS TEAM STRUCTURE

Way of organizing a project team in which there is no obvious leader, decisions are reached through consensus, and project tasks tend to reflect the input of all team members. Promotes extensive interaction and communication, but without strong consensual leadership the team can drift. Works best when the team is small, objectives are clear, and the task being accomplished is of high importance.

E-GOVERNMENT

Use by the U.S. government of Web-based Internet applications and other information technologies, combined with processes that implement these technologies.

EIGHTY-HOUR RULE

Method of breaking down each project activity or task into work packages that require no more than 80 hours of effort to complete.

EIGHTY-TWENTY (80/20) RULE

"Rule" devised by Vilfredo Pareto, who observed that 80 percent of the wealth in a particular region is owned by 20 percent of the population. As applied to quality management it is translated as meaning that 80 percent of the problems in quality are attributed to 20 percent of the operations. *See also* Pareto analysis.

ELABORATED

Worked out with care and detail; developed thoroughly.

ELAPSED TIME

Conventional concept of time with a 60-minute hour and 365-day year. Accounts for all time, not just time spent on the project.

E-LEARNING

Short for electronic learning. Form of distance learning that is Internet based. *Also called* e-training.

ELECTRONIC DATA INTERCHANGE (EDI)

Technique for electronically transferring and storing formatted information between computers using established and published formats and codes, as authorized by the applicable Federal Information Processing Standards (FIPS).

ELECTRONIC FUNDS TRANSFER (EFT)

Transfer payment transaction instruction given to the Federal Reserve System.

ELEPHANT IN THE ROOM

Important, obvious, and controversial topic of which everyone present is aware but that they refuse to discuss given its controversial nature.

ELEVATOR (LIFT) STATEMENT

Short (within two minutes), succinct, verbal statement describing the project and its intended customers and benefits. Name is derived from an unexpected encounter with an executive in riding an elevator (lift) and being able to condense the key points of a project and communicate the same to the executive in the time it takes to ascend or descend to the desired floor or level.

EMOTIONAL INTELLIGENCE THEORY

Relatively recent model of behavior described by Daniel Goleman in his 1995 book *Emotional Intelligence*, which provides another way to understand and assess people's behaviors, management styles, and interpersonal skills, among other things, using a measure called emotional quotient (EQ). The basic tenet of EQ is that IQ (intelligence quotient) is too narrow a gauge of a person's capabilities and that success is more predicated on a broad measure of capabilities not related to raw intelligence. Goleman identified the five "domains" of EQ as—

* Knowing your emotions

* Managing your own emotions

* Motivating yourself

* Recognizing and understanding other people's emotions

* Managing relationships; that is, managing the emotions of others

EMOTIONAL QUOTIENT (EQ)

See emotional intelligence theory.

EMPIRICAL RULE

Heuristic used in quality management relating to three standard deviations of the mean. For data sets having a normal, bell-shaped distribution, we can expect that 68% of all values fall within one standard deviation of the mean, 95% of all values fall within two standard deviations of the mean, and 99.7% of all values fall within three standard deviations of the mean.

EMPLOYEE STOCK OWNERSHIP PLAN (ESOP)

Plan in which employees take over, or participate in, the management of the organization that employs them by becoming shareholders of stock in that organization.

EMV

See expected monetary value.

END ACTIVITY

Activity in a network diagram with no logical successors.

END ITEM
Final production product when assembled, or completed, and ready for issue or deployment.

END OF STORY
There is no more to be said; the talking is over. Often said after a decision has been made, as in "We are going to outsource our data entry; end of story."

ENDORSEMENT
Written approval that signifies personal understanding and acceptance of the thing approved and recommends further endorsement by higher levels of authority if necessary; signifies authorization if endorsement of commitment is by a person with appropriate authority.

END PRODUCT
Deliverable resulting from project work.

END USER
Person or group for whom the project's product or service is developed.

ENGINEERING BUILD-UP ESTIMATE
See bottom-up estimate.

ENGINEERING CHANGE NOTICE
Formal release of an engineering change to the performing organizations.

ENGINEERING CHANGE ORDER
Directive to incorporate project improvements that have been designed after release of the initial product design.

ENGINEERING CHANGE PROPOSAL
Request initiated by either party to make changes to the drawings or specifications of a contract.

ENGINEERING COST ESTIMATE
See definitive estimate.

ENGINEERING ESTIMATE
See definitive estimate.

ENGINEERING REVIEW BOARD (ERB)

Committee of senior personnel from the functional engineering organizations convened to provide technical oversight for, and assistance to, the project manager. Usually convened at the request of the project manager. Members typically are appointed by the director of engineering or by the director's designee.

ENHANCEMENT

Change or group of changes to the scope of an existing project that provides additional functionality, features, or capabilities.

ENTERPRISE

(1) Company or organization.

(2) Subpart of a company or organization.

(3) Business of a customer.

ENTERPRISE ARCHITECTURE (EA)

(1) Generally, a planning and change management discipline that helps the organization align technology (people, processes, information) with strategic goals; and helps clarify where the organization is, where it is going, and what needs to be done to get there.

(2) Strategic information asset blueprint that defines the business, the information necessary to operate the business, the technologies necessary to support the business operations, and the transitional process needed to implement new technologies in response to changing business needs.

ENTERPRISE MODEL

Approach used to describe aspects of a business or organization, including mission, goals, objectives, processes, information requirements, and business activities.

ENTERPRISE PROJECT MANAGEMENT (EPM)

Comprehensive implementation and practice of project management based on the recognition that the sum total of an organization's work is a portfolio of simultaneous and interconnected projects that need to be managed collectively as well as individually. EPM is brought about by the consistent efforts of the project or program management office—or other organizational entities—to support project managers throughout the organization. Organizations that implement EPM generally regard project management as a key competency and, therefore, develop education and training programs, career paths, and associated reward systems to firmly establish project management as a professional discipline with its own identity. Additionally, such organizations encourage the consistent application of project management practices through the deployment of a methodology as well as by providing on-the-job support through a program management office or center of excellence. *See also* project office.

ENTERTAINMENT COSTS

Costs of amusement, diversions, social activities, and any directly associated costs such as tickets to shows or sports events, meals, lodging, rentals, transportation, and gratuities.

ENTITY RELATIONSHIP DIAGRAMS

Models that illustrate the logical structure of databases, typically used in the first stage of information-system design to describe information needs and/or the type of information that is to be stored in the database during requirements analysis.

ENTRANCE CRITERIA

Minimum accomplishments required to be completed by each project or program prior to entry into the next phase or effort.

ENVIRONMENT

(1) Aggregate of all cultural, political, geographical, physical, and technical conditions surrounding and influencing a project.

(2) Boundaries of a business area.

EOQ

See economic order quantity.

EPM

See enterprise project management.

EQ

See emotional quotient.

EQUAL EMPLOYMENT OPPORTUNITY (EEO)

In the United States, the legal right, granted through a series of laws and regulations, guaranteeing individuals the opportunity to hold a job without being discriminated against for a variety of reasons. These laws include—

• Title VII of the Civil Rights Act of 1964 (Title VII), which prohibits employment discrimination based on race, color, religion, sex, or national origin;

• Equal Pay Act of 1963 (EPA), which protects men and women who perform substantially equal work in the same establishment from sex-based wage discrimination;

• Age Discrimination in Employment Act of 1967 (ADEA), which protects individuals who are 40 years of age or older;

• Title I and Title V of the Americans with Disabilities Act of 1990 (ADA), which prohibit employment discrimination against qualified individuals with disabilities in the private sector, and in state and local governments;

• Sections 501 and 505 of the Rehabilitation Act of 1973, which prohibit discrimination against qualified individuals with disabilities who work in the federal government; and

• The Civil Rights Act of 1991, which, among other things, provides monetary damages in cases of intentional employment discrimination.

The U.S. Equal Employment Opportunity Commission (EEOC) enforces all of these laws. EEOC also provides oversight and coordination of all federal equal employment opportunity regulations, practices, and policies.

EQUAL OPPORTUNITY EMPLOYER

Employer who is committed to following affirmative action legislation in terms of employment opportunities.

EQUIPMENT

Machines, tools, or other hardware items necessary to complete a project or task.

EQUIPMENT PROCUREMENT

Acquisition of equipment or material to be used in the project.

EQUIPMENT SCHEDULING AND LOADING

Effective and efficient loading of machines to perform defined operations using their maximum capability to ensure attainment of the manufacturing schedule.

EQUITABLE ADJUSTMENT

Fair price adjustment under a contract clause for changed work, including an adjustment in profit; a change in the delivery schedule, if appropriate; and a change in any other affected terms of the contract.

EQUITY FINANCING

Method of obtaining funds by issuing either common or preferred stock, or both.

EQUITY THEORY OF MOTIVATION

Advanced by behavioral psychologist John Stacey Adams in 1963, the equity theory states that people are more likely to be motivated if they are treated fairly; on the other hand, if they feel unfairly treated they will be disaffected and demotivated.

EQUIVALENT UNITS

Approach used to determine the budget and calculate earned value (EV) using a given value placed on each unit completed. Applies best to manufacturing efforts.

ERB

See engineering review board.

ERGONOMICS

Study or science of how people interact with their work areas, and more specifically their computer workstations, monitor, seating, keyboards, and other physical elements of their workplace.

ERROR OF COMMISSION

(1) Error resulting from an action taken.

(2) In accounting, the error occurs when one or both of the double entries are made in the correct class of account but the wrong account within that class.

ERROR OF OMISSION

(1) Error that occurs as a result of an action not taken.

(2) In accounting, the error occurs when both entries required for a transaction are completely omitted from the books.

ES

See early start date.

ESCALATION

(1) Conversion of past to present prices or present to future prices through the use of a price index.

(2) Process of resolving disagreements or disputes by bringing such issues to a higher authority.

ESCALATOR CLAUSE

Provision in a contract providing for cost increases to be passed on.

ESCROW

Money, securities, or other property held by a third party until the conditions of a contract or agreement are met.

E-SIGNATURE (ELECTRONIC SIGNATURE)

Electronic sound, symbol, or process attached to or logically associated with a contract or other record and executed or adopted by a person with the intent to sign the record. Can be a typed name a person attaches to an e-mail message or a digitized image of a signature that is associated with a special algorithm that verifies the authenticity of the electronic document. In the U.S., the Electronic Signatures in Global and National Commerce Act, signed into law in June 2000, governs the use of e-signatures. Speeds the contracting process and makes it easier for businesses to conduct e-commerce as well as more traditional forms of commerce.

ESOP

See employee stock ownership plan.

ESTIMATE

Assessment of likely quantitative result, usually applied to project costs and durations. Should include some indication of accuracy (for example, ± X percent). Generally used with a modifier (such as preliminary, conceptual, or feasibility). Some disciplines use modifiers that imply specific accuracy ranges (such as order-of-magnitude, budget, and definitive), which traditionally have been used in engineering and construction projects but increasingly are used in other industry applications.

ESTIMATE AT COMPLETION (EAC)

Expected total cost of an activity, group of activities, or total project when the work is complete. Forecast of total project costs based on project performance to date. The *PMBOK® Guide* provides three methods of calculating EAC: EAC = ACWP + ETC; BAC / CPI; and ACWP + BCWS. *Also called* forecast at completion *or* latest revised estimate. *See also* earned value *and* estimate to complete.

ESTIMATED COST

Anticipated cost of performance of a project.

ESTIMATED FINAL COST

Anticipated cost of a completed project or component. Sum of the committed cost to date and the estimated cost to complete. *Also called* forecast final cost. *See also* estimate at completion.

ESTIMATE TO COMPLETE (ETC)

Expected additional cost needed to complete an activity, a group of activities, or the total project. Most techniques for forecasting ETC include an adjustment to the original estimate based on project performance to date. *See also* earned value *and* estimate at completion.

ESTIMATING

Forecasting the cost, schedule, and resource requirements needed to produce a specific deliverable.

ESTIMATING COSTS

Process of forecasting a future result in terms of cost, based upon information available at the time.

ESTIMATING EQUATION

Quantitative relationship use to estimate cost or price. The relationship may be linear or nonlinear and may include one or more independent variables.

ESTIMATING FACTOR

Multiple used to estimate cost or price based on a linear relationship with a product characteristic or an element of cost.

ESTIMATING GUIDELINES

Procedures for estimating project work effort, cost, or schedule, including formulas and criteria for assessing the major factors affecting the cost estimate.

ESTIMATING SYSTEM

Policies, procedures, and practices for generating time, cost, or resource estimates and other data included in business cases, proposals, or project and program estimates submitted to interested parties in the expectation of receiving approval to proceed or contract award. Components include—

- Organizational structure

- Established lines of authority, duties, and responsibilities

- Internal controls and managerial reviews

- Flow of work, coordination, and communications

- Estimating methods, techniques, accumulation of historical costs, and other analyses used to generate cost estimates

ETC

See estimate to complete.

ETHICAL MANAGEMENT STYLE

Management approach in which the project manager is honest, sincere, and able to motivate and press for the best and fairest solution.

ETHICS

System of moral principles and rules that becomes the standard for professional conduct.

E-TRAINING (ELECTRONIC TRAINING)

See e-learning.

EUROPEAN CENTRAL BANK (ECB)

Bank founded to oversee monetary policy for the countries that have converted their local currencies to the Euro. Formulates monetary policy, key interest rates, and the supply of reserves to the European System of Central Banks.

EUROPEAN FOUNDATION FOR QUALITY MANAGEMENT (EFQM) EXCELLENCE MODEL

Nonprescriptive framework based on 9 criteria and 32 sub-criteria used to assess an organization's progress towards business excellence. Based on the premise that customer satisfaction, people satisfaction, and impact on society are achieved through excellence that focuses on policy and strategy, people management, resources, and processes.

EUROPEAN QUALITY AWARD

Award established and presented by the European Foundation for Quality Management (EFQM) to those European firms that demonstrate commitment to business excellence in accordance with the EFQM Excellence Model. *See also* European Foundation for Quality Management (EFQM) Excellence Model.

EV

See earned value.

EVA

See economic value added.

EVALUATE

To appraise against a set value. Includes using determining factors and other criteria to quantitatively compare one project, proposal, or program with another for decision-making purposes.

EVALUATION CRITERIA

Rationale used to weight or score proposals submitted by prospective contractors; may be either objective or subjective.

EVENT

(1) Activity that does not use resources; a milestone.

(2) End state for one or more activities that occurs at a specific point in time. Used to show a critical point in a project, such as a decision point or the start or completion of a task or group of tasks.

(3) Significant occurrence that obligates the organization to take action.

(4) Key component of risk. Usually a description of the negative or positive incident associated with a risk.

EVENT CHART

See milestone chart.

EVENT MAINTENANCE

One or more maintenance actions required to effect corrective and preventative maintenance due to any type of failure or malfunction, false alarm, or scheduled maintenance plan.

EVENT-ON-NODE

Network diagramming technique in which events are represented by boxes (or nodes) connected by arrows to show the sequence in which the events are to occur. Used in the Program Evaluation and Review Technique (PERT).

EVENT-ORIENTED SCHEDULE

Timeline of project activities focused on events rather than activities.

EVMS

See Earned Value Management System.

EXAMINATION

Element of inspection consisting of investigation of supplies and services to determine conformance to specified requirements without using special laboratory equipment or procedures.

EXCEPTION REPORT

Document that includes only significant variances from the project baselines (rather than all variances). *See also* significant variance.

EXCEPTION REPORTING

Process of documenting those situations where significant variances from project specifications (baselines) have occurred. *See also* significant variance.

EXCHANGE RATE

Rate at which one currency is converted into another. Rates fluctuate over time based on macroeconomic factors and can influence revenue and costs when used on a project that is conducted across several countries' economic systems. In such instances, it is advisable to agree as to the timing of the currency conversion (for example, the date on which the goods were received, or when the invoice is raised versus received). Additionally, it is advisable to agree on the exchange rate to be used because there are many to choose from and they often differ by a slight margin. Many Web sites set exchange rates and financial newspapers around the world, such as the *Financial Times* and *The Wall Street Journal*, report on exchange rates.

EXECUTED CONTRACT

Signed, consummated contract, the terms and conditions of which have been completely fulfilled by the parties.

EXECUTING PROCESSES

Any process or activity undertaken to complete the work identified in the project or program management plan leading to the accomplishment of the stated objectives, including the coordination of people and other resources. *See also* project/program management process groups.

EXECUTION

Operation of carrying out a task, activity, initiative, project, or program according to a specific plan of action.

EXECUTION PHASE

See development phase.

EXIT CRITERIA

Specific accomplishments that must be satisfactorily demonstrated before a project or program can progress further in the current life-cycle phase or transition to the next life-cycle phase. Exit criteria normally are selected to track progress in important technical, schedule, or management risk areas. They serve as gates that, when successfully passed or exited, demonstrate that the project or program is on track to achieve its final program goals and should be allowed to continue with additional activities within a life-cycle phase or be considered for continuation into the next life-cycle phase.

EXIT INTERVIEW

Interview conducted by a project manager or employer with a team member or employee who is leaving the project or company for the purpose of obtaining feedback about the general feelings of the person to help improve the organization or project environment.

EXPECTANCY THEORY

Theory of motivation, which holds that people will tend to be highly motivated and productive if they believe that their efforts will likely lead to successful results and that they will be rewarded for their success.

EXPECTATIONS

Anticipated changes in performance as a result of project implementation. May be in the areas of business, productivity, operations, culture, and others.

EXPECTED MONETARY VALUE (EMV)

In risk management, the result of multiplying the probability of a variable's occurrence with its estimated monetary impact. Although a theoretical figure, it provides some sense of the value of the loss incurred should the risk occur. For example, if there is a 50 percent probability of snow, and snow will result in a $100 loss, the expected monetary value of the snow is $50 (0.5 x $100).

EXPECTED TIME

Statistically calculated time estimate used in PERT estimating to determine the number of work periods an activity will consume. *See also* probabilistic estimating.

EXPECTED VALUE

See expected monetary value.

EXPENDABLE ITEM

Item of relatively low value or one that is consumed after being used.

EXPENDITURE

Cost incurred in the normal course of business or the execution of a project to generate revenues or deliver results. *See also* expenses.

EXPENSE

Amount of assets or services used during a period.

EXPENSES

Daily costs incurred in running and maintaining a business or project. *See also* expenditure.

EXPERIENCE CURVE

See learning curve.

EXPERT AUTHORITY

Influence derived from an individual's knowledge or expertise, rather than from some outside source. *Also called* technical authority.

EXPERT INTERVIEW

Risk-identification technique in which qualified individuals are consulted to determine the risks on a project.

EXPERT JUDGMENT

Opinions, advice, recommendations, or commentary proffered, usually upon request, by a person or persons recognized, either formally or informally, as having specialized knowledge, proficiency, or training in a specific area.

EXPERT POWER

See expert authority.

EXPERT SYSTEM

Computer software that uses the knowledge of recognized experts in an area and makes inferences about a problem based on decision rules and data input to the software.

EXPLOIT

Risk response strategy that eliminates the uncertainty associated with an opportunity by ensuring that it will occur. *See also* acceptance.

EXPLORATORY FORECASTING

Forecasting method that extrapolates from past experience and looks toward the future; used in gap analysis to estimate future budget demands of projects in a portfolio.

EXPOSURE

(1) Impact value of a risk multiplied by its probability of occurring; another name for the expected value for threats.

(2) Loss provision made for a risk; requires that a sufficient number of situations in which this risk could occur have been analyzed.

EXPRESS AUTHORITY

Authority given explicitly, and usually in writing, to an individual to conduct the business affairs at hand.

EXPRESS WARRANTY

Promise that is actually spoken or written in an agreement. *See also* implied warranty.

EXTENDED MASS LAYOFF

In the U.S., layoff of at least 31 days in duration and involving 50 or more individuals from a single establishment filing initial claims for unemployment insurance during a consecutive five-week period.

EXTERNAL AUDIT

Audit performed by anyone outside the project team.

EXTERNAL DEPENDENCY

Dependency that involves a relationship between project and nonproject activities.

EXTERNAL FEEDBACK

Evaluative information about the performance of the project team from individuals outside the project and, typically, outside the organization.

EXTERNAL RISK

Risk beyond the control or influence of the project team (for example, a hurricane or typhoon). *See also* internal risk.

EXTRAPOLATION FROM ACTUAL COSTS

Extrapolation method used to estimate actual final costs based on actual costs of a prototype or preproduction version. Primarily used in estimating the production cost of system hardware, it assumes a relationship (technical, performance) between cost of prototypes and production units.

EXTREME PROGRAMMING (XP)

One of a variety of agile software development methods purported to increase the speed of development, reduce errors, and increase customer satisfaction. Built around rapid iterations, XP has 12 core practices, including the practice of all programmers working side by side in pairs, continually seeing and discussing one another's code. Developed by Kent Beck while he served as project leader on the Chrysler Comprehensive Compensation project. *See also* Twelve Rules of Extreme Programming.

F

FAC

See forecast at completion.

FACE THE MUSIC

Accept the consequences of one's actions.

FACILITATING MANAGEMENT STYLE

Management approach in which the project manager makes himself or herself available to answer questions and provide guidance when needed but does not interfere with day-to-day tasks.

FACILITATOR

Person external to a group whose purpose is to help the group work more effectively.

FACILITIES CAPITAL

Net book value of tangible and intangible capital assets subject to amortization.

FACILITIES CONTRACT

Contract under which the buyer provides work space, equipment, tools, and so on to a contractor or subcontractor for use in performing one or more related contracts for supplies and services.

FAGAN STYLE SOFTWARE INSPECTION

Type of manual defect detection method used in the software development process developed by Michael Fagan at IBM Corporation. Fagan Inspection is a group review method used to validate if the output of the process complies with the exit criteria specified for the process. Examples of activities for which Fagan Inspection can be used are—

- Requirements specification

- Software/information system architecture (for example, in DYA)

- Programming (for example, in iterations in XP or DSDM)

- Software testing (for example, when creating test scripts)

FAILURE

Event in which any part of an item does not perform as required by its performance specification. The failure may occur at a value in excess of the minimum required in the specification, that is, past design limits or beyond the margin of safety.

FAILURE MODE

Describes the way the failure occurs and its impact on equipment or system operation.

FAILURE MODES AND EFFECT ANALYSIS (FMEA)

Analysis process that examines various ways in which a product or service may fail and the effect of those failures on the system. Using FMEA, a project team can identify the most important possible failure modes so that action can be taken to reduce the risk of failure.

FAILURE RATE

Measure, usually expressed as a percentage, of nonconformance to specifications. Calculated by dividing the number of failed items by the number of total items being tested.

FAIR AND REASONABLE PRICE

Price considered to be fair to both parties based on agreed-upon conditions, promised quality, and timeliness of contract performance.

FAIR AND SQUARE

Honest and straightforward.

FAIR LABOR STANDARDS ACT (FLSA)

U.S. federal law enacted in 1938 that enforces a group of minimum standards that employers must abide by when hiring employees. Regulates such things as minimum wages per hour and maximum hours of work. Also provides that employees are paid one and a half times their regular hourly wage for work beyond 40 hours per week.

FAIR MARKET PRICE

Price at which bona fide sales have been made for assets of like type, quality, and quantity in a particular market at the time of acquisition.

FAIR MARKET VALUE

Price at which a willing seller will sell and a willing buyer will buy, in an arms-length transaction, when neither is under compulsion to sell or buy and both have reasonable knowledge of all the relevant facts.

FAIR USE

Concept in copyright law allowing a party to quote or reproduce a small portion of copyrighted material not requiring the permission of the copyright holder provided proper attribution is accorded said owner.

FAIT ACCOMPLI

A thing accomplished and presumably irreversible. A negotiator using this tactic hopes that the other party will accept a position because related actions or outcomes have already occurred.

FALLBACK POSITION

Alternative (second-choice) position.

FAS

See free alongside ship.

FAST DECISION PROCESS

Process in which a small, empowered, cross-functional or cross-organizational team, with the help of a trained facilitator, makes decisions quickly. Differs from other processes because it concentrates on producing deliverables.

FAST-TRACKING

(1) Compressing the project schedule by overlapping activities normally performed in sequence, such as design and construction. Sometimes confused with concurrent engineering.

(2) Choosing a certain employee or employees for rapid advancement.

FATIGUE

Physical weakening of material because of age, stress, or vibration.

FATIGUE ALLOWANCE

Time included in the production standard to allow for decreases or losses in production that might be attributed to worker fatigue. (Usually applied as a percentage of the leveled, normal, or adjusted time.)

FAULT TOLERANCE

Method used to make a computer or network system resistant to software errors and hardware malfunctions.

FAULT TREE

Diagram that shows the logical combination of causes leading to a particular failure. Because the cause-and-effect sequences are not limited, a precise analysis can be conducted.

FBS

See feature breakdown structure.
See functional breakdown structure.

FDD

See feature driven development.

FEASIBILITY

Assessment of the capability for successful implementation; the possibility, probability, and suitability of accomplishment.

FEASIBILITY ESTIMATE

See order-of-magnitude estimate.

FEASIBILITY PHASE

See concept phase.

FEASIBILITY STUDY

Examination of technical and cost data to determine the economic potential and practicality of project applications. Involves the use of metrics such as the time value of money so projects may be evaluated and compared on an equivalent basis. Interest rates, present value factors, capitalization costs, operating costs, and depreciation are all considered.

FEATURE BREAKDOWN STRUCTURE (FBS)

In agile project management, a graphic, architectural representation of the features to be included in the product under development. Used as a communications tool between the customer and the development teams so that there is no confusion as to the product that is to be built.

FEATURE CARDS

In agile project management, a technique for identifying product features in which one feature is written on a 4 x 6-inch index card. The total of the cards forms the product scope.

FEATURE DRIVEN DEVELOPMENT (FDD)

One of a variety of agile software development methods. FDD arose out of a collaboration with Jeff De Luca and Peter Coad and their flagship Singapore Project. Attempting to save a failing project that was two years under development with no code having been developed, FDD was developed with the following core values:

• A system for building systems is necessary in order to scale to larger projects.

• A simple, well-defined process works best.

• Process steps should be logical and their worth obvious to each team member.

• Process pride can keep the real work from happening.

• Good processes move to the background so the team members can focus on results.

• Short, iterative, feature-driven life cycles are best.

FEDERAL INFORMATION PROCESSING STANDARDS (FIPS)

Standards for information processing issued by the National Institute of Standards and Technology of the U.S. Department of Commerce; includes a numeric designation for geographic areas such as states, counties, and metropolitan areas.

FEDERALLY FUNDED RESEARCH AND DEVELOPMENT CENTER (FFRDC)

Activity that is sponsored under a broad charter by a U.S. government agency or research agencies for the purpose of performing, analyzing, integrating, supporting, and managing basic or applied research and development, and that receives 70 percent or more of its financial support from the government. In an FFRDC, a long-term relationship is typical; most or all of the facilities are owned or funded by the government; and the

FFRDC has access to government and supplier data, employees, and facilities beyond that which is common in a normal contractual relationship. The National Science Foundation maintains the master list of FFRDCs.

FEDERAL RESERVE BANK

One of 12 banks that make up the U.S. Federal Reserve System, whose role it is to monitor the commercial and savings banks in its region to ensure that they follow Federal Reserve Board regulations and to provide those banks with access to emergency funds. Each of the Federal Reserve Banks is owned by the member banks in its district.

FEDERAL RESERVE BOARD (FRB)

Governing board of the Federal Reserve System that includes seven members appointed by the president of the United States, subject to Senate confirmation, and serving 14-year terms. The Board establishes policies on matters such as reserve requirements and other bank regulations, sets the discount rate, and tightens or loosens the availability of credit in the U.S. economy.

FEDERAL RESERVE SYSTEM

System to regulate the U.S. monetary and banking system established by the Federal Reserve Act of 1913. The system comprises 12 member banks, their 24 branches, and all national and state banks. Primary responsibilities of the system are to set reserve requirements for member banks, supervise the printing of currency, and act as a clearinghouse for the transfer of funds throughout the banking system.

FEDERAL SUPPLY SCHEDULE PROGRAM

Program to provide U.S. federal agencies with a simplified process for acquiring commonly used supplies and services in varying quantities at lower prices while obtaining discounts associated with volume buying. Indefinite-delivery contracts (including requirements contracts) are awarded, using competitive procedures, to commercial firms to provide supplies and services at stated prices for given periods of time, for delivery within the 48 contiguous states, Washington, D.C., and possibly Alaska, Hawaii, and overseas.

FEE

Amount paid to the contractor beyond its costs under a cost-reimbursement contract. In U.S. federal procurement, "fee" is the term for the profit the government agrees to pay on a cost-reimbursement contract, and in most cases, the amount of fee reflects a variety of factors, including risk.

FEEDBACK

(1) Information extracted from a process or situation and used to control, plan, or modify immediate or future input to the process or situation.

(2) In organizations, the process of sharing concerns or observations between persons or groups with the specific intent of improving future performance.

FEE FOR PROFESSIONAL SERVICES

Amount paid under contract for professional and consultant services when the work is performed satisfactorily.

FEE SCHEDULE

List of prices to be paid and benefits to be received under listed procedures or benefits.

FEE SIMPLE

Absolute ownership of real and entire property by the owner, including the unencumbered right of disposition during his or her life and upon death.

FEINTING

Use of a pretense or action designed to mislead. In negotiations, this tactic normally involves the use of a true but misleading statement or behavior. It gives the other negotiator a false impression or deceives the negotiator into believing something that is not true.

FENWICK-vanKOESVELD TEST

Test that refers to the practice of asking, three times, who caused the failure that has occurred in order to get to the originator of the problem. Usually carried out by a team of persons that does not work with him or her (internal audit teams). No special technique is required. *See also* Five Whys.

FF

See finish-to-finish.

FFP

See firm-fixed-price contract.

FFRDC

See Federally Funded Research and Development Center.

FICA (FEDERAL INSURANCE CONTRIBUTIONS ACT)

U.S. law requiring U.S. employers to match the amount of Social Security tax deducted from an employee's paycheck.

FICTITIOUS NAME

Widely referred to as a DBA (doing business as). Used frequently by sole proprietors or partnerships to provide a name, other than those of the owners or partners, under which the business will operate.

FIDUCIARY

Person, group of persons, or organization that holds a position involving the confidence or trust of customers; usually relates to investments or other financial matters.

FIELD COST

Cost associated with establishing, operating, and maintaining the project site rather than the corporate office.

FIELDED SYSTEM

Operational system that is installed at the user site.

FIELD INSPECTION

Inspection done at the job site or work site where the item will be used or service delivered.

FIELD TEST(ING)

(1) In information technology, applications testing that is performed at the user site.

(2) In new product development, product use testing with users from the target market.

FIFO

See first in, first out.

FIFTY-FIFTY METHOD OF PROGRESS REPORTING

Method used in earned value management to estimate the amount of each task that has been completed. As soon as a task has started, half the effort is assumed to be completed and half the BCWS value associated with the task is entered into the project accounts book. Only after the task is actually completed is the remaining half of the BCWS value entered into the accounts. This approach provides a good statistical approximation of the BCWP for the project when there are many tasks under way of approximately the same magnitude.

FILTERING

(1) Selectively screening the thoughts and ideas of the communicator according to one's own frame of reference, attitudes, beliefs, expectations, and relationship to the communicator.

(2) Sorting technique that is used to measure the importance of risks based on predetermined criteria or filters. A series of questions is designed to separate risks of high priority from those of lower priority. Risks that do not survive the filter are removed from the priority listing.

FINAL COMPLETION

Certification that the entire work has been performed to the requirements of the contract, except for those items arising from the provisions of warranty.

FINAL CONVICTION

Conviction, whether entered on a verdict or plea, including a plea of nolo contendere (Latin for "I do not wish to contest"), for which a sentence has been imposed.

FINAL PAYMENT

Final settlement, paid at contract completion, of the contractually obligated amount, including any retention.

FINAL SYSTEM DESIGN

Full-scale, approved product design prepared from customer requirements and the initial system design.

FINANCIAL CLOSEOUT

Accounting analysis of how funds were spent on the project.
Signifies a point in time when no further charges should be
made against the project.

FINANCIAL CLOSURE PLAN

Course of action to be used to execute financial closeout in a
project or program.

FINANCIAL CONTROL

See cost control.

FINANCIAL MANAGEMENT

Process of managing financial resources, including management decisions concerning accounting and financial reporting,
forecasting, and budgeting.

FINANCIAL STATEMENT

Written record listing the financial status of an individual or
organization, including assets and liabilities.

FINANCIAL TIMES STOCK EXCHANGE (FTSE) 100

Unmanaged index of the 100 most highly capitalized blue chip
companies trading on the London Stock Exchange. Representing approximately 81 percent of the United Kingdom market, it
is used as a basis for investment products such as derivatives and
exchange-traded funds.

FINANCING

Raising funds required for the project using instruments and
methods such as stocks, mortgages, bonds, innovative financing
agreements, or leases.

FINDER'S FEE

Amount of money paid to an individual or concern for the sole
purpose of bringing together, for business gain, two or more
parties who otherwise did not know one another. The fee is
usually a percentage of the business deal negotiated by the parties but also may be a flat rate paid by one or all of the involved
parties.

FINISH DATE

Point in time associated with an activity's or project's completion. Usually qualified by terms such as actual, planned, estimated, scheduled, early, late, baseline, target, or current.

FINISH FLOAT

Amount of excess time an activity has at its finish before a successor activity must start. Also referred to as slack time.

FINISH-TO-FINISH (FF)

Relationship in a precedence diagramming method network in which one activity must end before the successor activity can end. *See also* logical relationship.

FINISH-TO-FINISH LAG

Minimum amount of time that must pass between the finish of one activity and the finish of its successor(s). If the predecessor's finish is delayed, the successor activity may have to be slowed or halted to allow the specified time period to pass. All lags are calculated when a project has its schedule computed. Finish-to-finish lags often are used with start-to-start lags.

FINISH-TO-START (FS)

Relationship in a precedence diagramming method network in which one activity must end before the successor activity can start. The most commonly used relationship in the precedence diagramming method. *See also* logical relationship.

FINISH-TO-START LAG

Minimum amount of time that must pass between the finish of one activity and the start of its successor(s). The default finish-to-start lag is zero. If the predecessor's finish is delayed, the successor activity's start will have to be delayed. All lags are calculated when a project has its schedule computed. In most cases, finish-to-start lags are not used with other lag types.

FIPS

See Federal Information Processing Standards.

FIRM-FIXED-PRICE (FFP) CONTRACT

Type of contract in which the buyer pays the contractor a set amount, as defined by the contract, regardless of the   contractor's costs. In fixed-price contracts, the performance risk is borne mostly by the seller, not the buyer.

FIRM OFFER

Offer from a seller to a buyer, usually in writing, that is valid for a set period of time.

FIRMWARE

Combination of a hardware device and computer instructions or computer data that reside as read-only software on the hardware device. The software cannot be readily modified under program control.

FIRO-B® (FUNDAMENTAL INTERPERSONAL RELATIONS ORIENTATION-BEHAVIOR™)

Assessment tool developed by William Schutz in 1958 to assess how teams performed in the U.S. Navy, it is used to help individuals and teams better understand their preferences in satisfying three basic social needs:

• Inclusion (the degree to which one belongs to a group, team, or community)

• Control (the extent to which one prefers to have structure, hierarchy, and influence)

• Affection (one's preference for warmth, disclosure, and intimacy)

For each factor, FIRO-B® assesses individuals as to how much they express the needs and how much they want to have the needs expressed to them from others. It is very helpful for understanding individual and team behavior.

FIRO-B® AWARENESS SCALE

Test used to determine how people fit into a group according to three dimensions: inclusion, control, and affection.

FIRST-ARTICLE TESTING

Evaluating the first items produced before or in the initial stage of production to see whether they conform to specified contract requirements.

FIRST FEASIBLE DEPLOYMENT

In agile project management, the iteration of a product that potentially could be deployed in the user's environment.

FIRST IN, FIRST OUT (FIFO)

Example of queuing theory, typically using a method of inventory rotation to ensure that the oldest inventory (first in) is used first (first out).

FIRST-TIER SUBCONTRACTOR

Subcontractor holding a subcontract with a prime contractor.

FIRST-TO-MARKET

First product or service that creates a new product or service category in an industry or sector. Often provides a significant competitive advantage to the organization until such time as other "me too" products or services are introduced from competitors.

FISCAL YEAR (FY)

Accounting period for which annual financial statements are regularly prepared, generally a period of 12 months, 52 weeks, or 53 weeks. May or may not coincide with calendar year.

FISHBONE DIAGRAM

See Ishikawa diagram.

FISH OR CUT BAIT

Make a decision now or move on to something else.

FIT

Externally imposed constraint for which a project deliverable may have to adapt or conform.

FITNESS FOR USE

Effectiveness of the design, manufacturing, and support processes in delivering a system that meets the operational requirements under all anticipated operational conditions.

FIVE NINES RELIABILITY

Measure of the percentage of time an automated system, such as a computer network, is available in a given period of time and expressed as 99.999. A computer network that is available for use 99.999 percent means that it will be unavailable (downtime) for only 5 minutes and 15 seconds or less in one year.

FIVE WHYS

Root cause analysis technique attributed to Taiichi Ohno at Toyota in which one asks "why" five times to determine the cause of failure. There can be more than one cause to a problem as well. Root cause analysis generally is carried out by a team of individuals rather than by a single individual.

FIXED ASSET

Property or equipment, such as machines, buildings, or land, used for the production of goods and services.

FIXED CHARGE

Expenses incurred each time a batch of product is manufactured or produced. Includes the cost of ordering raw material; engineering costs for machine setup and preparation for the production run; and costs for work-order processing.

FIXED COST

Cost that does not vary with volume of output or business, such as property taxes, insurance, depreciation, security, and minimum water and utility fees.

FIXED-PRICE CONTRACT

Type of contract with a firm pricing arrangement established by the parties at the time of contracting. A fixed-price contract is not subject to adjustment on the basis of the costs the contractor incurred performing the contract. Other types of fixed-price contracts (fixed-price contract with economic price adjustment, fixed-price incentive contract, fixed-priced redetermination prospective contract, and fixed-price redetermination retroactive contract) are subject to price adjustment on the basis of economic conditions or the contractor's performance of the contract. These types of fixed-price contracts are primarily used by the U.S. government but have commercial applicability as well.

FIXED-PRICE-INCENTIVE (FPI) CONTRACT

Type of contract in which the buyer pays the contractor for the actual allowable cost incurred, not to exceed a ceiling price defined in the contract, and the contractor can earn more or less profit depending on its ability to meet defined performance or cost criteria. In fixed-price contracts, the performance risk is borne mostly by the seller, not the buyer.

FIXED-PRICE-INCENTIVE-FIRM (FPIF) CONTRACT

Type of contract that uses an incentive whereby the contractor's profit is increased or decreased by a predetermined share of an overrun or underrun. A firm target is established from which to later compute the overrun or underrun. A ceiling price is set as the maximum amount the buyer will pay. Necessary elements for this type of contract are: target cost, or the best estimate of expected cost; target profit, or the fair profit at target cost; share ratio(s), to adjust profit after actual costs are documented; and ceiling price, or the limit the buyer will pay.

FIXED-PRICE LEVEL-OF-EFFORT CONTRACT

Type of firm-fixed-price contract requiring the contractor to provide a specified level of effort over a stated period of time on work that can be stated only in general terms.

FIXED PRICE WITH ECONOMIC PRICE ADJUSTMENT (FPEPA) CONTRACT

Type of contract providing for upward or downward revision of the stated contract price upon the occurrence of a specified contingency. Adjustments may reflect increases/decreases in actual costs of labor or material, or in specific indices of labor or material costs.

FLAT OUT

Using all one's efforts. Doing something at top speed.

FLAT RATE

Per-unit price that remains fixed regardless of the volume purchased.

FLAVOR OF THE MONTH

Idea, management technique, tactic, strategy, or approach that becomes very popular in a short period of time but quickly goes out of style and use.

FLOAT

Amount of time that an activity may be delayed from its early start without delaying the project end date. Derived by subtracting the early start from the late start or early finish from the late finish; it may change as the project progresses and as changes are made to the project plan. *Also called* slack, total float, *and* path float. *See also* free float.

FLOATING TASK

Task that can be performed earlier or later in the schedule without affecting the project duration or critical path.

FLOWCHART

Diagram consisting of symbols depicting a physical process, a thought process, or an algorithm. Shows how the various elements of a system or process relate and which can be used for continuous process improvement.

FLOW DIAGRAM

Graphic representation of work flow and the logical sequence of the work elements without regard to a time scale. Used to show the logic associated with a process rather than a duration for completion of work.

FLOW-DOWN CLAUSES

Clauses prescribed by the buyer that a prime contractor incorporates into any subcontracts.

FLOW PROCESS CHART

Graphical representation of the sequence of all operations, transportation, inspections, delays, and storage occurring during a process or procedure.

FLSA

See Fair Labor Standards Act.

FLYAWAY COSTS

Costs related to the production of a usable end item of military hardware. Includes the cost of creating the basic unit (airframe, hull, chassis, and so forth), an allowance for changes, propulsion equipment, electronics, armament, other installed government-furnished equipment, and nonrecurring "start-up" production costs.

FLY-BY-NIGHT

Used to describe a firm of questionable integrity, ethics, and objectives. Often such firms operate out of a basement, garage, or post-office box and are difficult to contact when their products or services do not prove satisfactory.

FMEA

See failure modes and effect analysis.

FOB

See free on board.

FOCAL POINT

Principal point of contact for coordination and exchange of information related to a particular issue or area. *See also* point of contact.

FOCUS GROUPS

Requirements elicitation technique that involves getting concerned parties together in one place at one time to get a general understanding of requirements or determine connections between processes.

FOG INDEX

Method developed by Robert Gunning to measure the readability of a written work in English based on a combination of two criteria: the average number of words per sentence and the percentage of words containing three or more syllables.

FOLLOWER

Task that logically succeeds a particular task in time.

FOLLOW-UP AUDIT

Audit conducted to determine whether the recommendations resulting from a previous audit were implemented and were effective in correcting or preventing the problems noted. Can be either a full or partial audit.

FORBEARANCE

Intentional failure of a contracting party to enforce a contractual requirement, term, or condition for future consideration by the other party. Although it is seen as a nonwaiver or as a one-time waiver of rights, it is not a total relinquishment of rights under the agreement.

FORCED ANALYSIS

Process of reanalyzing a project schedule even if no new data have been entered. The feature is used to analyze the project by itself after it has been analyzed with other projects in multi-project processing (or vice versa).

FORCE FIELD ANALYSIS

Quality technique that identifies the various pressures promoting or resisting change.

FORCE MAJEURE

French term meaning "greater force," it is a clause found in many contracts freeing both parties from liability or obligation to perform due to an extraordinary event that is beyond the control of either party, including strikes, war, pestilence, floods, earthquakes, civil riots, and the like.

FORCING

See conflict resolution.

FORECAST

Estimate or prediction of future conditions and events based on information and knowledge available at the time of the estimate, including financial and schedule information, resource require-ments, or any other element of a project.

FORECAST AT COMPLETION (FAC)

See estimate at completion.

FORECAST FINAL COST

See estimated final cost.

FORECASTING

Estimating or predicting future conditions and events. Generally done during the planning process but can occur at any phase in the project life cycle. Often confused with budgeting, which is a definitive allocation of resources rather than a prediction or estimate.

FOREIGN EXCHANGE

Instruments such as paper currency, notes, checks, and bills of exchange employed in making payments between countries.

FORMAL ACCEPTANCE

Documentation signifying that the customer or sponsor has accepted the product of the project or phase. May be conditional if the acceptance is for a phase of the project.

FORMAL AUTHORITY

Influence based on an individual's position in the organization and conferred upon that person by the organization. *Also called* legitimate authority.

FORMATIVE QUALITY EVALUATION

Ongoing evaluation process to ensure that project results conform to preestablished quality standards.

FORMING

See Tuckman's Model of Team Development (Stage 1).

FORMULA ESTIMATING

Method of work effort estimation using a prescribed method or formula to list and quantify major factors that affect project or product development.

FORTUNE 500

Annual listing in Fortune magazine of the 500 largest firms by annual revenue headquartered in the United States. Forbes magazine also publishes a list of the 500 biggest U.S. publicly owned corporations. *See also* Fortune Global 500.

FORTUNE GLOBAL 500

Annual listing in Fortune magazine of the 500 largest industrial corporations by revenue in the world.

FORWARD CONTRACT

Actual purchase or sale of a specific quantity of a commodity, government security, financial security, or other financial instrument at a price specified now for delivery and settlement in the future. Airlines typically use forward contracts to purchase jet fuel years in advance as a hedge against higher future prices.

FORWARD PASS

Calculation of the early start and early finish dates for the uncompleted portions of all network activities. *See also* network analysis *and* backward pass.

FORWARD PRICING

Using progressively escalated labor rates to convert direct labor hours to direct labor monetary values and using progressively escalated overhead rates, direct material, and subcontract monetary values to develop an escalated price estimate. *See also* negotiated bidding rates.

FORWARD SCHEDULING

Method in which the project start date is fixed and task duration and dependency information is used to compute the corresponding project completion date.

FPEPA

See fixed price with economic price adjustment contract.

FPI

See fixed-price-incentive contract.

FPIF

See fixed-price-incentive-firm contract.

FRAGNET

See subnet.

FRANCHISE

(1) License granted by one company (franchisor) to an individual or other company (franchisee) to operate a retail food, drug, or other retail establishment under certain specific terms and conditions for a fee.

(2) Right granted to an individual or firm to market a company's goods or services in a specific territory for a fee.

FRANCHISE TERRITORY

(1) Geographical area that a utility supplier has a right to serve based upon a franchise, a certificate of public convenience and necessity, or other legal means.

(2) Geographical area that a franchise has the rights in which to operate. In many instances those rights are exclusive.

FRAUD

Intentional deception; dishonesty. Usually consists of misrepresentation, concealment, or other forms of nondisclosure.

FRB

See Federal Reserve Board.

FREE ALONGSIDE SHIP (FAS)

Pricing scheme in which the seller agrees to pay for the shipment of goods from factory to pier.

FREE AND CLEAR

Without encumbrances; unencumbered.

FREEBIE

Something, usually a product, that is given away for free as a business promotion to generate customer interest.

FREE FLOAT

Amount of time that an activity may be delayed without delaying the early start of any immediately succeeding activities. *Also called* secondary float.

FREE ON BOARD (FOB)

Pricing scheme in which the seller agrees to pay for the shipment of goods to a specific point and no farther.

FREE TRADE AGREEMENT

Agreement between two or more countries that has, as its main purpose, the reduction or elimination of duties for goods flowing between the signatories.

FREE TRADE ZONE (FTZ)

Geographical area, usually a port of entry, designated by the country for duty-free entry of goods. As long as the goods do not go into the country from the FTZ, no duty is assessed.

FREEZE POINT

Specific date or time certain after which no additional requirements will be accepted for the development of a product or service.

FREQUENCY PLOT

Graphical display of how often data values occur within a given time frame.

FRONT END/UP FRONT

Planning or resource commitment at the beginning of the development process to anticipate later requirements and reduce future problems. *See also* early on.

FS

See finish-to-start.

FTE

See full-time equivalent.

FTSE

See Financial Times Stock Exchange 100.

FTZ

See free trade zone.

FULL AND OPEN COMPETITION

Method in U.S. federal procurement in which all responsible sources are permitted to compete for a contract.

FULL AUDIT

Audit that includes all elements of the project.

FULL MONTY, THE

Complete; the whole thing.

FULL-TIME EQUIVALENT

Numerical measure of the amount of staff hours involved in a project or other areas of employment and expressed as being equivalent to one or more persons. FTE is not necessarily the number of full-time positions on a project. For example, if 1.0 FTE equals a 40-hour workweek, that could mean one person is working 40 hours or two part-time people are working 20 hours each. In either case the FTE is 1.0. FTE, then, is not necessarily actual headcount; rather, it is the equivalent of actual headcount.

FUNCTIONAL BASELINE

Initial approved functional configuration identification. *See also* functional configuration identification.

FUNCTIONAL BREAKDOWN STRUCTURE (FBS)

Hierarchical structure showing the function of a product or service. Used in value analysis techniques.

FUNCTIONAL CONFIGURATION AUDIT

Audit to ensure that the functional requirements have been met by the delivered configuration item. *See also* audit.

FUNCTIONAL CONFIGURATION IDENTIFICATION

Current, approved technical documentation for a configuration item (CI) that prescribes: (1) all the necessary functional characteristics; (2) the tests required to demonstrate achievement of specified functional characteristics; (3) the necessary interface characteristics associated with the CI, its key functional characteristics, and its lower-level CIs, if any; and (4) the design constraints.

FUNCTIONAL DECOMPOSITION DIAGRAM

Hierarchical model that shows all the essential business processes without showing any sequence or relationships between them. Traditionally used as the basis for defining requirements.

FUNCTIONAL DEPARTMENT

Specialized department within an organization that performs a particular function, such as engineering, manufacturing, or marketing.

FUNCTIONALITY

(1) Particular set of functions or capabilities associated with computer software or hardware or an electronic device.

(2) Functions to be performed or capabilities to be delivered from the output or deliverable of a project to its intended users or customers.

FUNCTIONAL MANAGER

See line manager.

FUNCTIONAL ORGANIZATION

Organizational structure in which staff members are grouped hierarchically by specialty, such as production, marketing, engineering, and accounting at the top level, with each area further divided into subareas. (For example, engineering can be subdivided into mechanical, electrical, and so on). Coordination is accomplished by functional line managers and upper levels of management.

FUNCTIONAL ORGANIZATION EXPERTS

Customer-provided or internal personnel who are process and knowledge experts, provide validation, and work on technical aspects of the project.

FUNCTIONAL REQUIREMENTS

Characteristics of the deliverable described in ordinary, nontechnical language understandable to the customer. Customer plays a major, direct role in their development.

FUNCTIONAL REQUIREMENTS DOCUMENT

Formal document of the business (functional) requirements of a system; the baseline for system validation.

FUNCTIONAL SPECIFICATION(S)

Description of work to be performed in terms of the end purpose or results, rather than in terms of the specific procedures, processes, or equipment to be used in the performance of the work. May include a description of the qualitative nature of the end product and also may include a statement of the minimum essential characteristics the product must exhibit to satisfy its intended use.

FUNCTIONAL TESTING

Testing that ignores the internal mechanism of a system (or system component) and focuses solely on the outputs generated in response to selected inputs and execution conditions. *Also called* black box testing. *See also* white box testing.

FUNCTION POINT

Unit of measurement to express the amount of business functionality an information system provides to a user. *See also* function-point analysis.

FUNCTION-POINT ANALYSIS

Approach to estimating software costs that involves examining the project's initial high-level requirements statements, identifying specific functions, and estimating total costs based on the number of functions to be performed. Defined in 1979 by Alan Albrecht of IBM Corporation.

FUNCTION-QUALITY INTEGRATION

Process of ensuring that quality plans and programs are integrated, consistent, necessary, and sufficient to permit the project team to achieve defined product quality.

FUNDING

Organizational process by which monetary resources for a project are approved and formally allocated to the project.

FUNNY MONEY

(1) Costs and expenses charged to one functional component from another functional component within the same

organization simply for accounting purposes. No "real" money actually changes hands.

(2) In U.S. federal procurement, the use by contract negotiators to describe percentages, factors, or other estimating relationships that distract the other party from considering their effect on the total contract cost.

FUZZY FRONT END

Very early period in new product development where an organization is attempting to determine exactly what to develop and how based on any number of ideas from which it can choose.

FY

See fiscal year.

G

G&A

See general and administrative expense.

GAAP

See generally accepted accounting principles.

GAIN SHARING

Approach in which an organization shares the benefits of improvements, including profits, with its employees. Handled through such mechanisms as suggestion awards paid directly to individuals; employee stock ownership plans; and profit sharing, in which all employees receive a percentage of base pay as a bonus.

GAME PLAN

Approach to completing a task, activity, project, or program.

GANTT CHART

Graphic display of schedule-related information. Generally, activities or other project elements are listed down the left side of the chart, dates are shown across the top, and activity durations are displayed against the x and y axes as date-placed horizontal bars. Named after its developer, Henry Gantt.

GAO

See Government Accountability Office.

GAP ANALYSIS

(1) Examination of the difference between the current state and the desired or optimum state.

(2) Technique to help visualize the budget options available in project portfolios. Uses exploratory and normative forecasting and compares the curve associated with the total budget requirements of existing projects with that of the total anticipated budget for all projects, even those that are not under way. An anticipated gap can be determined and analyzed.

GARAGE BILL SCHEDULING

Scheduling tool that details every task, no matter how small, that must be completed to achieve a deliverable.

GARBAGE IN, GARBAGE OUT (GIGO)

Used in information processing to denote that the output of a computer program will be no better than the quality of the data that were input to the program.

GDP

See gross domestic product.

GEERT HOFSTEDE™ CULTURAL DIMENSIONS

Based on a large research project into national culture differences across subsidiaries of a multinational corporation (IBM) in 64 countries, and followed by numerous other studies, Professor Geert Hofstede from the Netherlands defined five national cultural differences that are crucial to the understanding of doing business globally. These areas of cultural difference include the following:

• Power distance—The extent to which the less-powerful members of organizations and institutions (like the family) accept and expect that power is distributed unequally.

• Individualism versus collectivism—In certain societies the ties between individuals are loose and in other societies members, from birth, are expected to be part of and integrated into strong, cohesive groups.

- Masculinity versus femininity—Refers to the distribution of roles between the genders where values contain a dimension from very assertive and competitive on one side (masculine) to modest and caring on the other (feminine).

- Uncertainty avoidance—Addresses a society's tolerance for uncertainty and ambiguity. A culture that avoids uncertainty will be characterized by strict laws and rules, while cultures that accept uncertainty usually have a "live and let live" philosophy of being.

- Long-term versus short-term orientation—Values associated with long-term orientation are thrift and perseverance; values associated with short-term orientation are respect for tradition, fulfilling social obligations, and protecting one's "face."

GENCHI GENBUTSU

Japanese term meaning "go see the problem." In quality management, practical experience is valued over theoretical knowledge. Therefore, in order to correct a quality problem, one must first observe the problem to fix it.

GENERAL AND ADMINISTRATIVE (G&A) EXPENSE

Management, financial, or other expense incurred by or allocated to an organizational unit for the general management and administration of the organization as a whole.

GENERAL AND ADMINISTRATIVE EXPENSE RATE

Indirect cost rate used by a concern to recover G&A expense.

GENERAL LEDGER

Formal ledger containing all of a business's financial statements of accounts.

GENERALLY ACCEPTED ACCOUNTING PRINCIPLES (GAAP)

Widely accepted set of standards, rules, conventions, and procedures for reporting financial information and used mainly in the U.S. Established by the Financial Accounting Standards Board (FASB).

GENERAL MANAGEMENT

Broad subject dealing with every aspect of managing an organization whose work is a continuous stream of activities. General management and project management share similar skills.

GENERAL PROVISIONS

Legal relationships and responsibilities of the parties to a contract, including how the contract will be administered; usually standard for an organization or project.

GENERAL REQUIREMENTS

Nontechnical specifications defining the scope of work, payments, procedures, implementation constraints, and other nontechnical requirements concerning the contract.

GENERAL SEQUENCING

Overview of the order in which activities are performed.

GERT

See Graphical Evaluation and Review Technique.

GET WELL

To solve a contract, project, or program problem. Usually implies requirement for, or discovery of, additional funding.

GIGO

See garbage in, garbage out.

GIVEN

Premise, fact, or assumption generally universally accepted at the outset.

GLASS CEILING

Unofficial barrier to workplace advancement placing women and minorities at a disadvantage with respect to promotional opportunities.

GLUT

Overproduction of a good or service.

GMT

See Greenwich Mean Time.

GNP

See gross national product.

GOAL

Basic component for measuring progress in attaining project objectives.

GO BY THE BOARDS

To be finished with. To be done.

GOING CONCERN, A

Viable business organization; one with the financial capacity to perform. Generally, refers to the liquidity of a concern. If the concern is illiquid, its viability as a business is questionable.

GOING RATE

Expression that means the cost of the average of suppliers of like products or services in the service area. The connotation is that the cost to be paid will be no more than and no less than the competition.

GOLD-PLATING

Providing more than the customer or specifications require, and thus spending more time and money than necessary to achieve quality.

GO/NO-GO

(1) Major decision point in a project life cycle.

(2) Measure that allows a manager to decide whether to continue, change, or end an activity or project.

(3) Type of gauge that tells an inspector if an object's dimension is within certain limits.

GOOD COP/BAD COP

See good guy/bad guy.

GOOD FAITH

Acting with honesty and lack of intention to obtain an unfair advantage or to defraud another party.

GOOD GUY/BAD GUY

Negotiation tactic that involves role playing by members of the negotiating team. One member plays an easygoing, good-guy role, while another team member plays the hard-core or difficult bad guy. The bad guy's position may even involve a serious personal threat. *Also called* good cop/bad cop.

GOODWILL

Unidentifiable intangible asset that originates under the purchase method of accounting for a business combination when the price paid by the acquiring company exceeds the sum of the identifiable individual assets acquired less liabilities assumed, based upon their fair values. Goodwill may arise from the acquisition of a company as a whole or a portion thereof.

GOT MY MOJO WORKING

My magical power is having a positive influence. Mojo, which was used in the early 20th century to mean voodoo, and often is used in the lyrics of blues songs, is now defined in business terms as influence.

GOVERNMENT ACCOUNTABILITY OFFICE (GAO)

Formerly the General Accounting Office. An agency of the U.S. government legislative branch, responsible solely to the Congress, that audits all negotiated government office contracts and investigates all matters relating to the receipt, disbursement, and application of public funds. Determines whether public funds are expended in accordance with appropriations.

GOVERNMENT CONTRACT QUALITY ASSURANCE

Various functions, including inspection, performed by the U.S. federal government to determine whether a contractor has fulfilled the contract obligations pertaining to quality and quantity.

GOZINTO CHART

Representation of a product that shows how the elements required to build it fit together. The term literally comes from the phrase "What goes into it?"

GRADE

Category or rank given to items that have the same functional use but do not share the same requirements for quality; low quality is always a problem, but low grade may not be.

GRAMM-LEACH BLILEY ACT OF 1999

Public law passed by the United States Congress, officially called the Financial Modernization Act of 1999, that includes provisions to protect consumers' personal financial information held by financial institutions. There are three principal parts to the privacy requirements:

• Financial Privacy Rule—Governs the collection and disclosure of customers' personal financial information by financial institutions

• Safeguards Rule—Requires all financial institutions to design, implement, and maintain safeguards to protect customer information

• Pretexting provisions—Protect consumers from individuals and companies that obtain their personal financial information under false pretenses, a practice known as "pretexting"

GRAPEVINE

Informal and unofficial communication path within an organization. Grapevine information has been shown to be accurate but usually incomplete.

GRAPH

Display or diagram that shows the relationship between activities; pictorial representation of relative variables. Examples include trend graphs, histograms, control charts, frequency distributions, and scatter diagrams.

GRAPHICAL EVALUATION AND REVIEW TECHNIQUE (GERT)

Network analysis technique that allows for conditional and probabilistic treatment of logical relationships (for example, some activities may not be performed). *See also* conditional diagramming method.

GRASS-ROOTS ESTIMATE

See bottom-up estimate.

GRAVEYARD SHIFT
Work shift between midnight and 8 a.m.

GREEN BELT
Designation given to an employee of an organization who has been trained on Six Sigma skills and tools and who will lead a process improvement or quality improvement team. Their level of skill and knowledge in Six Sigma is less than that of a Black Belt or Master Black Belt, but their level of product knowledge in the improvement area must be high. *See also* Black Belt *and* Master Black Belt.

GREENWICH MEAN TIME (GMT)
Solar time at the Royal Observatory in Greenwich, England (at longitude 0 degrees 0 minutes), which is used as the basis of standard time throughout the world. Any location on earth is either at GMT, minus one or more hours from GMT, or plus one or more hours from GMT. For example, during standard time New York City is –5 GMT; during Daylight Savings Time it is –4 GMT. During U.K. Standard Time, London is at GMT. However, when the U.K. is on British Summer Time, London is +1 GMT. GMT never changes. GMT is now called Coordinated Universal Time (but abbreviated as UTC). *Also called* Zulu *or* Z time. *See also* International Date Line.

GROSS
(1) Entire amount of income before any deductions are made.

(2) Any total amount before any deductions (for example, gross income or gross labor).

GROSS DOMESTIC PRODUCT (GDP)
Value of all the goods and services produced by workers and capital within a country (or region), such as the United States, regardless of nationality of workers or ownership. GDP includes production within national borders, regardless of whether the labor and property inputs are domestically or foreign owned.

GROSS INCOME
See gross profit.

GROSS MARGIN

Ratio of gross profit to sales revenue expressed as a percentage.

GROSS NATIONAL PRODUCT (GNP)

Sum of the market values of all final goods and services produced by a country's permanent residents and firms regardless of their location whether at home or abroad.

GROSS PROFIT

Difference between revenue earned and direct costs of goods or services sold.

GROSS SALES

Income received from total sales for goods and services, not reduced by discounts, returns, or allowances, over a given period of time.

GROUP COMMUNICATION

Meetings, presentations, negotiations, and other activities conducted by the project manager to convey information to the project team and other stakeholders.

GROUP DYNAMICS

Social interaction of the participants in a group. Can be positive or negative depending on the makeup and personality characteristics of the persons in the group.

GROUP NORMS

Behavior norms applied or observed in group members; these often dictate the degree to which a group can successfully accomplish a project.

GROUPTHINK

Behavior in which all members of a group adopt a unanimous position, at the expense of rationally considering all alternatives, in order to maintain group cohesion. Coined by Irving Janis in 1972.

GROUPWARE

Generic term used to describe any software application program that runs on a network and that allows groups of people to work collectively and collaboratively.

GUANXI

Chinese word for "relationship." The concept is applied in business where developing the right relationships and network of influential people helpful to one's cause or objectives can mean the difference between success and failure. By getting the right "guanxi," usually with the relevant authorities, the project manager or organization minimizes the risks, frustrations, and disappointments when doing business in China. Although relationships can help any project manager in any country, in China there is an especially heavy emphasis on doing business with people who are known and trusted.

GUARANTEE

Pledge or promise; for example, the system is guaranteed to perform according to the stated specifications.

GUERRILLA MARKETING

Term coined by Jay Conrad Levinson in his popular 1984 book of the same name, it is an unconventional system of promotions on a very low budget that relies on time, energy, and imagination instead of big marketing budgets. Nowadays the term means any aggressive, unconventional marketing methods the aim of which is to damage the market share of competitors.

GUIDELINE

Document that recommends methods and procedures to be used to accomplish an objective.

GUIDE TO THE SOFTWARE ENGINEERING BODY OF KNOWLEDGE

Publication of the IEEE Computer Society that establishes a baseline for the body of knowledge for the field of software engineering designed to promote the advancement of the theory and practice in the discipline. The guide contains the following 10 knowledge areas:

- Software requirements
- Software design
- Software construction
- Software testing
- Software maintenance
- Software configuration management
- Software engineering management
- Software engineering process
- Software engineering tools and methods
- Software quality

GWILLIAM MOTIVATIONAL MODEL

Theory of motivation that asserts that employees are motivated more by primal urges than by any loyalty to their workplace or organization.

H

HAMMOCK

Group of related activities that is shown as one aggregate activity and reported at a summary level. May or may not have an internal sequence. *See also* subnet.

HANDLING

Coordination and integration of all operations embracing packaging, protection, and movement of material by available equipment for short distances.

HANDS DOWN

Easily; with little effort.

HANGER

Unintended break in a network path. Usually occurs as a result of missing activities or missing logical relationships.

HANG SENG INDEX

Free-float adjusted market capitalization-weighted stock index of 40 companies trading on the Hong Kong Stock Exchange. It is the main indicator of market performance in Hong Kong.

HARD ASSETS

Physical assets (land, buildings, equipment) and financial assets (cash, credit, financial instruments).

HARD COPY

Printed information output as contrasted with electronic presentation.

HARD COSTS

Purchase price of actual assets. For example, the purchase price of a new computer system would be the hard cost.

HARD LOGIC

See mandatory dependency.

HARD SAVINGS

Savings associated with Six Sigma projects that allow an organization to produce the same output using fewer employees, or to produce additional output without increasing the number of employees. *See also* soft savings.

HCA

See Head of the Contracting Activity.

HEAD COUNT

(1) Number of people in a given project, group, or organization.

(2) Act of counting people in a given project, group, or organization (as in "to take a head count").

HEAD OF THE CONTRACTING ACTIVITY (HCA)

In U.S. federal procurement, the official who has overall responsibility for managing the contracting activity.

HEARTBURN APPEAL

(1) Appeal issue that seeks to reverse or amend a decision by a U.S. congressional committee adversely affecting the budget. In particular it is an appeal issue identified as being of major concern to the Secretary of Defense (SECDEF) that is addressed to the chairperson of the next committee scheduled to mark up the budget request.

(2) Any specific negative reaction to a proposal.

HEDGE YOUR BETS

To avoid committing oneself to a course of action.

HERZBERG'S THEORY OF MOTIVATION

Theory of motivation developed by Frederick Herzberg in which he asserts that individuals are affected by two opposing forms of motivation: hygiene factors and motivators. Hygiene factors such as pay, attitude of supervisor, and working conditions serve only to demotivate people if they are not provided in the type or amount required by the person. Improving hygiene factors under normal circumstances is not likely to increase motivation. Factors such as greater freedom, more responsibility, and more recognition serve to enhance self-esteem and are considered the motivators that energize and stimulate the person to do a better job. *See also* Motivation-Hygiene Theory.

HEURISTIC

(1) Problem-solving technique that results in an acceptable solution; often arrived at by trial and error.

(2) Rule of thumb.

HIDDEN AGENDA

Objectives of a person or group of persons not made known to others during the course of a project and that tend to subvert the stated objectives of the project or work contrary to them.

HIERARCHICAL MANAGEMENT

Traditional functional, or line, management in which areas and subareas of expertise are created and staffed with human resources. Organizations so established are ongoing in nature.

HIGH-PERFORMANCE WORK TEAM

Group of people who work together in an interdependent manner such that their collective performance exceeds that which would be achieved by simply adding together their individual contributions. Characteristics of such a team include strong group identity, collaboration, anticipating and acting on other team members' needs, and a laser-like focus on project objectives.

HISTOGRAM

One of the seven tools of quality. In statistics, a graphical display of tabulated frequencies. A histogram is the graphical version of a table that shows what proportion of cases falls into each of several or many specified categories. A histogram differs from a bar chart in that it is the area of the bar that denotes the value, not the height, a crucial distinction when the categories are not of uniform width. The categories usually are specified as nonoverlapping intervals of some variable. The categories (bars) must be adjacent. Examples would be a timeline chart that shows the use of a resource over time or a chart showing the characteristics of a problem on the horizontal (x) axis and the relative frequency of those characteristics on the vertical (y) axis.

HISTORICAL COST

Actual cost incurred in performing the work.

HISTORICAL ESTIMATING

Method of estimating work effort and costs using documented data from past projects or from similar tasks as the major input to the estimating process.

HISTORIC RECORDS

Project documentation used to predict trends, analyze feasibility, and highlight possible problem areas or pitfalls on subsequent similar projects.

HIT THE GROUND RUNNING

To get off to a brisk and effective start.

HOLDBACK

Portion of a construction loan that is not funded until the project is nearing completion or the borrower has satisfied certain contractual performance requirements, such as leasing a majority of the space in the building. The amount held back often is equal to the construction firm's projected profit when the building is completed.

HOLD HARMLESS CLAUSE

Clause in a contract where one party agrees to protect another from claims.

HOLDING COMPANY

Company that owns or controls other companies. Control can occur through the ownership of 50 percent or more of the voting rights or through the exercise of a dominant influence, such as enough voting stock.

HOLISTIC

Oriented toward viewing the whole rather than considering each piece individually.

HOST

1) Computer that controls communications in a network that administers a database.

2) Computer on which a program or file is installed.

3) Computer used to develop software intended for another computer.

HOUSE OF QUALITY

First matrix in a four-phase quality function deployment (QFD) process. Called so because of the correlation matrix that is roof-shaped and sits on top of the main body of the matrix. The correlation matrix evaluates how the defined product specifications optimize or suboptimize one another.

HOUSTON, WE HAVE A PROBLEM

Originally, a statement made by astronaut John Swigert, Jr., on the Apollo 13 moon flight, to report a near-fatal situation in space; now used in a humorous manner to report any kind of problem.

HSI

See human systems integration.

HUMAN FACTORS

Systematic application of relevant information about human abilities, characteristics, behavior, motivation, and performance. It includes principles and applications in the areas of human engineering, anthropometrics, personnel selection, training, life support, job performance aids, and human performance evaluation.

HUMAN RESOURCE GANTT CHART

Variation of the horizontal bar Gantt chart. Graphically illustrates how personnel resources are allocated, task by task, and how those resources are distributed throughout the life of a project. Used to track and plan personnel allocations and to identify when resources are overallocated.

HUMAN RESOURCE LOADING CHART

Vertical bar chart used to show personnel resource consumption by time period.

HUMAN RESOURCE MANAGEMENT

See project human resource management.

HUMAN RESOURCES

Personnel pool that is available to a project or organization.

HUMAN SYSTEMS INTEGRATION (HSI)

Includes integrated and comprehensive analysis, design, assessment of requirements, concepts and resources for system manpower, personnel, training, safety and occupational health, habitability, personnel survivability, and human factor engineering.

HURDLE RATE

In a discounted cash-flow analysis, required rate of return expected from an organization in order to proceed with a project, product, or new service. *See also* cutoff point.

HYGIENE FACTORS

According to Frederick Herzberg's Motivation-Hygiene Theory, factors related to job dissatisfaction that must be addressed to retain employees, such as pay, attitude of supervisor, or working conditions. *See also* Motivation-Hygiene Theory *and* Herzberg's theory of motivation.

HYPERCRITICAL ACTIVITIES

Activities on the critical path with negative float. Caused by constraints such as forced or target dates.

HYPERINFLATION

Extremely rapid growth in the rate of inflation so that money loses value and physical goods replace currency as a medium of exchange.

I

IA

See information assurance.

ICA

See independent cost analysis.

ICE

See independent cost estimate.

ICP

See inventory control point.

IDEA GENERATION

See concept generation.

IDEA PHASE

See concept phase.

IDEATION

See concept generation.

IDLE CAPACITY

Unused capacity of partially used facilities.

(1) It is the difference between that which a facility could achieve under 100 percent operating time on a one-shift basis, less operating interruptions resulting from time lost for repairs, setups, unsatisfactory materials, and other normal delays, and the extent to which the facility actually was used to meet demands during the accounting period.

(2) Multiple-shift basis may be used in the calculation instead of a one-shift basis if it can be shown that this amount of usage could normally be expected for the type of facility involved.

IDLE TIME

Time interval during which the project team, equipment, or both do not perform useful work.

IF

IF

See Industrial Fund.

IFB

See invitation for bids.

IGCE

See Independent Government Cost Estimate.

IGI

See incoming goods inspection.

IGNORE

Risk response strategy in which nothing is done to take advantage of a potential opportunity. *Also called* acceptance.

ILS

See integrated logistics support.

IMMEDIATE-GAIN ACTUARIAL COST METHOD

Any of the several actuarial cost methods under which actuarial gains and losses are included as part of the unfunded actuarial liability of the pension plan, rather than as part of the normal cost of the plan.

IMMEDIATE WARRANTY OF MERCHANTABILITY

Implication by sale of the item that it is reasonably fit for the ordinary purposes for which items are used. Items must be of at least average, fair, or medium-grade quality and must be comparable in quality to those that will pass without objection in the trade or market for items of the same description.

IMP

See integrated master plan.

IMPACT

Estimate of the effect that a risk will have on schedule, costs, product quality, safety, and performance.

IMPACT ANALYSIS

Qualitative or quantitative assessment of the magnitude of loss or gain to be realized should a specific risk or opportunity event—or series of interdependent events—occur.

IMPLEMENTATION PHASE

See development phase.

IMPLEMENTERS

Persons responsible for executing project activities and tasks to produce work results.

IMPLIED CONTRACT

Contract created by actions and not specifically written or spoken.

IMPLIED WARRANTY

Promise that is implicitly included in a transaction regardless of whether it is expressly written. For example, the implied warranty of merchantability states that goods or products must be reasonably fit for the ordinary purposes(s) for which they are used. *See also* express warranty.

IMPONDERABLES

Risks that are unknown and unknowable. *See also* unknown unknowns.

IMPOSED DATE (EXTERNAL)

(1) Predetermined calendar date set without regard to network-logical considerations or resource requirements.

(2) Specified date that is required by the project sponsor, the project customer, or other external factors for completion of certain deliverables.

IMPREST FUND

Cash fund of a fixed amount established by an advance of funds, without charge to an appropriation, from an agency finance or disbursing officer to a duly appointed cashier, for disbursement as needed from time to time in making payment in cash for relatively small amounts.

IMPROVEMENT CURVE

Estimating technique based on the concept that the resources (labor and/or material) required to produce each additional unit of a product decline as the total number of units produced over the item's entire production history increases. The concept further holds that decline in unit cost can be predicted mathematically.

IMS

See integrated master schedule.

INACCURACY ALLOWANCE

Allocation of time or money to cover possible inaccuracy in schedule or cost estimates.

INCENTIVE

Any of a number of factors that will motivate an individual or an organization to produce superior or faster results, including additional money, time off, recognition, and the like. In contracting, an incentive typically takes the form of monetary terms to turn out a product that meets significantly advanced performance goals, to improve on the contract schedule up to and including final delivery, to substantially reduce costs of the work, or to complete the project under a weighted combination of some or all of these objectives.

INCENTIVE CONTRACT

Negotiated pricing arrangement that gives the contractor higher profits for better performance or lower profits for worse performance in stated areas (cost, schedule, or technical performance).

INCOME

Amount of money (or its equivalent) received during a period of time in exchange for labor or services, from the sale of goods or property, or as profit from financial investments.

INCOME STATEMENT

See profit and loss statement.

INCOME STREAM

Regular flow of money generated by a project, business, or investment.

INCOME TAX

Tax paid on money made or profit realized from employment, business, or capital.

INCOMING GOODS INSPECTION (IGI)

Verification check to confirm that the product or products have arrived in good condition before they can be accepted. In certain instances, acceptance tests may need to be performed to confirm that the product or products meet specifications.

IN-CONTROL

Process that is free of special or assignable causes of variation but not necessarily free of common, or random, causes of variation. Control chart data will indicate if a process is in or out of control.

INCORPORATED

End result of going through the incorporation process. *See also* incorporation.

INCORPORATION

Legal process through which a company receives a charter and the state in which it is based allows it to operate as a corporation.

INCREMENTAL

Increasing gradually by regular degrees or additions.

INCREMENTAL COST

Increase or decrease in costs as a result of one more or one less unit of output.

INCREMENTAL DEVELOPMENT MODEL

Phased approach to project completion whereby certain project functionalities and capabilities are delivered in phases. Allows stakeholders to realize certain benefits earlier than if they were to wait for the total project to be completed.

INCUMBENT CONTRACTOR

Current contractor on an ongoing contractual requirement program.

INDEFINITE-DELIVERY CONTRACT

In U.S. federal procurement, a type of contract in which the period of performance is not specified in the original contract but is established by the contracting officer during performance.

INDEFINITE-QUANTITY CONTRACT

In U.S. federal procurement, a type of contract with an indefinite quantity, within stated minimum or maximum limits, of specific supplies or services to be furnished during a fixed period; deliveries are scheduled by placing orders with the contractor.

INDEMNIFICATION

Act of reimbursing a person for a loss already incurred. Two general types exist: common-law and contractual.

INDEPENDENT COST ANALYSIS (ICA)

Analysis of program, project, or component life cycle cost (LCC) estimates conducted by an impartial body disassociated from the management of the program or project.

INDEPENDENT COST ESTIMATE (ICE)

(1) Estimate of project costs conducted by individuals outside the normal project management structure.

(2) Estimate of anticipated project costs by the project team; used to compare the reasonableness of contractor proposals.

INDEPENDENT EVENT

Event in which the outcome of one event cannot be affected by the outcome of another event. In project management the concept is applied to determine the probability, or likelihood, of a risk event occurring and to determine expected value in decision-tree analysis.

INDEPENDENT GOVERNMENT COST ESTIMATE (IGCE)

Estimate of the cost for goods and/or estimate of services to be procured by contract. Such estimates are prepared by U.S. government personnel, independent of contractors, and are used as a basis against which to gauge reasonableness of prospective contractors' proposed costs.

INDEPENDENT RESEARCH AND DEVELOPMENT (IR&D)

Technical effort by industry that is not sponsored by, or required in performance of, a contract and that consists of projects falling within the areas of basic and applied research, development, systems, and other concept-formulation studies. Also refers to discretionary funds that industry can allocate to projects.

INDEPENDENT VERIFICATION AND VALIDATION (IV&V)

Process used to verify and validate software or some other product, by a group other than the one that created or implemented the original design.

INDEX OF LEADING ECONOMIC INDICATORS

Set of 10 statistics, collected and reported on monthly, used by economists to help forecast upturns or downturns in the economy including the index of consumer expectations and building permits for new private housing units. Created by the U.S. Department of Commerce, the index is now tracked by The Conference Board.

INDIRECT COST

(1) Cost not directly identified with one final cost objective. May be identified with two or more final or one or more intermediate cost objectives.

(2) Cost allocated to the project by the performing organization as a cost of doing business. *Also called* overhead cost *or* burden. *See also* direct cost.

INDIRECT COST ALLOCATION BASE

Base used to calculate indirect cost rates. It should be selected so as to permit allocation of indirect costs on the basis of the benefits accruing to the several cost objectives.

INDIRECT COST POOL

Group of incurred costs identified with two or more cost objectives but not identified specifically with any final cost objective.

INDIRECT COST RATE

Percentage or dollar factor that expresses the ratio of indirect expense incurred in a given period to direct labor cost, manufacturing cost, or another appropriate base for the same period. *Also called* burden rate.

INDIRECT PREJUDICE

Cost that results from a product failure or a failure to meet contractual commitments, such as loss of market share for the customer's organization. Can be calculated by average growth compared with reduced growth because of loss of production capability. Generally not covered by insurance.

INDUCTIVE STATISTICS

See inferential statistics.

INDUSTRIAL ENGINEERING

Art and science of using and coordinating personnel, equipment, and materials to attain a desired quantity of output at a specified time and at an optimum cost. This may include gathering, analyzing, and acting upon facts pertaining to building of facilities, layouts, personnel organization, operating procedures, methods, processes, schedules, time standards, wage rates, wage payment plans, costs, and systems for controlling the quality and quantity of goods and services.

INDUSTRIAL FUND (IF)

Revolving fund established at U.S. DOD industrial-type activities in which products or services are provided to external users. The purposes of the fund are to provide a more effective means of controlling costs; establish a flexible means for financing, budgeting, and accounting; encourage the creation of buyer-seller relationships; place budgeting and accounting on a more commercial basis; and encourage cross-servicing between military departments. Charges to the fund are made for procurement of materials, services, and labor, and the fund is reimbursed by proceeds from the sale of products and services.

INDUSTRIAL MOBILIZATION

Process of marshaling the industrial sector to provide goods and services, including construction, required to support military operations and the needs of the civil sector during domestic or national emergencies. It includes the mobilization of materials, labor, capital, facilities, and contributory items and services. Mobilization activities may result in some disruption to the national economy.

INFERENTIAL STATISTICS

Methods of using sample data taken from a statistical population to make actual decisions, predictions, and generalizations related to a problem of interest. *Also called* inductive statistics.

INFLATION

(1) Proportionate rate of change in the general price level, as opposed to the proportionate increase in a specific price. Inflation is usually measured by a broad-based price index, such as the Consumer Price Index (CPI).

(2) Factor in cost evaluation and cost comparison that must be predicted as an allowance for the price changes that occur with time and over which the project manager has no control, such as the cost of living index, interest rates, and other cost indices.

INFLUENCING THE ORGANIZATION

Ability of a project or program manager to "get things done." Requires an understanding of both the formal and informal structures of all the organizations, powers, and politics involved.

INFORMATION ARCHITECTURE

Emerging practice and discipline that involves the design of organization, labeling, navigation, and searching systems to help people find and manage information more successfully. Its application ranges from the design of technical reports to Web sites and can encompass, at the highest levels of architecture, how an organization will design and construct systems, and systems of systems, to provide relevant information to its users in the most cost-efficient manner.

INFORMATION ASSURANCE (IA)

Information operations that protect and defend information and information systems by ensuring their availability, integrity, authentication, confidentiality, and nonrepudiation. This includes providing for the restoration of information systems by incorporating protection, detection, and reaction capabilities.

INFORMATION DISTRIBUTION

Timely provision of needed information to project stakeholders in a variety of formats.

INFORMATION GATHERING AND ANALYSIS

Specific actions taken to gain information about project requirements, system elements, or critical acquisition processes for which the level of knowledge is insufficient to permit an informed decision to be made with respect to other risk-handling options.

INFORMATION OVERLOAD

Exposure to such quantity, type, and complexity of information input that one's ability to comprehend, assimilate, and use such information is increasingly diminished.

INFORMATION REQUIREMENT

Information needed to perform day-to-day operations.

INFORMATION SYSTEM

Complex, interactive structure of people, equipment, processes, and procedures designed to produce information collected from both internal and external sources for use in decision making.

INFORMATION TECHNOLOGY (IT)

(1) Any equipment or interconnected system or subsystem of equipment that is used in the automatic acquisition, storage, manipulation, management, movement, control, display, switching, interchange, transmission, or reception of data or information by the executive agency. IT includes computers, ancillary equipment, software, firmware, and related services, including support services.

(2) Application of engineering solutions in order to develop computer systems that process data.

INFORMATION TECHNOLOGY ARCHITECTURE (ITA)

Integrated framework for evolving or maintaining existing IT and acquiring new IT to achieve an organization's strategic goals.

INFORMATION TECHNOLOGY INFRASTRUCTURE

Data, information, processes, organizational interactions, skills, and analytical expertise, as well as systems, networks, and information exchange capabilities.

INFORMATION TECHNOLOGY INFRASTRUCTURE LIBRARY (ITIL)

Set of concepts and techniques for managing IT infrastructure, development, and operations; in short, it is a best-practices guide for the practice of IT service management. ITIL consists of a series of books addressing the various areas of IT service management and includes a supporting qualification program so an individual can become certified in its application in an organization. The names ITIL and IT Infrastructure Library are registered trademarks of the United Kingdom's Office of Government Commerce (OGC). ITIL gives a detailed description of a number of important IT practices, including comprehensive checklists, tasks, and procedures that can be tailored to any IT organization.

INFORMATION WARFARE (IW)

Actions taken to achieve information superiority by affecting an adversary's information, information-based processes, information systems, and computer-based networks while defending one's own information, information-based processes, information systems, and computer-based networks.

INFRASTRUCTURE

Resources such as personnel, buildings, or equipment required for a project or program.

INHERENT AVAILABILITY

Availability of a system with respect only to operating time and corrective maintenance. Ignores standby and delay times associated with preventive maintenance as well as Mean Logistics Delay Time (MLDT) and may be calculated as the ratio of Mean Time Between Failure (MTBF) divided by the sum of MTBF and Mean Time To Repair (MTTR), that is $IA = MTBF / (MTBF + MTTR)$.

INHERENTLY GOVERNMENTAL ACTIVITIES

Term used in U.S. government activities. Defines an activity as one that is so intimately related to the public interest that it must be performed by federal employees. These activities normally fall into two categories: the act of governing, that is, the discretionary exercise of government authority; and monetary transactions and entitlements.

INHERENT RELIABILITY AND MAINTAINABILITY (R&M) VALUE

Any measure of reliability or maintainability that includes only the effects of item design and installation, and assumes an ideal operating and support environment.

IN-HOUSE

Work performed by one's own employees as opposed to an outside contractor.

INITIAL PROJECT PLAN

(1) Top-down, high-level plan used to document the early approach to a project; usually contains resource manager commitments and a preliminary technical solution.

(2) Method for communication during the delegation of a project responsibility and acceptance of a project commitment.

INITIAL TERM

First time period covered under an agreement or contract (the term) at the end of which the agreement will either end or be renewed (sometimes automatically) under a specific set of conditions as described in the contract.

INITIATING PROCESSES

Procedures for recognizing that a program, project (including a project that is part of a program), or phase should begin and committing to start it. *See also* project/program management process groups.

INITIATION

Process of formally recognizing that a new project exists or that an existing project should continue into its next phase.

IN-KIND

Value of goods or services provided for which an equivalent amount of money would have otherwise been paid.

INNOVATION

Creation or invention of a new idea, method, device, or service and the actions needed to bring such idea, method, device, or service into final form. In many for-profit organizations the definition also includes the ability to generate a certain level of revenue and profit from the innovation.

INNOVATION ENGINE

Combination of people, processes, culture, and tools in an organization that provides for, encourages, and facilitates the creation of new ideas, methods, devices, and services for the good of the organization, its stakeholders, shareholders, and customers.

IN-PROCESS REVIEW

Formal review conducted (usually annually) during the operations and maintenance phase to evaluate system performance, user satisfaction with the system, adaptability to changing business needs, and new technologies that might improve the system.

IN-PROCESS REVIEW REPORT

Formal document detailing the findings of the in-process review. *See also* in-process review.

IN PRODUCTION

In IT, a fully documented system, built according to a systems development life cycle, fully tested, with full functionality, accompanied by training and training materials and with no restrictions on its distribution or duration of use.

IN-PROGRESS ACTIVITY

Activity that has started but has not been completed as of a given date.

INPUT

(1) Information or other items required to begin a process or activity.

(2) Documents or documentable items to be acted upon.

(3) Information, thoughts, or ideas used to assist in decision making.

INPUT LIMITS

Limitations imposed on the resources needed to execute the plan.

INPUT MILESTONE

Imposed target dates or target events that are to be accomplished and that control the plan with respect to time.

INPUT/OUTPUT

(1) Process of entering information into a system (input) and its subsequent results (output).

(2) Collection of hardware devices that enables input (for example, a keyboard or card reader) and output (for example, a monitor or printer). Collectively known as I/O.

INPUT PRIORITIES

Imposed priorities or sequence desired with respect to the scheduling activities within previously imposed constraints.

INPUT RESTRAINT

Imposed external constraint, such as dates reflecting input from others, target dates reflecting output required by others, or float allocation.

IN-SERVICE DATE

Time when the project's product or service is placed in a state of readiness or availability so that it can be used for its specifically assigned function.

INSOLVENCY

State that occurs when a business is unable to pay its debts as they fall due.

INSPECTION

Examination or measurement of work to verify whether an item or activity conforms to a specific requirement.

INSPECTION BY ATTRIBUTES

Inspection in which either the unit of product or characteristics of the product are classified as defective or nondefective, or the number of defects in the unit of product is counted with respect to a given requirement.

INSPECTION BY VARIABLES

Inspection in which certain quality characteristics of the sample are evaluated with respect to a continuous numerical scale and are expressed as precise points along this scale. Records the degree of conformance or nonconformance of the unit with specified requirements for the quality characteristics involved.

INSPECTION CYCLE

System in which supplies and equipment in storage are subjected to, but not limited to, periodic, special inspection and continuous action to ensure that material is maintained in a ready-for-issue condition.

INSPECTION-IN-PROCESS

Inspection performed during the manufacturing or repair cycle to help prevent defects from occurring and to inspect the characteristics and attributes that cannot be examined at final inspection.

INSPECTION LEVEL

Indication of the relative sample size for a given amount of product.

INSPECTION RECORD

Recorded data concerning the results of inspection action.

INSPECTION SYSTEM REQUIREMENT

(1) Requirement to establish and maintain an inspection system according to a directed (for example, government) specification.

(2) Requirement referenced in contracts when technical requirements necessitate control of quality by in-process and final end-item inspection.

INSTALLATION

Fixed or relatively fixed location together with its real estate, buildings, structures, utilities, and improvement thereon. It usually is identified with an existing or potential organization and its missions or functions.

INSTANT PUDDING

Term used by W. Edwards Deming, and initially coined by James Bakken of the Ford Motor Company in his book *Out of the Crisis*, to describe an obstacle to achieving quality and to illustrate the erroneous supposition that quality and productivity improvement can be achieved quickly through an affirmation of faith rather than through sufficient effort and education.

INSURABLE RISK

Risk that can be covered by an insurance policy. *Also called* pure risk.

INSURANCE

(1) Premium paid to a person or organization to cover some or all of the cost of a risk impact. *See also* impact.

(2) Protection against a risk of loss or harm.

INSURANCE ADMINISTRATION EXPENSES

Costs of administering an insurance program (for example, actuarial fees, service fees paid to insurance companies, trustees, or technical consultants, or the costs of operating a risk-management department).

INTANGIBLE CAPITAL ASSET

Asset that has no physical substance, has more than minimal value, and is expected to be held by an enterprise for continued use or possession beyond the current accounting period for the benefits it yields.

INTEGRATED BASELINE REVIEW

Review of a contractor's performance measurement baseline (PMB). It is conducted by program managers and their technical staffs or integrated product teams (IPTs) on contracts requiring compliance with DOD earned value management system (EVMS) criteria requirements within six months after contract award.

INTEGRATED COST/SCHEDULE REPORTING

Output of earned value analysis.

INTEGRATED LOGISTICS SUPPORT (ILS)

Composite of all considerations necessary to ensure the effective and economical support of a system over its life cycle. Principal elements include—

- Maintenance planning
- Supply support
- Technical data
- Facilities
- Staffing and personnel
- Training and training support
- Support equipment
- Computer resources support
- Packaging, handling, storage, and transportation
- Design interfaces

INTEGRATED MASTER PLAN (IMP)

Event-based plan that depicts the overall structure of the program and the key processes, activities, and milestones. It defines the accomplishments and criteria for each event in the plan.

INTEGRATED MASTER SCHEDULE (IMS)

In U.S. DOD programs, a time-phased schedule that serves as a tool for time-phasing work and assessing technical performance. Schedule activities in the IMS are traceable to the CWBS elements used in EVMS, allowing commonality for integrated program assessment of cost, schedule, technical performance, and associated risks.

INTEGRATED PRODUCT AND PROCESS DEVELOPMENT (IPPD)

Term used in U.S. DOD to describe a management technique that simultaneously integrates all essential acquisition activities through the use of multidisciplinary teams to optimize the design, manufacturing, and supportability processes. IPPD facilitates meeting cost and performance objectives, from product concept though teamwork through integrated product teams (IPTs).

INTEGRATED PRODUCT DEVELOPMENT TEAM (IPDT)

Group of people from different disciplines whose collective effort is required to complete a given product development project and who meet at frequent and regular intervals to plan, execute, and monitor project performance. They meet at the outset to plan the entire project even though many of its members may not be involved with project execution until many months, or years, after the project begins. It has been shown that this type of team can accelerate project completion because all team members agree on the project's objectives at the beginning of the project; understand their roles, as well as the roles of the others, in project execution; and know the exact time when they are required to work on the project.

INTEGRATED PRODUCT TEAM (IPT)

See integrated product development team (IPDT).

INTEGRATED PROJECT PROGRESS REPORT

Documentation that measures actual cost and schedule data against the budget by using BCWP, BCWS, and ACWP.

INTEGRATED PROJECT TEAM

Term used interchangeably with integrated product team. Technically speaking, if the end result of a project is a service rather than a tangible or intangible product, the team is not an integrated product team. It is an integrated project team.

INTEGRATION

Actions taken within a program office (PO) using the integrated product and process development (IPPD) process to ensure that the various functional disciplines of systems acquisition management are appropriately considered during the design, development, and production of a system.

INTEGRATION AND TEST PHASE

Life-cycle phase during which subsystem integration, system, security, and user acceptance testing are conducted; done prior to the implementation phase.

INTEGRATION DOCUMENT

Formal document that describes how the software components, hardware components, or both are combined, and the interaction between them.

INTEGRATION TEST

Testing in which software components, hardware components, or both are combined and tested to evaluate the interaction between them.

INTEGRITY

In IT, the degree to which a system (or system component) prevents unauthorized access to, or modification of, computer programs or data.

INTELLECTUAL CAPITAL

Intangible assets of an organization such as employee know-how and expertise, intellectual property, and organizational systems. Although difficult to quantify, one way to estimate its worth is to compare a company's book value with its share price. For example, if the company's book value is $10 per share and its stock is selling for $40 per share (market value), the difference often is attributed to intellectual capital. *See also* book value *and* market value.

INTELLECTUAL PROPERTY

Concept, idea, notion, thought, or process, including a computer program, that is definable, measurable, and proprietary in nature. Includes inventions, trademarks, patents, industrial designs, copyrights, and technical information, including software, data designs, technical know-how, manufacturing information and know-how, techniques, technical data packages (U.S. DOD), manufacturing data packages, and trade secrets.

INTENTION TO BID

Communication, written or oral, from prospective contractors indicating their willingness to perform the specified work. May take the form of a letter, statement of qualifications, or response to a request for proposals or request for quotations.

INTERCHANGEABILITY

Condition that exists when two or more items possess such functional and physical characteristics as to be equivalent in performance and durability, and are capable of being exchanged one for the other without alteration of the items themselves or of adjoining items, except for adjustment, and without selection for fit and performance.

INTERCONNECTION

Linking together of interoperable systems.

INTERDEPENDENCIES

Relationships among organizational functions in which one function, task, or activity is dependent on others.

INTEREST

Amount paid for the use of money.

INTERESTED PARTY

Person or persons who are affected by the result of a project or program.

INTEREST EXPENSE

Cost of borrowing money. It is shown as a financial expense item within the income statement.

INTEREST RATE

Typically the annual rate of interest, expressed as a percentage, charged for the use of money. The rate is derived by dividing the amount of interest by the amount of principal borrowed. For example, if a bank charged $1,000 a year to borrow $10,000, the interest rate would be 10 percent.

INTERFACE

(1) Common boundary or connection between persons, between systems, or between persons and systems.

(2) System external to the system being analyzed that provides a common boundary or service that is necessary for the other system to perform its mission; for example, a system that supplies power, cooling, heating, air services, or input signals.

INTERFACE ACTIVITY

(1) Activity connecting a node in one subnet with a node in another subnet to represent logical interdependence.

(2) Points of interaction or commonality between the project activities and outside influences.

INTERFACE CONTROL DOCUMENT

Specifies the interface between a system and an external system(s).

INTERFACE MANAGEMENT

(1) Process of identifying, documenting, scheduling, communicating, and monitoring interfaces related to the product and the project. The three major types of interfaces are personal and interpersonal; organizational; and system or technical.

(2) Management of communication, coordination, and responsibility between two organizations, phases, or physical entities that are interdependent.

INTERFACE REQUIREMENT SPECIFICATION (IRS)

Type of item performance specification that defines the required software interfaces for a given software item (SI) in the allocated baseline, the requirements for which are described by a software requirements specification (SRS). The IRS is frequently combined with the SRS.

INTERFACING

Act of communicating and working with various interface components on a project to achieve the project's objectives.

INTERNAL AUDIT

Self-audit conducted by members of the project team or a unit in the organization.

INTERNAL CONTROL

Process of monitoring and dealing with deviations from the project plan.

INTERNAL DOCUMENTATION

Written information that is associated with the development process, the quality system, and the product; is retained in the project files; and is not part of the final product.

INTERNAL PROJECT SOURCES

Historical data on similar procurements, cost and performance data on various contractors, and other internal information used in a proposed procurement.

INTERNAL RATE OF RETURN (IRR)

(1) Annual rate of earnings on an investment. IRR equates the value of the cash returns with invested cash and considers the application of compound interest factors. The formula is as follows:

$$\sum_{i}^{n} \frac{\text{Periodic cash flow}}{(1+i)^t} = \text{Investment amount}$$

where i = internal rate of return, t = each time interval, n = total number of time intervals, and $\sum$ is summation.

(2) Discount rate at which net present value (NPV) investment is zero. *See also* net present value.

INTERNAL REVENUE CODE

(1) Statutes that make up U.S. federal tax law.

(2) Generic name for any group of laws, statutes, and regulations describing tax law for a political jurisdiction.

INTERNAL RISK

Risk under the control or influence of the project team. *See also* external risk.

INTERNATIONAL DATE LINE

Imaginary line that runs from the North Pole to the South Pole and is, with some exceptions, 180° away from the Greenwich Meridian (0 degrees, 0 minutes of longitude). It is the line where each new day starts (in local time). It most corresponds to the time zone boundary separating +12 and −12 hours GMT. Crossing the line travelling east results in a day or 24 hours being subtracted, and crossing west results in a day being added. *See also* Greenwich Mean Time.

INTERNATIONAL ORGANIZATION FOR STANDARDIZATION (ISO)

Voluntary organization consisting of national standardization bodies of each member country. Prepares and issues standards identified as "ISO-XXXX."

INTERNATIONAL PROJECT MANAGEMENT ASSOCIATION (IPMA)

Association of project management associations headquartered in Zurich, Switzerland, made up of, for the most part, European countries' project management associations. Has developed a four-level certification program for project managers.

INTERNET PORTAL

See portal.

INTEROPERABILITY

Measure of the ability of two or more systems (or system components) to exchange information and use the information that has been exchanged.

INTERPERSONAL INTERFACES

Formal and informal reporting relationships among various project stakeholders.

INTERRELATIONSHIP DIGRAPH

Graphical representation of all the factors in a complicated problem, system, or situation.

INTERVENOR

Alternative name for a stakeholder in the nuclear power plant-construction industry.

IN THE BAG
Outcome that is virtually secured and accomplished.

IN THE BLACK
State of making money; being profitable.

IN THE RED
State of losing money.

INTIMIDATING MANAGEMENT STYLE
Management approach in which the project manager frequently reprimands team members to uphold his or her image as a demanding manager, at the risk of lowering team morale.

INTRAPRENEUR
In-house entrepreneur. In-house entrepreneurship is developed by blending entrepreneurial creativity with the stability of a large corporation.

INVENTORY BASIS
In U.S. federal procurement, the preferred basis for settlement proposals under fixed-price contracts terminated for convenience.

INVENTORY CLOSEOUT
Settlement and credit of inventory if purchased from project funds.

INVENTORY CONTROL POINT (ICP)
Organizational element within a distribution system that is assigned responsibility for systemwide direction and control of materiél, including such management functions as the computation of requirements, the initiation of procurement or disposal actions, the development of worldwide quantitative and monetary inventory data, and the positioning and repositioning of materiél.

INVENTORY TURNOVER
Ratio showing how many times the inventory of a firm is sold and replaced over a specific period.

INVENTORY TURNS

Measure of the length of time it takes a company to entirely replenish its inventory, including new materials as well as finished goods. The higher the number of "turns," the better the business is performing because customers are buying its products at a faster rate. Calculated by dividing annual sales by average value of the inventory. For example, if a company had sales of $100,000 last year and the average retail value of its inventory over the past year was $50,000, then the number of inventory turns equals two.

INVESTMENT

(1) Expenditure of an organization's funds on a project or program with the expectation that such project or program will have a positive return to the organization based on an established and agreed-upon set of criteria for said investment.

(2) In finance, the purchase of a financial product or other item of value with an expectation of favorable future returns. In general terms, investment means the use of money in the hope of making more money.

INVESTMENT BANKER

Underwriter (usually a firm) that serves as a middleman between a corporation issuing new securities and the public.

INVESTOR'S METHOD

See internal rate of return.

INVISIBLE WORKERS

Employees who telecommute and do not go to work in an office.

INVITATION FOR BIDS (IFB)

In U.S. federal procurement, solicitation document used in sealed-bidding procurements; generally, equivalent to a request for proposals.

INVOICE

(1) Written account or itemized statement addressed to the purchaser of merchandise shipped or services performed with the quantity, prices, and charges listed.

(2) Contractor's bill or written request for payment for work or services performed under the contract.

IN WRITING

Any worded or numbered expression that can be read, reproduced, and later communicated, which includes electronically transmitted and stored information. Also referred to as written.

IPDT

See integrated product development team.

IPMA

See International Project Management Association.

IPPD

See integrated product and process development.

IPT

See integrated product team.

IR&D

See independent research and development.

IRON-COLLAR

Name given to robots that perform tasks previously carried out by humans (blue-collar workers) such as one would find in an automobile manufacturing plant.

IRR

See internal rate of return.

IRS

See interface requirement specification.

ISHIKAWA DIAGRAM

One of the seven tools of quality. Diagram used to illustrate how various causes and subcauses create a specific effect. Named after its developer, Kaoru Ishikawa. *Also called* cause-and-effect diagram *or* fishbone diagram.

ISO

See International Organization for Standardization.

ISO 9000

Set of documented standards to help organizations ensure that their quality systems meet certain minimal levels of consistent performance.

ISO 21500

New and in-progress international guide to project management that will use BS 6079-1, Guide to Project Management (British Standards Institute), as its base document. The new ISO 21500 will be published sometime after 2010.

ISOMORPHIC TEAM STRUCTURE

Organization of a project team so that it closely reflects the physical structure of the project deliverable; for example, if the project is to produce a book, then each team member writes one chapter. The project manager is responsible for integrating the team's pieces into a cohesive final product.

ISSUE

Formally identified item related to a project that, if not addressed, may—

- Affect its schedule
- Change its direction
- Diminish its quality
- Increase its cost

It is distinguished from a risk in that it is an extant problem, whereas a risk is a future event. In many organizations, the terms are used interchangeably.

ISSUE MANAGEMENT

Structured, documented, and formal process or set of procedures used by an organization or a project to identify, categorize, and resolve issues. *See also* issue.

ISSUES REGISTER

Record of the identified issues on a project or program that need to be addressed and resolved in order to successfully complete a task, phase, or activity, or the project or program itself. Issues usually are assigned to one or more individuals on the team to resolve.

IT

See information technology.

ITA

See information technology architecture.

ITEM PERFORMANCE SPECIFICATION

Program-unique specification usually approved as part of the allocated baseline. States all necessary design requirements of a configuration item (CI) in terms of performance. Essential physical constraints are included. Item performance specifications state requirements for the development of items below the system level. They specify all the required item functional characteristics and the tests required to demonstrate achievement of those characteristics.

ITERATION

(1) One execution and result of an iterative process; for example, numerous redrafts of a document, or reworking of a funding profile, in order to satisfy everyone involved.

(2) Action or process of repeating or iterating.

ITERATIVE

(1) Repetitious or reoccurring activity or cycle.

(2) Process in which a series of activities is performed in sequence and repeatedly, with each set of activities reviewed and validated prior to moving on to the next.

(3) In requirements elicitation, creating requirements definitions through successive cycles of refinement and user validation.

ITIL

See Information Technology Infrastructure Library.

IV&V

See independent verification and validation.

IW

See information warfare.

J

JA

See job analysis.

JAD

See joint application design.

JEOPARDY

Future event or series of events that, if it occurs, will have a negative impact on the project. *Also called* threat.

JISHUKEN

Japanese word that means a management-driven activity in which managers and executives regularly identify areas that need continuous improvement; it stimulates "kaizen," or change for the better.

JIT

See just in time.

JOB

Homogeneous cluster of work tasks, the completion of which serves an enduring purpose for the organization. Within a job, there may be pay categories dependent on the degree of supervision required by the employee while performing assigned tasks, which are performed by all persons with the same job.

JOB ANALYSIS (JA)

Detailed examination of a job to determine the duties, responsibilities, and specialized requirements necessary for its performance.

JOB CLASS OF EMPLOYEES

Employees performing in positions within the same job.

JOB COSTING

Allocation of all time, material, and expenses to a project; provides for budgeting, forecasting, collecting, and reporting on the spending and revenue associated with specific projects.

JOB DESCRIPTION

Written outline, by job type, of the skills, responsibilities, knowledge, authority, and relationships involved in an individual's job. *Also called* position description.

JOB LOT

Relatively small number of a specific type of part or product that is produced at one time.

JOB ORDER

(1) Formal instruction to perform certain work according to specifications, estimates, and so forth.

(2) Descriptive of a cost system whereby costs are accumulated by job orders.

JOB SHOP

Manufacturing enterprise devoted to producing special or custom-made parts of products, usually in small quantities for specific customers.

JOINT APPLICATION DESIGN (JAD)

Facilitated group sessions held during software design and development between the technical design team and the customer(s). These structured workshops aim to speed up the development process, and when held frequently, improve customer satisfaction by maintaining close communication with the customer to determine exactly what the customer expects the system to do. A trained facilitator keeps the group on task during each session. In requirements elicitation, this technique can be especially valuable in crisis situations. Conceived in 1977 by Chuck Morris of IBM as an innovative way of getting users together to work out plans to install distributed systems.

JOINT VENTURE

Contractual partnership between organizations for a particular transaction to achieve common goals for mutual profit. Differs from a partnership in that a joint venture does not entail a continuing relationship between the parties.

JOURNAL

In accounting transactions, where transactions are recorded as they occur.

JUDICIAL MANAGEMENT STYLE

Management approach in which the project manager exercises sound judgment and applies it to project issues as the need arises.

JUST IN TIME (JIT)

Approach used to manage resources, requirements, and production so that the right material arrives at the right place just in time for use.

K

KAIKAKU

Japanese term for a rapid and revolutionary change, as opposed to kaizen, which describes a smaller and evolutionary change. *See also* kaizen.

KAIZEN

(1) Japanese term that literally means "change for the better." Refers to small, continuous improvements to products and services.

(2) Name of the book written by Masaaki Imai, who is credited with advancing and promoting the application of its principles.

KAIZEN BUDGETING

Budgeting approach that projects costs on the basis of future improvements rather than current practices and methods. The key is that the budget cannot be achieved unless improvements are made.

KAIZEN EVENT

Any action whose output is intended to be an improvement to an existing process. The action is defined and executed by a small group of individuals who have control over a specific process. *See also* kaizen.

KALDOR-HICKS CRITERION

Criterion of equity that asserts that one social state is better than another if there is a net gain in efficiency and if those that gain can compensate the losers.

KANBAN TECHNIQUE

Japanese term describing a method used for improving process flow by use of tags, status display boards, small designated material transfer spaces, designated containers, and similar mechanisms to give more visibility and control to the flow of material. Dedicated space is set up so the quantity of material can be held to the amount calculated as appropriate for just-in-time processing. The limited number of dedicated containers also serves as a control on the rate of production, helping to reinforce the just-in-time, demand-based system for material flow.

KANO ANALYSIS

Quality measurement tool used to prioritize customer requirements based on customer satisfaction. Based on the supposition that identified requirements may not be, and probably are not, of equal importance to all customers. Named after Professor Noriako Kano, who advanced the notion that there are five categories of customer preferences:

- Attractive
- One-dimensional
- Must-be
- Indifferent
- Reverse

These five categories have been reduced to four drivers of customer preferences in many applications:

- The "surprise and delight" factors

- The "more is better" factors

- The "must be" things

• The "dissatisfiers," the things that cause your customers not to like your product

KANSEI ENGINEERING
Japanese term describing a consumer-oriented technology process used to develop products that use the consumer's feelings (kansei) as a guideline in creating the product.

KEY CRITERIA
Important measures or values used in scoring models to ensure that the selection process results in the best available choice consistent with overall objectives.

KEY DECISION POINT
Major decision point that separates the phases of a project or program.

KEY EVENT
See milestone.

KEY-EVENT SCHEDULE
See milestone schedule.

KEY INTERFACE
Interfaces in functional and physical characteristics that exist at a common boundary with cofunctioning items, system, equipment, software, and data.

KEY PERFORMANCE INDICATORS (KPIs)
Metrics that have been identified as being critical to gather, monitor, and control for the successful performance of a business, program, or project.

KEY PERFORMANCE PARAMETERS (KPPs)
Attributes or characteristics of a system that are considered critical or essential to the client, customer, or user.

KEY PERSONNEL
List of identified persons considered critical to the success of a project.

KEY SUCCESS FACTORS (KSFs)

Identified list of specific skills or talents, competitive capabilities, or any other actions, approaches, processes, practices, or procedures that an organization must have and do to satisfy customers.

KICKBACK

Money, fee, commission, credit, gift, gratuity, thing of value, or compensation of any kind that is provided, directly or indirectly, to any person, contractor, prime contractor employee, subcontractor, or subcontractor employee for the purpose of improperly obtaining or rewarding favorable treatment in connection with an action or inaction, prime contract, or subcontract relating to a prime contract.

KICKOFF MEETING

Meeting held to acquaint stakeholders with the project and one another; presumes the presence of the customer and serves as an initial review of project scope and activities. Usually conducted after contract award or a decision to initiate a project.

KILL POINT

See control gate.

KINESICS

Study of communication through body movement.

KIRKPATRICK'S FOUR LEVELS OF TRAINING EFFECTIVENESS

Assessment scheme developed by Donald Kirkpatrick, PhD, in 1959 to determine the effectiveness level of a training program. The levels are

- Level 1: Reaction

How the participant reacted to the program; a measure of customer satisfaction most commonly captured on the "smiley sheet" evaluation form.

- Level 2: Learning

Defined as the extent to which participants change attitudes, improve knowledge, and/or increase skills as a result of the training program.

- Level 3: Behavior

Defined as the extent to which the changed behavior learned in the training program is applied on the job.

- Level 4: Results

Defined as the final results achieved as a result of attending the training, measured in a variety of ways, such as increased production, improved productivity, or decreased costs.

KISS MODEL

Pragmatic philosophy of conducting business in which the objective is to keep things, such as procedures, reports, and any other aspect of work, as simple as possible to get the job done. The acronym humorously describes the basic premise of simplicity, which is "keep it simple, stupid."

KIVIAT GRAPH

Multifaceted graphic representation technique for displaying the results of many changing variables simultaneously. Used to display productivity, quality, and other targets together.

KNOW-HOW

Knowledge, skills, and ability to do something correctly.

KNOWLEDGE MANAGEMENT

Collection of systems, processes, and procedures designed to acquire and share the intellectual assets of an organization. According to its proponents, knowledge management is the key that will give an organization a competitive advantage in the marketplace and enable it to serve its customers more efficiently. In project management, having a formal lessons-learned process is a form of knowledge management that can significantly aid project managers in avoiding the same mistakes others have made in the past.

KNOWLEDGE TRANSFER

Flow of knowledge, skills, information, and competencies from one person to another. Can happen through any number of methods, including coaching, mentoring, training courses, and on-the-job experience.

KNOWN KNOWNS

In risk management, risks that are foreseen and have been identified and documented in the project's risk listing. For example, when scope changes are certain and the extent of the scope changes is known at the outset.

KNOWN UNKNOWNS

In risk management, those future situations that it is possible to plan for or predict in part. For example, when schedule changes are certain but the extent of the changes is unknown.

KNOW WHICH WAY THE WIND BLOWS

To be aware of one's surroundings, especially the opinions of management and stakeholders.

KOTTER'S "EIGHT STEPS TO SUCCESSFUL CHANGE"

Described by John Kotter in his books *Leading Change* (1996) and *The Heart of Change* (2002), the eight steps are a pragmatic approach to understanding and managing change. Kotter asserts that successful change is based on understanding and relating to the emotional response to change. People first need to see and feel the change before it will occur. The eight steps call on managers to—

• Create a sense of urgency. Inspire people to move. Make objectives real and relevant.

• Develop the guiding influence. Make sure the right people are leading the change effort. One person alone cannot do it.

• Articulate a clear vision. Describe for the organization what the end result of change is.

• Communicate, communicate, communicate. It is critical that communication about the change take place on multiple levels.

• Empower everyone to action. Reward and recognize those who champion the change effort.

- Create short-term wins. Target easy opportunities first so everyone will see change happening and will get on board.

- Never let up. Sustained effort and commitment is needed so everyone recognizes that the effort is important and that management is committed to the end.

- Hold the gains. Make change stick by reinforcing the values espoused in the change program.

KPIs

See key performance indicators.

KPPs

See key performance parameters.

KSFs

See key success factors.

KÜBLER-ROSS FIVE STAGES OF GRIEF MODEL

Model developed by Swiss psychoanalyst Elisabeth Kübler-Ross to describe the five stages of grief an individual goes through when confronted with his or her mortality. The stages are denial, anger, bargaining, depression, and acceptance. This model often forms the underpinnings of modern organizational change models.

L

LABOR

Effort expended by people for wages or salary. Generally classified as either direct or indirect. Direct labor is applied to meeting project objectives and is a principal element used in costing, pricing, and profit determination; indirect labor is a component of indirect cost, such as overhead or general and administrative costs.

LABOR EFFICIENCY

Ratio of earned hours to actual hours spent on a prescribed task during a reporting period. When earned hours equal actual hours, the efficiency equals 100 percent.

LABOR-HOUR CONTRACT

Type of contract in which a fixed amount is paid for each hour of work performed by a specific labor class.

LABOR MARKET

Place where individuals exchange their labor for compensation. Labor markets are identified and defined by a combination of the following factors:

- Geography
- Education and/or technical background required
- Experience required by the job
- Licensing or certification requirements
- Occupational membership
- Industry

LABOR PRODUCTIVITY

Rate of output of a worker or group of workers per unit of time, usually compared with an established standard or expected rate of output.

LABOR-RATE STANDARD

Preestablished measure, expressed in monetary terms, of the price of labor.

LABOR RELATIONS COSTS

Costs incurred in maintaining satisfactory relations between an employer and its employees, including the costs of shop stewards, labor management committees, employee publications, and other related activities.

LABOR-TIME STANDARD

Preestablished measure, expressed in temporal terms, of the price of labor.

LAG

Modification of a logical relationship in a schedule such that there is a delay in the successor task. For example, in a finish-to-start dependency with a five-day lag, the successor activity cannot start until five days after the predecessor has finished. *See also* lead.

LAGGING INDICATORS

(1) In project management or general management, performance measures that represent the consequences of actions previously taken. They frequently focus on results at the end of a time period and characterize historical performance. Sales revenue may be considered a lagging indicator.

(2) Economic statistics that follow changes in economic activity to provide evidence of direction.

LAG RELATIONSHIP

One of four types of relationships involving a lag between the start or finish of a work item and the start or finish of another work item: finish-to-start; start-to-finish; finish-to-finish; and start-to-start.

LAISSEZ-FAIRE MANAGEMENT STYLE

Management approach in which team members are not directed by management. Little information flows from the project team to the project manager, or vice versa. This style is appropriate if the team is highly skilled and knowledgeable and wants no interference by the project manager.

LANDED COST

Total expense of receiving goods at a place of retail sale, including the retail purchase price, transportation costs, duties, value-added taxes, excise tax, and other taxes.

LANDING COST

Initial charges for landing imported goods, such as those for receiving goods from dockside vessels or from barges to lighters. They also may cover wharfage or delivery from the dock to land conveyance or warehouse.

LAST IN, FIRST OUT (LIFO)

Method of inventory rotation to ensure that the newest inventory (last in) is used first (first out).

LATE FINISH DATE (LF)

Latest possible point in time that an activity may end without delaying the project finish date. Used in the critical path method. *See also* late start date.

LATENT DEFECT

Defect that exists at the time of acceptance but cannot be dis-
covered by a reasonable inspection.

LATERAL COMMUNICATION

Communication across lines of an organization of equivalent
authority.

LATERAL THINKING

Term coined by Edward de Bono to describe a type of idea-
generation technique that uses a reasoning approach that is not
immediately obvious and does not follow step-by-step logical
analysis. Lateral thinking techniques are characterized by the
shifting of thinking patterns away from a predictable form of
reasoning. Ideas generated through lateral thinking may not be
ideas that can be implemented but may lead to other ideas than
can be applied to the problem at hand. Often called "out of the
box" thinking.

LATE START DATE (LS)

Latest possible point in time that an activity may begin without
delaying the project finish date. Used in the critical path method.
See also late finish date.

LATEST REVISED ESTIMATE

See estimate at completion.

LAUNCH

Act of officially introducing a new product, service, method, or
device into the market or the organization so that the intended
target audience can avail themselves of it and benefit from it.

LAW OF DIMINISHING RETURNS

Economic theory stating that beyond a certain production or
quality level, productivity or quality increases at a decreasing rate.
A diminishing return is one where for every dollar invested to
increase productivity, or quality, one can expect less than a dollar
of productivity or quality gains in return.

LCC

See life-cycle cost.

LCM

See life-cycle management.

LEAD

Modification of a logical relationship in a schedule such that there is an acceleration of the successor task. For example, in a finish-to-start dependency with a five-day lead, the successor activity can start five days before the predecessor has finished. *See also* lag.

LEADER

Individual who uses his or her influence in a group to motivate others to do something. Often used to refer to the project manager, who is the individual vested with formal authority for achieving project aims.

LEADER-COMPANY CONTRACTING

U.S. federal procurement approach used to establish a second source for a product that is being or has been developed by a single contractor. *Also called* leader-follower procurement.

LEADER-FOLLOWER PROCUREMENT

See leader-company contracting.

LEADERSHIP

(1) Use of influence to direct the activities of others toward the accomplishment of some objective.

(2) Ability to persuade others to do things enthusiastically.

(3) Human factor that binds a group together and motivates it toward goals.

LEADING

Establishing direction and aligning, motivating, and inspiring people.

LEAD TIME

Time required to wait for a product, service, material, or resources after ordering or making a request for such things.

LEAD USERS

Any person or persons for whom finding a solution to a particular need is so important that they modify a current product, or invent a new product, to solve the problem themselves because no one else is doing so or will do so. When the number of lead users reaches a critical mass, product manufacturers recognize a broader target audience and create the product on a mass scale using the lead users' ideas as a baseline.

LEAN DEVELOPMENT

One of a variety of agile software development methods. Developed by Robert Charette, it draws on the techniques of lean manufacturing found in the automotive industry in the 1980s. Lean development has 12 principles that focus on management strategies:

- Satisfying the customer is the highest priority.

- Always provide the best value for the money.

- Success depends on active customer participation.

- Every lean development project is a team effort.

- Everything is changeable.

- Deliver domain, not point, solutions.

- Complete, do not construct.

- An 80 percent solution today is better than a 100 percent solution tomorrow.

- Minimalism is essential.

- Needs determine technology.

- Product growth is feature growth, not size growth.

- Never push lean development beyond its limits.

LEARNING CURVE

(1) Graphical or numerical relationship between the average cost or unit cost of an item and the quantity produced.

(2) Tool used to project the amount of direct labor or material that will be used to manufacture a product on a repetitive basis.

LEARNING CURVE THEORY

Parametric model that says that each time we double the number of times we have performed a task, the time it takes to perform the task will decrease in a regular pattern.

LEARNING/IMPROVEMENT CURVE

Mathematical way to explain and measure the rate of change of cost (in hours or dollars) as a function of quantity.

LEARNING ORGANIZATION

Organization (project, department, division, and so forth) that has created an environment in which creative thinking is encouraged and collective aspirations are set free. Popularized by Peter Senge in his book *The Fifth Discipline: The Art and Practice of the Learning Organization*.

LEARNING RATE

Percentage of worker hours per unit required to increase the output to a specified level.

LEASE

Essentially a contract where the owner (lessor) of the asset (leased asset) provides the asset for use by the lessee at a specified price or other consideration, with an understanding that at the end of such period, the asset will be either returned to the lessor or disposed of per the lessor's instructions.

LEASEHOLD

Agreement between the lessee and lessor specifying the lessee's rights to use the leased property for a specific purpose and given time at a specified rental payment.

LEASEHOLD IMPROVEMENTS

Repairs and/or improvements, usually prior to occupancy, made to a leased facility by the lessee. The cost is then added to fixed assets and amortized over the life of the lease.

LEFT-BRAINED

Term used to describe individuals or ways of thinking that are closely aligned with analytical processes and business practices. Terms such as return on investment (ROI), process, bottom-line, and timing are associated with left-brained thinking. *See also* right-brained.

LEFT HAND DOESN'T KNOW WHAT THE RIGHT HAND IS DOING, THE

Any situation, either on a project or within an organization as a whole, where one group of individuals is working on something that is completely unknown to another group that could benefit by being aware of what is going on.

LEGAL ENTITY

(1) Classification of the type of business, such as corporation or partnership, that is formed upon its establishment and that determines its taxation, as well as what individual protection from monetary liabilities the owners are afforded. Although the corporation has been standard for many years, other options include limited partnership (LP), limited liability partnership (LLP), and limited liability corporation (LLC).

(2) Person or organization that has the legal standing to enter into contracts and may be sued for failure to perform as agreed in the contract. For example, a child under legal age is not a legal entity, while a corporation is a legal entity because it is a person from the law's perspective.

LEGAL OPINION

Written statement by a lawyer describing what is legal or lawful in accordance with the governing laws of the land.

LEGITIMACY

State or condition of complying with established rules and standards. Negotiators often rely on commonly accepted standards (for example, past practice, official policy, or written documents) to support a negotiation position. Win-lose negotiators might use questionable or nonexistent standards to support their negotiation position.

LEGITIMACY THEORY

Idea that a business is bound by a social contract in which it agrees to perform various socially desired actions in return for approval of its objectives and other rewards by the public and its customers, thus guaranteeing its continued existence.

LEGITIMATE AUTHORITY

See formal authority.

LESSEE

Party to whom the possession of specified property has been conveyed for a period of time in return for rental payments.

LESSONS LEARNED

Documented information, usually collected through meetings, discussions, or written reports, to show how both common and uncommon project events were addressed. This information can be used by other project managers as a reference for subsequent project efforts.

LESSONS-LEARNED REVIEW

Audit or evaluation conducted immediately upon project completion by the project team to learn from recent successes and failures. The results of the review are documented for use by project team members and other interested parties as a reference and guide for future project activities. *Also called* postproject evaluation and review.

LESSOR

Party who conveys specified property to another for a period of time in return for the receipt of rent.

LETTER CONTRACT

Preliminary, written contractual instrument that authorizes the immediate start of an activity before a pricing arrangement for the work to be done has been defined; a means to permit contractors to start work immediately after a requirement is identified.

LETTER OF CREDIT (LOC)

Legal document issued by a buyer's bank that assures the seller that payment will be made. Usually confirmed by the seller's bank, protection is given to the seller that payment will be made if the goods are shipped correctly, and protection is given to the buyer that the goods will be shipped before payment is made.

LETTER OF INTENT (LOI)

Document that describes the preliminary understanding between two or more parties who intend to make a contract or join together in another action in the future.

LEVEL FINISH SCHEDULE

Date an activity is scheduled to stop using the resource allocation process.

LEVELING

See resource leveling.

LEVEL OF EFFORT (LOE)

Support-type activity (such as vendor or customer liaison) that does not lend itself readily to measurement of discrete accomplishment and generally is characterized by a uniform rate of activity over a specific time period.

LEVEL-OF-EFFORT CONTRACT

Type of contract stating the amount of work in terms of effort, usually person-hours, person-months, or person-years, to be performed by specified labor classes over a given period of time.

LEVEL-OF-EFFORT COST ACCOUNT

Cost account that is necessary to a project but is more time-oriented than task-oriented. Examples include project management, scheduling, and field-engineering support. When these functions are charged directly to a contract, they continue for the life of the project but have no measurable output.

LEVEL OF INFORMATION SYSTEM INTEROPERABILITY (LISI)

Model applied to information systems to indicate a figure of merit for interoperability between systems. Within the LISI model, systems are evaluated by their use, application, sharing, and/or exchange of common procedures (to include technical standards), software applications, infrastructure, and data. Interoperability levels range from 0 to 4, with 4 indicating that systems are interoperable across the enterprise. The interoperability levels are defined in the following manner: 0 (Isolated); 1 (Connected); 2 (Functional); 3 (Domain); and 4 (Enterprise).

LEVEL OF OPENNESS

Extent to which a system, subsystem, or component conforms to open standards. The level of openness determines the extent to which a system can use multiple suppliers, insert new technology, and assign control on design, interfaces, repair, and implementation to the contractor/supplier.

LEVEL START SCHEDULE

Date activity is scheduled to begin using the resource allocation process. Equal to or later in time than the early start.

LF

See late finish date.

LIABILITY PERIOD

Time during which a prime contractor or subcontractor is liable for a failure of a product that has been delivered.

LICENSE

Official grant of permission needed to do a particular thing, exercise a certain privilege, or engage in a particular business or occupation. Licenses may be granted by governments, businesses, or individuals.

LICENSEE

Party to whom a license is provided.

LICENSING AGREEMENT

Arrangement whereby an organization that owns specific technology or information authorizes its use by another organization under certain conditions.

LICENSOR

Party that grants the license to the licensee.

LIEN

Legal claim to real or personal property that is used to secure a loan and that must be paid when the property is sold.

LIFE CYCLE

Entire useful life of a product or service, usually divided into sequential phases, including initiation, development, execution, operation, maintenance, and disposal or termination. *See also* project life cycle.

LIFE-CYCLE COST (LCC)

Sum total of all costs associated with the life cycle, including developing, acquiring, operating, supporting, and (if applicable) disposing of the product or service developed or acquired; LCC helps managers decide among alternatives. *See also* project life-cycle cost.

LIFE-CYCLE MANAGEMENT (LCM)

Management process, applied throughout the life of a system, that bases all programmatic decisions on the anticipated mission-related and economic benefits derived over the life of the system.

LIFE INSURANCE

Contract that pays the beneficiary a set sum of money upon the death of the policyholder. These plans pay benefits usually in the form of a lump sum, but they may be distributed as an annuity.

LIFO

See last in, first out.

LIKERT SCALE

Psychometric response scale, named after Rensis Likert, who published a report describing its use in 1932, which is used in questionnaires measuring the strength of agreement with a clear statement. For example:

Statement: "I found the system easy to use."

- Strongly disagree
- Somewhat disagree
- Undecided
- Somewhat agree
- Strongly agree

LIMITATION-OF-COST CLAUSE

Key clause in cost-reimbursement contracts to obligate the contractor to use its best efforts to perform the specified work and all obligations under the contract within the target, or estimated, cost.

LIMITATION OF FUNDS

Sum of funds available for expenses beyond which no work can be authorized for performance during a specified period.

LIMITATION-OF-FUNDS CLAUSE

Clause included in all incrementally funded cost-reimbursement contracts specifying that a contractor must notify the buyer in writing when the contractor determines that additional funds must be allotted to the contract to continue or to complete performance.

LIMITED AUTHORITY

Restrictions on authority to negotiate on behalf of one's company or organization. When large organizations are involved, most negotiators have limited authority. For example, government negotiator authority is limited by the funds available and any required management approvals. Negotiators using this tactic claim they have very little or no authority to negotiate a key issue or issues. Win-lose negotiators use limited authority to identify your negotiation limits without making any commitment or divulging any information themselves.

LIMITED LIABILITY

Restriction of one's potential losses to the amount invested in the business.

LIMITED PARTNERSHIP

Form of ownership of an entity in which one or more persons, with unlimited liability, called general partners, manage the partnership, while one or more other persons contribute only the capital. Members of the latter group are called limited partners.

LIMITING QUALITY

Maximum number of defects in product quality (or the worst product quality) that the consumer is willing to accept at a specified probability of occurrence.

LINEAR ORGANIZATION CHART

Used in addition to an organization chart to show the work package position in the organization by showing who participates, and to what extent, when an activity is performed or a decision is made. Shows the extent or type of authority exercised by each person in performing an activity in which two or more people have overlapping involvement.

LINEAR RELATIONSHIP

Relationship between two variables that can be expressed as straight-line graphs (for example, scatterplot).

LINE FUNCTION

Part of a corporation that is responsible for producing its goods or performing its services. In a service organization the line functions may be operations and sales. *See also* line manager.

LINE ITEM

(1) Smallest unit of a product whose status is tracked in a status system and that is usually a deliverable.

(2) Item of supply or service for which the contractor must bid a separate price.

LINE MANAGER

Manager of a group that makes a product or performs a service. *Also called* functional manager.

LINE OF BALANCE

Technique used to interpret and present graphically the essential factors involved in a production process, from selection and assembly of raw materials to completion of the end product. The flow of materials and components is integrated into the manufacture of end items according to phased delivery requirements. This technique provides information on project status, showing progress, timing, and phasing of related project activities, but lacks predictive features. It is most useful in production programs from the point when incoming or raw materials are received to the time end products are shipped.

LINE OF CREDIT

Specified amount of unsecured credit made by a bank or a vendor to a specified borrower for a specified time period.

LINE ORGANIZATION

See line function.

LINK

See logical relationship.

LINKED ACTIVITY

Activity dependent on the performance of another activity in precedence diagramming.

LINUS'S LAW

Philosophy of software development that asserts that with enough members on a development team, someone somewhere can glance at a module and detect an error that another programmer cannot see. Named after Linus Torvalds, the creator of Linux.

LIP SERVICE

Expression of agreement that is not supported by real conviction or action.

LIQUID ASSET

Cash, cash equivalents, and any asset that can quickly be converted into cash (for example, checks and easily convertible securities).

LIQUIDATED DAMAGES

Provision in a contract that specifies a sum for which one of the parties will be liable upon breach of contract or failure to perform.

LIQUIDATION

Selling all the assets of a debtor and using the cash proceeds of the sale to pay off creditors.

LIQUIDITY

Company's ability to meet current obligations with cash or other assets that can be quickly converted into cash.

LISI

See level of information system interoperability.

LITIGATION

Legal proceeding in a court of law; a judicial contest to determine and enforce legal rights.

LIVING DEAD

Venture capital investments that neither fail nor are easily liquidated. Venture capitalists deem that the living dead are failed investments because they do not provide the targeted return anticipated.

LLI

See long-lead-item materials.

LLT

See long-lead-time materials.

LOADED RATES

Charges for human and material resources that incorporate both hourly or per-use charges and all additional general and administrative costs associated with their use.

LOADING FACTOR

Scheduling allowance to adjust for project rework, administrative, nonproject, and nature-of-the-work time.

LOC

See letter of credit.

LOCKOUT

Temporary withholding or denial of employment during a labor dispute in order to enforce terms of employment upon a group of employees. A lockout is initiated by the management of an establishment.

LOCK, STOCK, AND BARREL

The whole thing.

LOE

See level of effort.

LOGIC

See network logic.

LOGICAL RELATIONSHIP

Dependency between two project activities or between a project activity and a milestone. The four types of logical relationships in the precedence diagramming method are (1) finish-to-start—the "from" activity must finish before the "to" activity can start; (2) finish-to-finish—the "from" activity must finish before the "to" activity can finish; (3) start-to-start—the "from" activity must start before the "to" activity can start; and (4) start-to-finish—the "from" activity must start before the "to" activity can finish. *Also called* link.

LOGIC DIAGRAM

See network diagram.

LOGISTICS INTEROPERABILITY

Form of interoperability in which the item to be exchanged is assemblies, components, spares, or repair parts. Logistics interoperability often will be achieved by making such assemblies, components, spares, or repair parts interchangeable; a lower level of interchangeability may exist when a degradation of performance or some limitations are operationally acceptable.

LOI

See letter of intent.

LONG-LEAD-ITEM (LLI)/LONG-LEAD-TIME (LLT) MATERIALS

Components of a system or piece of equipment for which the times to design and fabricate are the longest and, therefore, to which an early commitment of funds may be desirable in order to meet the earliest possible date of system completion.

LONG-TERM DISABILITY INSURANCE

Insurance coverage that provides a monthly benefit to employees who, due to a nonwork-related injury or illness, are unable to perform the duties of their normal occupation or any other for periods of time extending beyond their short-term disability or sickness and accident insurance.

LOOP

Network path that passes the same node twice. Loops cannot be analyzed using network analysis techniques such as CPM and PERT but are allowed in GERT.

LOSE FACE

To be humiliated and ashamed. To lose one's reputation. A powerful concept in Asian countries, in particular Japan.

LOSE-LOSE

Outcome of conflict resolution that results in both parties being worse off than before. Based on the strategy that it is better for each party to get something than nothing, even if that something does not accomplish either party's goals.

LOSS

Failure to earn a profit on a contract because the costs of performance (both direct and indirect) have exceeded the amount paid to the contractor under the terms of the contract.

LOSS LEADER

(1) In contracting, winning a contract at lower-than-acceptable prices in the hopes of negotiating change orders during the contract life to recover costs and fees.

(2) In retailing, selling a featured item of merchandise at a loss in order to draw customers.

LOT

Collection of units of product identified and treated as a unique entity and from which a sample can be drawn and inspected to determine whether there is conformance with acceptability criteria. *Also called* batch.

LOT ACCEPTANCE

Test based on a sampling procedure to ensure that the product meets quality standards and specifications. No acceptance or installation should be permitted until this test for the lot has been successfully completed.

LOT FORMATION

Process of collecting, segregating, or delineating production units into homogeneous, identifiable groups by type, grade, class, size, composition, or condition of manufacture.

LOT SIZE

Number of units of product that constitute a lot.

LOW BALLING

See buying in.

LOW-BALL OFFER

Artificially low-priced bid offered by a seller to induce a buyer to select him or her, over other competitors, to perform the service or provide the products required. Once the bid is won, the seller attempts to earn what actually is required to do the job by negotiating artificially high-priced change orders during the contract or work period.

LOWER CONTROL LIMIT

Three standard deviations below the mean. If this value is below zero, the lower control limit is set at zero.

LOWEST OVERALL COST

Considering price and other factors, the least expenditure of funds over the life cycle of a system or an item.

LOWEST RESPONSIVE, RESPONSIBLE BIDDER

In U.S. federal procurement, a contractor in a sealed bid procurement who is entitled to receive the contract award.

LOW-HANGING FRUIT

Easiest task or most readily achievable goal; a "quick win."

LS

See late start date.

LUMP SUM

Agreed-upon sum of money paid in full at one time.

M

MAD

See mean absolute deviation.

MADE REDUNDANT

Term used in the United Kingdom and certain other countries that means laid off or let go from a job because the company no longer needs the position.

MAINTAINABILITY

Design and installation characteristic expressed as the probability that a specified condition will be restored in a given period of time when maintenance is performed according to prescribed procedures and resources.

MAINTENANCE

In software engineering, the activities required to keep a software system operational after implementation. *See also* adaptive maintenance, corrective maintenance, enhancement, *and* perfective maintenance.

MAINTENANCE GUARANTEE

Assurance that a product will be maintained during a specified period of time.

MAINTENANCE MANUAL

Formal document that provides systems maintenance personnel with the information necessary to maintain the system effectively.

MAINTENANCE QUALITY ASSURANCE

Determination that material maintained, overhauled, rebuilt, modified, or reclaimed conforms to the prescribed technical requirements.

MAINTENANCE REVIEW

Formal review of both the completed and pending changes to a system with respect to the benefits achieved by completing recommended changes. Also provides information about the amount of maintenance required based on activity to date. Part of the post-implementation review report.

MAJOR DEFECT

Defect that is not critical but still is likely to result in failure or materially reduce the usability of the unit of product for its intended purpose.

MAJOR DEFECTIVE

Product unit that contains one or more major defects and also may contain minor defects but does not contain a critical defect.

MAKE-OR-BUY ANALYSIS

Management technique used to determine whether a particular product or service can be produced or performed cost-effectively by the performing organization or should be contracted out to another organization. The analysis considers both the direct costs of procuring the product or service and any administrative costs in managing the contractor.

MALCOLM BALDRIGE NATIONAL QUALITY AWARD

Award presented annually to U.S. corporations in various categories that have demonstrated a commitment to quality. Established by the U.S. Department of Commerce and administered by the National Institute of Standards and Technology. Nominees complete a detailed application that solicits specific information regarding their quality activities in the following categories: leadership; strategic planning; customer and market focus; information and analysis; human resource focus; process management; and business results.

MANAGEMENT AND OPERATING (M&O) CONTRACT

In U.S. federal procurement, an agreement under which the government contracts for the operation, maintenance, and support, on its behalf, of a government-owned or -controlled research, development, special production, or testing establishment wholly or principally devoted to one or more major programs of the contracting federal agency.

MANAGEMENT BY CRISIS

Management style that focuses on solving critical or urgent problems when and if they occur but doesn't do anything to prevent or minimize them before they occur.

MANAGEMENT BY EXCEPTION

Management approach in which managers concern themselves with only those variances that appear exceptionally large, significant, or otherwise peculiar.

MANAGEMENT BY OBJECTIVES (MBO)

Management approach or methodology, developed by Peter Drucker in the early 1950s, that encourages managers to give their subordinates more freedom in determining how to achieve specific objectives. Management and the subordinate jointly develop clear objectives, requirements, and milestones and ensure that they are realistic, measurable, and achievable. Subordinate performance and compensation are measured by progress achieved against these goals at regular intervals.

MANAGEMENT BY PROJECTS

Management approach that treats many aspects of ongoing operations in an organization as projects, applying project management principles and practices to them.

MANAGEMENT BY WALKING AROUND (MBWA)

Approach to gaining insight into project and operational activities advocated by Bill Hewlett and David Packard of Hewlett-Packard, and popularized by Tom Peters and Bob Waterman in the 1982 business classic *In Search of Excellence*. MBWA requires that managers get up from their desks and walk around their facilities and offices with the express intent of engaging their employees and team members in conversations about how things are really going rather than just relying on written reports. *Also called* "management by wandering around."

MANAGEMENT CONTROL OBJECTIVES

Goals, conditions, or levels of control a manager establishes to provide reasonable assurance that resources are safeguarded against waste, fraud, and mismanagement.

MANAGEMENT CONTROL POINT

Any milestone, juncture, phase gate, or point in the project life cycle where management can decide to move forward with a project or not depending on specific criteria that may include such things as performance to date, business case relevance, customer satisfaction, and other criteria deemed important to the organization.

MANAGEMENT CONTROL SYSTEM

Strategic tool for holding managers accountable and responsible for their individual and collective performance. Also provides feedback to managers on how they are performing, in which direction the organization is headed, and what type of correction may be required to stay on course.

MANAGEMENT CONTROL TECHNIQUES

Any form of organization, procedure, or document flow that is relied on to accomplish control objectives. *See also* management control objectives.

MANAGEMENT INFORMATION SYSTEM

Orderly and disciplined accounting and reporting methodology, usually automated, that provides for the accurate recording of data and the timely extrapolation and transmission of management information used in decision-making processes.

MANAGEMENT PLAN

Document that describes the overall guidelines under which the project is organized, administered, and managed to ensure timely accomplishment of project objectives.

MANAGEMENT RESERVE

Separately planned quantity of money or time intended to reduce the impact of missed cost, schedule, or performance objectives that are impossible to plan for (sometimes called "unknown unknowns").

MANAGEMENT REVIEW

Group assessment of project or program status and performance by management to determine whether the project or program will move to the next phase, repeat the last phase, or be terminated.

MANAGEMENT STYLE

One of the following management approaches that a project manager may adopt, depending on the situation: authoritarian; autocratic; combative; conciliatory; consensual; consultative-autocratic; democratic; disruptive; ethical; facilitating; intimidating; judicial; laissez-faire; participative; promotional; secretive; shared leadership; or shareholder management style. *See individual entries for definitions of each management style.*

MANAGERIAL QUALITY ADMINISTRATION

Process of defining and monitoring policies, responsibilities, and systems that are necessary to ensure quality standards are met throughout the project.

MANAGERIAL RESERVE

See management reserve.

MANDATORY DEPENDENCY

Dependency inherent in the nature of the work being done, such as a physical limitation. *Also called* hard logic.

MAN-HOUR/MONTH/YEAR

Effort equal to that of one person during one hour/month/year. Also referred to as staff-hour/month/year.

MAN-MACHINE INTERFACE (MMI)

Degree of compatibility between the individual user and the equipment being used.

MANPOWER

Total supply of persons available and fit for service. Indexed by requirements, including jobs lists, slots, or billets characterized by descriptions of the required people to fill them.

MANUFACTURER

Typically, a company that makes a product.

MANUFACTURING

Process of making an item using machinery, often on a large scale and characterized by division of labor.

MANUFACTURING ENGINEERING

Preproduction planning and operation analysis applied to specific projects. Other similar functions include sustaining (ongoing) engineering, production engineering, and production planning.

MAPPING

One of the seven tools of quality. A graphical depiction of a process, using various symbols to denote workflow and decision points, that helps identify waste and other quality problems. Is often used as a communication mechanism so employees can see exactly what happens in a process. The most common form of mapping is the process map, which denotes every step in a workflow process and describes what happens in each step.

MAQUILADORA

Manufacturing operation at the U.S.-Mexico border that includes two plants, one on each side of the border. Done to take advantage of the free trade allowed between the two countries and to take advantage of low Mexican wages and U.S. distribution facilities.

MARGIN

Gain accrued over and above the cost of the product or service delivered. *See also* gross margin *and* operating margin.

MARGINAL COST

Cost that reflects an increase or decrease in cost based on the result of one more or one less unit of output. Used to determine the value of increasing or decreasing production, or assigning additional personnel to a project.

MARKET DISRUPTION ANALYSIS

Systematic analysis that seeks to uncover the reasons why a particular trend or event caused a shift of market power from established to emerging players. Such shifts often occur when companies ignore market signs that their business models are becoming obsolete or they fail to adapt to changing technological innovation, shifting consumer preferences, or regulatory intervention.

MARKET DRIVEN

Allowing the marketplace to influence new product or service ideas developed and introduced by an organization.

MARKET INVESTIGATION

Phase of market research conducted in response to a specific need for material or services.

MARKET POSITION

Strength of a company or product within the target market.

MARKET REQUIREMENTS

List of needs that describes the business environment in which a product or service is targeted to be sold.

MARKET RESEARCH

(1) Gathering and analysis of information to help determine the size, characteristics, and potential of a market. Market research helps a company determine what people and companies want before developing a new product or service, so they can see if it will be successful in the marketplace at the price and other terms and conditions for which it will be offered for sale.

(2) In U.S. federal procurement, the gathering and analysis of information on potential suppliers who offer products and services required by federal agencies, in order to determine specifications and to estimate the costs of obtaining such products and services from the open market.

MARKET SEGMENT

Group of consumers, within a broader market, with similar characteristics and needs.

MARKET SEGMENTATION

Dividing an overall market into homogenous groups of consumers based on selected criteria to tailor the marketing message in order to gain more sales.

MARKET SHARE

Company's sales in a product or service area as a percent of the total market sales in that area.

MARKET SURVEILLANCE

All the activities that project managers and their team members perform continuously to keep themselves abreast of technology and product developments in their areas of expertise.

MARKET SURVEY

Collection and analysis of data from potential sellers to determine the ability to satisfy buyer requirements. Includes activities such as writing or calling knowledgeable experts, reviewing catalogs and marketing brochures, attending demonstrations, or conducting a formal request for information.

MARKET TESTING

Phase in the new product development life cycle where a new product as well as its marketing plan are tested together in a real commercial environment.

MARKET VALUE

What a firm is worth; calculated by multiplying the number of shares outstanding by the current share price. May be higher or lower than book value. *See also* book value.

MARKOV CHAIN

Method used to evaluate a system's mean time until failure. The system is modeled as a finite-state machine with working states and fault states, and a probability is associated with the transitions between states.

MARKUP

(1) *See* gross profit.

(2) Setting of a retail price on a product or service by some percentage increase over and above its wholesale cost.

(3) In U.S. government budgeting procedures, a line-by-line review and approval/disapproval/modification of a budget by congressional committees.

MASK RELATING STYLE

Style of relating in which a person learns to put on a mask because it is expected of him or her or because it may be the only means of survival. It can be a short- or long-term behavior pattern. Masks may be required in any area of life: a highly regulated environment, a job, a marriage, and so forth. It is easy to make an error in identifying another person's Motivational Value System™ if the person is using a borrowed relating style or a mask relating style. This leads to wrong predictions as to how an individual might behave.

MASLOW'S HIERARCHY OF NEEDS

Theory of motivation developed by Abraham Maslow in which a person's needs arise in an ordered sequence in the following five categories: physical needs, safety needs, love needs, esteem needs, and self-actualization needs.

MASTER BLACK BELT

Designation given to Six Sigma quality experts who are responsible for the strategic implementation of process improvement within an organization. Those holding such a designation are responsible for training other Six Sigma facilitators such as Black Belts and Green Belts, and for selecting, chartering, and overseeing critical process improvement projects within the organization. Additionally, they act as a company resource on all matters relating to Six Sigma. *See also* Green Belt *and* Black Belt.

MASTER PROGRAM SCHEDULE (MPS)

In the U.S. DOD, the top-level summary schedule for the program. It is prepared by the government and includes all policy and contractual events and activities. It is derived from the program WBS and provides the baseline for all subordinate schedules. It sometimes is called the program structure/schedule.

MASTER PROJECT SCHEDULE

See milestone schedule.

MASTER SCHEDULE

See milestone schedule.

MATERIAL BREACH

Most serious form of breach, it discharges the party that is not at fault from any further obligations under the contract. *See also* breach.

MATERIAL REQUIREMENTS PLANNING (MRP)

Planning and material-ordering technique based on the known or forecast final-demand requirements for each item, lead times for each fabricated or purchased item, and existing inventories of all items.

MATERIAL REVIEW BOARD

Formal board established in many U.S. federal procurements to review, evaluate, and dispose of specific nonconforming supplies or services and to ensure that corrective action is initiated and accomplished so future nonconformances do not occur.

MATERIALS MANAGEMENT

Organizational process, procedures, rules, and regulations for the ordering, storage, and movement of materials.

MATÉRIEL

Equipment, apparatus, and supplies used by a project, a program, or an organization.

MATÉRIEL MANAGEMENT

Direction and control of those aspects of logistics that deal with matériel, including identification, cataloging, standardization, requirements determination, procurement, inspection, quality control (QC), packaging, storage, distribution, disposal, maintenance, mobilization planning, industrial readiness planning, and item management classification; encompasses matériel control, inventory control, inventory management, and supply management.

MATHEMATICAL PROGRAMMING

Category of mathematical techniques for solving resource allocation and other constrained optimization problems; includes, for example, integer and linear programming.

MATRIX ORGANIZATION

Project organizational structure in which the project manager shares responsibility with the functional managers to assign priorities and direct the work of individuals assigned to the project. In a strong matrix organization, the balance of power over the resources is in favor of the project manager. In a weak matrix organization, functional managers retain most of the control over project resources.

MATURITY LEVEL

Defined point in an achievement scale that establishes the attainment of certain capabilities. *See also* capability maturity model.

MAXIMUM FEE

Dollar amount negotiated in a cost-plus-incentive-fee contract as the maximum amount of profit that the contractor can receive.

MBO

See management by objectives.

MBWA

See management by walking around.

MCCLELLAND'S MOTIVATIONAL NEEDS THEORY

Theory of motivation advanced by David McClelland in his 1988 publication *Human Motivation* in which he described three types of motivational needs:

• Achievement motivation (n-ach) characterized by an individual who seeks achievement of attainable and realistic goals and who needs a sense of accomplishment.

• Authority/power motivation (n-pow) characterized by a person who needs to be influential and effective and who needs to be the leader. Additionally, there is motivation towards increasing personal status and prestige within the organization.

• Affiliation motivation (n-affil) characterized by a person who needs friendly relationships and thrives on social interaction. Being a team player, this person has a need to be liked and held in popular regard.

MCGREGOR'S THEORY X AND Y

Theory of motivation advanced by Douglas McGregor stating that managers have one of two sets of assumptions about workers. Theory X managers view workers as machines who require a great deal of external control. Theory Y managers view workers as organisms who grow, develop, and exercise control over themselves.

M-COMMERCE (MOBILE COMMERCE)

Practice of conducting business-to-consumer transactions, usually over the Internet, using wireless, mobile devices such as cell phones, electronic organizers, personal digital assistants, and other forms of electronic apparatus. Such wireless Internet access requires the use of wireless application protocol (WAP), the standard used for such electronic communications. Examples of m-commerce applications include receiving stock quotes, driving directions, or the location of the nearest coffee bar through a cell phone.

M CURVE

Illustration of the volume of ideas generated over a specific time period. The illustration looks like two arches from the letter M.

MDA

See Milestone Decision Authority.

MEAN

Average value of a set of numbers.

MEAN ABSOLUTE DEVIATION (MAD)

Average absolute difference between observed values in a data set and the arithmetical mean (average) for those values.

MEAN DOWN TIME

Measure of maintainability derived by dividing the sum of the elapsed clock time that a system or product is unavailable due to failures by the number of occurrences over a selected time frame, usually one year.

MEAN LOGISTICS DELAY TIME (MLDT)

Indicator of the average time a system is awaiting maintenance. Generally includes time for locating parts and tools; locating, setting up, or calibrating test equipment; dispatching personnel; reviewing technical manuals; complying with supply procedures; and awaiting transportation. The MLDT is largely dependent upon the logistics support structure and environment.

MEAN MAINTENANCE TIME (MMT)

Measure of item maintainability taking into account both preventive and corrective maintenance. Calculated by adding the preventive and corrective maintenance time and dividing by the sum of scheduled and unscheduled maintenance events during a stated period of time.

MEAN TIME BETWEEN FAILURE (MTBF)

Measure of maintainability derived by dividing the sum of elapsed clock time between system failures by the number of occurrences over a selected time frame, usually one year.

MEAN TIME BETWEEN MAINTENANCE (MTBM)

Measure of reliability that represents the average time between all maintenance actions, both corrective and preventive.

MEAN TIME TO REPAIR (MTTR)

Measure of maintainability derived by dividing the sum of the elapsed clock time to perform corrective actions by the number of corrective actions required in a selected time frame, usually one year.

MEASUREMENT

In project management, the process of collecting, analyzing, and reporting metrics data.

MEASUREMENT OF COST

Accounting methods and techniques used to define cost components, determine the basis for cost measurement, and establish criteria for use of alternative cost measurement techniques.

MEASUREMENT OF DISPERSION

Indication of how closely values in a data set are clustered around the mean.

MEASURE OF CENTRAL TENDENCY

Central value, mean, mode, or median around which data observations such as historical prices tend to cluster. It is the central value of the distribution.

MEDIAN

Middle value of a set of numbers ordered from lowest to highest.

MEDIATION

Process of bringing parties engaged in a dispute or disagreement together to settle their differences through a meeting with a disinterested party, or mediator. In mediation, unlike binding arbitration, the mediator has no authority to force a settlement.

MEETING OF THE MINDS

Mutual assent of the parties to a contract, agreement, or course of action.

MEGAPROJECT

Extremely large and complex project ($100 million+) designed to accomplish an extensive scope of activities and requiring many more resources than most projects.

MEHRABIAN'S COMMUNICATION MODEL

Named after Professor Albert Mehrabian of the University of California at Los Angeles (UCLA), who established the now-classic statistic for the effectiveness of spoken communications:

- 7% of meaning is in the words that are spoken.

- 38% of meaning is paralinguistic (the way that the words are said).

- 55% of meaning is in facial expression.

Mehrabian's model has become one of the most widely referenced statistics in communications theory and practice. It is commonly used to explain the importance of meaning, as distinct from words.

MEMORANDUM FOR THE RECORD

In-house memo covering information that would otherwise not be recorded in writing for posterity and a paper trail of events and decisions. *See also* audit trail.

MEMORANDUM OF UNDERSTANDING (MOU)

De facto agreement that is generally recognized by all parties as binding even if no legal claim could be based on the rights and obligations delineated therein.

MERCHANTABILITY

Fitness for a particular purpose. Used to measure implied warranties. Products are merchantable if they are reasonably fit for ordinary purposes for which the goods are to be used.

MERGED CHANNEL

Marketing approach that uses numerous ways to remotely target consumers, including catalogs, cell phones, call centers, e-commerce sites, and physical storefronts. The objective of a well-functioning merged channel approach is to allow the consumer to make a purchase in any environment they prefer from the same company.

MERGER

Reorganization in which one corporation absorbs the corporate structure of another corporation.

MERIT RAISE

Increase in the salary and compensation of an individual based on superior job performance. Also referred to as merit increase or merit pay.

METHODOLOGY

See project management methodology.

METHODS ENGINEERING

Technique that subjects each operation of a given piece of work to close analysis in order to eliminate every unnecessary element or operation and in order to find the quickest and best method of performing each necessary element or operation. It includes the improvement and standardization of methods, equipment, and working conditions; operator training; the determination of

standard times; and the devising and administering of various
incentive plans.

METHODS STUDY

Systematic recording of all activities performed in a job or position of work, including standard times for the work performed.
Work simplification notes are written during the study.

METRICS

Units of measurement used to assess, calculate, or determine
progress performance in terms of monetary units, schedule,
quality results, or other relevant factors.

MICROCULTURE

Specific culture that exists within a particular organizational unit
or project.

MICROMANAGEMENT

Closely detailed scrutiny of a project's or program's activities
by one's superiors in the organization's hierarchy. May result in
second-guessing, reviews, changes, or further program justification. A usurpation of authority or responsibility.

MICROSEGMENTATION

Marketing strategy that narrows and refines a market into
smaller and more refined segments to better identify a company's prospects for its goods and services (for example, women
making more than $100,000 per year with two children and a
professional position in the financial industry). Segmenting a
market at this level can help companies hone their marketing
message to would-be customers.

MIDPOINT PRICING

Using a single set of rates that are the weighted average of a
future time period; used instead of progressively escalated rates
to develop an escalated price estimate.

MIGRATION

Movement of files and data between software applications.

MIGRATION PLANNING

Developing a plan to move from one software environment to
another.

MILESTONE

(1) Event with zero duration and requiring no resources. Used to measure the progress of a project or program and signify the completion or start of a major deliverable or other significant metric, such as costs incurred, hours used, payment made, and so on.

(2) Identifiable point in a project, program, or set of activities that represents a reporting requirement or completion of a large or important set of activities. *Also called* key event.

MILESTONE CHART

Scheduling technique used to show the start and completion of milestones on a time-scale chart. Normally, planned events are expressed using hollow triangles and completed events are shown as solid triangles. Rescheduled or slipped events usually are displayed as hollow diamond symbols. When the late milestones are completed, the diamonds are filled in. *Also called* event chart.

MILESTONE DECISION AUTHORITY (MDA)

In U.S. DOD, the person designated overall responsibility for a program. The MDA has the authority to approve entry of an acquisition program into the next phase of the acquisition process and is accountable for cost, schedule, and performance reporting to a higher authority, including Congress.

MILESTONE METHOD

Approach to calculating earned value that works well when work packages last longer then three months. First, objective milestones are established, preferably one or more for each month of the project. Then, the assigned work package budget is divided, based on a weighted value assigned to each milestone.

MILESTONE PAYMENTS

Payments made as a result of reaching a specific project or program milestone.

MILESTONE SCHEDULE

Schedule consisting of key events or milestones—generally, critical accomplishments planned at time intervals throughout the project—and used to monitor overall project performance.

May be either a network or bar chart and usually contains minimal detail at a highly summarized level. *Also called* key-event schedule, master schedule, *or* summary schedule.

MILITARY TIME

Time measured on a 24-hour clock, a convention of timekeeping in which the day runs from midnight to midnight and is divided into 24 hours. It is the most commonly used time notation in the world. It also is the international standard notation of time (ISO 8601). Also referred to as "24-hour time" and "railway time."

MIND MAPPING

Nonlinear, radial diagramming of words, ideas, or topics around a main concept. Popularized by educational consultant Tony Buzan, who reportedly studied the notebooks of Leonardo da Vinci while developing the concept.

MINIMUM FEE

Dollar amount negotiated in a cost-plus-incentive-fee contract as the minimum amount of profit that the contractor can receive.

MINOR DEFECT

(1) Defect that probably will not materially reduce the usability of the unit of product or the project for its intended purpose.

(2) Departure from established standards that has minimal impact on the effective use or operation of the unit.

MINOR DEFECTIVE

Unit of product that contains one or more defects, but none of these defects are critical or major.

MINOR RISK

Risk event that does not cause significant problems, no matter what its probability.

MINUTE-TAKING

Recording the discussions of a meeting. Also called "taking the minutes," it is done by a specific individual called the recorder or recording secretary.

MISREPRESENTATION OF FACT

False statement of substantive fact, or any conduct made with intent to deceive or mislead.

MISSION

Specific purpose that all or part of the organization is dedicated to achieving.

MISSION STATEMENT

Description prepared and endorsed by members of the organization that answers these questions: "What do we do? For whom do we do it? How do we go about it?" Used as a guide for making decisions in projects.

MITIGATION

Risk response strategy that decreases risk by lowering the probability of a risk event's occurrence or reducing the effect of the risk should it occur. *See also* acceptance, avoidance, *and* transfer.

MIXED ORGANIZATION

Organizational structure that includes both functions and projects in its hierarchy.

MLDT

See mean logistics delay time.

MMI

See man-machine interface.

MMT

See mean maintenance time.

MNC

See multinational corporation.

M&O

See management and operating contract.

MOCK-UP

Physical or virtual demonstration model, built to scale, and used early in the development of a product development project to verify proposed design, fit, critical clearances, operator interfaces, and other physical characteristics of the item to be produced.

MODE

Most frequent value of a set of numbers.

MODEL

Way to look at an item, generally by abstracting and simplifying it to make it understandable in a particular context.

MODERN PROJECT MANAGEMENT (MPM)

Broad range of project management activities (scope, cost, time, quality, risk, stakeholder management, and so forth) as distinguished from the narrower, traditional view of project management that only focuses on cost and time.

MODIFICATION

Change to a project's scope or the terms of a contract; usually written. Examples are change orders, notices of termination, supplemental agreements, and exercises of contract options.

MODULE

(1) Independently compilable software component made up of one or more procedures or routines, or a combination of procedures and routines.

(2) Training course or part of a training course.

MOMENT(S) OF TRUTH (MOT)

Point when a customer comes into contact with the products, services, systems, people, or procedures of an organization, resulting in a judgment of the quality of the organization's product or service. First articulated by Jan Carlzon while head of Scandinavian Airlines and published in his book of the same name in 1989.

MONITOR

Acquire and analyze data on an ongoing basis so that action can be taken when progress fails to match plans and meet objectives.

MONITORING ACTUALS VERSUS BUDGET

Continually measuring actual cost against the budget to establish a variance, analyze the reasons for a variance, and take the necessary corrective action. Also, monitoring, managing, and controlling changes in the final cost.

MONITORING AND CONTROLLING PROCESSES

Any process or activity that compares actual project or program results to the plan to ensure that the project's or program's identified and expected objectives will be achieved. Requires data gathering and analysis to identify variances, and coordinates corrective actions as required. *See also* project/program management process groups.

MONTE CARLO ANALYSIS

Schedule or cost risk assessment technique that entails performing a project simulation many times to calculate a likely distribution of results. *See also* schedule simulation.

MOONLIGHTING

Holding more than one paid job by an individual. The term derives from the fact that the second job held is usually evening work.

MOORE'S LAW

Prediction by Gordon Moore, cofounder of Intel Corporation, that the number of transistors on the microchip would double every 18 months. Today, Moore's law is applied liberally in the notion that computing power will double every 18 months.

MOST LIKELY TIME

In PERT estimating, the most realistic number of work periods the activity will consume.

MOT

See moment(s) of truth.

MOTIVATING

Inducing an individual to work toward his or her goals.

MOTIVATIONAL VALUE SYSTEM™

Set of seven identifiable motivational values that serve as a basis for judging ourselves and others, for engaging in behavior that enhances our sense of self-worth, and for focusing our attention on certain things while ignoring others. The Motivational Value System™ acts as an internal filter through which life is interpreted and understood. It is based on the theory that all people want to feel worthy. Most interactions among people are best understood as strivings by the individuals to achieve or enhance feelings of self-worth. Assessed in the Strength Deployment Inventory® (SDI®) instrument developed by Personal Strengths Publishing.

MOTIVATION-HYGIENE THEORY

Theory of motivation described by Frederick Herzberg that asserts that two sets of factors must be considered to satisfy a person's needs—those related to job satisfaction (motivators) and those related to job dissatisfaction (hygiene or maintenance factors). To retain employees, managers must focus on improving negative hygiene factors, such as pay, but to get employees to devote a higher level of energy to their work, managers must use motivators, such as recognition. *See also* Herzberg's theory of motivation.

MOTIVATORS

According to Frederick Herzberg's Motivation-Hygiene Theory, factors related to job satisfaction that must be addressed to motivate employees, such as recognition or greater responsibility. *See also* Herzberg's theory of motivation *and* Motivation-Hygiene Theory.

MOU

See memorandum of understanding.

MOURNING

See Tuckman's Model of Team Development (Stage 5).

MOVING AVERAGE COST

Inventory costing method in which an average unit cost is computed after each acquisition by adding the cost of newly acquired units to the cost of the units of inventory on hand and dividing this number by the new total number of units.

MOVING THE GOALPOSTS

Changing the objective during the project, usually to the disadvantage of one of the involved parties.

MPM

See modern project management.

MPS

See Master Program Schedule.

MRP

See material requirements planning.

MTBF

See mean time between failure.

MTBM

See mean time between maintenance.

MTTR

See mean time to repair.

MULTIDISCIPLINARY

Encompassing effort by many types of people representing different skills and backgrounds in the organization.

MULTILEVEL CONTINUOUS SAMPLE PLAN

See sample plan, multilevel, continuous.

MULTINATIONAL CORPORATION (MNC)

Corporation that manages production establishments or delivers services in at least two countries. Very large MNCs such as ABB® and Motorola® have operations in many countries. The home office or headquarters of an MNC may function more like a large, local company given its size and influence on the local economy.

MULTIPLE-PROJECT SCHEDULING

Process of developing a project schedule based on constraints imposed by other projects.

MULTIPLE SAMPLE PLAN
See sample plan, multiple.

MULTIUSER
Having more than one user.

MULTIYEAR CONTRACTING
Special contracting method covering more than one year of requirements, but the total funds to be obligated are not available at the time of contract award.

MURPHY'S LAW
Informal and unfounded principle of business stating that whatever can go wrong, will go wrong. Ed Murphy, a development engineer, coined the term in 1949 as a result of errors made by a laboratory technician.

MUTUALLY EXCLUSIVE EVENTS
Set of events where the occurrence of one event excludes the occurrence of any other event.

MYERS-BRIGGS TYPE INDICATOR
Test developed by Isabel Briggs Myers and Katharine Cook Briggs to categorize people according to where they lie on four scales, each reflecting a different dimension of human behavior: extrovert-introvert; sensing-intuitive; thinking-feeling; and judging-perceiving. These scales comprise 16 different psychological types, each associated with a number of well-documented behavioral traits.

N

N/A
See not applicable.

NASDAQ COMPOSITE INDEX

Stock market index of more than 3,000 stocks and other securities listed on the NASDAQ Stock Market, which is the largest electronic screen-based equity securities trading market in the U.S. It is owned by the National Association of Securities Dealers (NASD), and NASDAQ is an acronym for National Association of Securities Dealers Automated Quotation System. Because non–U.S. companies are also listed, it is not exclusively a U.S. index. However, because many of the listed companies are in the technology sector the index is often referred to by financial reporters as "tech-heavy."

NATURAL VARIATION

Quality concept that asserts that making any product or delivering any service with absolute consistency is impossible. This type of variation can be predicted through the application of statistical techniques.

NDA

See nondisclosure agreement.

NEAR-CRITICAL ACTIVITY

Activity that has little total float or that otherwise could become critical as a result of certain situations occurring.

NEAR-CRITICAL PATH

Path that is not critical at the outset of the project but could become critical as a result of certain situations occurring; the path through the network that contains the least total float.

NEAR-TERM ACTIVITY

Activity that will either begin or be underway and will be completed soon.

NEED

Gap between what is and what should be. It should not be confused with a "want," which is desirable but nonessential.

NEEDS REQUIREMENTS LIFE CYCLE

Process of identifying and articulating needs of the intended users, sponsors, or beneficiaries of a project to ensure that the project will satisfy those needs. The cycle begins when needs first emerge and ends when those needs are subsequently articulated, either in functional or technical terms.

NEGATIVE CASH FLOW

Situation in which a business is spending more than it is earning in any given accounting period.

NEGATIVE FLOAT

Situation in which the difference between the late (start or finish) date and the early (start or finish) date of an activity is a negative number, indicating that the late date is earlier in time than the early date. This situation comes into existence when a forced end date of an activity is used to calculate the backward pass without considering the predecessor activity's start date and duration. Negative float means the activity cannot be completed on time unless and until certain decisions are made to correct the situation.

NEGOTIATED BIDDING RATES

Rates agreed to with the customer based on a reasonable projection of the direct costs as related to a projection of the indirect costs, usually reaching three years into the future. *See also* forward pricing.

NEGOTIATED CONTRACT

Contract obtained by direct agreement between a buyer and seller through bargaining and negotiation as opposed to using sealed bids. *See also* negotiation.

NEGOTIATED FINAL RATES

Actual rates agreed upon by the customer after the fact. Actual costs are adjusted to exclude those items that the customer refuses to allow, such as entertainment costs.

NEGOTIATING

(1) Process of bargaining with individuals concerning resources, information, and activities. Conferring with others to come to terms or reach an agreement.

(2) Process in which parties with different interests reach an acceptable agreement through communication and compromise.

NEGOTIATION

(1) Contracting through the use of both competitive and non-competitive proposals and discussions.

(2) Any contract awarded without using sealed bidding procedures.

NEGOTIATION OUTCOMES

In general, there are three possible outcomes to every negotiation. These outcomes are known as win-win, win-lose, and lose-lose. Any negotiation can conceivably result in any of these outcomes, but different negotiation styles can make one more likely. *See also* win-win, win-lose, *and* lose-lose.

NEGOTIATION PLAN

Approach to conducting a specific negotiation. It includes—

• Background (for example, contract, contractor, and negotiation situation)

• Major and minor negotiation issues and objectives (both price and nonprice)

• Negotiation priorities and positions on key issues (including minimum, objective, and maximum positions on price)

• Negotiation approach

NEGOTIATIONS

Exchanges between parties with the sole purpose of reaching agreement on a specific matter such as personnel resources, contracts, or other important issues associated with project and program execution.

NET

Generally speaking, the amount of money remaining after all relevant deductions have been made from the starting, or gross, amount.

NET 10, 30 ...

Refers to payment terms on an invoice. For example, "Net 10, 2 percent, 30" would mean that if a purchaser pays the invoice within 10 days, a 2 percent reduction in the invoice amount will be given, but the full invoice amount is due within 30 days.

NET BOOK VALUE

Dollar amount shown in the accounting system for assets, liabilities, or equity. When comparing one company with another, net book value is the excess of total assets over total liabilities.

NET EARNINGS

See net profit.

NET INCOME

See net profit.

NET LOSS

Situation in which the expenses for an accounting period exceed income.

NET PRESENT VALUE (NPV)

Financial calculation that takes into account the time values of a stream of income and expenditure at a given interest rate. *See also* present value.

NET PROFIT

Amount of money earned after all expenses, including direct and indirect costs, have been deducted from total revenue. *Also called* net earnings *or* net income.

NETREPRENEURS

Businesspersons or entrepreneurs who establish business enterprises on the Internet.

NETWORK

(1) Graphic depiction of the relationships of project activities. *See also* network diagram.

(2) Communication facility that connects end systems; interconnected series of points, nodes, or stations connected by communication channels; an assembly of equipment through which connections are made between data stations.

NETWORK ANALYSIS

Identification of early and late start and finish dates for uncompleted portions of project activities. *Also called* schedule analysis. *See also* critical path method, Program Evaluation and Review Technique, *and* Graphical Evaluation and Review Technique.

NETWORK-BASED SCHEDULING

Process of determining the logical relationships among WBS work packages, activities, and tasks, and then arranging these to establish the shortest possible project duration. Examples of these techniques include PERT, CPM, and PDM.

NETWORK DIAGRAM

Schematic display of the logical relationships of project activities, usually drawn from left to right to reflect project chronology. *Also called* logic diagram and often incorrectly referred to as a PERT chart.

NETWORKING

Art of building alliances and making connections, usually informally, through a variety of professional and social activities.

NETWORK LOGIC

Sequence of activities in a network affecting the order in which the work (that is, project activities) will be performed.

NETWORK PATH

Continuous series of connected activities in a project network diagram.

NET WORTH

Difference between total liabilities and total assets.

NEUTRAL PERSON

Impartial third party who serves as a mediator, fact finder, or arbitrator, or otherwise functions to help opposing parties resolve the issues in controversy.

NEW BLUE-COLLAR

Worker in today's modern manufacturing plant who is more highly skilled and educated than workers of the past.

NEW COMPONENT

In portfolio management, a new project, program, or other initiative added to the portfolio.

NIH

See not invented here syndrome.

NIKKEI 225

Stock market index (Nikkei heikin kabuka) for the Tokyo Stock Exchange. The Nikkei average is the most watched index of Asian stocks, and has been calculated daily by the Nihon Keizai Shimbun (Nikkei) newspaper since 1971.

NINETY-NINETY (90-90) RULE OF PROJECT SCHEDULING

Informal, tongue-in-cheek observation that states that the first 90 percent of the project takes 90 percent of the time and the remaining 10 percent takes the other 90 percent of the time.

NO-BRAINER, A

Decision whose option is so clear and simple that it requires very little, if any, thought to make.

NODE

Junction point joined to some or all of the other dependency lines in a network; an intersection of two or more lines or arrows. *See also* arrow diagramming method *and* precedence diagramming method.

NOMINAL GROUP TECHNIQUE

Specific structured process of team brainstorming and creative problem-solving that draws on individual and group strengths but prevents domination by any one individual. Consists of five separate steps: (1) silent generation—individual team members write responses to a problem statement in silence; (2) round robin—each team member recites his or her responses, which are written on a flip chart, white board, or other mechanism such that all parties can view the list at the same time; (3) clarification—the group discusses the remarks; (4) selection and ranking—each team member selects and ranks in priority order the top 3–10 ideas collected; and (5) final selection and ranking—the facilitator tallies the results and prepares the group's ranked set of ideas.

NOMINAL INTEREST RATE

Interest rate that is not adjusted to remove the effects of actual or expected inflation. Market interest rates are generally nominal interest rates.

NONBINDING ARBITRATION

Arbitration in which the parties are not legally bound to the decision of the arbitrator. *See also* arbitration.

NONCONFORMANCE

Deficiency in characteristics, documentation, or procedures that makes the quality of material, service, or product unacceptable or indeterminate.

NONDISCLOSURE AGREEMENT (NDA)

Legally binding document in which an organization promises to use another's proprietary data only for specific purposes and not to reveal or disclose these data to any other organization or individual.

NONPERSONAL SERVICES CONTRACT

Contract under which the personnel performing the services are not subject, either by the contract's terms or by the manner of its administration, to the supervision and control that usually exist between the buyer and its employees.

NONPROFIT ORGANIZATION

(1) Corporation, foundation, trust, or institution operated for scientific, educational, or medical purposes, not organized for profit, and whose net earnings do not benefit any private shareholder or individual.

(2) In the United States, a university or other institution of higher education or an organization granted nonprofit status under the Internal Revenue Code, or any nonprofit scientific or educational organization qualified under a state nonprofit organization statute.

NONRECURRING COST

Project-incurred cost that is not expected to recur on any future work. *See also* recurring cost.

NONVERBAL COMMUNICATION

Means of conveying a message, or part of a message, either consciously or subconsciously, through body language, physical environment, and personal attributes such as physical appearance, vocal cues, and touch. Research has shown that between 70 and 90 percent of the entire interpersonal communication spectrum is nonverbal. *See also* Mehrabian's communication model.

NONWORK UNIT

Calendar unit in which certain types of work will not be performed on an activity, such as holidays.

NORMAL COST

Annual cost attributable, under the actuarial cost method in use, to years subsequent to a particular valuation date.

NORMAL INSPECTION

Inspection, under a sampling plan, that is used when no evidence exists that the quality level of the product being submitted is better or worse than the specified quality level.

NORMATIVE FORECASTING

Method for assessing the future in terms of what is required to reach a particular objective. Used in gap analysis for determining the contents of a project portfolio to ensure that the objective can be achieved.

NORMING

See Tuckman's Model of Team Development (Stage 3).

NOT APPLICABLE (N/A)

Term used in a variety of circumstances that means does not apply or is not relevant.

NOTICE TO PROCEED

Formal and official notice issued to a contractor to begin contract performance.

NOT INVENTED HERE SYNDROME (NIH)

Attitude that prevents individuals and groups from using and benefiting from the ideas of other individuals or groups because of personal pride; cultural, ethnic, or national prejudice; or other bias.

NOT/NO EARLIER THAN

Date before which an activity may not start or end; a constraint.

NOT/NO LATER THAN

Date after which an activity may not start or end; a constraint.

NOT TO EXCEED (NTE)

Term found in contract pricing agreements prohibiting the contractor from incurring costs over a specified amount.

NOVATION AGREEMENT

Legal instrument executed by the contractor (transferor), the successor in interest (transferee), and the buyer by which, among other things, the transferor guarantees performance of the contract, the transferee assumes all obligations under the contract, and the buyer recognizes the transfer of the contract and related assets.

NPV

See net present value.

NTE

See not to exceed.

NULL HYPOTHESIS

In statistics, and especially in quality management, a hypothesis advanced to be nullified or refuted in order to support a different hypothesis. When used, the null hypothesis is presumed true until statistical evidence in the form of a hypothesis test indicates otherwise. In science, the null hypothesis is used to test differences in treatment and control groups, and the assumption at the outset of the experiment is that no difference exists between the two groups for the variable being compared. *See also* type I error *and* type II error.

O

OBJECTIVE

(1) End toward which effort is directed; a predetermined result.

(2) Organizational performance criteria to be achieved and measured in the use of organizational resources.

OBJECTIVE QUALITY EVIDENCE

Statement of fact, either quantitative or qualitative, about the quality of a product or service based on observations, measurements, or tests that can be verified. Evidence describing the item, process, or procedure can be expressed in terms of specific quality requirements or characteristics that are identified in drawings, specifications, and other documents.

OBLIGATED BALANCE

Amount of money committed for specific purposes but not actually spent.

OBLIGATION

Duty to make a future payment of money. The duty is incurred as soon as an order is placed or a contract is awarded for the delivery of goods and the performance of services. The placement of an order is sufficient. An obligation legally encumbers a specified sum of money, which will require outlay(s) or expenditures in the future.

OBS

See organizational breakdown structure.

OCCUPATION

Set of activities or tasks that employees are paid to perform. Employees who perform essentially the same tasks are in the same occupation, whether or not they work in the same industry. Some occupations are concentrated in a few particular industries; other occupations are found in many industries.

OCCUPATIONAL GROUPS

Group of related occupations; for example, sales occupations and service occupations.

OCCUPATIONAL ILLNESS

Any abnormal condition or disorder caused by exposure to factors associated with employment. It includes acute and chronic illnesses or diseases that may be caused by inhalation, absorption, or ingestion of, or direct contact with, substances that otherwise damage the health of the person exposed to them.

OCCUPATIONAL INJURY

Any injury, such as a cut, fracture, sprain, or amputation, that results from a work-related event or from a single instantaneous exposure in the work environment.

OCF

See operating cash flow.

OE

See operational effectiveness.

OFFER

Response to a solicitation or tender that, if accepted, would bind the contractor to perform the resulting contract.

OFFEROR

Party who makes an offer and seeks acceptance from the buyer.

OFF THE RECORD

Statements made in confidence by an individual who does not want them attributed to him or her.

OFF-THE-SHELF ITEM

Item produced and placed in stock by a manufacturer or contractor, or stocked by a distributor, before orders or contracts are received for its sale.

OJT

See on-the-job training.

O&M

See operations and maintenance.

ON ACCOUNT

Partial payment made towards satisfaction of a debt.

ONE HUNDRED PERCENT INSPECTION

Inspection in which specific characteristics of each product unit are examined or tested to determine conformance with requirements.

ONE-OFF

Happening one time only.

ONE-STOP, ALL-STOP FLOW CONTROL

Production approach in which coordination and communication among process stages are regulated as a balanced flow process. All stages of a process function as a unit. If one stage of the process has a major problem and must shut down for correction, all other stages of the process will stop automatically after reaching a predetermined quantity of completed work in the holding area.

ONE-STOP SHOP

Used to describe a place or company that can satisfy all the requirements of a customer.

ON-THE-JOB TRAINING (OJT)

Learning a new skill or technique by doing it while on the job.

OPEN-DOOR POLICY

Management approach that encourages employees to speak freely and regularly to management regarding any aspect of a business or project. Adopted to promote the open flow of communication and to increase the success of business operations or project performance by soliciting the ideas of employees. Tends to minimize personnel problems and employee dissatisfaction.

OPEN-ENDED PROBLEM

Problem without a single correct answer and whose boundaries can be challenged.

OPEN-SOURCE LICENSING

License for a software product that permits users to read, access, change, and reuse the source code of the product.

OPEN STANDARDS

Widely accepted and supported standards set by recognized standards organizations or the marketplace. These standards support interoperability, portability, and scalability, and are equally available to the general public at no cost or for a moderate license fee.

OPEN SYSTEMS ENVIRONMENT (OSE)

Comprehensive set of interfaces, services, and supporting formats, marked by interoperability of application, as specified by IT standards and profiles. An OSE enables information systems to be developed, operated, and maintained independent of application-specific technical solutions or vendor products.

OPERATING CASH FLOW (OCF)

Amount used to represent the money moving through a company resulting from its operations, as distinct from its purely financial transactions.

OPERATING CHARACTERISTIC CURVE

Plotted curve showing the percent of lots or batches that may be expected to be accepted under a specific sampling plan for a given process quality.

OPERATING COSTS

(1) Primary costs necessary to operate and maintain a capability or system.

(2) In accounting, the expense of maintaining property (for example, paying property taxes and utilities and insurance); it does not include depreciation or the cost of financing or income taxes. *Also called* operating expenses.

OPERATING EXPENSES

All selling and G&A expenses. Includes depreciation but not interest expense.

OPERATING INCOME

Revenue less the cost of goods sold and related operating expenses that are applied to the day-to-day operating activities of the company. It excludes financial items such as interest income, dividend income, and interest expense; extraordinary items; and taxes.

OPERATING MARGIN

Ratio of operating income to sales revenue.

OPERATING PROFIT

Gross profit minus operating expenses.

OPERATING TIME

Time during which the system is operating in a manner acceptable to the operator.

OPERATION

Military action using deployed forces.

OPERATIONAL BASELINE

Identifies the project deliverable or system accepted by the users in the operational environment after a period of onsite testing using production data. *See also* baseline.

OPERATIONAL DEFINITION

Description in specific terms of what something is and how it is measured by the quality control process. May include metrics.

OPERATIONAL EFFECTIVENESS (OE)

Measure of the overall ability of a system to accomplish a mission when used by representative personnel in the environment planned or expected for operational employment of the system, considering organization, doctrine, tactics, supportability, survivability, vulnerability, and threat.

OPERATIONAL ENVIRONMENT

Environment that addresses all operational requirements and specifications required of the final system, including its platform and packaging.

OPERATIONAL RELIABILITY AND MAINTAINABILITY (R&M) VALUE

Any measure of R&M that includes the combined effects of item design, quality, installation, environment, operation, maintenance, and repair.

OPERATIONS AND MAINTENANCE (O&M)

(1) Actions taken to ensure the functionality and effectiveness of a system, facility, device, component, piece of machinery, or any ongoing process once it is put into use.

(2) Phase in the product life cycle that immediately follows the acceptance of the product by the end-user, sponsor, or client. Responsibility for this phase typically rests with the product manager, not the project manager.

OPERATIONS MANUAL

Formal document that provides a detailed operational description of a device, a component, a piece of machinery, a system and its interfaces, or any other item that requires personnel to have knowledge of its assembly.

OPM3®*

See Organizational Project Management Maturity Model.

OPM3® PRODUCTSUITE

Set of automated tools and services developed under the stewardship of the Project Management Institute by Det Norske Veritas that increases the ability of assessors and consultants to help organizations increase their capability in project management. OPM3® ProductSuite is only available to PMI® Certified OPM3® Assessors and Consultants.

---

*"OPM3" is a certification mark of the Project Management Institute, Inc., which is registered in the United States and other nations.

OPPORTUNITY

(1) Future event or series of events that, if they occur, will have a positive impact on a project.

(2) Benefit to be realized from undertaking a project.

OPPORTUNITY ASSESSMENT

Examination of the uncertainty associated with the possible occurrence of an event that is expected to have a positive impact on a project.

OPPORTUNITY COST

Rate of return that would have been earned by selecting an alternative project rather than the one selected. Opportunity cost is used as one variable in project selection.

OPTIMISTIC TIME

In PERT estimating, the minimum number of work periods the activity will consume.

OPTIMIZATION STRATEGY

Carefully organized steps used to maximize the occurrence or impact of a project opportunity.

OPTION

Contractual clause permitting an increase in the quantity of supplies beyond that originally stipulated or an extension in the time for which services on a time basis may be required.

ORDER-OF-MAGNITUDE ESTIMATE

Approximate estimate that is accurate to within –25 percent to +75 percent and is made without detailed data. Usually produced from a cost capacity curve, with scale-up or scale-down factors that are appropriately escalated, and approximate cost capacity ratios. Used in the formative stages of an expenditure program for initial project evaluation. *Also called* preliminary estimate, conceptual estimate, *or* feasibility estimate. *See also* estimate.

ORDINARY INCOME

Income derived from the regular operating activities of a business, but exclusive of capital gains.

ORGANIZATION

Company, corporation, firm, or enterprise, either public or private, which may or may not be incorporated.

ORGANIZATIONAL BREAKDOWN STRUCTURE (OBS)

Graphical depiction used to show the work units or work packages that are assigned to specific organizational units.

ORGANIZATIONAL CHANGE MANAGEMENT

Structured approach to transitioning individuals, teams, departments, divisions, or entire organizations from a current, or AS-IS, state to a future, or TO-BE, state with as little disruption and angst as possible. Organizational change management is characterized by a shift in peoples' attitudes and behaviors to accept, if not completely embrace, the TO-BE state.

ORGANIZATIONAL CONFLICT OF INTEREST

Situation where an individual is unable to render impartial assistance or advice to his or her employer because of other activities or relationships with other persons.

ORGANIZATIONAL CULTURE

System of shared beliefs, mores, values, norms, and symbols that represents the unique character of a company or organization and provides the context for action and behavior in it.

ORGANIZATIONAL INTERFACES

Formal and informal reporting and working relationships among different organizational units.

ORGANIZATIONAL OBJECTIVES

Specified goals that define an organization and its endeavors; organizational objectives serve as a focus towards which employees' efforts are directed.

ORGANIZATIONAL PLANNING

Process of identifying, documenting, and assigning project roles, responsibilities, and reporting relationships.

ORGANIZATIONAL POLITICS

System of rules, behaviors, power, and relationships that people use to influence outcomes advantageous to their position, desires, and objectives.

ORGANIZATIONAL PROJECT MANAGEMENT MATURITY MODEL (OPM3®)

Global standard developed by the Project Management Institute to help organizations better understand their enterprise-wide project management practices and to measure their maturity, or stage of process development, against identified best practices. OPM3® is used to—

• Describe the importance of organizational project management and how to recognize enterprise competency

• Conduct an assessment to determine its maturity

• Develop an improvement plan to increase it organizational project management maturity

OPM3® is used to assess maturity in project, program, and portfolio management.

ORGANIZATIONAL RESOURCES

Human and nonhuman resources available to the organization to fulfill its mission, objectives, and goals.

ORGANIZATIONAL STRATEGY

Means through which the use of resources accomplishes end purposes.

ORGANIZATIONAL STRUCTURE

Alignment of human resources and functions of the organization, usually depicted on a chart or graph, that shows the relative authority and hierarchy of personnel. There are three types of structure:

• Functional (*See* functional organization.)
• Matrix (*See* matrix organization.)
• Line (*See* line organization.)

ORGANIZATION CHART

Graphic display of reporting relationships that provides a general framework of the organization.

ORGANIZATION COST

Cost relating to business organization or reorganization expenses, such as incorporation fees and costs of attorneys, accountants, brokers, promoters, organizers, management consultants, and investment counselors, whether or not they are employees of the organization.

ORIGINAL DURATION

First estimate of the number of work units needed to complete an activity. Most common time units are hours, days, weeks, and months.

ORIGINAL INSPECTION

First inspection of a particular quantity of product, as distinguished from the inspection of a product that has been resubmitted after prior rejection.

OSE

See open systems environment.

OTHER BID CONSIDERATIONS

Evaluation of the organization's personnel and financial resources, facilities, performance record, responsiveness to contract terms and conditions, and general willingness to perform the work.

OTHER DIRECT COSTS

Group of accounting elements that can be attributed to specific tasks or activities. Examples include travel, living, and postage costs.

OUTCOME

Final condition or result at the end of a sequence or path of events.

OUTLAYS

See expenditure.

OUT-OF-COURT SETTLEMENT

Any dispute, disagreement, or controversy between the parties to an agreement that is resolved through means other than a court of law.

OUT OF HIDE

Means of funding a program, perhaps not planned or scheduled, out of existing military department funds without receiving any outside help from the U.S. Congress or Office of the Secretary of Defense (OSD).

OUTPUT

(1) Documents or deliverable items that are a result of a process.

(2) In information processing, the result of what the computer is programmed to do.

OUTSOURCING

Process of awarding a contract or otherwise entering into an agreement with a third party, usually a supplier, to perform services or create products that currently are being performed by an organization's employees. Organizations may outsource elements of their operations for any of the following reasons: the service or product can be performed or produced cheaper, faster, or better by a third party; there is an insufficient number of employees in the organization to perform the required work; the organization lacks the skills necessary to perform the work; or the service—for example, janitorial service—is not a core business function contributing to the organization's revenue growth and technical expertise, and accordingly management does not want to focus time and attention on it. *See also* contracting out.

OUTSTANDING

(1) Amount owed as a debt.
(2) Word used to mean fantastic or superb.

OVERALL CHANGE CONTROL

(1) Activities concerned with influencing the factors that create change to ensure it is beneficial, or that determine a change has occurred and manage it. *See also* change control.

(2) Coordination of changes across an entire project.

OVERALL RISK RATING

Overall probability and impact for each risk as a combined risk ranking. The overall risk rating can be presented as a qualitative or quantitative (expected value) rating.

OVERHEAD COST

See indirect cost (2).

OVERHEAD RATE

Percentage rate determined by dividing an organization's indirect costs for an accounting period by the base used to allocate indirect costs to work accomplished during the period of performance.

OVERRUN

Amount of the cost of performance that is greater than the amount estimated.

OVERSIGHT

Review activity by any person or body to determine the status of a project or program or to ascertain whether the organization's rules are being followed; can serve as a basis for future policy-making. Often done by a PMO.

OVER THE TOP

To an excessive degree; beyond reasonable and acceptable limits.

OVERTIME

Time worked by an employee in excess of the agreed-upon normal working hours. Typically compensated for by either a higher rate of pay per hour or compensatory time.

OWNERSHIP OF QUALITY RESPONSIBILITY

Ultimate responsibility of the individual performing a task to ensure that the requirements or specifications are met.

P

P2M

See Project and Program Management for Enterprise Innovation.

PACKAGING

Process and procedures used to protect material. It includes cleaning, drying, preserving, packing, and unitization.

PADDING

Arbitrarily inflating the time and/or cost estimates for work packages in the WBS by those responsible for their completion. Because padding is largely invisible to the project manager, it is difficult to prevent the additional time and/or cost from being used, and the project manager is not truly in control of the project.

PAIRWISE COMPARISON

Multivoting technique used to rank-order a set of factors (for example, requirements, projects, and so on) when the members of a group cannot reach agreement on the priorities of each of the factors. Each factor is compared with every other factor and voted on by the group to determine which of the two compared is more important. After all the comparisons and voting are complete, the votes are tallied. The factor with the largest number of votes is the group's highest priority; the other factors are ranked by descending order of votes.

PAL

See process asset library.

PARALLEL TASKS

Independent tasks that proceed concurrently.

PARAMETER

Determining factor or characteristic. Usually related to performance in developing a system.

PARAMETRIC COST ESTIMATING

Estimating approach that uses a statistical relationship between historical data and other variables (for example, lines of code in software development) to calculate an estimate.

PARAMETRIC MODELING

Practice of using project characteristics (parameters) in a mathematical model to predict project costs. Considered to be reliable when the historical information used to develop the model is accurate, parameters used in the model are readily quantifiable, and the model is scalable.

PARENT ORGANIZATION

Firm or organization within which the project is being conducted.

PARETO ANALYSIS

One of the seven tools of quality named after Vilfredo Pareto. Recognizes that a small number of problem types account for a significant overall percentage of the total number of problems that occur in the manufacture of a process or delivery of a service. Often called ABC analysis or the 80/20 rule. For example, 80 percent of the downtime of a computer system is attributable to 20 percent of the computer's components.

PARETO DIAGRAM

Histogram, ordered by frequency of occurrence, that shows the number of results that were generated by each identified cause. Usually includes a second scale to reflect percentage of results for each cause.

PARETO OPTIMAL SOLUTION

Solution in which making a party better off requires making another party worse off by the same or a greater amount.

PARETO'S LAW

Principle, espoused by Joseph Juran and based on the work of nineteenth-century Italian economist Vilfredo Pareto, stating that a relatively small number of causes (the "vital few") typically will produce a large majority of problems or defects. Improvement efforts usually are most cost-effective when focused on a few high-impact causes.

PARKINSON'S LAW

"Work expands so as to fill the time available for its completion." Stated by C. Northcote Parkinson, 1909–1993, English political scientist, historian, and writer, from his book *Parkinson's*

Law: The Pursuit of Progress, published in 1958. Parkinson was a bureaucrat working for the British in India during the colonial era.

PAROL EVIDENCE

Evidence presented verbally; in contract law, any verbal or oral evidence not included in the written agreement.

PAROL EVIDENCE RULE

Rule in contract law that prohibits the contracting parties from altering a written contract by contradictory verbal statements or contemporaneous oral agreement.

PARTIAL AUDIT

Audit that covers a subset of the project elements.

PARTIAL PAYMENT

Payment made upon delivery and acceptance of one or more complete deliverables or units as required under the contract, even though other quantities or items remain to be delivered.

PARTICIPATIVE ESTIMATING

Estimating approach in which the primary estimator depends on other people to provide or review estimates for part or all of a work estimate.

PARTICIPATIVE MANAGEMENT STYLE

Management approach in which the project manager solicits information from and shares decision-making authority with the project team.

PARTNERING

Approach used at the beginning of the contract that encourages assimilation of the contractor's employees into the project as full partners to achieve contract objectives.

PARTNERSHIP

Working relationship, formalized in a legal agreement, of two or more parties to achieve common business goals.

PARTY-AT-INTEREST

See stakeholder.

PASS/FAIL FACTOR

(1) Any minimum level of acceptability below which the item or thing under consideration will not be considered as acceptable.

(2) In U.S. federal procurement, the minimum level of acceptable compliance with a requirement that must be offered for a proposal to be considered. If a proposal fails to meet minimum requirements, it will not be given further consideration.

PASSIVE QUALITY ASSURANCE

Quality assurance that is reactive and corrective in nature; the quality system is fixed only in response to problems.

PASS THE BUCK

Pass the responsibility on to someone else.

PAST PERFORMANCE INFORMATION

Relevant information, for future source selection purposes, regarding a contractor's actions under previously awarded contracts. It includes, for example: the contractor's record of conforming to contract requirements and to standards of good workmanship; the contractor's record of forecasting and controlling costs; the contractor's adherence to contract schedules, including the administrative aspects of performance; the contractor's history of reasonable and cooperative behavior and commitment to customer satisfaction; and generally, the contractor's businesslike concern for the interest of the customer.

PATCHWORK DELIVERABLES

(1) Deliverables that lack cohesiveness, reflecting many ad hoc decisions rather than a comprehensive vision.

(2) Deliverables that are the result of a requirements definition method in which specifications are developed as they occur.

PATENT

Form of legal protection that provides a person or legal entity with exclusive rights to exclude others from making, using, or selling a concept or invention for the duration of the patent. There are three types of patents available: design, plant, and utility. Patents in the U.S. are issued by the U.S. Patent and Trademark Office.

PATENT DEFECT

Any defect that exists at the time of acceptance and is not a latent defect.

PATH

Set of sequentially connected tasks, activities, lines, or nodes in a project network diagram.

PATH CONVERGENCE

Point at which parallel paths of a series of activities meet. Notable because of the tendency to delay the completion of the milestone where the paths meet.

PATH FLOAT

See float.

PAYBACK PERIOD

Financial project evaluation criterion used to determine the amount of time before the net cash flow from a project becomes positive. *Also called* payout time period.

PAY-FOR-PERFORMANCE

Compensation scheme for employees and team members in which their level of pay is tied directly to specific business goals and management objectives. Organizations adopt this approach to improve individual accountability; align shareholder, management, and employee interests; and enhance performance.

PAYMENT

Obligation to compensate the contractor according to the terms of the contract.

PAYMENT AUTHORIZATION

Process that allows funds to be transferred to an account to pay a contractor for delivered goods or services according to contractual terms.

PAYMENT BOND

Bond to secure the payment of subcontractors, laborers, and so on, by the prime contractor.

PAYOUT TIME PERIOD

See payback period.

PAY PERIOD

Specific period of time used to determine the pay earned by an employee. Pay periods are one week, two weeks, or monthly in most organizations.

PBR

See program benefits review.

PBS

See project breakdown structure.

PC

See percent complete.

PCO

See procuring contracting officer.

PDCA

See plan-do-check-act cycle.

PDM

See precedence diagramming method.

PDR

See preliminary design review.

PE

See program element.

P/E

See price-to-earnings ratio.

PECHA KUCHA

Japanese for "chit chat," a presentation format in which someone's creative work can be easily and informally shown to others. Devised by Astrid Klein and Mark Dytham of Klein-Dytham Architecture, Tokyo, its use now applies to business meetings where presenters are limited to showing only 20 PowerPoint® slides for 20 seconds each (the 20-20 format), for a total of 6 minutes 40 seconds. Done primarily to time box presentations and to force presenters to get to the point.

PEER AUDIT

Audit conducted by a group of peers rather than full-time or assigned auditors.

PEER GROUP ANALYSIS

Practice of comparing one's company with one or more competitors or other companies using such factors as industry, size, revenue, and geographical location. The most common analysis is the study of compensation packages to ensure that the company remains competitive in its industry. Other analyses include financial performance, marketing strategies, and inventory control.

PEER REVIEW

Review of a project or phase of a project by individuals with equivalent knowledge and background who are not currently members of the project team and have not participated in the development of the project.

PENALTY

Money or other cost a person or company must pay for breaking a law or violating part or all of a contract.

PENETRATION PRICING

Establishing a lower price for one's product compared with the competition's in order to rapidly enter a market.

PERCENT COMPLETE (PC)

Estimate, expressed as a percent, of the amount of work completed on an activity or group of activities, typically based on resource use. Used in calculating earned value.

PERCENT DEFECTIVE

Percent of defectives of any given quantity of units of product. Calculated by 100 times the number of defective units of product divided by the total number of units of product. *See also* defective.

PERCENT SPENT

Estimate, expressed as a percent, of how much of the total budget has been spent on an activity or a group of activities as of a specified date. Used in earned value analysis.

PERCEPTUAL MAPPING

Quantitative market research tool used to understand what customers think of current and future products.

PER DIEM

Latin for "by the day." A daily allowance given to employees; for example, travel expenses.

PERFECTIVE MAINTENANCE

Software maintenance performed to improve the performance, maintainability, or other attributes of a computer program.

PERFORMANCE

(1) Determination of achievement used to measure and manage project quality.

(2) Operational and support characteristics of a system that allow it to effectively and efficiently perform its assigned mission over time. The support characteristics include both supportability aspects of the design and support elements necessary for system operation.

PERFORMANCE-BASED CONTRACTING

Structuring all aspects of an acquisition around the purpose and outcomes of the work to be performed, as opposed to either the manner by which the work is to be performed or broad and imprecise statements of work. In U.S. federal procurement, also referred to as performance-based service contracting

PERFORMANCE BOND

Bond used to secure the performance and fulfillment of all the undertakings, terms, and conditions of a contract.

PERFORMANCE IMPROVEMENT

Primary output of project team development. It may manifest itself in improvements in individual and team skills, behaviors, and capabilities.

PERFORMANCE MEASURE

Quantitative or qualitative method or characteristic for describing performance; a measure used to track progress (or lack thereof) toward a strategic objective or intermediate result. Performance measures, sometimes called performance indicators, serve to determine whether progress is being made, rather than why such progress is or is not being made. *See also* key performance indicators.

PERFORMANCE MEASUREMENT BASELINE (PMB)

See budgeted cost of work scheduled.

PERFORMANCE REPORTING

Collecting and disseminating information about project performance to provide project stakeholders with information about how resources are being used to achieve project objectives. Includes status reporting, progress reporting, and forecasting.

PERFORMANCE REQUIREMENTS

(1) Results that are required to be achieved at the activity, task, or project level.

(2) Results a contractor is required to achieve based on the contract's terms and conditions.

PERFORMANCE REVIEW

Meeting held periodically to assess a project's progress including earned value management analysis, forecasting, and status reporting.

PERFORMANCE SPECIFICATION

Technical requirement that describes the operational characteristics desired for an item in order to convey what the final product should be capable of accomplishing, rather than how it should be built or what its measurements, tolerances, or other design characteristics should be. If a contract contains performance specifications, the contractor accepts general responsibility for product design and engineering and for achieving the performance requirements in the contract.

PERFORMING

See Tuckman's Model of Team Development (Stage 4).

PERFORMING ORGANIZATION

Enterprise whose employees are most involved in doing the project work.

PERSONAL SERVICES CONTRACT

Contract that by its express terms or as administered makes the contractor's personnel appear to be, in effect, employees of the buyer's organization.

PERSONAL STRENGTH

Behavior trait that is consistent with the person's Motivational Value System™. It is a means to enhance mutual gratification between one's self and another person without violating the integrity of either person and is therefore considered a strength. Using the appropriate personal strengths at the appropriate time allows mutual affirmation and respects the integrity of both parties. *See also* personal weakness.

PERSONAL WEAKNESS

Personal strength that is perceived by others as being exhibited and practiced by the person in the extreme. To be overtrusting or gullible is a weakness; it lessens the likelihood of mutual gratification and is an invitation to resistance or withdrawal by the other party. To be overly self-confident or arrogant also is a weakness; it lessens the likelihood of mutual gratification and is an invitation to resistance or withdrawal by the other party. To be overpersevering or stubborn is a weakness; it lessens the likelihood of mutual affirmation and is an invitation to hostility or withdrawal by the second party. *See also* personal strength.

PERT

See Program Evaluation and Review Technique.

PERT CHART

Graphic portrayal of milestones, activities, and their dependency upon other activities for completion and depiction of the critical path. *See also* Program Evaluation and Review Technique.

PERT/COST

Approach to project cost management in which cost and time estimates are calculated for each activity. The cost is then monitored closely so the financial effect of making any changes can be calculated. A variety of analyses can be performed, including estimating how much it will cost to "crash" certain activities in the project.

PERT ESTIMATING

See Program Evaluation and Review Technique.

PESSIMISTIC DURATION

In PERT estimating, the maximum number of work periods the activity will consume. *Also called* pessimistic time.

PESSIMISTIC TIME

See pessimistic duration.

PETTY CASH

Account and location where actual cash (for example, currency and coins) is kept to reimburse individuals for minor, out-of-pocket expenditures.

PGMP^{SM}

See Program Management Professional.

PHASE

See project phase.

PHASED PLANNING

Approach used to plan only to the level of detail that is known at the time. The output of each project phase includes a phase plan and an updated project plan. The phase plan is prepared at the task or work package level and provides the detailed work to be completed in the next phase of the project; the updated project plan is the overall plan for the remainder of the project.

PHASE-END REVIEW

See control gate.

PHASE EXIT

See control gate.

PHASE GATE

See control gate.

PHASE GATE REVIEW

See control gate.

PHASE REVIEW

See control gate.

PHYSICAL CONFIGURATION AUDIT

Audit to ensure that all physical attributes listed in the design requirements have been met by the configuration item being delivered.

PHYSICAL CONSTRAINT

Any constraint that mandates the sequence of activities in a network due to physical operating constraints (for example, the second floor of a building cannot be started until the first floor is completed).

PIECE PART

Single piece not normally subject to disassembly without destruction or impairment of use, such as resistors, transistors, relays, and gears.

PILOT

Trial apparatus or operation used to validate a proposed solution in a live environment.

PIPELINE

In new product development, the total number of new product ideas that are being considered or developed at any one time.

PIPELINE MANAGEMENT

Cross-functional process that integrates product strategy, project management, and functional management to continually optimize the project management and execution of the organization's product development activities.

P&L

See profit and loss statement.

PLAN

Intended future course of action.

PLAN-DO-CHECK-ACT (PDCA) CYCLE

Universal improvement methodology, advanced by W. Edwards Deming and based on the work of Walter Shewhart, designed to continually improve the processes by which an organization produces a product or delivers a service. Following is a brief explanation of what happens in each phase of the cycle:

- Plan: Plan ahead for change. Analyze and predict the results.

- Do: Execute the plan, taking small steps in controlled circumstances.

- Check: Check and study the results.

- Act: Take action to standardize or improve the process.

PLANNED ACTIVITY

Activity or task that has not started or finished prior to the current date.

PLANNED FINISH DATE

See scheduled finish date.

PLANNED START DATE

See scheduled start date.

PLANNED VALUE (PV)

Sum of approved cost estimates (including any overhead allocation) for activities or portions of activities scheduled to be performed during a given period. *Also called* budgeted cost of work scheduled. *See also* earned value.

PLANNING PACKAGE

Logical aggregation of work within a cost account that can be identified and budgeted in early baseline planning but is not yet defined into work packages.

PLANNING PHASE

Phase in a generic project life cycle where the project plan or program plan is prepared.

PLANNING PROCESSES

(1) Any process undertaken to define and describe project or program scope, develop a management plan, and identify and schedule the activities and tasks that are part of the project or program.

(2) Any activity associated with devising and maintaining a workable scheme to accomplish the business need that the project or program was undertaken to address. *See also* project/program management process groups.

PLANNING, PROGRAMMING, BUDGETING AND EXECUTION (PPBE) PROCESS

Primary resource allocation process of the U.S. DOD. It is one of three major decision support systems for defense acquisition, along with Joint Capabilities Integration and Development System (JCIDS) and the Defense Acquisition System. It is a formal, systematic structure for making decisions on policy, strategy, and the development of forces and capabilities to accomplish anticipated missions.

PLANS AND SPECIFICATIONS

Drawings, specifications, and other data for and preliminary to construction.

PLATFORM

Hardware and systems software on which applications software is developed or installed and operated.

PLUG DATE

Date externally assigned to an activity that establishes the earliest or latest date the activity is allowed to start or finish.

PM

See project management.

PMB

See performance measurement baseline.

PMBOK® GUIDE

Abbreviation referring to the Project Management Institute's publication entitled *A Guide to the Project Management Body of Knowledge*, which identifies that subset of the project management body of knowledge that is generally recognized as good practice. *See also* project management body of knowledge.

PMD

See Program Management Directive.

PMI®

See Project Management Institute, Inc.

PMI® CERTIFIED OPM3® ASSESSOR™

Individual certified by PMI® to conduct an OPM3® assessment using PMI® proprietary tools. Certification requires the individual to undergo an entrance assessment, successfully pass an entrance examination, be subject to an experience requirement screening, participate in training, and successfully pass a final examination. There is also a requirement to maintain the certification.

PMI® CERTIFIED OPM3® CONSULTANT™

Individual certified by PMI® to develop an improvement plan for an organization that has been the subject of an OPM3® assessment. One cannot become a Consultant without first being certified an Assessor. To be certified as a Consultant one needs to take a training program and successfully pass the exam.

PMI® RISK MANAGEMENT PROFESSIONAL (PMI-RMP)ᔆᴹ*

(1) Professional certification awarded by the Project Management Institute to individuals who have met established minimum requirements in knowledge, education, and experience in project risk management.

(2) Individual holding such certification.

PMIS

See project management information system.

PMI® SCHEDULING PROFESSIONAL (PMI-SP)ᔆᴹ**

(1) Professional certification awarded by the Project Management Institute to individuals who have met established minimum requirements in knowledge, education, and experience in project scheduling.

(2) Individual holding such certification.

PMO

See program management office.
See project management office.

---

*"PMI-RMP" is a certification mark of the Project Management Institute, Inc., which is registered in the United States and other nations.

**"PMI-SP" is a certification mark of the Project Management Institute, Inc., which is registered in the United States and other nations.

PMP®

See Project Management Professional.

POC

See point of contact.

POINT OF CONTACT (POC)

Agreed-to, official communication point between two interfacing organizations. Usually one person. *Also called* single point of contact.

POKA YOKE

Japanese term that means to avoid (yokeru) inadvertent errors (poka); more commonly known as mistake proofing. A poka yoke device is one that prevents incorrect parts from being made or assembled, or easily identifies a flaw or error. Sometimes called "idiot proofing."

POLICY DEPLOYMENT

Process of developing and promulgating policies in the organization; translating senior management's objectives into more specific and quantifiable objectives for each unit in the organization.

POPULATION

In quality management, the entire body or collection of items or samples that is the focus of concern.

PORTAL

Web site designed to provide a broad array of services, information, and references on a specific topic through a combination of its own content and links to other Web sites. As a "doorway" to the Web, a portal typically, but not always, provides these services for free with the expectation that visitors to the site will buy products and services from the organizations that advertise on the site.

PORTFOLIO

Collection of projects, programs, and other initiatives grouped together for management and control purposes whose individual objectives and benefits are aimed at satisfying the organization's strategic objectives.

PORTFOLIO BALANCING

Process used by an organization to identify the most advantageous mix of projects and programs to satisfy the organization's strategic objectives.

PORTFOLIO MANAGEMENT

Business process, usually conducted at the highest level within an organization, that decides: which projects, programs, and other initiatives will be undertaken in a given period of time; the criteria for selecting those initiatives; and the active management of the initiatives through their life cycles to ensure that benefits will be realized, including their termination as required.

POSITIONAL NEGOTIATION

Negotiating approach in which immediate needs are stated on the assumption that the environment will not, or cannot, change.

POSITION DESCRIPTION

See job description.

POSITIVE FLOAT

See float.

POSTCONTRACT EVALUATION

Objective review and analysis of both parties' performance, the technical problems encountered, and the corrective actions taken.

POST-IMPLEMENTATION REVIEW

Formal review to evaluate the effectiveness of the output of the product or service of the project after being used in an operational environment by its users usually for at least three months.

POST-IMPLEMENTATION REVIEW REPORT

Formal document detailing the findings of the post-implementation review. *See also* post-implementation review.

POSTPROJECT ANALYSIS AND REPORT

Formal analysis and documentation of the project's results, including cost, schedule, and technical performance, versus the original plan.

POSTPROJECT EVALUATION AND REVIEW

See lessons-learned review.

POUND OF FLESH

Something which is owed that is ruthlessly required to be paid back.

POWER

Ability to influence the behaviors, decisions, opinions, methods, strategies, and commitment of others. Like conflict, power may be used in either a positive or a negative way.

POWER OF ATTORNEY

(1) Authority given one person or corporation to act for and obligate another, as specified in the instrument creating the power.

(2) In corporate suretyship, an instrument under seal that appoints an attorney-in-fact to act on behalf of a surety company in signing bonds. *See also* attorney-in-fact.

PPBE

See Planning, Programming, Budgeting and Execution Process.

PPI

See producer price index.

PPM

See project portfolio management.

PPR

See program performance review.

PREAWARD MEETINGS

Meetings to rank prospective contractors and examine the contractors' facilities or capabilities before final contract award.

PREAWARD SURVEY

Evaluation of a prospective contractor's capability to perform under the terms of a proposed contract.

PREBID CONFERENCE

See bidders conference.

PRECEDENCE DIAGRAMMING METHOD (PDM)

Network diagramming technique in which activities are represented by boxes (or nodes) and linked by precedence relationship lines to show the sequence in which the activities are to be performed. The nodes are connected with arrows to show the dependencies. Four types of relationships are possible: finish-to-finish; finish-to-start; start-to-finish; and start-to-start. *Also called* activity-on-node (AON) *or* activity-on-arc.

PRECEDENCE RELATIONSHIP

Term used in PDM for a logical relationship.

PRECISION

How closely all instances of a characteristic of a product or service are to being the same.

PRECONTRACT COST

Cost incurred by a contractor before the contract's effective date.

PREDECESSOR ACTIVITY

Activity or task that must begin or end before another activity or task can begin or end. In ADM, the activity that enters a node; in PDM, the "from" activity.

PREDICTION INTERVAL

Range of values that contains, with a high degree of confidence, the true value of the cost or price that is subject to being predicted using a regression. For example, a prediction interval could permit a person to state that they are 90 percent confident that the range includes the true value of the dependent variable.

PREFEASIBILITY PHASE

See concept phase.

PREFERENTIAL LOGIC

See discretionary dependency.

PREFERRED LOGIC

See discretionary dependency.

PRELIMINARY DANGER ANALYSIS

Technique in which the potential danger of each system component is identified. No cause-effect link is drawn between components and dangers. Generally used as the basis for other dependability techniques.

PRELIMINARY DESIGN REVIEW (PDR)

Review, conducted during system acquisition, of each configuration item to (1) evaluate the selected design approach in terms of progress, technical adequacy, and risk resolution; (2) determine the item's compatibility with the development specification's performance and engineering requirements; and (3) establish the existence and compatibility of the physical and functional interfaces among the item and other items in the project.

PRELIMINARY ESTIMATE

See order-of-magnitude estimate.

PREMATURE TERMINATION

Situation in which a decision is made to terminate a project before its objectives have been met. Many reasons exist for it, but generally speaking it is an action taken by management because either the project cannot be completed within a reasonable time and cost range, or the end product or service of the project is no longer needed.

PREPONDERANCE OF THE EVIDENCE

Legal standard for being adjudicated as guilty in a civil case in the U.S. When deciding if the fact at issue is true or not, there is more evidence to support it than refute it. *See also* beyond a reasonable doubt.

PREPROPOSAL CONFERENCE

In U.S. federal procurement, a meeting held by the contracting officer with prospective contractors during the solicitation period of a procurement by negotiation.

PREQUALIFICATION

Determination of the contractor's responsibility prior to issuing a solicitation, request for proposal, or tender.

PRESENT VALUE

Amount of money today that is equivalent to a payment, or series of payments, or revenues to be received in the future. Determined by multiplying each future cash flow by a present value factor, also called the discount factor, which represents the opportunity cost of the funds. For example, if the opportunity cost of money is 10%, the present value (that is, today's value) of $100 received one year from now is $91 [1 / (1 + 0.10)]. Present value is used to perform "like to like" comparisons.

PRESOLICITATION CONFERENCE

In U.S. federal procurement, a meeting held by the contracting officer with prospective contractors as a preliminary step in negotiated acquisitions to: develop or identify interested sources; request preliminary information based on a general description of the supplies or services involved; explain specifications and requirements; and aid prospective contractors in preparing proposals prior to making a large expenditure of effort, time, and money.

PREVENTIVE MAINTENANCE

All actions performed in an attempt to retain an item in a specified condition by providing systematic inspection, detection, and prevention of incipient failures.

PRICE

(1) Monetary amount paid, received, or asked in exchange for supplies or services, which is expressed as a single item or unit of measure for the supplies or services.

(2) In U.S. federal procurement, cost plus any fee or profit applicable to the contract type.

PRICE ADJUSTMENT

Modification of the price as stated in the terms of a contract.

PRICE ANALYSIS

(1) Examination and evaluation of a prospective price, without performing cost analysis, by determining the reasonableness of the price offered with reference to similar items or services offered for sale in the marketplace.

(2) In U.S. federal procurement, the process of examining and evaluating a proposed price without evaluating its separate cost elements and proposed profit.

PRICE CEILING

Government-imposed limit on how high a price can be charged on a product.

PRICE COMPETITION

In U.S. federal procurement, competition in a procurement when offers are solicited and received from at least two responsible contractors capable of completely or partially satisfying requirements.

PRICE ELASTICITY

Measure of the degree to which customers respond to price changes. If a product is responsive to price changes (people buy more when prices are lowered, or people buy less if prices are raised) then the product is said to be elastic. A product is inelastic if a significant change in price is accompanied by a minor amount of change in demand.

PRICE INDEX NUMBER

Quantity that measures relative price changes from one time period to another.

PRICE LEVEL INDEX

Factor used to convert constant dollar amounts from one year to another.

PRICE-RELATED FACTORS

In U.S. federal procurement, elements that can be quantified and used with price to determine the most advantageous bid for the government. They include foreseeable costs or delays to the government resulting from such factors as differences in inspection, locations of supplies, and transportation; changes made, or requested by the bidder, in any of the provisions of the invitation for bids, if the change does not constitute a ground for bid rejection; advantages or disadvantages to the government that might result from making more than one award; federal, state, and local taxes; origin of supplies; and, if foreign, the application of the Buy American Act or any other prohibition on foreign purchases.

PRICE-TO-EARNINGS RATIO (P/E)

Price of a share of stock divided by its earnings per share. Also known as the "multiple." Provides investors with an idea of how much they are paying for a company's earning power. The higher the ratio, the more expensive the stock.

PRICING

Process of establishing a reasonable amount or amounts to be paid for supplies or services.

PRICING ARRANGEMENT

Basis agreed to by contractual parties for payment of amounts for specified performance, generally through a specific type of contract, either cost-reimbursement or fixed-price.

PRIMARY FAILURE

Failure of a system because of age, poor design, poor construction, or improper installation of a component.

PRIME CONTRACT

Contract agreement or purchase order entered into by a contractor with a buyer. *See also* privity of contract.

PRIME CONTRACTOR

Organization that is managerially, commercially, and technically capable of accepting a contract from a buyer and is responsible for coordinating the activities of a number of subcontractors, integrating their deliverables, and managing risks to meet the buyer's requirements in terms of performance, cost, schedule, and other relevant factors. "Prime" distinguishes the contract from any subcontract entered into between the prime contractor and a supplier or vendor called a subcontractor, or between one subcontractor and another, lower-level subcontractor.

PRIME RATE

Interest rate that banks charge their preferred customers. Changes in the prime rate influence changes in other rates such as mortgage interest rates or interest rates on car loans.

PRINCE2

See Projects in Controlled Environments (Version 2).

PRINCIPLED NEGOTIATION

Negotiation approach with its primary objective being the achievement of a win-win result. *See also* win-win.

PRIORITIZATION MATRIX
Tool for comparing the elements of a set of criteria against one another. In quality planning, it is used to determine the relative value of project requirements.

PRIORITY RULES
Formal methods, such as ratios, used to rank items to determine which one should be next.

PRIVATE EQUITY
(1) Refers to the equity securities of unlisted (nonpublicly traded) companies.

(2) Term used to denote the source of funds used for the acquisition of, or substantial investment in, a company by a firm that uses such funds for said purpose (often called a "private equity" firm).

PRIVATIZATION
Process aimed at shifting organizations, functions, and responsibilities, in whole or in part, from the government to the private sector.

PRIVITY OF CONTRACT
Legal relationship and responsibilities between parties to the same contract.

PROBABILISTIC ESTIMATING
Method of estimating that generally uses three values to compute a statistically weighted estimate. *See also* Program Evaluation and Review Technique.

PROBABILITY
Likelihood of occurrence.

PROBABILITY ANALYSIS
Risk quantification technique that entails specifying a probability distribution for each variable and then calculating values for situations in which any one or all of the variables are changed at the same time.

PROBABILITY FUNCTION

Function that assigns a probability to each and every possible outcome.

PROBABILITY OF ACCEPTANCE

Percent of inspection lots expected to be accepted when the lots are subjected to a specific sampling plan.

PROBLEM DEFINITION

Process of distinguishing between causes and symptoms to determine the scope of effort to pursue on the project. Answers the question: "What problem(s) are we trying to solve?"

PROBLEM / NEED STATEMENT / GOAL

Documentation that defines the problem to be resolved, reinforces the need to develop a solution, and describes the overall objectives of the customer or end user.

PROBLEM RESOLUTION

Interaction between two or more parties with the specific intent of finding a mutually acceptable solution to a technical or other problem that affects project accomplishment.

PROBLEMS

(1) Negative risk events, known or unknown, that have materialized and have had a negative impact on project objectives.

(2) Any issues that impede the orderly execution of a project task or activity and that need to be resolved by the stakeholders so progress can be advanced.

PROBLEM SOLVING

Also called confrontation. *See* conflict resolution.

PROCEDURES

(1) Step-by-step instructions on ways to perform a given task, activity, or process; may be accompanied by a statement of purpose and policy for a task, examples of the results of a task, and so forth.

(2) Prescribed method to perform specified work.

PROCESS

(1) Series of interconnected actions, steps, or procedures leading to a result.

(2) High-level sequence or flow of tasks performed during production of a product or delivery of a service.

PROCESS ADJUSTMENT

Immediate corrective or preventive action as a result of quality control measurements; generally handled according to procedures for overall change control.

PROCESS ANALYSIS

Structured approach used to identify and understand what an organization does; defines business processes and the necessary data used through specific diagramming techniques. Helps managers improve the performance of their business.

PROCESS ASSET LIBRARY (PAL)

Repository of all interrelated actions and activities performed in an organization to achieve a specific set of products, results, or services.

PROCESS AVERAGE

Average percent of defective units or average number of defects per hundred units of product submitted by the manufacturer for original inspection.

PROCESS CAPABILITY

Ability of a process to produce a defect-free product or service in a controlled manner of production or controlled service environment. Key metrics and indicators can be used to determine performance; some will address overall performance, others potential performance.

PROCESS DEFINITION

Dividing a process into its component parts so that it can be described in detail.

PROCESS FLOWCHART

Diagram showing how various elements of a system relate. *Also called* system flowchart.

PROCESS LAYOUT

Method of plant layout in which the machines, equipment, and areas for performing the same or similar operations are grouped together; layout by function.

PROCESS MAP

Workflow or other diagram that graphically depicts the chronological flow of work in a hierarchical manner to illustrate how a product or transaction is processed. It is a visual representation either of the workflow within a process or of the whole operation. A high-level process map, sometimes called the "30,000-foot view," can be constructed in successive levels of detail down to the "micromap." A properly constructed process map will provide those who are unfamiliar with the process a good understanding of how it works.

PROCESS MATURITY

How close a developing or extant process is to being complete and capable of continuous improvement through quantitative measure and feedback.

PROCESS MEASURABLES

Indicators, metrics, or other quantifiable characteristics that directly measure the performance of key processes that affect customer expectations. Once data are collected and analyzed, specific actions can be taken to improve the performance of these indicators, which in turn should improve process performance and, ultimately, customer satisfaction.

PROCESS MODEL

Approach to show how processes are linked together in a business unit.

PROCESS OWNER

Individual(s) responsible for the design, execution, and performance of a process in an organization. Additionally, the process owner is responsible for ensuring that the process continues to provide value to the organization and for identifying future improvement opportunities.

PROCESS REVIEW

Formal review of the effectiveness of a process.

PROCESS SHEET

Document, originating in manufacturing engineering and sent to the production floor, that describes and illustrates methods and tools to be used in fabricating or assembling specific parts or subassemblies.

PROCESS SPECIFICATION

Specification that is applicable to a service performed on a product or material. Examples of processes include heat treatment, welding, plating, packing, microfilming, and marking. Process specifications cover manufacturing techniques that require a specific procedure to achieve a satisfactory result.

PROCESS STABILITY

Ability or capacity of a process to perform in a predictable manner over time. A run diagram provides graphic evidence of process stability.

PROCESS STANDARD SHEET

Tool for reducing work performance variation that contains managerial information, such as policies, rules, objectives, goals, and targets, and technical information, such as critical dimensions, work methods, measurement techniques, materials, equipment, process control methods, and specifications. Has sufficient detail and clarity to serve as a guide to job accomplishment so someone new can perform the job correctly the first time by following the standard.

PROCUREMENT

Process of acquiring goods or services from outside the immediate project organization, beginning with determining the need for the supplies or services and ending with the contract's completion and closeout.

PROCUREMENT AUDIT

Structured review of the procurement process, from procurement planning through contract administration, to identify successes and failures on a contract or group of contracts associated with an individual project or program. The lessons learned can be used later on the same project or program or on other projects or programs in the performing organization.

PROCUREMENT/BUYER NEGOTIATIONS
See contract negotiations.

PROCUREMENT CONSIDERATIONS OTHER THAN COST
Evaluation of staff and financial resources, facilities, performance record, responsiveness to contract terms and conditions, and a general willingness to perform the work as part of the evaluation process of a contractor's proposal.

PROCUREMENT COST CONSIDERATIONS
Assessment of the contractor's approach, realism, and reasonableness of cost, taking into account a forecast of economic factors affecting cost and cost risks reflected in the cost proposal.

PROCUREMENT DOCUMENTS
Documents issued to prospective contractors when requesting bids or quotations for supply of goods or services.

PROCUREMENT MANAGEMENT PLAN
Document that describes the management of the procurement processes, from solicitation planning through contract closeout.

PROCUREMENT PERFORMANCE EVALUATION
Comprehensive review of the original specification, statement of work, scope, and contract modifications for use in lessons learned to avoid similar problems in future procurements.

PROCUREMENT PLANNING
Process to determine what and when to procure.

PROCUREMENT PREQUALIFICATION
Review of potential contractor's experience, past performance, capabilities, resources, and current workloads.

PROCUREMENT RANKING
Qualitative or quantitative evaluation of the capabilities and qualifications of prospective contractors for the purpose of selecting one or more of them to provide the proposed supplies or services.

PROCUREMENT RELATIONSHIP WITH CWBS

Relationship of the supplies or services to be procured with the overall work and their interface with other project activities.

PROCUREMENT RESPONSE

Communications, positive or negative, from prospective contractors in response to the request to supply goods or services.

PROCUREMENT SOURCE EVALUATION

Overall review of capabilities and ranking of prospective contractors for the purpose of requesting proposals or entering into negotiations for the award of the contract.

PROCUREMENT STRATEGY

Plan or method outlining the approach an organization, program, or project will use to procure goods and services, and the overall objectives that are intended to be achieved.

PROCUREMENT TECHNICAL CONSIDERATIONS

Contractors' technical competency, understanding of the technical requirements, and ability to produce technically acceptable supplies or services.

PROCURING CONTRACTING OFFICER (PCO)

In U.S. federal procurement, a contracting officer who enters into contracts on behalf of the government.

PRODUCER PRICE INDEX (PPI)

Family of indexes that measures the average change over time in selling prices charged by domestic producers of goods and services to their clients. PPIs measure price change from the perspective of the seller. This contrasts with other indexes that measure price change from the purchaser's perspective, such as the consumer price index (CPI). Sellers' and purchasers' prices may differ due to government subsidies, sales and excise taxes, and distribution costs.

PRODUCIBILITY

Relative ease of manufacturing an item or system. This relative ease is governed by the characteristics and features of a design that enables economical fabrication, assembly, inspection, and testing using available manufacturing techniques.

PRODUCIBILITY REVIEW

Review of the design of a specific hardware item or system to determine the relative ease of producing it using available production technology, considering the elements of fabrication, assembly, inspection, and test.

PRODUCT

End result of a project or a specific task, activity, or process; either a tangible, physical product or a clearly specified event.

PRODUCT ANALYSIS

Process to develop a better understanding of the project's product. May include techniques such as systems engineering, value engineering, value analysis, function analysis, and quality function deployment.

PRODUCT BASELINE

(1) Initially approved documentation describing all the necessary functional and physical characteristics of the product to be developed.

(2) In information technology, the set of completed and accepted system components and the corresponding documentation that identifies these products.

PRODUCT BREAKDOWN STRUCTURE

Hierarchical structure used to decompose the product into constituent parts, as in a bill of materials.

PRODUCT DEFINITION

Form, fit, and function of a deliverable or set of deliverables.

PRODUCT DESCRIPTION

Documentation delineating the product characteristics or service that the project was undertaken to create.

PRODUCT DEVELOPMENT PROCESS

Structured and usually documented approach that organizations follow to design, develop, and introduce new products to the marketplace. Stages include concept, selection, design, development, testing, availability, and maintenance.

PRODUCT DOCUMENTATION

Written information about the product that is a part of the final work product.

PRODUCT EVALUATION TRIALS

Requirements elicitation technique used to gather and refine user requirements for a specific product. In this method a small group of users obtains the product and tests it, evaluating its suitability for its intended application and reworking requirements as needed.

PRODUCTION

Process of converting raw materials by fabrication into required material. It includes the functions of production-scheduling, inspection, quality control (QC), and related processes.

PRODUCTION CONTROL

Procedure of planning, routing, scheduling, dispatching, and expediting the flow of materials, parts, subassemblies, and assemblies within the plant from the start of production to the finished product in an orderly and efficient manner.

PRODUCTION ENGINEERING

Application of design and analysis techniques to produce a specified product. Included are the functions of planning, specifying, and coordinating the application of required resources; performing analyses of producibility and production operations, processes, and systems; applying new manufacturing methods, tooling, and equipment; controlling the introduction of engineering changes; and employing cost-control techniques.

PRODUCTION MANAGEMENT

Effective use of resources to produce on-schedule the required number of end units that meet specified quality, performance, and cost specifications. It includes, but is not limited to, industrial resource analysis, a producibility assessment, producibility engineering, planning, production engineering, industrial preparedness planning, postproduction planning, and productivity enhancement.

PRODUCTION MANAGEMENT TECHNIQUE

Technique used to determine the progress of a production program.

PRODUCTION PERMIT

In the U.S. DOD, written authorization, before production or provision of a service, to depart from specified requirements for a specific quantity or a specific time. *Also called* deviation permit.

PRODUCTION PLAN

Document that describes employment of the manufacturing resources needed to produce the required products or systems, on time and within cost constraints.

PRODUCTION PLANNING

Broad range of activities initiated early in the acquisition process, and continued through a production decision, to ensure an orderly transition from development to cost-effective production or construction.

PRODUCTION PLAN REVIEW

In the U.S. DOD, a review conducted to approve or disapprove a contractor-prepared and -submitted production plan.

PRODUCTION PROVEOUT

Technical test conducted prior to production testing with prototype hardware to determine the most appropriate design alternative. This testing also may provide data on safety, the achievability of critical system technical characteristics, how to refine hardware configurations and make them more rugged, and determination of technical risks.

PRODUCTION READINESS

Preparedness of a system to proceed into production. A system is ready for production when the producibility of the production design and the managerial and physical preparations necessary for initiating and sustaining a viable production effort have progressed to the point where a production commitment can be made without incurring unacceptable risks that will breach thresholds of schedule, performance, cost, or other established criteria.

PRODUCTION SCHEDULES

Time controls used by management to ensure that production operations run efficiently and economically.

PRODUCTION SURVEILLANCE

In the U.S. DOD, contract administration function used to determine contractor progress and identify any areas that might delay performance.

PRODUCTIVITY

Measure of economic efficiency that shows how effectively economic inputs are converted into output. Productivity is measured by comparing the amount of goods and services produced with the inputs used to produce them.

PRODUCT LIABILITY

Responsibility of a producer or others to make restitution for loss related to personal injury, property damage, or other harm caused by a product.

PRODUCT LIFE CYCLE

Total period of time that a product exists in the marketplace, from concept to termination.

PRODUCT LINE

Group of products marketed by an organization that have certain characteristics, customers, and uses in common and may share the same, or common, technologies and distribution channels.

PRODUCT MANAGER

Person responsible for overseeing all the activities that concern a particular product or product line, including gathering customer requirements such as the features products should contain, providing support once the product is launched, and gathering feedback from users or customers for improvement. Sometimes called a brand manager.

PRODUCT-ORIENTED PROCESSES

Methods used to specify and create the project product; defined by the project life cycle but vary by application area.

PRODUCT-ORIENTED SURVEY

Review and evaluation that determines the adequacy of the technical requirements relating to product quality and conformance to design specifications.

PRODUCT-ORIENTED WBS

See work breakdown structure.

PRODUCT PLATFORMS

Building blocks that are common across a range of products or a particular product line and that serve as the basis for a series or family of products over a number of years.

PRODUCT QUALITY REVIEW

Action taken by the buyer to determine that the quality of supplies or services accepted complies with specified requirements.

PRODUCT REVIEW

(1) In IT, a formal review of a product software or document to determine if it meets its requirements. Can be conducted as a peer review.

(2) Any review, formal or informal, whose purpose is to determine if a product meets the needs, requirements, specifications, or expectations of its target audience. *See also* product verification.

PRODUCT SCOPE

Features, functions, and characteristics to be included in a product.

PRODUCT VERIFICATION

Analysis conducted to ensure the product produced from a project or program conforms to the stakeholders' requirements, desires, and expectations.

PROFIT

Amount realized after the total project costs, both direct and indirect, are deducted from the price. *Also called* operating profit.

PROFITABILITY

Measure of the total project income compared with the total monies expended at any given period of time. Includes techniques such as economic value added, payout time period, return on investment, net present value, and discounted cash flow.

PROFIT AND LOSS STATEMENT (P&L)

Written summary of the revenues, costs, and expenses of a corporation during an accounting period. *Also called* income statement.

PROFIT CENTER

Segment of a company or business organization that is responsible for producing profits on its own, which will then be aggregated with other profit centers in the company to produce the entire company's profits.

PROFIT OBJECTIVE

In U.S. federal procurement, an amount that the contracting officer, in preparing to negotiate price based on a cost analysis, concludes is the appropriate negotiated profit or fee for the specific procurement.

PRO FORMA FINANCIAL STATEMENT

Financial projection that shows how an actual financial statement will look if certain specified assumptions are realized.

PROGRAM

(1) Group of related projects managed in a coordinated way to obtain benefits not available from managing the projects individually; may include an element of ongoing activities or tasks that are not within the scope of the individual projects but that contribute to the program's intended benefits.

(2) In the U.S. DOD, a major acquisition program.

(3) As a verb, to schedule funds to meet requirements and plans, or to write computer code.

(4) Major, independent part of a software system.

(5) Combination of program elements (PEs) designed to express accomplishment of a definite objective or plan.

PROGRAM BENEFITS REVIEW (PBR)

Comprehensive performance review to determine the extent to which the program is achieving its stated targets and benefits and whether the processes used in such achievement conform to the program management processes of the organization to be used for such purposes.

PROGRAM BRIEF

Document that describes the overall business objectives and vision for a program. Term used mostly in the United Kingdom.

PROGRAM BUDGETING

Aggregating income and expenditures by project or program, often in addition to aggregating by organizational unit or activity.

PROGRAM DIRECTOR

Individual responsible for the success of the program and who provides strategic direction for, makes executive decisions in behalf of, and manages the internal and external relationships for the overall benefit of the program. *See also* program manager.

PROGRAM ELEMENT (PE)

In the U.S. DOD, a basic building block of the Future Years Defense Program. The PE describes the program mission and identifies the organization responsible for performing the mission. A PE may consist of forces, manpower, materiél (both real and personal property), services, and associated costs, as applicable.

PROGRAM EVALUATION AND REVIEW TECHNIQUE (PERT)

Event-oriented, probability-based network analysis technique used to estimate project duration when there is a high degree of uncertainty with the individual activity duration estimates. PERT applies the critical path method to a weighted average duration estimate. The formula is as follows:

$$\frac{O + 4(ML) + P}{6},$$

where O = optimistic time, ML = most likely time, and P = pessimistic time.

PROGRAM GOVERNANCE

Process or set of processes used by an organization to define, develop, manage, monitor, and close out a program. It is primarily aimed at ensuring that the program's objectives are met and benefits delivered, and it includes a process for terminating a program if it appears the program will not meet identified objectives and benefits.

PROGRAM GOVERNANCE BOARD

Management team responsible for executing all aspects of program governance.

PROGRAM MANAGEMENT

(1) Coordinated management of a related series of projects over a period of time, in order to accomplish broad business goals to which the individual projects contribute, including benefits realization, stakeholder management, and program governance.

(2) In the U.S. DOD, the process whereby a single leader exercises centralized authority and responsibility for planning, organizing, staffing, controlling, and leading the combined efforts of civilian and military personnel and organizations in the management of a specific defense acquisition program or programs, throughout the system life cycle.

PROGRAM MANAGEMENT DIRECTIVE (PMD)

Official Headquarters (HQ) U.S. Air Force document used to direct acquisition responsibilities to the appropriate Air Force major commands, agencies, Program Executive Offices (PEOs), or designated acquisition commander. All Air Force acquisition programs require PMDs.

PROGRAM MANAGEMENT OFFICE (PMO)

Organizational entity established to assist program managers throughout the organization in implementing program management principles, practices, methodologies, tools, and techniques. May also provide assistance on individual programs through coaching and mentoring. In many organizations, the program management office is a support function and is not responsible for program execution. Its main objective is implementing effective program practices throughout the organization. As a practical matter, in organizations that practice both project and program management, the program management office also functions as a project management office.

PROGRAM MANAGEMENT PLAN

Document that describes the tactical means by which the program will be executed. Consists of the following subsidiary plans: quality plan, human resource plan, risk management plan, contracting plan, communications plan, transition plan, and interface plan, among other components.

PROGRAM MANAGEMENT PROFESSIONAL (PgMP^{SM})

(1) Professional certification awarded by the Project Management Institute to individuals who have met the established minimum requirements in knowledge, skills, experience, and application in the discipline of program management.

(2) Individual holding such certification.

PROGRAM MANAGER

(1) Individual typically responsible for a number of related projects aimed at achieving an overall business objective, each with its own project manager.

(2) In the U.S. DOD, the designated individual with responsibility for and the authority to accomplish program objectives for development, production, and sustainment to meet the user's operational needs. The program manager shall be accountable for credible cost, schedule, and performance reporting to the Milestone Decision Authority (MDA).

(3) As defined by the U.S. Federal Acquisition Institute, the person responsible for program plans, funding, schedules, and timely completion within cost limitations. Planning responsibilities include developing acquisition strategies and promoting full and open competition.

PROGRAM OFFICE

Organizational entity established to complete a number of projects that collectively satisfy a strategic or tactical organizational objective, usually headed by a program manager and staffed by professionals from various disciplines. When implementing a program office, it is not uncommon for the staff, including the project managers, to report directly to the program manager in a supervisor-employee relationship. However, not all organizations adopt this specific approach, opting instead for a matrix form of organization.

PROGRAM ORGANIZATIONAL STRUCTURE

Alignment of human resources and functions of the program organization, usually depicted on a chart or graph to show the relative hierarchy of personnel.

PROGRAM PERFORMANCE REVIEW (PPR)

Formal, structured review and analysis, usually conducted under the auspices of a steering committee or program governance board, to assess and determine the status of the program relative to its business objectives.

PROGRAM PROCUREMENT AUDIT

Procurement audit performed at the program level. *See also* procurement audit.

PROGRAM RISK

Any identified risk that will affect achievement of the program's business objectives. Such risk can include stakeholder issues, delivery of value, ensuring the availability of resources, and successfully executing the transition plan. Program risk tends to be found at the interproject level, as opposed to the risks inherent in individual projects.

PROGRAM SCOPE STATEMENT

Scope statement developed at the program level. *See also* scope statement.

PROGRAM SPECIFICATION

Description of the design logic in a software component, generally using pseudo-code.

PROGRAM TRANSITION PLAN

Plan that is executed in the closing phase of a program that contains such activities as—

- Initiating benefits realization measurement
- Releasing resources
- Acknowledging individual performance
- Performing administrative closure
- Obtaining stakeholders' acceptance of program results
- Transferring ongoing activities to the functional organization

PROGRAM WORK BREAKDOWN STRUCTURE (PWBS)

WBS structure that encompasses an entire program. It consists of at least three levels, with associated definitions, and is used by a program manager and contractors and suppliers if applicable to develop and extend a contract work breakdown structure (CWBS). It contains uniform terminology, definitions, and placement in the product-oriented family tree structure.

PROGRESS PAYMENTS

Interim payments for work done according to contract terms that may specify performance milestones or be tied to completion of a particular stage of the project or staying below certain cost targets.

PROGRESS REPORTING

Production of status reports that describe on a regular basis what the project team has accomplished.

PROGRESS TREND

Indication of whether the progress rate of a task or project is increasing, decreasing, or remaining the same during a specific period.

PROJECT

(1) Temporary undertaking to create a unique product or service. A project has a defined start and end point and specific objectives that, when attained, signify completion.

(2) In the U.S. DOD, synonymous with program in general usage; a planned undertaking having a finite beginning and ending, involving definition, development, production, and logistics support of a major weapon or weapon support system or systems. A project may be all of or part of a program.

PROJECT ACCOUNTING

Process of identifying, collecting, measuring, recording, and communicating actual project cost data.

PROJECT AND PROGRAM MANAGEMENT FOR ENTERPRISE INNOVATION

Publication of the Project Management Association of Japan (PMAJ) that describes best practices in project and program management. It is used as a foundation for PMAJ's professional certification system, which consists of three levels: Project Management Specialist (PMS), Project Management Registered (PMR), and Program Management Architect (PMA). *Also called* P2M.

PROJECT ARCHIVES

(1) Complete set of indexed project records.

(2) Any project-specific or historical databases containing information about a project or group of projects.

PROJECT AUDIT

Structured, formal review of a project, at any time in the project's life cycle, to assess progress performance relative to time, cost, and technical objectives; typically conducted by a third party.

PROJECT-BASED ORGANIZATION

Organization that derives its revenue, or accomplishes its mission, primarily from performing projects for others.

PROJECT BASELINE

Project management frame of reference established based on the detailed project plan and incorporating the project's cost, schedule, and quality objectives to provide a basis for measuring progress, comparing planned and actual events and expenditures, and identifying and executing changes to the project's scope of work.

PROJECT BREAKDOWN STRUCTURE (PBS)

Similar to the WBS but used in some application areas when the term WBS is incorrectly used to refer to a bill of materials.

PROJECT BUDGET

Amount and distribution of funds allocated to a project.

PROJECT BUSINESS CASE

Document containing the results and analysis of business assessments that provide the justification for pursuing a project opportunity.

PROJECT CALENDAR

Calendar identifying the specific work periods during the project life cycle when resources will be consumed.

PROJECT CHARTER

Document issued and signed by senior management that gives the project manager authority to apply organizational resources to project activities and formally recognizes the existence of a project. Includes a description of the business need the project was undertaken to address and a description of the product or service to be delivered by the project.

PROJECT CLOSEOUT

Process that provides for project acceptance by the project's sponsor, completion of various project records, final revision and issue of documentation to reflect the "as-built" condition, and retention of essential project documentation.

PROJECT COMMUNICATIONS MANAGEMENT

Processes needed to ensure proper collection, dissemination, storage, and disposition of project information to project stakeholders. Consists of communication planning, information distribution, performance reporting, and administrative closure.

PROJECT CONTROL

Any action taken by the project manager or team members with the intent of ensuring successful project completion. Usually based on the identification and collection of project performance information.

PROJECT CONTROL OFFICE

See project office.

PROJECT COORDINATOR

In some project organizational structures, an individual who reports to a higher-level manager in the organization (for example, at the CEO staff level), who has the authority to assign work to individuals in various functional organizations, and who shares authority and resources with functional managers. Considered a weak form of project management.

PROJECT COST BASELINE

See cost baseline.

PROJECT COST ESTIMATE

Sum total of all costs required to complete a project. In most organizations, the cost of maintaining and decommissioning the product or service created by the project is not included in this estimate. *See also* cost estimate.

PROJECT COST MANAGEMENT

Processes required to ensure that the project is completed within an approved budget. Consists of resource planning, cost estimating, cost budgeting, and cost control.

PROJECT COST SYSTEM

Cost accounting system that includes ledgers, asset records, liabilities, write-offs, taxes, depreciation expenses, raw materials, prepaid expenses, salaries, and so on for the project.

PROJECT DATA SHEET

In agile project management, a single-page description of project scope that is produced in the envision phase.

PROJECT DEFINITION

Process of thoroughly exploring all aspects of a proposed project, particularly the relationship between required performance, development time, and cost. The areas of technical uncertainty are examined, and possible tradeoffs are evolved in order to achieve a satisfactory balance between performance, development time, and cost.

PROJECT DEFINITION WORKSHEET

Generic name used to identify any number of tools or templates that capture important project information to ensure that the project team addresses, and agrees upon, key project elements. Such elements include background and summary, goals and key deliverables, milestones, assumptions, risks, cost estimates, legal issues, and other relevant information.

PROJECT DURATION

Elapsed time from project start date to project finish date.

PROJECT ENVIRONMENT

(1) Combined internal and external forces, both individual and collective, that assist or restrict attainment of the project objectives. These forces may be either business or project related, or may be a result of political, economic, technological, or regulatory conditions.

(2) Circumstances, objects, or conditions by which project team members are surrounded.

(3) Everything outside the project that delivers input or receives output from the project.

(4) Cultural, political, financial, moral, and ethical characteristics that affect how projects are completed.

PROJECT EVALUATION

Periodic examination of a project to determine whether the objectives are being met. Conducted at regular intervals, such as at the beginning or end of a major phase. May result in redirection of the project and decisions to change the scope, time, or cost baselines, for example, or to terminate the project. *See also* control gate.

PROJECT EXECUTION

See development phase.

PROJECT EXPEDITOR

In some project organizational structures, an individual who is a staff assistant to an executive who has the ultimate responsibility for the project. The project expeditor assumes the day-to-day responsibilities of the project manager and has authority over resources within his or her executive's department but not over resources from other departments.

PROJECT FINISH DATE

Latest calendar finish date of all activities on the project, based on network or resource allocation process calculations.

PROJECT HUMAN RESOURCE MANAGEMENT

Processes necessary to ensure effective use of the people involved with the project; consists of organizational planning, staff acquisition, and team development.

PROJECT INITIATION

See initiation.

PROJECT INTEGRATION

Process of bringing together diverse organizations, groups, parts, or activities to form a cohesive whole to successfully achieve project objectives.

PROJECT INTEGRATION MANAGEMENT

Processes necessary to ensure that the various project elements are coordinated effectively. Consists of project plan development, project plan execution, and overall change control.

PROJECT INVESTMENT COST

Aggregation of all the project cost elements (capital and operating) as defined by an agreed-upon scope of work.

PROJECTION

Estimate of future performance based on the review of historical information, present situation, and future outlook.

PROJECTITIS

Inappropriately intense loyalty to the project. Sometimes called "navel gazing."

PROJECTIZED ORGANIZATION

Organizational structure in which resources are assigned full time to the project manager, who has complete authority to assign priorities and direct the work of people on the project.

PROJECT JUSTIFICATION

Business need or purpose for which the project was undertaken; can be used to provide a basis for evaluating future investment trade-offs.

PROJECT LEADER

(1) Term generally synonymous with "project manager" but used more widely in Europe than elsewhere.

(2) Term preferred over "project manager" by some organizations because it more accurately reflects the leadership skills, in addition to the management competencies, required of the person in charge of a project.

PROJECT LIFE CYCLE

Collection of generally sequential project phases whose specific names and numbers are determined by the organization(s) involved in the project. Generally includes the major steps involved in conceptualizing, initiating, designing, developing, executing, and closing of the project's deliverables. It does not include maintenance and operations of the product of the project.

PROJECT LIFE-CYCLE COST

Sum total of all costs associated with the initiation, design, development, execution, and closeout of a project.

PROJECT MANAGEMENT (PM)

Application of knowledge, skills, tools, and techniques to project activities to meet or exceed stakeholder needs and expectations from a project.

PROJECT MANAGEMENT BODY OF KNOWLEDGE

Totality of knowledge within the project management discipline. As in other professions such as law, medicine, and accounting, the body of knowledge rests with the practitioners and academics involved in its application and advancement. The complete project management body of knowledge includes practices that have been widely applied and proven, as well as innovative and advanced practices with more limited use and application. *See also PMBOK® Guide.*

PROJECT MANAGEMENT CONTROLS

Processes or procedures designed to ensure that project performance information is collected, analyzed, and reviewed by appropriate stakeholders and used to decide any course of action to achieve the project's objectives. Examples include time tracking, scope change requests, and control gates.

PROJECT MANAGEMENT INFORMATION SYSTEM (PMIS)

(1) Systems, activities, and data that allow information flow in a project; frequently automated.

(2) Tools and techniques used to gather, integrate, and distribute output of the other project management processes.

PROJECT MANAGEMENT INSTITUTE (PMI®), INC.

International, nonprofit professional association dedicated to advancing the discipline of project management and state-of-the-art project management practices. *See also* Project Management Professional *and* Program Management Professional.

PROJECT MANAGEMENT METHODOLOGY

Highly detailed description of the procedures to be followed in a project life cycle. Often includes forms, charts, checklists, and templates to ensure structure and consistency.

PROJECT MANAGEMENT OFFICE (PMO)

Organizational entity established to assist project managers throughout the organization in implementing project management principles, practices, methodologies, tools, and techniques. In most implementations, the project management office is a support function and is not responsible for project execution. Its main objective is implementing effective project management practices throughout the organization. *Also called* center of excellence *or* center of expertise.

PROJECT MANAGEMENT PORTAL

Web site, usually developed for commercial gain, that provides services, information, and references on project management. *See also* portal.

PROJECT MANAGEMENT PROCESSES

Series of actions that describe and organize the work of a project.

PROJECT MANAGEMENT PROFESSIONAL (PMP®)

(1) Professional certification awarded by the Project Management Institute to individuals who have met the established minimum requirements in knowledge, education, and experience in the discipline of project management.

(2) Individual holding such certification.

PROJECT MANAGEMENT SOFTWARE

Specific computer applications designed to aid in planning and controlling project costs and schedules.

PROJECT MANAGEMENT TEAM

Members of the project team who are involved directly in project management activities.

PROJECT MANAGER

Individual responsible for managing the overall project and its deliverables. Acts as the customer's single point of contact for the project. Controls planning and execution of the project's activities and resources to ensure that established cost, time, and quality goals are met.

PROJECT METRICS

Measurable criteria that indicate the overall status or performance of a project or project management practice. Can be technical, administrative, or managerial in nature; data are collected regularly. Viewed by the organization as being necessary to gauge performance and make adjustments to processes and procedures. May include schedule performance, cost data, defect levels, customer satisfaction, employee morale, time-to-market performance, and so on.

PROJECT NETWORK DIAGRAM

Graphical depiction of the logical relationships between and among project activities.

PROJECT OBJECTIVES

(1) Identified, expected results and benefits involved in successfully completing a project.

(2) Quantifiable criteria that must be met for a project to be considered successful.

(3) Project scope expressed in terms of output, required resources, and schedule.

PROJECT OFFICE

Organizational entity established to complete a specific project or series of projects, usually headed by a project manager.

PROJECT ORGANIZATION

Structure or arrangement of project participants.

PROJECT PERSONNEL

Members of the project team directly employed on a project.

PROJECT PHASE

Collection of logically related project activities, usually resulting in the completion of a major deliverable. Collectively, the project phases compose the project life cycle.

PROJECT PLAN

Formal, approved document, in summarized or detailed form, used to guide both project execution and control. Documents planning assumptions and decisions, facilitates communication among stakeholders, and documents approved scope, cost, and schedule baselines.

PROJECT PLAN DEVELOPMENT

Compilation of the results of all the other planning processes into a consistent, complete document.

PROJECT PLAN EXECUTION

Completion of the project plan by performing the activities described therein.

PROJECT PLANNING

(1) Developing and maintaining the project plan; identifying the project objectives, activities needed to complete the project, and resources and quantities required to carry out each activity or task within the project.

(2) Approach to determine how to begin, sustain, and end a project.

PROJECT POLITICS

Actions taken by a project manager or other stakeholder to cause a group of people with different interests to work toward a common goal.

PROJECT PORTFOLIO

Collection of projects that fall under a single management umbrella. Each project may be related to or independent of another but the collection as a whole is aimed at achieving one or more organizational objectives. *See also* portfolio management.

PROJECT PORTFOLIO MANAGEMENT (PPM)

See portfolio management.

PROJECT PROCUREMENT MANAGEMENT

Part of project management that includes the processes required to acquire supplies and services from outside the performing organization. Consists of procurement planning, solicitation planning, solicitation, source selection, contract administration, and contract closeout.

PROJECT PROFIT BASELINE

Amount planned for in the project plan that will be realized once project costs (direct and indirect) are deducted from project revenue or price. Often used in expected value calculations to estimate best case, worst case, and most likely project outcomes.

PROJECT/PROGRAM MANAGEMENT PROCESS GROUPS

Five processes identified by the Project Management Institute that accomplish the function of project and program management. They include initiating, planning, executing, monitoring and controlling, and closing processes.

PROJECT QUALITY MANAGEMENT

Processes required to ensure that the project will satisfy its objectives and requirements. Includes quality planning, quality assurance, and quality control.

PROJECT QUALITY SYSTEM

Organizational structure, responsibilities, procedures, processes, and resources needed to effect project quality management.

PROJECT RECORDS

Collection of correspondence, reports, memoranda, and documents describing the project or related to it. May be in hardcopy or electronic form.

PROJECT RECOVERY

Process of identifying, executing, monitoring, and controlling specific actions or alternatives to reduce or eliminate the significant variances relative to project time, cost, and technical performance.

PROJECT REPORTING

Communicating information about project status and progress.

PROJECT REQUIREMENTS

See functional requirements *and* technical requirements.

PROJECT RESOURCES

See resources.

PROJECT REVIEW(S)

Periodic monitoring of project activities and tasks by an objective third party to ascertain its status and uncover any performance issues. Conducted based on a set schedule or at the completion of a major phase.

PROJECT RISK

(1) Cumulative effect of the probability of uncertain occurrences that may positively or negatively affect project objectives.

(2) Degree of exposure to negative events and their probable consequences (opposite of opportunity). Characterized by three factors: risk event, risk probability, and the amount at stake.

PROJECT RISK MANAGEMENT

Processes involved with identifying, analyzing, and responding to project risk; consists of risk identification, risk quantification, risk response development, and risk response control.

PROJECT RISK MANAGER

Person on the project team responsible for preparing and tracking a risk management plan and for integrating risk management issues into project planning and execution.

PROJECT SCHEDULE

Planned dates to perform activities and meet milestones.

PROJECT SCOPE

All the work required to deliver a project's product or service with the specified features and functions.

PROJECT SCOPE MANAGEMENT

Processes required to ensure that the project includes all the work required, and only the work required, to successfully complete the project; consists of initiation, scope planning, scope definition, scope verification, and scope change control.

PROJECT SEGMENTS

Subdivisions of the project delineated as manageable components.

PROJECT SELECTION METHODS

Techniques, practices, or procedures used to select a project or group of projects that best supports the organization's objectives. Divided into two broad categories: (1) benefit measurement methods—comparative approaches, scoring models, benefit contribution assessments, and economic models—and (2) constrained optimization methods—mathematical models using linear, nonlinear, dynamic, integer, and multiobjective programming algorithms.

PROJECT SERVICES

Expertise or labor needed to implement a project that is not available within the project manager's organization.

PROJECTS IN CONTROLLED ENVIRONMENTS (VERSION 2) (PRINCE 2)

Project management method covering the organization, management, and control of projects. First developed in 1989 by the Central Computer and Telecommunications Agency as a United Kingdom government standard for information technology project management. More general than the original method in that it focuses on a generic, best-practices approach to project management.

PROJECT SPONSOR

Person in an organization whose support and approval are required for a project to start and continue. The Software Engineering Institute (SEI) project sponsors can be divided into two categories: authorizing and reinforcing. The authorizing sponsor is generally a single individual who can commit all resources required to implement the project successfully, and can enforce the behavioral changes necessary. Reinforcing sponsors are often other managers whose support is required for successful implementation of the project.

PROJECT STAKEHOLDER

See stakeholder.

PROJECT STRATEGY

Plan with policies to provide general direction on how resources will be used to accomplish project goals and objectives.

PROJECT SUMMARY WBS

Special-purpose WBS that displays only the higher levels of the project WBS; used primarily for reporting to senior management or the customer.

PROJECT TEAM

Group of people with complementary skills, a common purpose, shared goals, and mutual accountability who share responsibility for accomplishing project goals and who report to the project manager.

PROJECT TEAM ROLES

Identified authority, accountability, and responsibility of project team members individually and as a whole.

PROJECT TERMINATION

See project closeout.

PROJECT TIME MANAGEMENT

Processes required to ensure that the project is completed on time; consists of activity definition, activity sequencing, activity duration estimating, schedule development, and schedule control.

PROJECT WBS

See work breakdown structure.

PROMOTIONAL MANAGEMENT STYLE

Management approach in which the project manager encourages team members to realize their full potential, cultivates team spirit, and lets team members know that good work will be rewarded.

PROOF OF CONCEPT

Collecting evidence to support acceptance of a proposed solution, usually through experimentation or a pilot. *See also* pilot.

PROPOSAL

(1) Procurement document prepared by a contractor to describe the contractor's ability and willingness to provide the requested product according to the requirements of the relevant solicitation document.

(2) Offer submitted by a contractor to enter into a contract, contract modification, or termination settlement. *See also* bid and quotation.

PROPOSAL EVALUATION TECHNIQUE

Method for selecting sellers that uses expert judgment to rate multiple bids or proposals against predetermined evaluation criteria.

PROPOSAL PROJECT PLAN

Plan issued early in a project that may be part of the contractor's proposal and contains key analysis, procurement, and implementation milestones; historical data; and any client-supplied information. Sometimes presented in bar or Gantt chart form or as a summary-level network, supported with narrative explanations and used for inquiry and contract negotiations.

PROTEST

(1) Written objection, submitted by an interested party, to a solicitation for offers or to the award or proposed award of a contract.

(2) In U.S. federal procurement, a concern over the award of a contract, submitted to the Government Accountability Office (GAO) or Procuring Contracting Office (PCO).

PROTOTYPE

Small or full-scale, and usually functioning, form of a newly developed product that is used to evaluate the product design.

PROVISION

Written term or condition used only in solicitations and applying before contract award; distinguished from clauses, which are terms and conditions in contracts.

PSYCHOGRAPHICS

Characteristics of consumers used for marketing purposes that, in addition to standard demographic data, include their lifestyles, opinions, interests, and attitudes.

PUBLIC-PRIVATE PARTNERSHIP

Contractual arrangement, sometimes referred to as a joint venture, between public- and private-sector partners. Can include a variety of activities that involve the private sector in the development, financing, ownership, and operation of a public facility or service. Typically includes infrastructure projects or facilities. In such a partnership, public and private resources are pooled and responsibilities divided so that the partners' efforts complement one another. Typically, each partner shares in income resulting from the partnership in direct proportion to the partner's investment. Such a venture, although a contractual arrangement, differs from typical service contracting in that the private-sector partner usually makes a substantial cash, at-risk, equity investment in the project, and the public sector gains access to new revenue or new delivery capacity without having to pay the private-sector partner.

PUBLIC RELATIONS

Activity designed to improve the environment in which a project organization operates with the aim of promoting the goals and objectives of the project to its stakeholders.

PULL SYSTEM

Resource flow in a production or manufacturing process in which only what has been consumed is replaced.

PUNCH LIST

Enumeration of the work remaining to fulfill the project scope.

PUNITIVE DAMAGES

Monetary compensation, over and above actual damages, sought by a buyer to punish a seller for nonperformance or other wrongful acts.

PURCHASE

Acquisition of items, mostly off-the-shelf or catalog, manufactured outside the purchaser's premises.

PURCHASE DESCRIPTION

Description of the essential physical characteristics and functions necessary to meet requirements.

PURCHASE ORDER

(1) Offer to buy certain supplies, services, or construction from sources based on specified terms and conditions.

(2) In U.S. federal procurement, an offer by the government to buy supplies or services, including construction and research and development, upon specified terms and conditions, using simplified acquisition procedures.

PURE RISK

See insurable risk.

PURSE-STRING AUTHORITY

Influence based on the amount of control an individual has over the money used to carry out the project.

PV

See planned value.

PWBS

See program work breakdown structure.

PYRRHIC VICTORY

Victory gained at too high a cost.

Q

QA

See quality assurance.

QAR

See quality assurance representative.

QBL

See qualified bidders list.

QC

See quality control.

QFD

See quality function deployment.

QML

See qualified manufacturers list.

QPL

See qualified products list.

QUALIFIED BIDDERS LIST (QBL)

List of contractors who have had their products examined and tested and who have satisfied all applicable qualification requirements for the product or have otherwise satisfied all applicable qualification requirements.

QUALIFIED MANUFACTURERS LIST (QML)

List of manufacturers who have had their products examined and tested and who have satisfied all applicable qualification requirements for the product.

QUALIFIED PRODUCT

Product examined, tested, and qualified for inclusion on an applicable qualified products list.

QUALIFIED PRODUCTS LIST (QPL)

List of products that the buyer has determined will satisfy project requirements, with accompanying names and addresses of the manufacturers or distributors and appropriate product identification and test reference data.

QUALIFIED SELLERS LIST

List or files of prospective contractors, including information on their relevant experience and other characteristics.

QUALITATIVE RISK ASSESSMENT

Nonnumeric description of a risk (such as high, medium, low), including the likelihood that it will occur, its impact, the methods for containing the impact, possible fallback or recovery measures, and ownership data.

QUALITY

(1) Total characteristics of an entity or item that affect its ability to satisfy stated or implied needs.

(2) Conformance to requirements or specifications.

(3) Fitness for use.

QUALITY ASSURANCE (QA)

(1) Process of regularly evaluating overall project performance to instill confidence that the project will satisfy relevant quality standards.

(2) Organizational unit responsible for quality assurance efforts.

QUALITY ASSURANCE PLAN

Detailed plan setting forth the process, procedures, checklists, methods, and techniques to be used on a project to ensure that quality requirements are met.

QUALITY ASSURANCE REPRESENTATIVE (QAR)

In U.S. federal procurement, an individual, located at a contractor's facility, who is responsible for the government's procurement quality assurance function. In executing that responsibility, the individual must determine whether the contractor has satisfied its contract obligations pertaining to item quality and quantity.

QUALITY AUDIT

Structured review of quality management activities to identify lessons learned and improve the performance of the project or other projects within the organization.

QUALITY-BY-DESIGN

Process used to design quality into a product or service at the outset. This reduces operations, maintenance, and warranty costs once the product is launched and put into use by the customer.

QUALITY CIRCLES

Small groups of employees that meet regularly to improve the process, product, or service of their organization. Key characteristic: they do not include any management representatives.

QUALITY CONFORMANCE INSPECTION

Examinations and tests performed on items or services to determine conformance with specified requirements.

QUALITY CONTROL (QC)

(1) Monitoring of specific project results to determine whether they comply with relevant quality standards and identification of ways to eliminate causes of unsatisfactory performance.

(2) Organizational unit with responsibility for quality control efforts.

QUALITY CONTROL MEASUREMENTS

Results of quality control testing and measures presented in a form for comparison and analysis.

QUALITY COUNCIL

Group of individuals, typically consisting of senior managers, that is responsible for coordinating the quality program in an organization.

QUALITY EVALUATION

Technical process of gathering measured variables or counted data for decision making in a quality process review.

QUALITY FUNCTION DEPLOYMENT (QFD)

Process used to provide better product definition and product development and to help a design team define, design, manufacture, and deliver a product or service that meets or exceeds customer needs. Strives to ensure that the customer's definition of product or service specifications is used, work is performed by strong cross-functional teams, and the major phases of product development are linked.

QUALITY GATE

Predefined completion criteria for a task, including audits, walk-throughs, and inspections, that provide an assessment of progress, processes used, and project products to be delivered.

QUALITY IMPROVEMENT

(1) Systematic approach to reduce or eliminate waste, rework, and losses in the production, process, or delivery of services.

(2) Action taken to increase the effectiveness and efficiency of the project to provide added benefits to project stakeholders.

QUALITY LOOP

Conceptual model of interacting activities that influence the quality of a product or service in various stages, ranging from needs identification to assessment of whether the needs have been satisfied. *Also called* quality spiral.

QUALITY MANAGEMENT

(1) Planning, organizing, staffing, and directing management activities with the objective of achieving the required quality.

(2) Overall management function involved in determining and implementing quality policy.

QUALITY MANAGEMENT PLAN

Document that describes how the project management team will implement its quality policy. The quality management plan becomes part of the overall project plan and incorporates quality control, quality assurance, and project quality improvement procedures.

QUALITY OF CONFORMANCE

Effectiveness of the design and manufacturing functions in executing the product manufacturing requirements and process specification.

QUALITY OF DESIGN

Effectiveness of the design process in capturing the operational requirements and translating them into detailed design requirements that can be manufactured or coded in a consistent manner.

QUALITY OF EARNINGS

Increased earnings due to increased sales and cost controls, in contrast with artificial profits created by favorable currency conversion or inflation of inventory.

QUALITY PATH

Activities that are most important to the project's quality.

QUALITY PHILOSOPHY

Established quality policies and procedures that are used to guide work throughout the organization and serve as the basis for performing project work.

QUALITY PLANNING

Identifying the specific quality standards that are relevant to the project and determining how to satisfy them.

QUALITY POLICY

Overall intentions and directions of the organization concerning quality, as formally expressed by top management.

QUALITY PREDICTOR

Measure for estimating the likelihood of conforming to specifications in the production of a product or delivery of a service.

QUALITY PROCESS REVIEW

Technical process of using data to determine how the actual project results compare with the quality specifications or requirements. If deviations occur, the review may result in changes in the project design, development, use, and so on, depending on the decisions of the client, involved stakeholders, and project team.

QUALITY PROCRASTINATION

Deferring, delaying, or postponing quality improvement decisions, actions, and programs to the last moment, and thereby placing the organization under time pressure to make needed changes.

QUALITY PRODUCT

Product that meets or exceeds the customer's expectations.

QUALITY PROGRAM

Program designed to maintain the quality of material and services, from concept through technology and system development, production, deployment, and disposal.

QUALITY RISK

Failure to complete tasks to the required level of technical or quality performance.

QUALITY SPIRAL

See quality loop.

QUALITY SURVEILLANCE

Ongoing monitoring and verification of the status of procedures, methods, conditions, processes, products, and services and the analysis of records related to stated requirements to ensure that quality requirements are being met.

QUALITY SYSTEM

(1) Organizational structure, responsibilities, procedures, processes, and resources used to implement quality management.

(2) Procedures, processes, people, management, tools, and facilities involved in ensuring that quality is built into a product or service.

QUALITY SYSTEM REVIEW

Formal evaluation by top management of the status and adequacy of the quality system in relation to the organization's quality policy and other relevant objectives.

QUANTITATIVE RISK ASSESSMENT

Numeric analysis of risk estimates, including probability of occurrence and quantification of impact, in order to forecast the project's schedule and costs and determine likely outcomes.

QUICK RESPONSE

Practice in supply chain management used by retailers and manufacturers where near-real-time-signals trigger replenishment responses, thereby improving inventory turnover and product allocation and helping retailers avoid running out of important stock.

QUID PRO QUO

Something given in return for being given something of equivalent value. In business, it typically takes the form of favors rather than an exchange of items.

QUORUM

Minimum number of officers and members of a committee or organization, usually a majority, who must be present for the valid transaction of business.

QUOTATION

In U.S. federal procurement, a document generally used when the award decision will be price-driven; does not constitute a binding offer. *See also* bid and proposal.

QUOTE

Statement of current price.

QUOTER

Person who has submitted a quote.

R

RACI MATRIX

Tool used to identify the various stakeholders in a project, or operating process, and their roles in it. The matrix divides project or process tasks into four responsibility types, which are then assigned to the different roles. RACI stands for—

• Responsible—Those who actually perform the task

• Accountable—The person(s) ultimately in charge of ensuring the task is completed correctly

• Consulted—Those whose opinions will be solicited

• Informed—Those stakeholders who need to be kept apprised of project developments

RAD

See rapid application development.

RADAR CHART

In quality management, a graphical display of the differences between actual and ideal performance. It aids in identifying strengths and weaknesses and determining actual performance.

RAINMAKER

Individual who brings in a significant amount of new business to a company because of his or her skills, connections, and reputation.

RAM

See responsibility assignment matrix.

RAMP UP

Process of increasing performance, as with an activity or production.

RANDOM CAUSE

Indeterminable reason that precipitates a special event, that is, one that is outside the control limits.

RANDOM SAMPLING

Sampling method in which each unit of the population has an equal chance of being selected.

RANGE

Difference between the largest and smallest values in a set of numbers.

RANGE ESTIMATING

Applying probabilistic modeling to cost estimates as an adjunct to traditional estimating, not as a substitute for it. Includes identifying the mathematical probability of a cost overrun, the amount of financial exposure, risks and opportunities ranked according to bottom-line importance, and the contingency required for a given level of confidence. Can also be used in schedule estimating. In its simplest form it is providing an estimate that has two numbers: the lowest amount and the highest amount (for example, $50,000 to $100,000).

RAPID APPLICATION DEVELOPMENT (RAD)

Process used in software development where the requirements definition and design phases are iteratively conducted; in this process, a rough set of requirements is used to create an initial version of the system, giving users an idea of the look, feel, and capabilities of the system. User evaluation and feedback provide the basis for revisions to the requirements, and the process is repeated until the requirements are considered to be complete. As the name indicates, its objective is to rapidly produce an application for the user with a high degree of accuracy.

RAPID PROTOTYPING

Building a sample product from preliminary system requirements and showing the customer the prototype of the deliverable to obtain his or her reactions and input. *See also* application prototyping.

RATE COST

Mathematical way of explaining and measuring the impact of changing production rates on a program's total cost.

RATE OF RETURN

Amount of gain or loss for a security in a particular period; consists of income plus capital gains relative to investment, usually quoted as a percentage.

RATES

Prices charged for goods and services. May include rate schedules, riders, rules, terms and conditions of service, and other tariff and service charges.

RATING FACTOR

Percentage of skill, effort, and method displayed by an operator during the period of the study, with 100 percent representing normal skill and effort.

RATIONAL UNIFIED PROCESS (RUP)

Iterative, adaptable software development process created by the Rational Software Corporation, which was acquired by the IBM Corporation in 2002. It includes a hyperlinked knowledge base with sample artifacts and detailed descriptions of many different types of software development and business analysis activities. RUP is a part of the IBM Rational Method Composer (RMC) product and is highly customizable. Designed from the start to include both a generic, public domain process, known as the Unified Process, and a more detailed specification known as the Rational Unified Process, which is marketed as a commercial product. The product is marketed as providing proven best practices for software and systems delivery and implementation of effective project management.

RAYLEIGH CURVE

Roughly bell-shaped curve that represents the buildup and decline of staff power, effort, or cost followed by a long trail representing staff power, effort, or cost devoted to enhancement or maintenance of software application.

RBS

See resource breakdown structure.

RBWA

See routing by walking about.

RDU

See remaining duration.

REAL DOLLAR VALUES

See constant dollar values.

REAL INTEREST RATE

Interest rate that has been adjusted to remove the effect of expected or actual inflation. Real interest rates can be approximated by subtracting the expected or actual inflation rate from a nominal interest rate.

REALIZATION FACTOR

Measure of overall performance used in a work measurement system. It is calculated by dividing the actual time to perform the work by the standard time.

REALIZATION GAP

Time interval between when a need is perceived by a user and the fulfillment of that need by a new product or service, or both.

REAL PROPERTY

Land and whatever is erected on it, growing on it, or affixed to it.

REAL TIME

(1) Pertains to a system or mode of software operation in which computation must be performed during the actual time that an external process occurs, in order to allow computational results to respond to external processes.

(2) Describes an immediate response to an outside stimulus.

REASONABLE CERTAINTY

Degree of certainty about something that a reasonable person would find sufficient in order to accept a conclusion or statement of fact about it.

REASONABLENESS OF COST

(1) When the cost of an item or service does not exceed that which would be incurred by someone conducting a competitive business.

(2) Element in the determination of whether a cost is allowable.

REASONABLE PERSON

Hypothetical person who exercises qualities of attention, knowledge, intelligence, and judgment that society requires of its members for the protection of their interest and the interest of others.

REASONABLE PRICE

Business decision reached jointly by a buyer and seller, a product of judgment influenced by bargaining strength and economic realities dictated by the marketplace.

REBASELINING

Establishing a new project baseline because of sweeping or significant changes in the scope of a project. Must be approved by all parties.

RECORD RETENTION

Period of time that records are kept for reference after contract or project closeout.

RECORDS

Includes books, documents, accounting procedures and practices, and other data, regardless of type and regardless of whether such items are in written form, in the form of computer data, or in any other form.

RECORDS DISPOSITION SCHEDULE

Schedule of when certain records that are no longer needed for the conduct of the regular business of an organization are disposed of, retired, or preserved.

RECORDS MANAGEMENT

Procedures established by an organization to identify, index, archive, and distribute all documentation associated with a project.

RECOVERABILITY

Ability of a software system to continue operating despite the presence of errors.

RECOVERY

(1) Act of correcting problems on a current project to improve its chances of success.

(2) Restoration of computing data after a system failure.

RECOVERY SCHEDULE

Special schedule showing efforts taken to recover time lost on a project.

RECRUITMENT PRACTICES

Policies, guidelines, or procedures concerning the initial assignment of staff.

RECURRING COST

Production cost, such as labor and materials, that varies with the quantity produced, as distinguished from nonrecurring cost. *See also* nonrecurring cost.

RED HERRING

Something that is used in order to divert attention from the real issue.

RED TEAM

Independent, peer-level review team usually used to provide feedback on proposals but useful for any documentation and presentation material.

REDUCED INSPECTION

Inspection under a sampling plan using the same quality level as that in a normal inspection but requiring a smaller sample.

REENGINEERING

Radical redesign of a business process to achieve dramatic improvements in productivity, cycle times, and quality.

REFERENCE BASE

Source of detailed cost information within a function or organization from which estimates and budgets may, in part, be established for work related to that function. For example, a piecemeal reference base of $10 per widget may be used to establish a $10,000 apportioned cost account budget for an activity to develop 1,000 widgets.

REFERENT AUTHORITY

Influence based on an individual's referring to a higher power as supporting his or her position or recommendation. ("The boss and I think this is a good idea.")

REFINEMENT

Rework, redefinition, or modification of the logic or data that already may have been developed as part of the project planning process to more accurately describe milestones, constraints, and priorities.

RegPM

Competency-based project management certification program developed by the Australian Institute of Project Management and consisting of three levels: Qualified Project Practitioner (QPP), Registered Project Manager (RPM), and Master Project Director (MPD). Launched in April 1997, it is based on the Australian National Competency Standards for Project Management. RegPM means Registered Project Manager.

REGRESSION ANALYSIS

Statistical technique used to establish and graphically depict the relationship of a dependent variable to one or more independent variables.

REGRESSION TEST

In software maintenance, the rerunning of test cases that previously executed correctly in order to detect errors introduced by the maintenance activity.

REGULATION

Written description of product, process, or service characteristics and what is needed to comply with applicable administrative provisions.

REIMBURSEMENT

Payment to a seller, employee, or other party for incurred expenses in project performance or any aspect of work associated with an organization.

REINSURANCE

Transaction that provides that a surety, for a consideration, agrees to indemnify another surety against loss that the latter may sustain under a bond it has issued.

REJECTION NUMBER

Minimum number of defects or defective units in a sample that will cause rejection of the entire lot represented by the sample.

RELEASE

(1) Configuration management activity wherein a specific version of software is made available for use.

(2) Agreement by a contracting party that the other party will not be liable for any future claims.

RELEASE (OF) CLAIMS

Certificate that releases and holds the buyer harmless from any future claims by the contractor.

RELIABILITY

Ability of an item to perform a required function under stated conditions for a stated period of time.

RELIABILITY ASSURANCE

Actions necessary to provide adequate confidence that the material conforms to established reliability requirements.

REMAINING AVAILABLE RESOURCES

Difference between the resource availability pool and scheduled resource requirements. Computed during the resource allocation process.

REMAINING DURATION (RDU)

Time required to complete an activity.

REMAINING FLOAT (RF)

Difference between the early finish date and the late finish date.

REMEDY

Right of a contracting party when the other party does not fulfill its contractual obligations.

REMUNERATION

Payment for goods or services or to recompense for losses. For example, a paycheck is remuneration for work.

REPATRIATION

Movement of the financial assets or profits of a company or an individual from a foreign country to the home country.

REPORTING

Communicating information regarding project status and progress.

REPRESENTATIVE SAMPLE

Sample in which the number of units selected in proportion to the size of sublots, subbatches, or parts of the lot or batch is identified by some rational criterion and selected at random.

REQUEST FOR PROPOSALS (RFP)

Type of bid document used to solicit proposals from prospective contractors for products or services. Used when items or services are of a complex nature; it assumes that negotiation will take place between the buyer and the contractor. *See also* tender.

REQUEST FOR QUOTATIONS (RFQ)

Similar to request for proposals but generally with a lower monetary amount involved in the procurement. Used to solicit proposals from prospective contractors for standard products or services without going through negotiation.

REQUEST FOR TECHNICAL PROPOSALS (RTP)

In U.S. federal procurement, a solicitation document used in two-step sealed bid. Normally in letter form, it asks only for technical information, not cost or pricing data.

REQUIRED OPERATIONAL CHARACTERISTICS

System parameters that are primary indicators of the system's ability to perform the required project functions and to be supported.

REQUIREMENT

(1) Capability needed by a user.

(2) Condition or capability that a project must meet or possess.

(3) In information technology, a system or system component that satisfies a contract, standard, specification, user, or stakeholder.

REQUIREMENTS ANALYSIS

Process of evaluating the customer's stated needs and validating them against specific organizational requirements and plans.

REQUIREMENTS ANALYSIS PHASE

Period of time in the systems development life cycle during which the requirements for a software product are formally defined, documented, and analyzed.

REQUIREMENTS ELICITATION

Systematic analysis, gathering, and documentation of the requirements that a project or solution must satisfy.

REQUIREMENTS MANAGEMENT

Process, tools, and techniques used by an organization to describe successfully and accurately what the project will produce and to document the results.

REQUIREMENTS SCRUB

In U.S. federal procurement, a review of user or government comments received in response to the announcement of an operational requirement. The scrub is used to validate and prioritize suggested or requested system functions and capabilities before release to industry.

REQUIREMENTS TRACEABILITY

Process of understanding, documenting, approving, and auditing the relationships between a system's components and functions and the requirements for which the system was developed. Each function and component of a system should be directly traceable to a requirement identified by a user, client, customer, or stakeholder.

REQUIREMENTS TRACEABILITY MATRIX

Tool that helps track functional requirements and their implementation through the development process.

REQUIREMENTS WORK PLAN (RWP)

Miniproject plan focusing solely on the scope, cost, and schedule of the analysis phase (requirements elicitation) of the project that is created by the business analyst. The RWP may become a component of the overall project plan.

RESCHEDULE

Change the logic, duration, or dates of an existing schedule because of corrective actions or externally imposed conditions.

RESCISSION

Release of a party from all obligations under a contract.

RESERVE

Money or time provided for in the project plan to mitigate cost, schedule, or performance risk. *See also* management reserve *and* contingency reserve.

RESIDUAL VALUE

Value of a fixed asset after depreciation charges have been subtracted from its original cost.

RESOURCE

(1) In management, the time, staff, and money available to perform a service or build a product.

(2) Asset required for a process step to be performed.

RESOURCE ALLOCATION

Process of assigning resources to the activities in a network while recognizing any resource constraints and requirements; adjusting activity start and finish dates to conform to resource availability and use.

RESOURCE AVAILABILITY DATE

Calendar date when a given resource or resource pool becomes available.

RESOURCE AVAILABILITY POOL

Number of resources available for a given allocation period.

RESOURCE BREAKDOWN STRUCTURE (RBS)

Variation of the organizational breakdown structure used to show which work elements are assigned to individuals.

RESOURCE CALENDAR

Calendar denoting when a resource or resource pool is available for work on a project.

RESOURCE CODE

Method used to identify a given resource type.

RESOURCE CONFLICT

Situation that arises because of the allocation of one resource to more than one task.

RESOURCE-CONSTRAINED SCHEDULING

Special case of resource leveling where the start and finish dates of each activity are calculated based on the availability of a fixed quantity of resources.

RESOURCE DESCRIPTION

Actual name or way to identify a resource code.

RESOURCE GANTT CHART

Variation of the horizontal bar Gantt chart used to show how resources are allocated over time, task by task, and how the resources will be distributed throughout the life of the project. Used to track and plan resource allocations and to identify when resources are overallocated.

RESOURCE HISTOGRAM

Vertical bar chart used to show resource consumption by time period. *Also called* resource loading chart.

RESOURCE LEVELING

(1) Practicing a form of network analysis in which scheduling decisions (start and finish dates) are driven by resource management issues such as limited resource availability or changes in resource levels.

(2) Leveling out the peaks and valleys of resource requirements so that a fixed amount of resources can be used over time.

(3) Ensuring that a resource is maximized but not used beyond its limitations.

RESOURCE-LIMITED PLANNING

Planning activities so that predetermined resource availability levels are not exceeded. Activities begin as soon as resources are available (subject to network logic constraints) as required by the activity.

RESOURCE-LIMITED SCHEDULE

Project schedule whose start and end dates for each activity have been established on the availability of a fixed and finite set of human and material resources.

RESOURCE LOADING
Designating the amount and type of resources to be assigned to a specific activity in a certain time period.

RESOURCE LOADING CHART
See resource histogram.

RESOURCE MANAGER
Person responsible for obtaining and controlling resources for an organization. They collaborate with project managers to assign individual resources to projects in order to accomplish the project's work. Typical duties include recruiting, training, and administrative management.

RESOURCE MATRIX
Structure used to allocate types of resources to tasks by listing the tasks in the WBS along the vertical axis and the resources required along the horizontal axis. Differs from a responsibility assignment matrix in that assignments of specific individuals typically are not depicted.

RESOURCE PLAN
Document used to describe the number of resources needed to accomplish the project work and the steps necessary to obtain a resource.

RESOURCE PLANNING
Process of determining the resources (people, equipment, material) needed in specific quantities, and during specific time periods, to perform project activities.

RESOURCE POOL
Collection of human and material resources that may be used concurrently on several projects.

RESOURCE POOL DESCRIPTION
Information about the resources that are potentially available for use on the project.

RESOURCE RATE

Unit rate, such as staff cost per hour or bulk material cost per cubic meter, for each resource needed in order to calculate project costs.

RESOURCE RELEASE PLAN

Documented record noting how and when resources, usually personnel, will be released from a project or program and assigned to other projects or programs in the organization.

RESOURCE REQUIREMENTS

Output of the resource planning process that describes the types and quantities of resources required for each element of the WBS. Resources are then obtained through staff acquisition or procurement.

RESOURCES

People, equipment, or materials required or used to accomplish an activity. In certain applications, such things as "nonrainy days" are described as a resource.

RESOURCE SELECTION

Process of choosing the type, amount, and sources of resources necessary to accomplish a work effort.

RESOURCE SPREADSHEET

Tool used to show the number of resource units needed on the project, by type, at different periods of time. By adding all resource requirements for each time unit, the total resource requirements for the project by time period can be calculated. The output of this spreadsheet can also be displayed as a resource histogram.

RESPONSE ANALYSIS MATRIX

Matrix grid that shows potential relationships between sets of high-priority project risks and potential risk response strategies. Ratings entered into the grid can indicate the positive or negative effects that response strategies might have on multiple identified project risks.

RESPONSE PLANNING

Process of formulating project risk management strategies, including allocating responsibility to the project's various functional areas. May involve avoidance, acceptance, mitigation, and the use of certain tools and techniques such as deflection and contingency planning.

RESPONSE SYSTEM

Ongoing process during the project to monitor, review, and update any project risks and make necessary adjustments.

RESPONSIBILITY

(1) Obligation of an individual or group to perform assignments effectively.

(2) Status of a prospective contractor that determines whether the contractor is eligible for contract award.

RESPONSIBILITY ASSIGNMENT MATRIX (RAM)

Structure used to relate the WBS to individual resources to ensure that each element of the project's scope of work is assigned to an individual. A high-level RAM defines which group or unit is responsible for each WBS element; a low-level RAM assigns roles and responsibilities for specific activities to particular people. *Also called* accountability matrix. *See also* resource matrix.

RESPONSIBILITY CHART

See responsibility assignment matrix.

RESPONSIBILITY MATRIX

See responsibility assignment matrix.

RESTRICTED COMPUTER SOFTWARE

In U.S. federal procurement, computer software developed at private expense that is a trade secret, that is commercial and privileged, or that is published and copyrighted computer software. Includes minor modifications of such computer software.

RESTRICTED RIGHTS

In U.S. federal procurement—

(1) The rights of the government in restricted computer software as set forth in a Restricted Rights Notice, if included

in a data rights clause of the contract, or as otherwise may be included or incorporated in the contract.

(2) The rights of the government in restricted computer software, as set forth in a Restricted Rights Notice or as otherwise may be provided in a collateral agreement incorporated in and made part of a contract, including minor modifications of such computer software.

RESTRICTED STOCK

Stock that is acquired through an employee stock option plan or other private means and that may not be transferred.

RESUBMITTED LOT

Lot that has been either rejected or subjected to examination or testing to remove all defective units; it later may be reworked or replaced and submitted again for acceptance.

RETAINAGE

Withholding of a portion of a contract payment until contract completion to ensure full performance of the contract terms.

RETURN ON ASSETS (ROA)

Time independent measure used to assess performance (efficiency) against assets used. ROA integrates the balance sheet and income statement.

RETURN ON EQUITY (ROE)

Amount, usually expressed as a percentage, earned on a company's common stock investment for a given period of time.

RETURN ON IDEAS

Qualitative or quantitative evidence collected showing the gain that has resulted from the implementation of a particular idea or group of ideas.

RETURN ON INVESTED CAPITAL

See return on investment.

RETURN ON INVESTMENT (ROI)

Amount of gain, expressed as a percentage, earned on an investment or group of investments. To calculate ROI, the benefit or return of an investment is divided by the cost of the investment, and the result is expressed as a percentage or ratio:

ROI = (Return from investment − Cost of investment) / Cost of investment

RETURN ON SALES (ROS)

Measure of operational efficiency that varies widely from industry to industry. ROS is net pretax profit as a percentage of net sales.

REVENUE

Amount of money earned as a result of completing a project, selling a product, or providing a service. *See also* turnover.

REVERSE ENGINEERING

Developing design specifications by inspection and analysis of an existing product. The goal often is to duplicate or improve upon the product's functionality.

REVERSE SCHEDULING

Method in which the project completion date is fixed and task duration and dependency information are used to compute the corresponding project start date.

REVIEW

Formal process during which an activity or product (for example, code or a document) is presented for comment and approval. Reviews are conducted for different purposes, such as peer reviews, user reviews, or management reviews, or performed at a specific milestone, such as phase reviews, usually to report progress. *See also* phase-end review.

REVISION

Change made to the start and/or finish dates of an approved project schedule. Generally, dates are revised only because of scope changes. In some cases, rebaselining is then required. *See also* rebaselining.

REWARD AND RECOGNITION SYSTEM

Formal management actions to promote or reinforce desired behavior. To be effective, such a system should make the link between performance and reward clear, explicit, and achievable and should consider individual differences. For example, what is considered a highly motivating reward by one person may not interest another.

REWARD AUTHORITY

Influence derived from an individual's being able to provide positive reinforcement for desired behavior. For example, a project manager provides recognition and bonuses to top performers, further motivating them to project success.

REWORK

Action taken to ensure that a defective or nonconforming item complies with requirements or specifications.

RF

See remaining float.

RFP

See request for proposals.

RFQ

See request for quotations.

RIGHT-BRAINED

Being inclined towards ways of thinking that are closely aligned with creativity, passion, and intuition. Terms such as design, aesthetics, and innovation are associated with right-brained thinking. *See also* left-brained.

RIGHTS IN TECHNICAL DATA

Term specific to U.S. DOD contracting. The right for the government to acquire technical data (TD). If the government has funded or will fund a part of or the entire development of an item, component, or process, then the government is entitled to unlimited rights in the TD. However, if the item, component, or process is developed by a contractor or subcontractor exclusively at private expense, the government is entitled to limited rights. Such data must be unpublished and identified as limited-rights data.

RIGID GATE

Review point in a stage-gate process at which all prior work and deliverables must be complete before the next stage can begin.

RING-FENCING

To separate something from normal judgment and scrutiny to guarantee its protection, especially the funding of a project.

RISK

See project risk.

RISK ACCEPTANCE

See acceptance.

RISK ALLOWANCE

Time or money budgeted to cover uncertainties because of inaccuracies in deterministic estimates or the occurrence of risk events. *See also* contingency reserve *and* management reserve.

RISK ANALYSIS

Analysis of the probability that certain undesirable and beneficial events will occur and their impact on attaining project objectives. *See also* risk assessment.

RISK AND OPPORTUNITY ASSESSMENT MODEL (ROAM)

Specific technique developed by ESI International to quantify the identified risks and opportunities associated with a particular project to help decide whether the project should be undertaken.

RISK APPRAISAL

Work involved in identifying and assessing risk.

RISK AREAS

Program areas that are the primary sources of program risk. Risk areas include but are not necessarily limited to: threat and requirements; technology; design and engineering; manufacturing; support; cost; and schedule.

RISK ASSESSMENT

(1) Review, examination, and judgment to see whether identified risks are acceptable according to proposed actions.

(2) Identification and quantification of project risks to ensure that they are understood and can be prioritized. *Also called* risk evaluation.

RISK ASSUMPTION

Risk-handling option in which selected project or program risks are accepted and monitored by the management team.

RISK AUDIT

Formal, methodical review of risk management to assess whether the identified risks and risk strategies are acceptable; helps determine overall progress performance of the risk management plan.

RISK AVOIDANCE

See avoidance.

RISK BUDGET

Cost and schedule allowance held in reserve and spent only if uncertainties or risks occur. A combination of contingency and management reserves.

RISK CONSEQUENCE

See impact.

RISK CONTINGENCY

See contingency.

RISK CONTROL

Risk-handling option that monitors a known risk and then takes specific actions to minimize the likelihood of the risk occurring and/or reduce the severity of the consequences.

RISK DATABASE

Database for risks associated with a project.

RISK DEFLECTION

See deflection.

RISK DESCRIPTION

Documentation of the risk element to identify the boundaries of the risk.

RISK DOCUMENTATION

Recording, maintaining, and reporting of all risk assessment results, risk-handling analysis, and risk monitoring results.

RISK EVALUATION

See risk assessment.

RISK EVENT

Discrete occurrence that may affect a project, positively or negatively. *See also* project risk.

RISK EVENT STATUS

(1) Measure of importance of a risk event. Also referred to as criterion value or ranking.

(2) Probability and impact of a risk as of the data date.

RISK EXPOSURE

(1) Impact value of a risk multiplied by its probability of occurring.

(2) Loss provision made for a risk; requires that a sufficient number of situations in which this risk could occur have been analyzed.

RISK FACTOR

Risk event, risk probability, or amount at stake.

RISK HANDLING

Process that identifies, evaluates, selects, and implements risk-handling options that reduce risk to acceptable levels with the best cost-benefit ratio.

RISK IDENTIFICATION

Determining the risk events that are likely to affect the project and classifying them according to their cause or source.

RISK LISTING

Comprehensive list of risks identified on a project and used by the project team to track the results of risk analysis, response planning, and any actions taken during the risk management process. *See also* risk register.

RISK MANAGEMENT

See project risk management.

RISK MANAGEMENT PLAN

Documentation of the procedures to be used to manage risk during the life of a project and the parties responsible for managing various areas of risk. Includes procedures for performing risk identification and quantification, planning risk response, implementing contingency plans, allocating reserves, and documenting results.

RISK MANAGEMENT STRATEGY

Formal statement of how risk management will be carried out for a project, what resources will be used, and, if applicable, what roles contractors and subcontractors will play.

RISK MITIGATION

See mitigation.

RISK MONITORING

Process that systematically tracks and evaluates the performance of risk items against established metrics throughout the project or program and develops further risk reduction handling options as appropriate.

RISK MONITORING AND CONTROL

Monitoring residual risks, identifying new risks, executing risk reduction plans, and evaluating their effectiveness throughout the project life cycle.

RISK PLANNING

Process of developing an organized, comprehensive, and iterative approach to identifying, mitigating, and continuously tracking risk. The process is tailored for each project or program.

RISK PORTFOLIO

Risk data assembled and collated for project management.

RISK PRIORITIZING

Filtering, grouping, and ranking risks following assessment.

RISK PROBABILITY

Assessment of the likelihood that a risk event will occur.

RISK QUALIFICATION

See qualitative risk assessment.

RISK QUANTIFICATION

See quantitative risk assessment.

RISK RATING SCHEME

Controlled, documented, and verifiable method of assigning risk levels to a project or program, or subset of a project or program, that is based on the probability of risk occurring and the consequence of failing to achieve the desired outcome.

RISK REGISTER

Record of the risks identified in a project or program that are monitored by the team to determine when or if they will occur. As a best practice, each identified risk should be assigned to one or more persons whose responsibility it is to monitor the risk triggers and implement the risk response plan should the risk occur. *See also* risk listing.

RISK RESPONSE CONTROL

Process of implementing risk strategies, documenting risk, and responding to changes in risk during the life of the project.

RISK RESPONSE DEVELOPMENT

Identification of specific actions to maximize the occurrence of opportunities and minimize the occurrence of specific risks in a project.

RISK RESPONSE PLAN

Specific actions the project team will initiate should the identified risks occur.

RISK SUMMARY

Description of each risk factor, including its effect, ownership, and recommendations for response development.

RISK SYMPTOM

Indirect manifestation of an actual risk event, such as poor morale serving as an early warning signal of an impending schedule delay or cost overruns on early activities pointing to poor estimating. *Also called* risk trigger.

RISK TRANSFER

(1) Risk-handling option that reallocates system requirements or design specifications between different system elements in order to reduce overall system risk, system element risk, or process risk.

(2) Risk-handling option that shares selected program risks between the buyer and the seller by means of various contractual arrangements.

(3) Any practice that transfers the management of risk from one party to another.

RISK TRIGGER

See risk symptom.

R&M

See inherent reliability and maintainability value *and* operational reliability and maintainability value.

ROA

See return on assets.

ROADBLOCK

Impediment to progress or obstruction that prevents people, teams, and organizations from meeting their objectives.

ROAM

See risk and opportunity assessment model.

ROBUST DESIGN

Design that is capable of properly performing its function under a wide range of conditions, including some anticipated level of customer misuse.

ROE

See return on equity.

ROI

See return on investment.

ROLE

Defined responsibility, usually a task, to be carried out by one or more individuals.

ROLLING WAVE BUDGETING

Budgeting approach in which a full-period projection is made using an unsupported, top-down budget at the beginning of the project. As time progresses, the top-down budget is replaced with a more detailed, bottom-up budget that extends three to six months into the near-term future. A top-down budget is then used again at the end of the project.

ROLLING WAVE PLANNING

Progressive detailing of the project plan as necessary to control each subsequent project phase.

ROLLOUT

Widespread, phased introduction of a project's product or service.

ROOT CAUSE

Known, identified reason for the presence of a defect or problem.

ROOT CAUSE ANALYSIS

Investigation of a business problem to determine its real origin.

ROS

See return on sales.

ROUTING

Term used in England to describe a sequenced list of the operations needed to manufacture a part, including the resources required at each phase of the production process.

ROUTING BY WALKING ABOUT (RBWA)

Term used in England to describe a method of flow charting a process by actually walking the course of the production process to ensure that what is depicted on the chart is what actually happens.

ROYALTY

Payment made by one party to another for use of its intellectual assets, conveyances, leases, or inventions. Based on a percentage of profit, sales, production, or other criteria agreed to by the parties.

RTP

See request for technical proposals.

RULE OF THUMB

(1) In cost estimating, a relationship commonly used to estimate product cost or price.

(2) Means of estimation made according to a rough-and-ready practical rule or heuristic and not based on science or exact measurement but rather past experience.

RUN DIAGRAM

One of the seven tools of quality; a graph showing the number of events plotted against a time line.

RUN RATE

How the financial performance of a company would look if one were to extrapolate current results out over a certain period of time. For example, in order to extrapolate how much money a company will make in a given year after completing the first quarter, the first quarter's results would be multiplied by four, assuming that the following three quarters would be roughly the same as the first.

RUP

See Rational Unified Process.

RUTHLESS TESTING

In agile project management, the comprehensive, rigorous, and diligent application of testing techniques designed to uncover problems in the product under development, with the objective being to identify as many problems as possible, as early in the life cycle as possible, to reduce technical debt and satisfy user requirements.

RWP

See requirements work plan.

S

SA

See systems analysis.

SACRED COW

Something too highly regarded to be subjected to criticism. In project management, certain projects are regarded as sacred cows because they were initiated at the direction of an executive without having gone through the customary business case process.

SALAMI TECHNIQUE

In negotiations, when the negotiator makes one demand at a time, rather than requesting everything at once. Meant to convey the "slicing" of salami on a deli machine.

SAMPLE

One or more units of product selected from a lot or batch at random or according to an established sampling plan for quality control purposes. *See also* representative sample *and* biased sample.

SAMPLE FRAME

Listing of all units in the universe from which a sample can be drawn.

SAMPLE FREQUENCY

Ratio of the number of units of product randomly selected for inspection to the number of units of product passing the inspection station.

SAMPLE PLAN

Documentation of the sample size or sizes to be used and the associated acceptance and rejection criteria.

SAMPLE PLAN, DOUBLE

Type of sampling plan in which the decision to accept or reject the first sample leads to a decision to take a second sample. Inspection of a second sample then leads to a decision to accept or reject.

SAMPLE PLAN, MULTILEVEL, CONTINUOUS

Type of sampling plan in which the inspection periods of 100 percent inspection and two or more levels of sampling inspection alternate; the sampling frequency may be constant or may change as a result of the inspection.

SAMPLE PLAN, MULTIPLE

Type of sampling plan in which the decision to accept or reject an inspection lot may be reached when at least one sample from that inspection lot has been inspected and will always be reached when a designated number of samples has been inspected.

SAMPLE PLAN, SEQUENTIAL

Type of sampling plan in which the sample units are selected one at a time. After inspection of each unit, a decision is made to accept, reject, or continue inspection until the acceptance or rejection criteria are met. Sampling ends when the inspection results of the sample units determine that the acceptance or rejection decision can be made. Sample size is not fixed in advance and depends on actual inspection results.

SAMPLE PLAN, SINGLE

Type of sampling plan in which a decision to accept or reject an inspection lot is based on only one sample.

SAMPLE PLAN, SINGLE-LEVEL, CONTINUOUS

Type of sampling plan in which the inspection periods of 100 percent inspection and sampling inspection are alternated, and the sampling rate remains constant.

SAMPLE SIZE

Number of units of product in the sample selected for inspection.

SAMPLE UNIT

Unit of product selected to be part of a sample.

SANDBAGGING

In project time and cost estimating, purposefully misrepresenting the amount of time or cost by providing an estimate that is much longer (time) or higher (cost) so that the project team has a comfortable margin within which to work.

SARBANES-OXLEY ACT (SOX)

U.S. law enacted in 2002 that contains sweeping reforms for issuers of publicly traded securities, auditors, corporate board members, and lawyers. It adopts tough new provisions intended to deter and punish corporate and accounting fraud and corruption, threatens severe penalties for wrongdoers, and protects the interests of workers and shareholders. This affects project and program managers who develop automated systems that contain and report on their firm's financial information.

SCALABLE MODEL

Cost estimating model that works as well for a very large project as for a very small one.

SCAMPER

Idea-generation technique developed by creativity expert Michael Michalko. It stands for: Substitute, Combine, Adapt/Adopt, Modify/Magnify/Minify, Put to other uses, Eliminate, Reverse/Rearrange. Using this technique as a checklist, participants ask themselves questions relating to each letter to unlock new ideas for improvement.

SCATTER DIAGRAM

Tool that shows the correlation between two different variables.

SCE

See software capability evaluation.

SCENARIO PLANNING

Technique that allows decision-makers to explore the implications of several alternative future states, thus avoiding the danger of single-point forecasts. Conducted in a nonthreatening group setting. Participants express beliefs, challenge assumptions, and alter their viewpoints to ultimately arrive at a strategic direction that is flexible and will remain so as actual events unfold.

SCHEDULE

Time-sequenced plan of activities or tasks used to direct and control project execution. Usually shown as a milestone chart, Gantt or other bar chart, or tabular listing of dates.

SCHEDULE ANALYSIS

See network analysis.

SCHEDULE BASELINE

Approved project schedule that serves as the basis for measuring and reporting schedule performance.

SCHEDULE CHANGE CONTROL SYSTEM

Procedures followed to change the schedule. Includes paperwork, tracking systems, and approval levels needed to authorize changes.

SCHEDULE COMPRESSION

See duration compression.

SCHEDULE CONTROL

Management of project schedule changes.

SCHEDULE DEVELOPMENT

Analysis of activity sequences, activity durations, and resource requirements used to develop the project schedule. Involves assigning start and end dates to the project activities. These dates can be determined initially by applying the activity duration estimates to the activities in the project network diagram.

SCHEDULED FINISH DATE

Point in time when work is scheduled to finish on an activity; normally, between the early and late finish dates. *Also called* planned finish date.

SCHEDULED START DATE

Point in time when work is scheduled to start on an activity; normally, between the early and late start dates. *Also called* planned start date.

SCHEDULE MANAGEMENT PLAN

Document used to define management of schedule changes; a subsidiary element of the overall project plan.

SCHEDULE PERFORMANCE INDEX (SPI)

Ratio of work performed to work scheduled (BCWP / BCWS). The project is behind schedule if the SPI is less than one, and ahead of schedule if the SPI is greater than one. *See also* earned value.

SCHEDULE REFINEMENT

Necessary rework, redefinition, or modification of the schedule logic or data developed during planning, based on project activity such as milestones, constraints, and priorities.

SCHEDULE REVISION

Changes to the scheduled start and finish dates in the approved project schedule.

SCHEDULE RISK

Risk that jeopardizes completing the project on schedule.

SCHEDULE SIMULATION

Use of the project network as a model of the project. The results are used to quantify the risks of various schedule alternatives, project strategies, paths through the network, or individual activities. Most schedule simulations are based on some form of Monte Carlo analysis.

SCHEDULE UPDATE

Schedule revision to reflect the most current status of the project.

SCHEDULE VARIANCE (SV)

(1) Difference between the scheduled completion of an activity and its actual completion.

(2) In earned value, BCWP less BCWS; an SV of less than zero shows that project activity is behind schedule.

SCHEDULE WORK UNIT

Calendar time unit when work can be performed on an activity.

SCHEDULING

(1) Fitting tasks into a logical timetable, using detailed planning of work with respect to time.

(2) Determining when each item of preparation and execution must be performed.

SCOPE

Sum of the products and services to be provided by the project.

SCOPE BASELINE

See baseline.

SCOPE BASELINE APPROVAL

Approval of the baseline by the appropriate authority, such as the project sponsor or senior management.

SCOPE CHANGE

Modification to the agreed-upon project scope as defined by the approved WBS.

SCOPE CHANGE CONTROL

Process of (1) influencing the factors that cause scope changes to help ensure that such changes are beneficial; (2) determining that a scope change has occurred; and (3) managing the changes if and when they occur.

SCOPE CHANGE CONTROL SYSTEM

Procedures used to change the scope of the project, including paperwork, tracking systems, and approval levels needed to authorize changes.

SCOPE CONSTRAINT

Restriction affecting project scope.

SCOPE COST

Estimated cost of performing the work as defined in the project scope statement.

SCOPE CREEP

Gradual increase of the project's scope such that it is not noticed by the project management team or the customer. Occurs when the customer identifies additional, sometimes minor, requirements that, when added together, may collectively result in a significant scope change and cause cost and schedule overruns.

SCOPE CRITERIA

Standards or rules composed of parameters considered in project definition.

SCOPE DEFINITION

Division of the major deliverables into smaller, more manageable components to (1) improve the accuracy of cost, time, and resource estimates; (2) define a baseline for performance measurement and control; and (3) clarify responsibility assignments.

SCOPE INTERFACES

Points of interaction between the project and its components or its respective environments.

SCOPE MANAGEMENT

See project scope management.

SCOPE MANAGEMENT PLAN

Document that describes the management of project scope, integration of any scope changes into the project, and identification and classification of scope changes.

SCOPE OF THE CONTRACT

Work contemplated by the contractor and the buyer at the time of contract award.

SCOPE OF WORK

Description of the totality of work to be accomplished or resources to be supplied under a contract. *See also* statement of work.

SCOPE PLANNING

Developing a written scope statement that includes the project justification, major deliverables, project objectives, and criteria that will be used to determine whether the project or phase has been successfully completed.

SCOPE REPORTING

Process of periodically documenting project status in terms of cost as it affects financial status, schedule as it affects time-constraint status, and technical performance as it affects quality.

SCOPE RISKS

Risks associated with scope, or the need for "fixes" to achieve the required technical deliverables.

SCOPE STATEMENT

Documented description of the project concerning its output, approach, and content. Such documentation helps managers make future project decisions and develops a common under-standing of the project's scope by stakeholders.

SCOPE VERIFICATION

Process of ensuring that all identified project deliverables have been completed satisfactorily.

SCREENING

Technique used to review, analyze, rank, and select the best alternative for the proposed action.

SCREENING INSPECTION

Inspection in which each item of product is inspected for desig-nated characteristics and defective items are removed.

SCREENING SYSTEM

Minimum performance requirements for one or more of the evaluation criteria used to select a contractor.

SCRUM

Analogy for how product development teams should operate to improve efficiency and overall outcomes. First described by Hirotaka Takeuchi and Ikujiro Nonaka in their Harvard Business Review article "The New New Product Development Game" (1986). In 1996, Ken Schwaber detailed how the scrum approach could be applied in the systems development process, making it one of the more widely used agile methods that accepts that the development process is unpredictable. The term is borrowed from the game of rugby: Scrum occurs when players from each team huddle closely together in an attempt to advance down the playing field. Scrum projects are split into iterations (sprints) consisting of the following three phases:

• Pre-sprint planning—The features and functionality to be developed are selected from a backlog of features.

• Sprint programming—Teams are assigned their sprint objectives and they begin development.

• Post-sprint meeting—Team members gather to discuss project progress and demonstrate the current system.

S-CURVE

Graphic display of cumulative costs, labor hours, or other quantities, plotted against time. The curve is flat at the beginning and end and steep in the middle. Generally describes a project that starts slowly, accelerates, and then tapers off.

SDI®

See Strength Deployment Inventory®.

SDLC

See systems development life cycle.

SDP

See software development plan.

SE

See systems engineering.

SEALED BIDDING

In U.S. federal procurement, a contracting method that solicits submission of competitive bids through an invitation for bids, followed by public opening of the bids and then contract award to the responsive and responsible contractor.

SEASONALITY

Variations in business economic activity that recur as a result of weather, holidays, and vacations. When interpreting financial reports, it is important to take seasonality into account.

SECDEF

Acronym meaning the U.S. Secretary of Defense.

SECOND SOURCE

Alternative source for supply or service used to help foster competition.

SECONDARY FAILURE

System failure because of the use of a component in extreme conditions, such as in very high heat or strong vibration.

SECONDARY FLOAT

See free float.

SECRETIVE MANAGEMENT STYLE

Management approach in which the project manager says or reveals little, to the detriment of the project.

SECTION 508

Refers to Section 508 of the Rehabilitation Act of 1993 (29 U.S.C. 794d), which requires U.S. federal agencies to develop, procure, maintain, or use electronic and information technology that is accessible to federal employees and members of the public with disabilities.

SECURITY RISK ASSESSMENT

Process that permits project team members to make informed decisions relating to the acceptance of identified risk-exposure levels or implementation of cost-effective measures to reduce those risks.

SECURITY TEST

Formal test performed on an operational system, based on the results of the security risk assessment, in order to evaluate compliance with security and data integrity guidelines, and address security backup, recovery, and audit trails. *Also called* Security Testing and Evaluation (ST&E).

SEI

See Software Engineering Institute.

SELF-INSPECTION

Process in which the individual performing a task also conducts the measurement to ensure that requirements or specifications are met.

SENSITIVITY ANALYSIS

Assessment of the impact a change will have on the expected outcome of a process or project. Such change may involve modifying the value of one or more of the variables or assumptions used to predict the outcome.

SEP

See systems engineering plan.

SEQUENTIAL SAMPLE PLAN

See sample plan, sequential.

SERVICE CONTRACT

Contract that directly engages the time and effort of a contractor to perform an identified task rather than to furnish a physical product.

SERVICE LEVEL AGREEMENT (SLA)

Agreement or contract between two parties that precisely details the level of service and technical support to be provided to the buyer by the seller, as well as the consequences for failure. Often used in IT contracts, SLAs spell out the obligations of the seller regarding response time, uptime of computer systems, maintenance requirements, and other technical and business services.

SERVICE LIABILITY
Responsibility of a producer or others to make restitution for loss related to personal injury, property damage, or other harm caused by a service.

SET-UP
Making ready or preparing for the performance of a job operation. Includes the teardown to return the machine or work area to its original or normal condition.

SET-UP COSTS
Costs associated with establishing a new manufacturing procedure; can include the cost of design, acquisition, machinery, and employee training.

SET-UP TIME
Time required to assemble or arrange fixtures and equipment in order to begin productive work, including adjustments and takedown of the original set-up.

SEVEN TOOLS OF QUALITY
Originally identified by Kaoru Ishikawa for use with quality circles. They include—

- Mapping
- Pareto Analysis
- Fishbone Diagram
- Histogram
- Run Diagram
- Correlation and Stratification
- Check Sheets

See individual entries for definitions.

7 WASTES

Forms of waste that occur in a manufacturing plant and that have since been applied to other business environments. Developed by Toyota's former chief engineer Taiichi Ohno, who asserted that the opposite of waste is value and that the seven wastes are a set rather than individual entities. Also, they are productivity—not quality—related. They include the wastes of—

- Overproduction
- Waiting
- Transporting
- Inappropriate processing
- Unnecessary inventory
- Unnecessary motions
- Defects

SEVERANCE PAY

Payment, in addition to regular salaries and wages, to workers whose employment is being involuntarily terminated.

SHAKEDOWN

Trial run before putting a procedure or new system into production in an attempt to locate all the bugs and problems. A term most often used in the shipbuilding industry, but it can be applied to any similar situation.

SHAKE-UP

Rapid change in the management of a project or organization usually through the firing or reassignment of personnel. The purpose of a shake-up is to improve work performance by taking a drastically different direction.

SHARED LEADERSHIP MANAGEMENT STYLE

Management approach in which the project manager holds that leadership consists of many functions, which can be shared among team members. Some common functions are timekeeping, record-keeping, planning, scheduling, and facilitating.

SHAREHOLDER

Owner of one or more shares of a corporation, usually evidenced by the holding of certificates or other formal documents.

SHAREHOLDER MANAGEMENT STYLE
Management approach in which little or no information input or exchange takes place within the team, but the team has the ultimate authority to make final decisions.

SHAREHOLDER VALUE ANALYSIS
Process that attempts to demonstrate to shareholders how certain management decisions affect a company's ability to earn more than its total cost of capital. Used at both the corporate and individual business unit levels, this process provides such information to decision-makers as a framework for measuring the trade-offs among reinvesting in existing businesses, investing in new businesses, and returning cash to stockholders.

SHELF LIFE
Expected length of time in inventory for a system, component, or subassembly.

SHORT-TERM DISABILITY INSURANCE
Insurance that provides short-term (typically 26 weeks in the U.S.) income protection to employees who are unable to work due to a nonwork-related accident or illness.

SHORT-TERM PLAN
(1) Short-term schedule showing detailed activities and responsibilities for a particular period (usually four to eight weeks).

(2) Management technique often used "as needed" or in a critical area of the project.

SHOULD COST
Estimate of contract price that reflects reasonably achievable contractor economy and efficiency.

SHOULD-COST ESTIMATE
Estimate of the cost of a product or service, used to assess the reasonableness of a prospective contractor's proposed cost.

SHOWSTOPPER
Event or condition serious enough to disrupt or halt a negotiation, project, or program.

SHRINKAGE

In business, the act of stealing goods. Euphemism in the retail industry for shoplifting.

SIC

See Standard Industrial Classification Code.

SIGMA

Lowercase Greek letter "s" (σ); refers to the standard deviation of a population. Sigma, or standard deviation, is used as a scaling factor to convert upper and lower specification limits to Z. A process with three standard deviations between its mean and a specification limit would have a Z value of 3 and commonly would be referred to as a 3 sigma process. The most widely known program for quality is Six Sigma, developed by Motorola, Inc., and now used in organizations worldwide. *See also* Six Sigma.

SIGNIFICANT VARIANCE

Difference between the plan and actual performance that jeopardizes the project objectives.

SIGN-OFF

Written approval of a course of action.

SIMPLE INTEREST

Interest computed on principal alone, as opposed to compound interest, which includes accrued interest.

SIMULATION

Technique used to emulate a process; usually conducted a number of times to understand the process better and to measure its outcomes under different policies.

SINGLE FAILURE POINT

Failure of an item that will result in failure of the entire system. Single failure points are normally compensated for by redundancy or an alternative operational procedure.

SINGLE-LEVEL CONTINUOUS SAMPLE PLAN

See sample plan, single-level, continuous.

SINGLE POINT OF CONTACT (SPOC)

See point of contact.

SINGLE SAMPLE PLAN

See sample plan, single.

SINGLE SOURCE

One supplier from whom is procured the entire quantity of goods or services required, even though other competitive suppliers are available.

SITUATION ANALYSIS

Review process used to identify and define facts and variables that might influence a situation.

SIX SIGMA

Quality concept developed by Motorola, Inc., and defined as a measure of goodness—the ability of a process to produce perfect work. Six sigma refers to the number of standard deviations from the average setting of a process to the tolerance limit, which in statistical terms translates to 3.4 defects per million chances for error.

SKILL SETS

Sets of specific abilities that individual resources can possess, such as cost estimating, budgeting, and cost management skills.

SKUNKWORKS

(1) Separate program management operation established to operate outside the normal process, either to expedite development or because of a high security classification.

(2) Any initiative conducted outside and apart from normal operating practices to speed development, keep the work secret, or otherwise improve efficiency.

SLA

See service level agreement.

SLACK

See float.

SLOWDOWN

Effort, typically organized by a union, in which employees decrease productivity in order to bring pressure upon management. Generally used as an alternative to a strike and seen as less disruptive.

SLUSH FUND

Account with funds that can be used by the project manager for any expenditure for which he or she sees fit. Often carries a negative connotation, as slush funds often are secretive and have been used for bribes by political officials.

SMART

Acronym whose letters stand for Specific, Measurable, Agreed-upon, Realistic, and Time-bound. SMART is used as an adjective to note that these characteristics apply. For example: a SMART objective or a SMART unit of work in a WBS.

SME

See subject matter expert.

SMOKE AND MIRRORS

Using trickery or deception to get one's way or influence a decision.

SMOOTHING

See conflict resolution.

SOCIOCULTURAL BARRIER

Real or perceived inhibitor of communication, association, or equality among groups of people.

SOE

See state-owned enterprise.

SOFT LOGIC

See discretionary dependency.

SOFT SAVINGS

Savings associated with Six Sigma projects that include such things as reduced time to market, the avoidance of costs or lost profit, improved employee morale, enhanced image for the organization, and other intangibles that may result in additional savings to an organization but are harder to quantify. *See also* hard savings.

SOFT SKILLS

Skills such as negotiation, team building, conflict management, and communication that focus on the "people" side of project management as opposed to technical or hard skills.

SOFTWARE

Computer's set of instructions to carry out various applications and tasks.

SOFTWARE CAPABILITY EVALUATION (SCE)

Formal evaluation of an organization's software process maturity, typically by a team of assessors. Often used by buyers to determine the seller's software process maturity. The Software Capability Maturity Model® (SWCMM®) and the Capability Maturity Model Integration® (CMMI®) of the Software Engineering Institute are the most common reference models used in these evaluations.

SOFTWARE DEVELOPMENT DOCUMENT

Contains all the information pertaining to the development of each unit or module, including the test cases, software, test results, approvals, and any other items that will help explain the functionality of the software.

SOFTWARE DEVELOPMENT PLAN (SDP)

Management plan, usually generated by the developer, outlining the software development effort.

SOFTWARE DOMAIN

Distinct functional area that can be supported by a class of software systems with similar requirements and capabilities. A domain may exist before there are software systems to support it.

SOFTWARE ENGINEERING

Application of a systematic, disciplined, quantifiable approach to the development, operations, and support of software; that is, the application of systems engineering to software. Typical software engineering tasks include analyzing the system requirements allocated to the software, developing the software requirements, developing the software architecture, designing the software, implementing the software in the code, integrating the software components, and testing the software to verify that the software satisfies the specific requirements allocated to the software component of a system or subsystem. It may include management issues such as directing program teams, scheduling, and budgeting.

SOFTWARE ENGINEERING BODY OF KNOWLEDGE

See Guide to the Software Engineering Body of Knowledge.

SOFTWARE ENGINEERING INSTITUTE (SEI)

U.S. government Federally Funded Research and Development Center (FFRDC), operated by Carnegie Mellon University in Pittsburgh, Pennsylvania, under contract to the U.S. Department of Defense. SEI's mission is to improve software engineering processes for the DOD. SEI has become well-known worldwide for its software Capability Maturity Model® (CMM®), Capability Maturity Model Integration® (CMMI®), and other models used by software development professionals to improve the processes with which they develop application programs.

SOFTWARE FAILURE

Inability, due to a fault in the software, to perform an intended logical operation.

SOFTWARE ITEM

Aggregation of software, such as a computer program or database, that satisfies an end-use function and is designated for purposes of specification, qualification, testing, interfacing, configuration management (CM), or other purposes. A software item is made up of computer software units (CSUs).

SOFTWARE MAINTAINABILITY

Ease with which a software system, or component, can be modified to correct faults or improve performance.

SOFTWARE QUALITY

Ability of software to satisfy its specified requirements.

SOFTWARE QUALITY ASSURANCE (SQA)

Process of evaluating overall software performance on a regular basis to provide confidence that it will satisfy the relevant quality standards. Also used to denote the organization responsible for performing SQA activities.

SOFTWARE RELIABILITY

Probability that software will not cause a system failure for a specified time under specified conditions.

SOFTWARE REUSE

Process of implementing or updating software systems using existing software assets; designed to reduce the time and cost of software development as well as to increase quality by using already-tested software components.

SOLD DOWN THE RIVER

Betrayed or cheated.

SOLE PROPRIETOR

Individual who owns a business, as opposed to stock in a corporation. A sole proprietor pays no U.S. corporate income tax but has unlimited liability for his or her business debts and obligations. *See also* sole proprietorship.

SOLE PROPRIETORSHIP

Form of business structure in which an individual and his or her company are considered a single entity for tax and liability purposes and in which the owner does not pay income tax separately for the company; instead, he or she reports business income or losses on his or her individual income tax return. A sole proprietorship is distinguished by the fact that there is only one owner for the business (hence, "sole") and the business is unincorporated.

SOLE SOURCE

Only source known to be able to perform a contract, or the one source among others that for a justifiable reason is considered to be the most advantageous for the purpose of contract award.

SOLICITATION

(1) Obtaining quotations, bids, offers, or proposals as appropriate.

(2) Document sent to prospective contractors requesting the submission of offers or information.

SOLICITATION PLANNING

Documenting product or service requirements and identifying potential sources.

SOP

See standard operating procedure.

SOPK

See System of Profound Knowledge.

SOR

See statement of requirements.

SOS

See System of Systems.

SOURCE CODE

Human-readable computer instructions and data definitions expressed in a form suitable for input to an assembler, compiler, or other translator.

SOURCE SELECTION

Process of choosing from among potential contractors.

SOURCE SELECTION PROCEDURES

Approaches used to maximize competition; minimize complexity of the solicitation, evaluation, and selection process; ensure impartial and comprehensive evaluation of proposals; and select the source whose proposal is most advantageous and realistic.

SOURCES OF RISK

Categories of possible risk events that may affect the project positively or negatively. Descriptions of risk sources should include rough estimates of the probability that a risk event from that source will occur, the range of possible outcomes, the expected timing, and the anticipated frequency of risk events from the source.

SOW

See statement of work.

SOX

See Sarbanes-Oxley Act.

S&P

See Standard and Poor's 500.

SPAN OF CONTROL

Number of individuals (direct reports) that a manager or project manager can effectively manage. The number will vary, but generally, a manager should have no more than 10 direct reports. Once that number is exceeded, the organizational structure needs to be reviewed and changed. *See also* division of labor.

SPECIAL CAUSE VARIATION

See special event.

SPECIAL EVENT

Variation in a product or delivery of a service that does not follow a normal distribution; event that falls outside the established control limits on a statistical process control chart.

SPECIALIST

Expert in a particular field who may be used as a resource for multiple projects in an organization. *Also called* subject matter expert (SME).

SPECIALTY TEAM STRUCTURE

Organizational structure in which team members apply their special expertise across a number of tasks so that their skills can be used where and when appropriate.

SPECIFICATION

Description of the technical requirements for a material, product, or service, including the criteria for determining that the requirements have been met. Generally, three types of specifications are used in projects: performance, functional, and design.

SPECIFICATION CONTROL

System to ensure that project specifications are prepared in a uniform fashion and are changed only with proper authorization.

SPENDING LEVEL

Real expenditure or cash outlay of any entity in a given category or budgetary area.

SPI

See schedule performance index.

SPIRAL DEVELOPMENT MODEL

Progressive method of software development in which successive, more complete versions of the product are developed and verified only to be scrapped and replaced by a more complete and technically comprehensive version. This development approach usually involves close interaction and feedback with the ultimate end user of the application program.

SPLINTERED AUTHORITY

Authority residing in several managers over the same project or operation.

SPLITTING

In scheduling resources, the practice of dividing an activity into two or more parts to more efficiently assign resources to it, in order to complete it in a given period of time.

SPOC

See single point of contact.

SPONSOR

Individual or group in the performing organization providing the financial resources, in cash or in kind, for the project.

SPONSORSHIP

Degree of commitment, support, and buy-in expressed and demonstrated by key stakeholders or sponsors of the project.

SPOT CASH

Immediate cash payment on a transaction.

SQA

See software quality assurance.

STAFF ACQUISITION

Process of obtaining the human resources needed to work on a project.

STAFFING MANAGEMENT PLAN

Document that describes when and how human resources will become part of a project team and when they will return to their organizational units; may be a part of an overall project plan.

STAFFING REQUIREMENTS

Determination of what kinds of skills are needed from what types of individuals or groups, how many, and in what time frames; a subset of the overall resource requirements.

STAGE GATE

See control gate.

STAKEHOLDER

Individual or organization actively involved in the project or whose interests may be affected, either positively or negatively, as a result of project execution or successful project completion. *Also called* party-at-interest.

STAKEHOLDER ANALYSIS

Assessment of project stakeholder information needs and sources, and development of reporting procedures to meet those needs. A key to stakeholder analysis is to attempt to convert those who are opponents of the project to a position of neutrality or being proponents of the effort, and to convert those who are neutral to being proponents.

STAKEHOLDER ANALYSIS CHART

Graphic depiction identifying the key stakeholders on a project or program on one axis and their level of influence on the other axis. Such a depiction readily unveils those who are proponents of the project, those who are neutral, and those who are opponents.

STAKEHOLDER MANAGEMENT

Action taken by the project manager or project team to curtail stakeholder activities that would adversely affect the project.

STAKEHOLDER TOLERANCES

Term that describes the capacity of each stakeholder and group of stakeholders to recognize and deal with risk.

STANDARD

(1) Basis for uniformly measuring or specifying performance.

(2) Document used to prescribe a specific, consensus solution to a repetitive design, operations, or maintenance situation.

(3) Document approved by a recognized body that provides, for common and repeated use, rules, guidelines, or characteristics for products, processes, or services; however, compliance is not mandatory.

(4) Document that establishes engineering and technical limitations and applications of items, materials, processes, methods, designs, and engineering practices.

STANDARD AND POOR'S (S&P) 500

Unmanaged index of the 500 largest, most actively traded stocks on the New York Stock Exchange. It provides a guide to the overall health of the U.S. stock market. Used as a benchmark against which financial and money managers are measured based on their financial performance.

STANDARD COST

(1) Cost computed with the use of preestablished methods.

(2) Goal or baseline cost used to expedite the process of costing transactions, determined from historical experience or derived from the best available information.

STANDARD DEVIATION

Square root of the variance; a measure of spread of data points about the mean. Represented by the Greek letter sigma (σ).

STANDARD ERROR OF ESTIMATE

Measure of divergence in the actual values of the dependent variable from their regression estimates. (Also known as standard deviation from regression line.) The deviations of observations from the regression line are squared, summed, and divided by the number of observations.

STANDARD INDUSTRIAL CLASSIFICATION (SIC) CODE

Industrial classification method used to report price index changes. A code number is assigned to specific industry groups.

STANDARD OPERATING PROCEDURE (SOP)

Detailed step-by-step procedure for repetitive operations.

STANDARD PROCEDURE

Documented prescription that a certain type of work be done in the same way wherever it is performed.

STANDARDS METHOD

Approach used in budgeting and measuring performance that requires that standards be established for the performance of the specific tasks; generally used in manufacturing.

STANDARD WAGE RATE

Normal or base salary of an employee before overtime or premium pay is computed.

START DATE

Point in time associated with an activity's start. Usually qualified by one of the following terms: actual, planned, estimated, scheduled, early, late, target, baseline, or current.

START-TO-FINISH

Relationship in a precedence diagramming method network in which one activity must start before the successor activity can finish.

START-TO-START

Relationship in a precedence diagramming method network in which one activity must start before the successor activity can start.

START-UP

(1) Period after the date of initial operation during which the unit is brought up to acceptable production capacity and quality. Often confused with the date of initial operation.

(2) New company, usually small, with an innovative idea or product.

STATEMENT OF REQUIREMENTS (SOR)

Type of statement of work in which the procurement item is presented as a problem to be solved, rather than a clearly specified product or service.

STATEMENT OF WORK (SOW)

Narrative description of products or services to be supplied under contract that states the specifications or other minimum requirements; quantities; performance dates, times, and locations, if applicable; and quality requirements. Serves as the basis for the contractor's response and as a baseline against which the progress and subsequent contractual changes are measured during contract performance. *See also* statement of requirements.

STATE OF THE ART

Level to which science and technology at any designated cutoff time have been developed in a given industry or group of industries, as in "the laptop's capabilities were determined by the state of the art at the time it went into production."

STATE-OWNED ENTERPRISE (SOE)

Government-created legal entity to undertake business or commercial activities. SOEs can be fully or partially owned by a government. In China, it is estimated that SOEs employ more than half of its approximately 750 million workers.

STATISTICAL PROCESS CONTROL

Method used in quality control to monitor product and service quality. Based on the collection and analysis of data obtained during the manufacture of a product or the delivery of a service. Plotted on a graph. Helps identify whether the process is producing the results expected and helps pinpoint causes of special variation.

STATISTICAL SAMPLING

Choosing part of a population of interest for inspection.

STATISTICAL SUMS

Sums used to calculate a range of total project costs from the cost estimates for individual work items in order to help quantify the relative risk of alternative project budgets or proposal prices.

STATUS

Condition of the project at a specified point, relative to time, cost, performance, or other key performance indicators.

STATUS REPORT

(1) Description of where the project currently stands; part of the performance reporting process.

(2) Formal report on the input, issues, and actions resulting from a status meeting.

STATUS REVIEW MEETING

Regularly scheduled meeting held to exchange information about a project.

STATUTES

In the U.S., written laws enacted by a federal or state legislative body.

STEERING COMMITTEE

Management team assembled to oversee a project, program, or other major initiative to which the leader of the initiative, for example the project manager or program manager, reports performance progress on a regular basis. The steering committee makes key decisions regarding direction, scope, control, and funding as part of its overall responsibilities. *See also* program governance board.

STI

See Straits Times Index.

STOCHASTIC

Probabilistic; not deterministic. Pertaining to a randomly determined sequence of observations, each of which is a sample of one element of a probability distribution.

STOCK

(1) Certificate documenting the shareholder's ownership in a corporation.

(2) Merchandise that an entity has on hand or in inventory.

STOCK CERTIFICATE

Certificate establishing ownership of a stated number of shares in a corporation's stock.

STOCK OPTION(S)

Contractual right granted by a company to the named holder of the option that allows the holder to purchase the company's stock at a fixed price stated on the stock option within a specified period of time. If the stock option is not exercised within the specified period of time, the contractual right lapses. Stock options are one way public companies provide financial incentives to employees to improve a company's revenues and earnings.

STOP LIGHT VOTING

Convergent-thinking voting technique in which participants vote their preferences using colored adhesive dots (red, yellow, and green). Can be employed in any area in which multivoting is helpful.

STOP-WORK ORDER

Formal directive to stop work because of nonconformance, funding, or technical limitations.

STORAGE QUALITY CONTROL

Technical inspection of material received from vendors that was not previously inspected at the source and for which acceptance at destination is required.

STORMING

See Tuckman's Model of Team Development (Stage 2).

STORYBOARD

In product development, a way to portray renderings or images of products or concepts used to demonstrate an approach or philosophy. The "board" typically refers to foam-core boards that are used in such applications.

STRAIGHT FROM THE HORSE'S MOUTH

From the highest authority; from someone in the know.

STRAIGHT-LINE METHOD OF DEPRECIATION

Method in which an equal amount of an asset's cost is considered an expense for each year of its useful life.

STRAITS TIMES INDEX (STI)

Market value-weighted stock market index based on the 30 representative companies listed on the Singapore Exchange.

STRATEGIC ALLIANCE

See strategic partnership.

STRATEGIC CHANGE

Cardinal change to the strategic intent of an organization that would cause a review of the mix of projects and programs in its portfolio, as well as the criteria for selecting such projects and programs, to ensure alignment with the changed direction.

STRATEGIC DESIGN AND IMPLEMENTATION

Development and execution of a plan for meeting an organization's goals and objectives through the planned use of resources.

STRATEGIC PARTNERSHIP

Voluntary formation of a business relationship among or between independent organizations in support of a long-term strategy of mutual interest and benefits; typically based on a documented agreement of mutual cooperation.

STRATEGIC PLAN

Document that articulates an organization's future direction and strategy, including its use of capital and people to achieve its goal during the period covered by the plan.

STRATEGIC PLANNING

Type of planning that establishes an organization's future mission, objectives, goals, and strategies.

STRATEGY

Action plan that guides the coordinated use of resources through programs, projects, policies, procedures, organizational design, and performance standards to achieve business goals and objectives.

STRAW BOSS

Group leader who has been delegated the authority to lead others but has no permanent title or status.

STRAWMAN

(1) Working draft copy circulated for comments or suggested changes.

(2) In real estate, one who purchases property that is, in turn, conveyed to another so as to conceal the identity of the purchaser.

STRENGTH DEPLOYMENT INVENTORY® (SDI®)

Self-scoring assessment tool, developed by Dr. Elias Porter, that measures an individual's Motivational Value System™, both when things are going well and when the person faces conflict or opposition. *See also* Motivational Value System™.

STRENGTHS-WEAKNESSES-OPPORTUNITIES-THREATS (SWOT) ANALYSIS

Analysis used to determine where to apply special efforts to achieve desired outcomes. Entails listing strengths and how best to take advantage of them; weaknesses and how to minimize their impacts; opportunities presented by the project and how best to take advantage of them; and threats and how to deal with them. Often used in competitive analysis to compare a company's products and services with those of its competitors.

STRIKE

Temporary work stoppage by a group of workers, not necessarily union members, to express a grievance or enforce a demand. A strike is initiated by the workers of an establishment.

STRONG MATRIX

Organizational structure in which the balance of power over resources shifts from the functional managers to the project manager, and the project manager has greater decision-making influence. *See also* weak matrix.

STRUCTURED WALK-THROUGH

Systematic, comprehensive review of the requirements, design, or implementation of a system by a group of qualified experts.

SUBCONTRACT

Contract or contractual action entered into by a prime contractor or subcontractor to obtain supplies, materials, equipment, or services under a prime contract.

SUBCONTRACTED ITEMS

Parts and services produced or performed by other than the prime contractor, according to the prime contractor's design, specifications, or directions, and applicable only to the prime contract.

SUBCONTRACTING PROCESS

Process of acquiring personnel, goods, and services from external sources for new or existing work.

SUBCONTRACTOR

(1) Competent and qualified organization or person procured to perform work within specified elements of the project's WBS; serves as an adjunct member of the project team.

(2) Contractor, distributor, vendor, or firm that furnishes supplies or services to a prime contractor or another subcontractor.

SUBJECT MATTER EXPERT (SME)

See specialist.

SUBNET

Subdivision of a project network diagram generally representing some form of subproject. *Also called* subnetwork *or* fragnet.

SUBNETWORK

See subnet.

SUBOPTIMIZATION

Optimization of a subelement of a system, perhaps to the detriment of the overall system.

SUBOPTIMIZE

(1) In quality, to do the best within one function or one area but with a potential cost to the larger whole.

(2) Generally, to use to less than the maximum degree of output, not to the fullest potential.

SUBPOENA

Writ issued by a court commanding a person to appear in court.

SUBPROJECT

Component of a project; often contracted out to an external enterprise or another functional unit in the performing organization.

SUBSIDIARY MANAGEMENT PLAN

Additional management plans included in the final project plan. For example, the communication management plan, the procurement management plan, the quality management plan, the risk management plan, and IT-specific management plans such as the security plan, the logistics plan, the transition plan, the configuration management plan, and the test strategy plan.

SUBSTANTIAL COMPLETION

(1) Point when the product is ready for use or is being used for the purpose intended and is so certified.

(2) Term used in construction contracting to mean substantial performance of contract requirements though not complete performance; often found when the contractor completes construction of the structure but fails to complete punch-list items, install ornamental features, finish site cleanup, and so on.

SUBSYSTEM

Collection of components that meets the definition of a system, but is considered part of a larger system.

SUBTASK

Portion of a task or work element.

SUCCESSOR ACTIVITY

Activity that starts after the start of a current activity.

SUMMARY LEVEL

Major subsystem level of a project WBS.

SUMMARY SCHEDULE

See milestone schedule.

SUMMARY WORK BREAKDOWN STRUCTURE

Top three levels of a full WBS; these levels usually represent the formal cost and schedule reporting levels for a contract.

SUMMATIVE QUALITY ASSURANCE

See summative quality evaluation.

SUMMATIVE QUALITY EVALUATION

Process of determining the lessons learned after the project is complete by documenting specific items that helped determine, maintain, or increase quality standards.

SUM-OF-THE-YEARS DIGITS (SYD)

Accelerated depreciation method in which a constant balance (cost minus salvage value) is multiplied by a declining depreciation rate.

SUNK COSTS

Costs that once expended can never be recovered or salvaged. Current thinking strongly suggests that sunk costs should not be considered a factor in deciding whether to terminate a project or allow it to continue to the next phase.

SUPPLEMENTARY AGREEMENT

Contract modification accomplished by the mutual action of the parties involved.

SUPPLEMENTARY CONDITIONS

Modifications, deletions, and additions to standard general conditions developed for particular goods or services.

SUPPLEMENTARY INFORMATION

Additional information collected from supplementary sources.

SUPPLIER

Person or organization responsible for the performance of a contract or subcontract.

SUPPLIER EVALUATION

Review and analysis of a response to a solicitation to determine the prospective supplier's ability to perform the work as requested. May include an evaluation of the prospective supplier's financial resources, ability to comply with technical criteria and delivery schedules, record of performance, and eligibility for award.

SUPPLIER RANKING

Qualitative or quantitative determinations of prospective contractors' qualifications relative to the provision of the proposed goods or services.

SUPPLY CHAIN

Start-to-end system of organizations, people, activities, processes, information, and resources required to move a product or service from supplier to customer.

SUPPLY CHAIN BLACK HOLE

Term used by retailers to describe a situation where a consumer purchases an item online to be picked up at the physical store, but the inventory systems cannot ensure the product will be available when the consumer shows up to collect.

SUPPLY CHAIN INTEGRATION

Synchronizing the efforts of all parties or stakeholders—suppliers, vendors, manufacturers, developers, dealers, distributors, and so on—to meet and exceed the needs and expectations of the customer, client, or end user. With a focus on relationship-building, such integration results in strong bonds of trust and communication aimed at ensuring that the right products are delivered to the right places at the right time and at the right cost.

SUPPORT STAFF

Individuals who provide assistance to the project or program team in areas such as financial tracking and project administration.

SURETY

Individual or organization that has agreed to be legally liable for the debt, default, or failure of a principal to satisfy a contractual obligation.

SURGICAL TEAM STRUCTURE

Organizational structure in which a single individual has primary responsibility for the final product. Specialists produce pieces of the final output, which are given to the primary resource for integration into a completed product. Administrative and support personnel handle day-to-day administrative tasks, and the primary resource is backed up by an assistant who is available to take over in the event of the sudden loss of the primary. This approach can lead to consistent output in a relatively short time; however, friction can develop among the specialists and support staff, and the backup is seldom able to fully assume the primary's duties when called upon to do so.

SURVIVABILITY

Measure of the ability of a system to continue to function, especially in the presence of errors.

SURVIVOR BENEFITS

In the U.S., a series of payments to the dependents of deceased employees. Survivor benefits are of two types. The "transition" type pays the named beneficiary a monthly amount for a short period, usually 24 months. Transition benefits may then be followed by "bridge benefits," which are a series of payments that last until a specific date, usually the surviving spouse's 62nd birthday.

SV

See schedule variance.
See systems view.

SWAG

Acronym that means "scientific wild anatomical guess" but is stated as a word. Estimate of the time or cost required to complete a project or element of a project based solely on the experience of the estimator. Typically done in haste, SWAG estimates are usually no more accurate than order-of-magnitude estimates.

SWEATSHOP

Workplace characterized by long hours and deplorable working conditions, including abusive management practices.

SWEBOK

Acronym meaning Software Engineering Body of Knowledge. *See also Guide to the Software Engineering Body of Knowledge.*

SWING SHIFT

Work shift in an industry from, roughly, midafternoon until midnight.

SWOT

See strengths-weaknesses-opportunities-threats analysis.

SYD

See sum-of-the-years digits.

SYSTEM

(1) Methodical assembly of actions or things forming a logical and connected scheme or unit.

(2) Set of functional capabilities.

SYSTEM ADMINISTRATOR

Person responsible for planning a system installation and use of the system by other users.

SYSTEM ANALYSIS

Management planning technique that applies scientific methods from many disciplines to major problems or decisions. The list of disciplines includes traditional military planning, economics, political science and social sciences, applied mathematics, and the physical sciences.

SYSTEM ARCHITECTURE

Manner in which hardware or software is structured; that is, how the system or program is constructed, how its components fit together, and what protocols and interfaces are used for communication and cooperation among the components, including human interaction.

SYSTEM CHANGE REQUEST

Formal change control document procedure used to request a change to a system baseline, provide information concerning the requested change, and act as the documented approval mechanism for the change.

SYSTEM DESIGN

Translation of customer requirements into comprehensive, detailed functional, performance, or design specifications, which are then used to construct the specific solution.

SYSTEM DESIGN DOCUMENT

Formal document that describes the system architecture, file and database design, interfaces, and detailed hardware/software design; used as the baseline for system development.

SYSTEM ENGINEERING

Logical sequence of activities and decisions to transform an operational need into a description of system performance parameters and a preferred system configuration.

SYSTEM FLOWCHART

See process flowchart.

SYSTEM INTERFACES

Physical interfaces among connecting parts of a system, or performance interfaces among various functional or product subsystems.

SYSTEM LIFE

Period of time that begins when an information technology application is installed and ends when the users' need for it disappears.

SYSTEM OF PROFOUND KNOWLEDGE (SOPK)

Concept advanced by W. Edwards Deming to improve quality in an organization, consisting of four main ideas:

• Knowledge of variation—a knowledge of common cause and special variation.

• Knowledge of systems—understanding that all the parts of a business are related in such a way that if you focus on optimizing one part, other parts may suffer.

• Knowledge of psychology—what motivates people.

• Theory of knowledge—how we learn things.

SYSTEM OF SYSTEMS (SoS)

Mix of existing and/or new systems being managed as a system. The overall objective for developing a SoS WBS is to provide the program management team a structure that captures the various systems' work and common elements that will be accomplished at the SoS level. The mix of constituent systems may include existing, partially developed, and yet-to-be-designed independent systems. A SoS is managed as a system, thus it is baselined and should have an assigned program manager. A SoS WBS is driven by the need to capture the common elements that support the integration of the various systems into the SoS.

SYSTEM SOFTWARE

Software designed to facilitate the operation of a computer system and associated computer programs such as operating systems, code compilers, and utilities. *See also* application software.

SYSTEM TESTING

Process of testing an integrated system from end-to-end to verify that it meets specified business requirements. Typically executed in a stable, production-like environment. System testing should not begin until all integration testing has been completed.

SYSTEMS ANALYSIS (SA)

In systems development, the process of studying and understanding the requirements (customer needs) of a system in order to develop a feasible design. Includes the examination of processes, procedures, workflow, data models, user needs, and other components of work in order to design a comprehensive automated solution to solve a business problem.

SYSTEMS APPROACH

Wide-ranging, synthesizing method of addressing problems that considers multiple and interacting relationships. Commonly contrasted with the analytic approach.

SYSTEMS DEVELOPMENT LIFE CYCLE (SDLC)

Formal model of a hardware/software project that depicts the relationship among activities, products, reviews, approvals, and resources. Also, the period of time that begins when a need is identified (initiation) and ends when the system is no longer available for use (disposition).

SYSTEMS ENGINEERING (SE)

Overarching process that a program team applies to transition from a stated capability to an operationally effective and suitable system. SE encompasses the application of SE processes across the project life cycle, adapted to each and every phase, and is intended to be the integrating mechanism for balanced solutions addressing capability needs, design considerations and constraints, as well as limitations imposed by technology, budgets, and schedules. The SE processes are applied early in concept definition and then continuously throughout the total life cycle.

SYSTEMS ENGINEERING PLAN (SEP)

Description of the program's overall technical approach, including processes, resources, metrics, applicable performance incentives, and the timing, conduct, and success criteria of technical reviews.

SYSTEMS MANAGER

Individual, or group, responsible for post-implementation system maintenance, configuration management, change control, and release control. This may or may not include members of the development team.

SYSTEMS THINKING

Emphasizes the value of viewing a system as a whole before examining its parts. By doing so, the environmental context of the system is better understood, resulting in greater appreciation and understanding of how the individual parts interact with the whole. Originated from a rigorous scientific discipline called general systems theory, which centers on the natural world and its living systems and governing laws.

SYSTEMS VIEW (SV)

Architectural view that identifies the kinds of systems, how to organize them, and the integration needed to achieve the desired operational capability. It also characterizes available technology and systems functionality.

T

TAGUCHI LOSS FUNCTION

Statistical model developed by Dr. Genichi Taguchi that demonstrates that the closer a finished product is to customer specifications, the less loss the performing organization will experience. *See also* Taguchi method.

TAGUCHI METHOD

Approach that uses statistical techniques to compute a "loss function" used to determine the cost of producing products that fail to achieve a target value.

TAKE IT OR LEAVE IT

Negotiation tactic that presents two alternatives: take the current offer as proposed or give up any chance of reaching an agreement. A negotiator using this tactic might use words such as "My best offer is on the table, and I have no room to compromise further."

TANGIBLE CAPITAL ASSET

Asset that has physical substance and more than minimal value and is expected to be held by an organization for continued use or possession beyond the current accounting period.

TARGET COMPLETION DATE

See target date.

TARGET COST

Negotiated amount of cost included in incentive contracts.

TARGET DATE

(1) Date an activity is planned to start or end.

(2) Date generated by the initial CPM schedule operation and resource allocation process.

TARGET FEE

Amount the contractor will receive if its total allowable costs equal total target costs in a cost-plus-incentive fee contract.

TARGET FINISH DATE (TF)

Date work is planned to finish on an activity.

TARGET MARKET

Selected market segment (group of consumers or potential customers) to whom an organization intends to market its products and services.

TARGET PLAN

Plan and schedule based on achieving the target date.

TARGET PROFIT

Amount of profit the contractor will receive if its total allowable costs equal total target costs in a fixed-price-incentive contract.

TARGET REPORTING

Reporting on the current schedule versus the established baseline schedule, or "target," and the variance between them.

TARGET START DATE (TS)

Date work is planned to start on an activity.

TARIFF

Usually, a country's tax on imports.

TARIFF, AD VALOREM

Tariff determined as a percentage of the value of the goods.

TASK

Well-defined component of project work; a discrete work item. There are usually multiple tasks for one activity. *See also* activity.

TASK DEFINITION

Unique description of each project work division.

TASK FORCE

(1) Team of skilled contributors who are charged with investigating a problem for the specific purpose of developing and implementing a solution.

(2) Form of project organization usually used for small, uncomplicated projects.

TASK FORCE ORGANIZATION

See projectized organization.

TASK-ORIENTED WBS

See work breakdown structure.

TASK TYPE

Identification of a task by resource requirement, responsibility, discipline, jurisdiction, function, or any other characteristic used to categorize it.

TAX

Charge against a legal entity's person or property or activity for the support of government; for example, income taxes, sales taxes, duties, and levies.

TAXABLE

Refers to goods, services, royalties, or funds subject to taxation.

TAX SHELTER

Any legal method a taxpayer can use to reduce tax liabilities.

TCO

See total cost of ownership.

TCPI

See to-complete performance index.

TD

See technical data.

T&E

See test and evaluation.

TEAM

See project team.

TEAM ARRANGEMENT

Arrangement in which (1) two or more companies form a partnership or joint venture to act as a potential prime contractor, or (2) a potential prime contractor agrees with one or more other companies to have them act as subcontractors.

TEAM BUILDING

(1) Planned and deliberate process of encouraging effective working relationships while diminishing difficulties or roadblocks that interfere with the team's effectiveness, competence, and resourcefulness.

(2) Process of influencing a group of diverse people, each with individual goals, needs, and perspectives, to work together effectively for the good of the project.

TEAM-BUILDING ACTIVITIES

Management and individual actions undertaken specifically and primarily to improve team performance.

TEAM DEVELOPMENT

(1) Development of individual and group skills to improve project performance.

(2) Enhancement of stakeholders' ability to contribute as individuals and to function as a team.

TEAMING AGREEMENT

Agreement between two organizations to work together as partners in a venture, recognizing that each has specific skills that will contribute to an effective team relationship. The agreement lists their specific responsibilities and obligations and itemizes the distribution of revenues, profits, or other benefits resulting from the arrangement.

TEAM MEMBERS

See project team.

TECHNICAL ANALYSIS

Review by personnel with special knowledge, skills, experience, or abilities in engineering, science, or management of the proposed types and quantities of materials, labor, processes, special tooling, facilities, the reasonableness of scrap and spoilage, and other factors set forth in the proposal(s) in order to determine the need for and reasonableness of the proposed resources, assuming reasonable economy and efficiency.

TECHNICAL AUTHORITY

See expert authority.

TECHNICAL BASELINE

Project's work breakdown structure.

TECHNICAL DATA (TD)

In U.S. DOD contracting, scientific or technical information recorded in any form or medium, such as manuals and drawings, necessary to operate and maintain a defense system. Documentation of computer programs and related software are TD. Computer programs and related software are not TD. Also excluded are financial data or other information related to contract administration.

TECHNICAL DEBT

In agile project management, the difference between a product's actual cost of change and its optimal cost of change. The further in the development cycle a problem is found and fixed, the higher the cost.

TECHNICAL INTERFACES

Formal and informal working and reporting relationships among different technical disciplines involved in a project.

TECHNICAL PROJECT LEADER

Person who serves primarily as the senior technical consultant on a team.

TECHNICAL QUALITY ADMINISTRATION

Process in which a plan is prepared to monitor and control the technical aspects of the project so they are completed satisfactorily. The plan includes policies and procedures to prevent or correct deviations from quality specifications or requirements.

TECHNICAL QUALITY SPECIFICATION

Establishment and documentation of the specific project requirements—including execution criteria and technologies, project design, measurement specification, and material procurement and control—needed to satisfy the expectations of the client, stakeholders, and project team.

TECHNICAL QUALITY SUPPORT

Provision of technical training and expertise from one or more support groups to a project in a timely manner.

TECHNICAL REQUIREMENTS

Description of the features of the deliverable in detailed technical terms to provide project team members with crucial guidance on what needs to be done on the project.

TECHNICAL RISK

Risk that arises from activities related to technology, design and engineering, manufacturing, and the critical technical processes of testing, production, and logistics.

TECHNICAL SPECIFICATION

See specification.

TECHNIQUE

Skilled means to an end.

TELECOMMUTING

Performing one's job or project responsibilities at a location that is remote from one's office, usually from home, through the use of computers and telecommunications devices. Has become popular among organizations because it reduces the amount of time an employee spends traveling to and from the office, reduces pollution and traffic congestion, and generally improves employee morale and productivity.

TEMPLATES

Set of guidelines that provides sample outlines, forms, checklists, and other documents.

TEMPORARY

Having a definite beginning and a definite end.

TENDER

(1) Solicitation of bids or proposals for goods or services. *See also* solicitation.

(2) Response to a solicitation submitted by a prospective contractor. *See also* offer *and* request for proposals.

TERM CONTRACT

In U.S. federal procurement, a type of cost-plus-fixed-fee contract in which the scope of work is described in general terms and the contractor's obligation is stated in terms of a specified level of effort for a stated period of time.

TERMINATION BY ADDITION

Ending the project by bringing it into the organization as a separate, ongoing entity.

TERMINATION BY EXTINCTION

Ending all activity on the project without extending it in some way, such as by inclusion or integration.

TERMINATION BY INTEGRATION

Ending the project by bringing all its activities into the organization and distributing them among existing functions.

TERMINATION BY MURDER

Ending the project suddenly and without warning, usually for a reason that is unrelated to the purpose of the project.

TERMINATION BY STARVATION

Reducing the project's budget significantly, so that progress stops, without formally ending the project.

TERMINATION FOR CONVENIENCE

Exercise of the buyer's, and in some contracts the contractor's, right to terminate a contract for no reason whatsoever other than it does not make sense to continue. In such cases, there is no fault or blame placed on either party.

TERMINATION FOR DEFAULT

Exercise of the buyer's contractual right to completely or partially terminate a contract because of the contractor's actual or anticipated failure to perform its contractual obligation.

TERMINATION MANAGER

Individual responsible for closing out the administrative details of a project.

TERMS AND CONDITIONS

All the contract clauses.

TEST

Process of exercising the product to identify differences between expected and actual results and performance. Typically testing is bottom-up: unit test, integration test, system test, and acceptance test.

TESTABILITY

Metric that measures the characteristics of a requirement that enable it to be verified during a test.

TEST ANALYSIS REPORT

Formal documentation of the software testing as defined in the test plan.

TEST AND EVALUATION (T&E)

Process in which a system or selected components are compared with requirements and specifications through testing.

TEST AND EVALUATION MASTER PLAN

Formal document that identifies the tasks and activities so the entire system can be adequately tested to ensure a successful implementation.

TESTBED

System representation consisting of actual hardware and/or software and computer models or prototype hardware and/or software.

TEST CASE

Specific set of test data and associated procedures developed for a particular test.

TESTING

Part of inspection that assesses the properties or elements, including functional operation, of supplies or their components by applying established scientific principles and procedures.

TEST PROBLEM REPORT

Formal documentation of problems encountered during testing; the form is attached to the test analysis report. *See also* test analysis report.

TEST READINESS REVIEW

Formal phase review to determine that test procedures are complete and the system is ready for formal testing.

TEST SCRIPT

In software testing, a set of instructions that will be executed, either manually or automatically, to ensure that the system functions as designed.

TF

See target finish date.

THEORY OF CONSTRAINTS (TOC)

Theory of continuous improvement of any system, advanced by Eliyahu M. Goldratt. Requires recognition of the important role of the system's constraints, which are anything that limits the system from achieving higher performance. In project management, the constraint is the critical path. TOC breaks down the process into five steps as follows: identify the constraints; decide how to exploit the constraints; subordinate everything else to the exploitation decision; elevate the constraints; and finally, return to the previous steps if the constraint has been broken. The process helps managers identify what to change, what to change it to, and finally, how to bring about the change to improve the system.

THEORY W MANAGEMENT

Approach to software project management in which the project manager tries to make winners of each party involved in the software process. Its subsidiary principals are "plan the flight and fly the plan" and "identify and manage your risks." Suggested by Barry Boehm.

THEORY X MANAGEMENT

Approach to managing people described by Douglas McGregor. Based on the philosophy that people dislike work, will avoid it if they can, and are interested only in monetary gain from their labor. Accordingly, the Theory X manager will act in an authoritarian manner, directing each activity of his or her staff.

THEORY Y MANAGEMENT

Approach to managing people described by Douglas McGregor. Based on the philosophy that people will work best when they are properly rewarded and motivated, and that work is as natural as play or rest. Accordingly, the Theory Y manager will act in a generally supportive and understanding manner, providing encouragement and psychological rewards to his or her staff.

THEORY Z MANAGEMENT

Approach to managing people described by William Ouchi. Based on the philosophy that people need goals and objectives, motivation, standards, the right to make mistakes, and the right to participate in goal setting. More specifically, it describes a Japanese system of management characterized by the employee's heavy involvement in management, which has been shown to result in higher productivity levels when compared with U.S. and Western counterparts. Successful implementation requires a comprehensive system of organizational and sociological rewards. Its developers assert that it can be used in any situation with equal success. *Also called* participative management style.

THINK LINKS

Stimuli (that is, thoughts, ideas, suggestions) used in divergent thinking to help participants make new connections using seemingly unrelated concepts from a list of people, places, or things. *See also* divergent thinking.

THIRD DEGREE, THE

Unusually detailed questioning and interrogation.

THOMAS-KILMANN CONFLICT MODE INSTRUMENT

Questionnaire used to measure how much competing, collaborating, compromising, avoiding, and accommodating behavior is displayed in conflict situations. Examines the extent to which individuals use assertive versus cooperative behavior in work situations.

THREAT

Future event or series of events that, if it occurs, will negatively affect the project. *Also called* jeopardy.

THREE-POINT ESTIMATING

Technique that allows for uncertainty in estimates by defining the distribution of possible task durations according to three duration estimates: the minimum, the maximum, and the target.

THRESHOLD

Time, monetary unit, or resource limit that, if exceeded, causes some type of management review to occur.

TIED ACTIVITY

Activity that must start within a specified time or immediately after its predecessor's completion.

TIGER TEAM

Group of objective specialists, convened by management, who evaluate, assess, and make recommendations for resolving problems associated with a particular area of concern. Often used to review a company's proposal prior to its being submitted to the prospective buyer.

TIGER TEAM REVIEW

What a tiger team does. *See also* tiger team.

TIGHTENED INSPECTION

Inspection under a sampling plan using the same quality level as that of normal inspection but requiring more stringent acceptance criteria.

TIGHT MATRIX

Physical placement of project team members in one location.

TIME-AND-MATERIALS CONTRACT

Type of contract that provides for the acquisition of supplies or services on the basis of direct labor hours, at specified fixed hourly rates, for the following: wages; overhead; general and administrative (G&A) expenses and profit; and materials at cost, including materials-handling costs.

TIME BOX

Defined period of time in which an activity, task, iteration, or other effort must be completed. Used in agile software development methods to fix the amount of time devoted to developing a particular iteration. Once the time is exhausted, work stops and whatever was developed is used for the next step in the process. Sometimes called "time boxing."

TIME-LIMITED SCHEDULING

Scheduling activities so that the limits on resource use are not exceeded, unless those limits would push the project beyond its scheduled finish date. Activities may not begin later than their late start date, even if resource limits are exceeded. Should not be used on networks with negative total float time.

TIME LINE

Schedule line showing key dates and planned events.

TIME NOW

Time at which all remaining work starts on a project. The then-current date on which the project schedule report was generated.

TIME-PHASE BUDGET

Project budget identifying expenditures for labor and materials for each task based on project time periods (for example, day, week, month).

TIME-SCALED NETWORK DIAGRAM

Project network diagram drawn in such a way that the position and length of an activity represents its duration. Essentially, a bar chart that includes network logic.

TIME-SERIES ANALYSIS

Identification of a trend related to time and using the trend to forecast future costs or events.

TIME TO MARKET

Total length of time taken to develop a new product, from idea to launch. The precise definition of the start and end events for purposes of measuring time to market will vary across industries and companies, and even with different product lines within a company.

TIME VALUE OF MONEY

Economic concept that purports that money available now is more valuable than the same amount of money at some point in the future, simply due to its potential earning power, and not inflation as many believe. Used in calculating the present value of money for financial analysis and other purposes. *See also* present value.

TIME VARIANCE

Scheduled time for the work completed less the actual time.

TO-BE STATE

Typically, a graphical representation of a work or business process that is an improvement over the AS-IS state, and how things will be done in the future to increase productivity, efficiency, and customer satisfaction. *See also* AS-IS state.

TOC

See Theory of Constraints.

TO-COMPLETE PERFORMANCE INDEX (TCPI)

Projected cost performance that must be met on all remaining project work to meet an identified objective, such as the BAC. TCPI = (Remaining work) / (Budget remaining) = (BAC – EV) / (BAC – AC)

TOLERANCE

(1) Specific range in which a result is considered to be acceptable.

(2) Range of values above and below the estimated project cost, schedule, or performance within which the final value is likely to fall.

TOM

See trade-off matrix.

TOOLS AND TECHNIQUES

(1) Mechanisms applied to input for the purpose of creating output.

(2) Set of activities, services, instruments, or materials that enables the individual or project team to create, develop, and complete deliverables.

TOP-DOWN BUDGET

General, nondetailed projections often used to determine the range of possible costs for a project.

TOP-DOWN ESTIMATING

Cost estimating that begins with the top level of the WBS and then works down to successively lower levels. *Also called* analogous estimating.

TOP LINE

Revenue figure of a company or its gross sales. Named such because the first line item (the "top" of the report) in an income statement consists of revenue figures. *See also* turnover.

TOP-LINE GROWTH

Growth in revenues.

TORT

Wrongful act that is neither a crime nor a breach of contract but renders the person committing the act liable to the victim for damages. An example would be a building owner's failure to repair a sidewalk, causing a person to fall and break a leg. The law provides remedy for damages from the fall.

TOTAL ALLOCATED BUDGET

Sum of all budgets allocated to a project, which consists of the performance measurement baseline and all reserves.

TOTAL CERTAINTY

Situation in which all information is available and everything is known.

TOTAL CONTRACT COST

Sum of direct and indirect costs allocable to a contract, incurred or to be incurred, less any allocable credits, plus any allocable cost of money.

TOTAL COST

Sum of allowable direct and indirect costs that are allocable to a project, including all contracts and subcontracts, and have been or will be incurred, less any allocable credits, plus any allocable costs of money.

TOTAL COST OF OWNERSHIP (TCO)

Sum total cost of owning, deploying, and using a product. TCO includes purchase price as well as support, maintenance, and disposition fees over the life-cycle of use of the product. It commonly is applied to computer hardware and software such as personal computers and is used to determine total life-cycle costs to the organization. *Also called* total ownership cost.

TOTAL CURRENT LIABILITIES

Claims to the company's assets that are due within one year or the cycle of operations, including accounts payable, notes payable, current maturities, and accrued liabilities.

TOTAL FLOAT

See float.

TOTAL OWNERSHIP COST

See total cost of ownership.

TOTAL QUALITY MANAGEMENT (TQM)

(1) Approach used to achieve continuous improvement in an organization's processes and products.

(2) Common approach to implementing a quality improvement program within an organization.

(3) Philosophy and set of guiding principles that encourage employees to focus their attention on ways of improving effectiveness and efficiency in the organization.

TOUCH LABOR

Defined as production labor that can be reasonably and consistently related directly to a unit of work being manufactured, processed, or tested. Hands-on labor effort.

TQM

See total quality management.

TRACEABILITY

(1) Ability to trace the history, application, or location of an item or activity by means of recorded identification.

(2) Ease with which a project can be traced forward from specifications to the final deliverable, or backward from the deliverable to the original specifications in a systematic way. *See also* requirements traceability.

TRACK RECORD

Project manager's, contractor's, or other person or company's reputation for completing work or otherwise producing results on a timely and economical basis.

TRADEMARK

Logo or insignia that differentiates one organization's goods from all others. Also, any mark, letter, design, picture, or combination thereof, in any form, that is used by a person to denominate goods that he or she makes; is affixed to the goods; and is neither a common nor generic name for the goods, nor a picture of them, nor merely a description of them.

TRADE NAME

Distinctive and unique name used to identify a product or company and build brand recognition. Organizations such as Coca-Cola®, Ford®, and IBM® aggressively protect their trade names within the global markets.

TRADE-OFF

The giving up or accepting of one advantage, or disadvantage, to gain another that has more value to the decision-maker. For example, accepting the higher cost, a disadvantage, of a project because there will be more functionality, an advantage, in the delivered product.

TRADE-OFF MATRIX (TOM)

Table that establishes the relative priorities of project scope, resources, and schedule, with one always being identified as the highest priority. Used as a decision-making tool after having been agreed to at the outset by project stakeholders.

TRAINING

Activities designed to increase the skills, knowledge, and capabilities of an individual or the project team.

TRANCHE

French for "slice," in program management it refers to a group of projects that delivers a new or otherwise recognizable part of a new or enhanced capability.

TRANSFER

Risk response strategy that seeks to shift the impact of a risk to a third party, along with ownership of the response. *Also called* deflection. *See also* acceptance, avoidance, *and* mitigation.

TRANSFORMATIONAL LEADERSHIP

Motivational approach to management based on the practice of encouraging employees to achieve greater performance through inspirational leadership. Such an approach is thought to develop employee self-confidence and result in higher achievement goals.

TREE SEARCH

Evaluation of a number of alternatives that logically branch from one another like limbs on a tree.

TREND ANALYSIS

(1) Use of mathematical techniques to forecast future outcomes based on historical results. Often used to monitor technical, cost, and schedule performance.

(2) Examination of project results over time to determine whether performance is improving or deteriorating.

TREND REPORT

Indicator of variations of project control parameters against planned objectives.

TRIAL BALLOON

Tentative plan offered to test the reaction of a particular audience.

TRIPLE CONSTRAINT

Term used to identify what generally are regarded as the three most important factors a project manager needs to consider in any project: time, cost, and scope (specifications). Typically represented as a triangle, each of these constraints, when changed, will affect one or both of the others. For example, if the scope of a project increases, generally time and cost also will increase.

TRUE-UP

To make level, square, balanced, or concentric. Used in project and program management as an expression meaning to bring into alignment with predetermined criteria or processes.

TS

See target start date.

T-TYPE MATRIX

Tool used to identify the root cause of problems resulting in design changes in new product development. Proper use of the matrix helps in understanding why the problem occurred and resulted in a design change; why the problem was not detected when it occurred; and how the design process can be improved so that similar problems can be eliminated or reduced in the future.

TUCKMAN'S MODEL OF TEAM DEVELOPMENT

Model of team development and behavior advanced by Dr. Bruce Tuckman in 1965 to which he later added the fifth stage of Adjourning in the 1970s. The model explains that as the team matures through these stages, the leadership style of the project manager will, and indeed must, also change. Beginning with a directing style, moving through coaching, then participating, and finishing the project delegating and almost detached. At this point the team may produce a successor leader and the previous leader can move on to develop a new team.

The progression is—

- Forming
- Storming
- Norming
- Performing
- Adjourning

Characteristics of each phase include—

- Stage 1: Forming – Team is highly dependent on the leader for direction and guidance. Roles and responsibilities of team members are unclear and confused. Team members test tolerance of the leader and the system, and often ignore processes.

• Stage 2: Storming – Conflict among team members as each attempts to establish primacy within the group. Frequent challenges to the team leader regarding purpose and direction of project. Clarity of purpose increases but plenty of uncertainties persist. Power struggles emerge and cliques and factions form. Team leader often must compromise to keep project moving forward.

• Stage 3: Norming – Team members accept individual roles and recognize authority of the leader. Agreement is often resolved through consensus, especially with respect to key decisions. Strong sense of commitment and unity is evident in team members. Team leader adopts a facilitative role to build consensus and direction and shares leadership in certain aspects of the project.

• Stage 4: Performing – Team shares a common vision, is self-directing to a large extent, and has a high degree of autonomy with respect to decision making. Although disagreements occur, they are resolved within the team with little help from the team leader. Although the team requires delegated tasks and projects from the leader, it does not need to be led, assisted, or instructed in its endeavors. Team leader delegates and oversees progress rather than actively managing the group.

• Stage 5: Adjourning – *Also called* mourning, this describes the breakup of the team as members move on to other projects. Some people will feel insecure during the breakup. Accordingly, the team leader/project manager should ensure that team members will be placed on other teams and projects that will contribute to their professional development.

TURNOVER

(1) Word used in the United States and other countries that means the ratio of the number of workers that must be replaced in a given time period to the average number of workers.

(2) Word used in the United Kingdom and other countries that means revenue earned per year.

TURNOVER RATE

In the U.S. as used by the Bureau of Labor Statistics, the number of total separations during the month divided by the number of employees who worked during or received pay for the pay period that includes the 12th of the month (monthly turnover); the number of total separations for the year divided by average monthly employment for the year (annual turnover).

TWELVE RULES OF EXTREME PROGRAMMING

• The Planning Game: At the start of each iteration, customers, managers, and developers meet to flesh out, estimate, and prioritize requirements for the next release. The requirements are called user stories and are captured on story cards in a language understandable by all parties.

• Small Releases: An initial version of the system is put into production after the first few iterations. Subsequently, working versions are put into production anywhere from every few days to every few weeks.

• Metaphor: Customers, managers, and developers construct a metaphor, or set of metaphors, upon which to model the system.

• Simple Design: Developers are urged to keep design as simple as possible—say everything once and only once.

• Tests: Developers work test-first; that is, they write acceptance tests for their code before they write the code itself. Customers write functional tests for each iteration, and at the end of each iteration all tests should run satisfactorily.

• Refactoring: As developers work, the design should be evolved to keep it as simple as possible.

• Pair Programming: Two developers sitting at the same machine write all code.

• Continuous Integration: Developers integrate new code into the system as often as possible. All functional tests must still pass after integration or the new code is discarded.

- Collective Ownership: The code is owned by all developers, and they may make changes anywhere in the code at any time they feel necessary.

- On-site Customer: A customer works with the development team at all times to answer questions, perform acceptance tests, and ensure that development is progressing as expected.

- 40-hour Weeks: Requirements should be selected for each iteration so that developers do not need to put in overtime.

- Coding Standard: Code should be written in the same way by all developers, using the same styles and formats to ensure clear communication and rapid code sharing.

See also extreme programming.

TYPE I ERROR

Type of statistical error also known as an "error of the first kind", an "α error," or a "false positive." In statistical terms, it means the error of rejecting a null hypothesis when it actually is true. A false positive normally means that a test claims something to be positive when that is not the case. For example, a pregnancy test with a positive result, indicating that the person taking the test is pregnant, has produced a false positive if the person is not pregnant. The null hypothesis in this instance is that the person is not pregnant. The test shows the person to be pregnant, but in reality that is not the case. Thus, we have a type I error. *See also* type II error *and* null hypothesis.

TYPE II ERROR

Type of statistical error also known as an "error of the second kind," a β error, or a "false negative." The error of failing to reject a null hypothesis when the alternative hypothesis is the true state of nature. For example, a pregnancy test with a negative result, indicating that the person taking the test is not pregnant, has produced a false negative in the case where the person is, in fact, pregnant. The null hypothesis in this instance is that the person is not pregnant. The test shows the person not to be pregnant, but in reality the person is pregnant. *See also* type I error *and* null hypothesis.

U

UCC

See uniform commercial code.

UML

See Unified Modeling Language.

UNACCEPTABLE RISK

Exposure to risks that are significant enough to jeopardize an organization's strategy, endanger human lives, or represent a significant financial exposure such that avoidance or mitigation is imperative.

UNALLOWABLE COST

Cost incurred by a contractor that is not chargeable to the project on which the contractor is working.

UNAVOIDABLE DELAY

In contracting, a delay that is beyond the control of the contractor.

UNBILLED REVENUE

Recognized revenue that has not been billed to the purchaser(s).

UNCERTAINTY

(1) Situation in which only part of the information needed for decision making is available.

(2) Lack of knowledge of future events.

UNCERTAINTY ALLOWANCE

Allocation of time or money to cover the potential occurrence of risk events. *See also* contingency reserve *and* management reserve.

UNCOMPENSATED OVERTIME

In the U.S., the hours worked without additional compensation in excess of an average of 40 hours per week by direct charge employees who are exempt from the Fair Labor Standards Act. Compensated personal absences such as holidays, vacations, and sick leave must be included in the normal work week for purposes of computing uncompensated overtime hours.

UNDERBUDGETED

Budgeted line item where the budgeted amount is not sufficient to cover the actual amount needed.

UNDERMINING

(1) Negotiation tactic that attempts to put the other party on the defensive using threats, insults, or ultimatums. Although this tactic often backfires because most people resent verbal attacks, it sometimes can be effective when used against an easily intimidated negotiator.

(2) Activity by an individual designed to subvert the objectives of the project.

UNDISTRIBUTED BUDGET

Budget applicable to contract effort that has not been identified to CWBS elements at or below the lowest level of reporting.

UNIDENTIFIED CASH RECEIPTS

Temporary holding account for funds that have been received but the account receivable of which has not yet been identified.

UNIFIED MODELING LANGUAGE (UML)

Modeling language, governed by the Object Management Group, that helps to specify, visualize, and document models of software systems, including their structure and design. Emphasizes the development of modular, reusable software components as the building blocks of a software system. Makes use of use case diagrams, sequence diagrams, class diagrams, and state chart diagrams.

UNIFORM COMMERCIAL CODE (UCC)

Code of U.S. laws governing various commercial transactions, including the sale of goods, banking transactions, and other matters. Developed to bring uniformity to the laws of the various states. Has been adopted, with some modifications, in all states except Louisiana, the District of Columbia, and the Virgin Islands.

UNINTERRUPTIBLE POWER SUPPLY (UPS)

Device that supplies electrical power during blackouts, brown-outs, spikes, or surges to ensure that information technology equipment receives clean electrical power to avoid the loss of data and computing capability.

UNIT

Smallest logical entity specified in the design of a software system; must be of sufficient detail to allow the code to be developed and tested independent of other units. *See also* module.

UNIT COST CURVE

Plot of the cost of each unit of a given quantity. The total cost for the given quantity, based on the sum of the cost of each individual unit.

UNITED STATES CODE (U.S.C.)

Consolidation and codification of the general and permanent laws of the U.S. arranged according to subject matter under 50 title headings, in alphabetical order to a large degree. Sets out the current status of the laws, as amended.

UNIT IMPROVEMENT CURVE

Improvement curve model based on the assumption that as the total volume of units produced doubles, the cost per unit decreases by some constant percentage.

UNIT OF PRODUCT

Item inspected to determine whether it is defective or nondefective, or to count the number of defects. May be a single article, a pair, a set, a length, an area, an operation, a volume, a component of an end product, or the end product itself. May or may not be the same as the unit of purchase, supply, production, or shipment.

UNIT PRICE CONTRACT

Contract in which the contractor is paid per unit of service, and the total contract value is a function of the quantities needed to complete the work.

UNIT TESTING

Physical testing of the code module or object that is performed by the developer or programmer. Typically performed immediately after the code is developed.

UNKNOWN UNKNOWNS

Risks that are not foreseen and therefore have not been planned for during the risk management process. Called unk-unks.

UNLIMITED RIGHTS

(1) The right to do what one pleases with another's intellectual property.

(2) In U.S. federal procurement, the rights of the government to use, disclose, reproduce, prepare derivative works, distribute copies to the public, and perform publicly and display publicly, in any manner and for any purpose, and to have or permit others to do so.

UNMANAGEABLE RISK

Risk for which it is impossible to reduce the likelihood of occurrence or amount at stake.

UNPRICED CHANGES

Authorized changes to a contract, the cost of which is negotiated during execution.

UNSOLICITED PROPOSAL

Written proposal submitted on the initiative of the prospective contractor, for the purpose of obtaining a contract, that is not in response to a formal or informal request.

UNWARRANTED CONFLICT

Type of conflict that arises when there is a clash of relating styles of the people involved. Frequently there already may be agreement between parties about the goal, but one person's way of achieving the goal threatens the other person's sense of self-worth. This also can occur when someone either overdoes a strength or is perceived as having overdone a strength.

UPDATE

Revision reflecting the most current information on the project.

UPPER CONTROL LIMIT

Three standard deviations above the mean.

UPS

See uninterruptible power supply.

U.S.C.

See United States Code.

USE CASE

Something a user or system needs to achieve through interaction with a system. Use cases must provide real business value to one or more users of the system.

USE CASE DIAGRAM

Diagram, part of the UML standard, used to describe the interaction between users (actors) and a system (use case). The use case diagram represents the availability of functionality under normal circumstances, without exceptions or errors in the function.

USE CASE SCENARIO

Text that flows out of a use case diagram, providing a detailed, step-by-step behavior of the interaction between the system and an actor in the accomplishment of a single business objective.

USEFUL LIFE

Amount of time during which a product will provide a return or value to its owner or user.

USER

Ultimate customer for the product; the people who actually will use it.

USER ACCEPTANCE TEST

Formal testing conducted to determine whether a system satisfies its acceptance criteria and to enable the user to determine whether to accept the system. *See also* acceptance testing.

USER FRIENDLINESS

See user friendly.

USER FRIENDLY

Primarily a term used in information technology, it refers to a machine (hardware) or program (software) that is compatible with a person's ability to operate it successfully and easily.

USER INTERFACE

Software, input/output devices, screens, procedures, and dialogue between the user of the system (people) and the system, or system component, itself.

USER PROFILING

Process of identifying the broad categories of users for the business solution, in order to validate and clarify the scope of the solution.

USER REQUIREMENTS

Specific product, service, or other business need that the project is intended to meet.

USER SATISFACTION REVIEW

Formal survey used to gather the data needed to analyze current user satisfaction with the performance capabilities of an existing system or application; administered annually or as needed.

UTILITY

State or quality of being useful functionally or operationally. Designed for or possessing a number of useful or practical purposes, rather than a single, specialized one.

UTILITY THEORY

Theoretical approach to measuring a person's willingness to take a risk in light of the different levels of reward, whether that reward be for the person taking the risk or for other potential beneficiaries.

V

VAC

See variance at completion.

VAK LEARNING STYLES

Arising from the work of psychologists and early learning specialists such as Fernald, Keller, Orton, Gillingham, Stillman and Montessori, VAK (visual-auditory-kinesthetic) has come into its own as a result of the interest shown by proponents of accelerated learning because its principles and benefits extend far beyond its early applications to all types of learning and development. VAK provides a means for understanding one's own as well as others' learning styles. The learning styles are—

- Visual: seeing and reading
- Auditory: listening and speaking
- Kinesthetic: touching and doing

Research on VAK shows that most people possess a dominant or preferred learning style; however, there is a certain population that has a mixed and evenly balanced blend of the three styles.

VALIDATION

Determining the correctness of the final product, system or system component with respect to the user's requirements. Answers the question, "Am I building the right product?" *See also* verification.

VALUE

What a thing is worth. Usually preceded by the word or words such as "fair" or "fair market," and usually defined in the document in which it is found.

VALUE ADDED

Difference, at each stage of production or provisioning of a service, between the price of a product or service and all materials or activities paid for to produce the product or provide the service.

VALUE-ADDED RESELLER (VAR)

Found in the technology sector, a company that sells other company's products.

VALUE-ADDED TAX (VAT)

Consumption tax where taxes are levied at each step of a manufacturing process where value is added to that product at that point in the manufacturing cycle, as well as at the point where the consumer purchases the end product.

VALUE ANALYSIS

Activity concerned with optimizing cost performance. Systematic use of techniques to identify the required functions of an item, establish values for those functions, and provide the functions at the lowest overall cost without loss of performance.

VALUE CHAIN

Series of interconnected, value-added activities, the sum total of which connect an organization's supply side with its demand side. Identifying and forging mutually beneficial relationships with all the stakeholders in the value chain enhances an organization's ability to produce a product for, or deliver a service to, its customers at the highest level of quality at competitive prices. *See also* supply chain integration.

VALUE ENGINEERING

Approach that examines each element of a product or system to determine whether there is a more effective and less expensive way to achieve the same function.

VALUE RELATING STYLE

Style of relating that a person normally prefers to use, that is, when the person is neither blocked nor coerced but is free to act in a way that makes the person feel good about himself or herself. This is the external expression of the Motivational Value System™. The value relating style is the style we ordinarily associate with a person as their characteristic style of behaving. *See also* Motivational Value System™.

VALUE STREAM MAP (VSM)

Tool used to document the flow of products or services through a system. The VSM differentiates the value-adding activities of a system from the nonvalue-adding ones. Recording the time taken for each activity shows what percentage of valuable time an object or person spends in a system. Any nonvalue-adding time indicates an opportunity for possible improvement within the system.

VAR

See value-added reseller.

VARIABLE COST

Unit of cost that varies with production quantity, such as the material or direct labor required to complete a product or project.

VARIABLE INTEREST RATE

Interest rate that moves up and down based on the changes of an underlying interest rate index, for example, a home mortgage or credit card might have a variable rate that is a certain spread over the prime rate.

VARIABLES SAMPLING

Sampling method in which the result is rated on a continuous scale that measures the degree of conformity.

VARIANCE

Actual or potential deviation from an intended or budgeted amount or plan. Difference between a plan and actual time, cost, or performance.

VARIANCE ANALYSIS

Comparison of actual project results with planned or expected results.

VARIANCE AT COMPLETION (VAC)

In the earned value method, the difference between the BAC and the EAC (VAC = BAC − EAC). A measure of the amount of expected overrun or underrun.

VARIANCE REPORT

Documentation of project performance related to a planned or measured performance parameter.

VARIANCE THRESHOLD

Predetermined cost, schedule, or performance parameter that, when realized, causes an action. For example, the project's cost-schedule variance threshold may be set at 20 percent, so that any variance greater than 20 percent would require an action, such as reporting the event to senior management, holding a project review, or redefining the project's scope.

VARIATION

(1) Change to a contractor's work order under the terms of the contract.

(2) Degree of change or divergence among the members of a set or group.

VAT

See value-added tax.

VC

See venture capitalist.

VENDOR

Distributor of commonly available goods or services when requirements and specifications are well defined.

VENDORS CONFERENCE

See bidders conference.

VENTURE CAPITAL

Capital committed to an unproven venture, usually by a firm specializing in such activities. The start-up money is called "seed money" and carries with it the greatest risk for the firm providing such funding. Once the project moves forward it may require additional financing at additional "rounds" or the "mezzanine level" before the company is finally brought to the market and the venture capital firm can earn its targeted return.

VENTURE CAPITALIST (VC)

Professional, equity-based investor. *See also* venture capital.

VERBAL PROTOCOLS

Requirements-elicitation technique that uses direct observation on processes, activities, and behaviors. The analyst observes the worker while the worker describes each action being taken during the process.

VERIFIABILITY

Measure of the relative effort needed to verify a requirement; a requirement is verifiable only if there is a finite, cost-effective process to determine that the software product or system meets the requirement.

VERIFICATION

Process of determining whether the products of a life cycle phase fulfill the requirements established during the previous phase. Answers the question, "Am I building the product right?" *See also* validation.

VERIFICATION AND VALIDATION PLAN

Formal document that describes the process used to verify and validate the requirements. Created during the planning phase and updated throughout the SDLC.

VERIFICATION, VALIDATION, AND TEST (VV&T)

Process used to prove that a solution meets both specification and user requirements, as evidenced by test and operational results.

VERSION

Commercial or customized software application that reflects major changes in functions. *See also* build.

VERSION DESCRIPTION DOCUMENT

Formal document that describes the exact version of a configuration item and its interim changes. It is used to identify the current version; provides a "packing list" of what is included in the release.

VERTICAL INTEGRATION

Extent to which a firm owns its upstream suppliers and its downstream buyers. Control upstream is referred to as backward integration (towards suppliers of raw material), while control of activities downstream (towards the eventual buyer) is referred to as forward integration. For example, if a company that manufactures tires has a high degree of integration it would own the rubber plantations where the raw material comes from as well as the retail stores where the tires are sold and mounted on vehicles.

VIRTUAL TEAM

Project team that is not physically in the same place and whose interaction occurs primarily through electronic networks such as the Internet, intranets, or other configurations to ensure that a team environment is established and maintained.

VISION

Basic theme or shared value that is important and meaningful to the members of an organization.

VISION BOX

In agile project management, an architectural overview of the product to be produced, ensuring that team members and stakeholders fully understand what it is that will be built.

VOCAL CUES

Nonverbal messages communicated by the sound of the human voice that can provide valuable information, especially during negotiations.

VOICE OF THE CUSTOMER

What the customer wants from the process; in other words, the conditions necessary for customer satisfaction.

VOICE OF THE PROCESS

What the process is currently producing.

VOLATILITY

In requirements management, the degree to which requirements are expected to change throughout the system's development life cycle; opposite of stability.

VSM

See value stream map.

VV&T

See verification, validation, and test.

W

WAIVER

Intentional or voluntary relinquishment of a known right, or conduct that warrants an inference that the right has been relinquished. Under the doctrine of waiver, a party can relinquish rights he or she has under the contract. For example, the right to strict performance is waived if the contractor delivers incomplete or defective products, or delivers after the scheduled date, and the project manager does not object or demand that the defects be corrected.

WALK-THROUGH

(1) Peer review and examination of the requirements, design, or implementation of a project by qualified experts to ensure that the project objectives will be met.

(2) Process used by software developers in which a group of knowledgeable peers mentally steps through the design and logic flow of a program, using test cases to identify errors and inconsistencies.

(3) Rehearsal of an operational procedure by simulating the execution of all its steps except those that are high risk or prohibitively expensive.

WARRANTED CONFLICT

Conflict that arises when the goals or aims of the individuals in question do not agree. This type of conflict is not a function of either party's value relating style, but rather a disagreement over a particular subject.

WARRANTY

Promise or affirmation made by a contractor regarding the nature, usefulness, or condition of the supplies or services to be furnished under the contract, based on one party's assurance to the other that the goods will meet certain standards of quality, including condition, reliability, description, function, or performance. Purpose is to establish a level of quality and to give a source of remedy for loss because of a defect in the quality of goods.

WARRANTY CLAUSE

Specific clause in a contract to provide the buyer with additional time after delivery to correct defects or make some other type of adjustment.

WARRANTY COSTS

Costs arising from fulfillment of any contractual obligation of a contractor to correct defects in the products, replace defective parts, or make refunds in the case of inadequate performance.

WARRANTY OF MERCHANTABILITY

Promise that goods are reasonably fit for the purpose for which they are sold and represented by the seller.

WAR ROOM

Command and control center for a specific project, which also serves as a conference area for the project client, senior management, and other project stakeholders. Has the added benefit of providing unmistakable identity to the project, whose team members may not work in close physical proximity.

WATER BEETLE

Name given to the process of regularly distributing parts to and between kanban locations at a site.

WBS

See work breakdown structure.

WBS DICTIONARY

Collection of work package descriptions that includes planning information such as schedule dates, cost budgets, and staff assignments.

WBS ELEMENT

Any entry at any level in the work breakdown structure.

WBS INDEX

List of work breakdown structure elements.

WC

See working capital.

WEAK MATRIX

Organizational structure in which the balance of power over project resources shifts in the direction of the functional manager, and the project manager has less decision-making influence and authority. *See also* strong matrix.

WEAKNESS

In U.S. federal procurement, a proposal flaw that increases the risk of unsuccessful contract performance. A significant weakness in the proposal is a flaw that appreciably increases the risk of unsuccessful contract performance.

WEIGHTING SYSTEM

Method for quantifying qualitative data to minimize the effect of personal prejudice. Used in project or contractor selection.

WET NOODLE

Tactic used by negotiators to keep from getting pinned down on any position by giving qualified or noncommittal responses. Users of this tactic avoid making firm commitments or concessions whenever possible.

WHAT-IF ANALYSIS

Process of evaluating alternative strategies by changing certain variables and assumptions to predict the outcome of such strategies.

WHITE BOX TESTING

(1) Software engineering verification technique used to determine if the software code works as expected.

(2) Testing technique that takes into account the internal mechanism of a system or component. *See also* black box testing.

WHITE PAPER

Narrative exposition on any topic advancing the thoughts and opinions of the author, the purpose of which may be to submit to scrutiny the author's idea by the readership, criticize a course of action proposed by the author's company or government, or advance a particular position. Often, but not necessarily, written and distributed anonymously.

WHOLE NINE YARDS, THE

All of it; the full measure.

WHOLESALE PRICE INDEX (WPI)

Composite index of wholesale prices of a representative group of commodities.

WINDFALL

Positive risk event, known or unknown, that has materialized.

WIN-LOSE

Outcome of conflict resolution that typically makes use of the power available to each party and treats conflict as a zero-sum game.

WIN-WIN

Outcome of conflict resolution that results in both parties being better off. Focuses on the objectives of both parties and the ways to meet those objectives while resolving the issue(s) at hand.

WITHDRAWING

See conflict resolution.

WITHHOLDING

Nonpayment of contract amounts by the buyer because the contractor failed to carry out some obligation under the contract.

WOMB-TO-TOMB

See cradle-to-grave.

WORK ACCEPTANCE

Conducting, documenting, and verification of work according to acceptance criteria provided in the technical specifications and contract documents.

WORKAROUND

Unplanned response to a negative risk event. Distinguished from contingency plan because it is not planned in advance of the risk event's occurrence.

WORK AUTHORIZATION

Permission for specific work to be performed during a specific period; generally used in cases where work is to be performed in segments because of technical or funding limitations. *Also called* work release.

WORK AUTHORIZATION SYSTEM

Formal procedure for sanctioning project work to ensure that it is done at the right time and in the proper sequence.

WORK BREAKDOWN STRUCTURE (WBS)

Hierarchically structured grouping of project elements that organizes and defines the total scope of the project. Each descending level is an increasingly detailed definition of a project component. Project components may be products (a product-oriented WBS) or tasks (a task-oriented WBS). *See also* contract work breakdown structure *and* program work breakdown structure.

WORK CYCLE

Pattern of motions and/or processes that is repeated with negligible variation each time an operation is performed.

WORK ELEMENT

See task.

WORKING CALENDAR

(1) Calendar dates that cover all project activities, from start to finish.

(2) Calendar that reflects project work and nonwork dates (for example, holidays or planned shutdowns) and is used as a basis for network and schedule calculations in project management software.

WORKING CAPITAL (WC)

Current assets minus current liabilities; also called net current assets or current capital. Reflects the ability to finance current operations.

WORKING TIME

Period of time in which actual work on a project can be, and should be, completed. Working time will vary from project to project depending on its unique requirements. For example, replacing a large private branch exchange computer used for telecommunications in an office building is commonly done on weekend days when most people are not in the office.

WORK ITEM

See task.

WORKLOAD

Sum total of work that a person, group, or organization is responsible for completing within a given time period. May be expressed qualitatively, which often is a perception of the load based on the ability of a specific person to do it, or quantitatively, which usually is based on historical data and experience.

WORK MEASUREMENT

Method to determine how long it should take an employee to perform the work and to identify opportunities for improvement.

WORK PACKAGE

Deliverable at the lowest level of the WBS. May be divided into activities and used to identify and control work flows in the organization.

WORK PACKAGE BUDGET

Resources that are formally assigned by the responsible performing organization to accomplish a work package, expressed in monetary units, hours, standards, or other definitive units.

WORK PATTERN

Complete set of life cycle phases, activities, deliverables, and reviews required to develop or maintain a software product or system; a formal approach to systems development.

WORK PERFORMED

Includes completed work packages and the completed portion of work packages begun but not yet completed.

WORK RELEASE

See work authorization.

WORK RESULTS

Outcome of activities performed to accomplish the project.

WORK SAMPLING STUDY

Statistical sampling technique employed to determine the proportion of delays or other classifications of activity present in the total work cycle.

WORK STATEMENT

See statement of work.

WORK UNIT

Calendar time unit when work may be performed on an activity.

WORKWEEK

Normal number of days or hours designated as the period of time in which project work will be conducted. Many organizations use eight hours a day, five days a week as a standard workweek. However, this is adjusted based on workplace rules and regulations, culture, working conditions, site location, and any other variable that necessitates a change to the norm. Project managers must base their cost and schedule estimates on the workweek applicable to their project.

WORLD TRADE ORGANIZATION (WTO)

International trade body formed by the agreement of member nations. The WTO is an evolution of the General Agreement on Tariffs and Trade (GATT) process designed to resolve trade disputes and eliminate or lower trade barriers.

WORST-CASE SCENARIO

(1) Project budget/cost baseline plus the sum of all negative impacts at 100 percent, or project profit baseline minus the sum of all negative impacts at 100 percent—not the expected value of all the negative impacts but all the negative impacts themselves.

(2) Worst possible outcome given the circumstances.

WORTH

Measure of value received for the resources expended.

WORTH WHAT PAID FOR (WWPF)

In quality management, a quantitative evaluation conducted by a customer who asks and answers the question, "Is the price I paid for the product or service worth the product or service I bought?"

WPI

See wholesale price index.

WRITE-DOWN

Reduction in the book value of an asset.

WRITE-OFF

Action taken to decrease the value of an item; for example, a tax write-off decreases tax liability, or a vehicle involved in an accident can be declared a write-off if the cost to repair it exceeds the value of the vehicle.

WTO

See World Trade Organization.

WWPF

See worth what paid for.

X

XP

See extreme programming.

Y

YAGNI

Acronym meaning "You Aren't Going to Need It" is a dictate of extreme programming that says architectural features that do not support the current version of the software the team is developing should be eliminated.

YEAR TO DATE (YTD)

Period that begins on January 1st of the current year or the fiscal year, up until today's date.

YIELD

Annual return on an investment, expressed as a percentage.

YTD

See year to date.

Z

ZD

See zero defect.

ZERO-BASED BUDGET

Form of budgeting where the costs and expenses of the prior year are not taken into consideration when establishing future expense or budgetary levels. Each category of expense starts from zero and the budget is built from that point and justified to management; thus "zero base."

ZERO DEFECT (ZD)

Quality standard, first articulated by Philip Crosby, that asserts that nothing less than 100 percent quality should be the goal of an organization.

ZERO–ONE-HUNDRED APPROACH

Method used to determine earned value as it applies to work packages that start and are expected to be completed within a month. No value is earned when the activity starts, but when it is completed, 100 percent of the value is earned.

ZERO-SUM GAME

Game in which the sum of the amounts won and lost by all parties is zero. Whatever is gained in such a game is always achieved at the expense of the other party. Many view implementing project management in an organization as a zero-sum game whereby project managers win power and authority at the expense of functional or line managers.

ZERO VARIANCE

Situation in which the planned date or cost is equal to the actual date or cost of an activity or project. This is a rare event in most projects.

Z TIME

See Greenwich Mean Time.

ZULU

See Greenwich Mean Time.

References

Ambler, Scott W. "Initiating an Agile Project." Dr. Dobb's Journal (June 1, 2006).

Cohen, David, Sunny Baker, Kim Baker, and G. Michael Campbell. *The Complete Idiot's Guide to Project Management.* 4th ed. Indianapolis, Ind.: Alpha, 2007.

Bamford, Robert, and William J. Deibler. *ISO 9001:2000 for Software and Systems Providers.* Boca Raton, Fla.: CRC Press, 2004.

Bartlett, John. *Managing Programmes of Business Change.* 3d ed. London: Intype London Ltd., 2002.

Bicheno, John, and Philip Catherwood. *Six Sigma and the Quality Toolbox.* Buckingham, United Kingdom: PICSIE Books, 2005.

Cockburn, Alistair. *Agile Software Development: The Cooperative Game.* 2d ed. New York: Addison-Wesley, 2006.

Cohen, Dennis J., and Robert J. Graham. *The Project Manager's MBA: How to Translate Project Decisions Into Business Success.* San Francisco: Jossey-Bass, 2001.

Englund, Randall L., and Alfonso Bucero. *Project Sponsorship: Achieving Management Commitment for Project Success.* San Francisco: Jossey-Bass, 2006.

Fagan, M.E. "Design and Code Inspections to Reduce Errors in Program Development." IBM Systems Journal 15, 3 (1976): 182–211.

Federal Acquisition Institute. *Glossary of Acquisition Terms.* Washington, D.C.: 1998.

Fleming, Quentin W., and Joel M. Koppelman. *Earned Value Project Management.* 3d ed. Newtown Square, Pa.: Project Management Institute, 2006.

Flannes, Steven W., and Ginger Levin. *Essential People Skills for Project Managers.* Vienna, Va.: Management Concepts, 2005.

Forsberg, Kevin, Hal Mooz, and Howard Cotterman. *Visualizing Project Management: Models and Frameworks for Mastering Complex Systems.* Hoboken, N.J.: John Wiley & Sons, 2005.

Garrett, Gregory A., and Rene G. Rendon. *U.S. Military Program Management: Lessons Learned and Best Practices.* Vienna, Va.: Management Concepts, 2006.

Highsmith, Jim. *Agile Project Management: Creating Innovative Products.* Boston: Addison-Wesley, 2004.

Hill, Gerard M. *The Complete Project Management Office Handbook.* 2d ed. New York: Auerbach Publications, 2007.

Jonasson, Hans. *Determining Project Requirements.* Boca Raton, Fla.: Auerbach Publications, 2007.

Kirkpatrick, Donald L. *Evaluating Training Programs: The Four Levels.* 3d ed. San Francisco: Berret-Koehler Publishers, Inc., 2006.

Lindvall, Mikael, David Cohen, and Patricia Costa. *Agile Software Development.* Rome, NY: Data and Analysis Center for Software, 2003.

Mersino, Anthony. *Emotional Intelligence for Project Managers: The People Skills You Need to Achieve Outstanding Results.* New York: AMACOM, 2007.

Project Management Institute. *Practice Standard for Earned Value Management.* Newtown Square, Pa.: Project Management Institute, 2005.

Project Management Institute. *Program Management Professional (PgMP) Examination Specification.* Newtown Square, Pa.: Project Management Institute, 2007.

Project Management Institute. *The Project Management Body of Knowledge.* Newtown Square, Pa.: Project Management Institute, 2004.

Project Management Institute. *The Standard for Portfolio Management.* Newtown Square, Pa.: Project Management Institute, 2006.

Project Management Institute. *The Standard for Program Management.* Newtown Square, Pa.: Project Management Institute, 2006.

Project Management Institute. *Practice Standard for Work Breakdown Structures.* 2d ed. Newtown Square, Pa.: Project Management Institute, 2006.

Pritchard, Carl. *The Project Management Communications Toolkit.* Norwood, Mass.: Artech House, Inc., 2004.

_____. *Risk Management: Concepts and Guidance.* 3d ed. Arlington, Va.: ESI International, 2005.

Rad, Parviz F., and Ginger Levin. *Project Portfolio Management: Tools and Techniques.* New York: IIL Publishing, 2007.

Rose, Kenneth H. *Project Quality Management: Why, What, and How.* Boca Raton, Fla.: J. Ross Publishing, Inc., 2005.

Takeuchi, Hirotaka, and Ikujiro Nonaka. "The New New Product Development Game." Harvard Business Review (January-February 1986).

U.S. Air Force Software Technology Support Center. *Software Project Management Technology Report,* Rev. 4.6, Apr 9, 2000.

U.S. Department of Defense. *Department of Defense Handbook: Work Breakdown Structure,* MIL-HDBK-881, July 30, 2005.

U.S. Department of Defense, Defense Systems Management College. *Scheduling Guide for Program Managers.* Fort Belvoir, Va.: Defense Systems Management College Press, October 2001.

U.S. Department of Justice. *The Department of Justice Systems Development Life Cycle Guidance Document.* Washington, D.C.: Department of Justice, Information Resources Management, January 2003.

U.S. Department of Labor Bureau of Labor Statistics online glossary at http://www.bls.gov/bls/glossary.htm.

U.S. Office of Personnel Management. *Alternative Dispute Resolution: A Resource Guide*. Washington, D.C.: U.S. Office of Personnel Management. Online version at http://www.opm.gov/er/adrguide_2002/index.asp.

Vargas, Ricardo Vania. *Practical Guide to Project Planning*. Boca Raton, Fla.: Auerbach Publishing, 2007.

Verzuh, Eric. *The Fast Forward MBA in Project Management*. 3d ed. Hoboken, N.J.: John Wiley & Sons, 2008.

Wideman, R. Max. *A Management Framework for Project, Program and Portfolio Integration*. Victoria, BC, Canada: Trafford Publishing, 2006.

Williams, David, and Tim Parr. *Enterprise Programme Management: Delivering Value*. Basingstoke, United Kingdom: Palgrave Macmillan, 2006.

Wood, Jane, and Denise Silver. *Joint Application Design*. New York: John Wiley & Sons, 1989.

A Note to Our Readers

If you discover that we have missed a term that you think should be included in the next edition, please take a moment to let us know. We will be much indebted to you for your effort in helping us keep this glossary current, accurate, and complete.

Send us the term or phrase—and your interpretation of it—and we will present it to our Technical Advisory Board for inclusion in the fourth edition. Note that ESI will edit all submissions for clarity and style and retain the copyright on the final printed definitions.

Send your entries or other comments to—

Vice President for Product Development
ESI International
901 N. Glebe Road, Suite 200
Arlington, VA 22203
Phone: 1-888-ESI-8884
Fax: 1-703-558-3001

ESI Study Tools and Publications

Risk Management: Concepts and Guidance.
Third edition. 2005. 416 pages. $54.95.
Carl L. Pritchard, PMP

Gain a higher-level perspective on risk management. This third edition contains 35 tool-packed chapters focusing on a systematic approach to risk management. It highlights specific techniques to enhance organizational risk identification, assessment, and management.

PMP® Exam: Practice Test and Study Guide. **Seventh edition. 2006. 408 pages. $39.95.**
J. LeRoy Ward, PMP, PgMP

This rigorous study guide provides 40 multiple-choice questions in each of the nine knowledge areas and the professional and social responsibility domain plus a composite 200-question practice test intended to simulate the PMP® certification exam. All answers are fully referenced and keyed to the five project management process groups. Also included is a bibliography and a study matrix to help you to focus on specific areas.

The Portable PMP® Exam Prep: Conversations on Passing the PMP® Exam. Three volumes, nine CDs. Third edition. $99.95.
Carl L. Pritchard, PMP and J. LeRoy Ward, PMP, PgMP

This three-volume set of nine CDs addresses the nine areas of the project management body of knowledge and includes a bonus session on professional responsibility. Ward and Pritchard's informative, engaging style is easy to listen to, plus you can take the CDs anywhere you go. In addition, there are sessions on preparing for the current exam and test-taking tips that ESI students have found indispensable.

PgMP℠ Exam: Practice Test and Study Guide. 2008. 276 pages. $44.95.
J. LeRoy Ward, PMP, PgMP

With the help of this essential book and CD-ROM, you will be ready to pass your Program Management Professional (PgMP℠) exam. The book includes study hints, a list of major topics covered on the exam, 20 multiple-choice practice questions for each domain, a comprehensive answer key, and a bibliographic reference for further study. Two challenging, 170-question practice tests, also delivered via CD-ROM to provide a real simulation of the PMI® exam, will give you an insider's look at the questions, phrases, terminology, and sentence construction that you'll encounter on the real exam. This essential study tool was created with one goal in mind: helping you to pass your exam and become PgMP℠ certified.

PMP® Exam Challenge! Fourth edition. 2005. 600 pages. $44.95.
J. LeRoy Ward, PMP, PgMP and Ginger Levin, D.P.A., PMP, PgMP

This easy-to-use, flashcard-format book lets you quiz yourself on all nine of the project management knowledge areas, as well as the professional and social responsibility domain. Each of the 600 questions includes references to the five project management process groups on the PMP® certification exam.

The Project Management Drill Book: A Self-Study Guide. 2003. 197 pages. $54.95.
Carl L. Pritchard, PMP

Gear up for the PMP® certification exam! Learn project management one drill at a time. ESI's *Project Management Drill Book* provides a provocative way to challenge you with hundreds of project management practice drills. From earned value to expected value, from precedence diagrams to decision trees, and from the WBS to professional responsibility, this data-packed volume builds your understanding of the language and your confidence in the practice of project management. Multiple-choice, fill-in-the-blank, and true-or-false drills deepen your understanding of available project management tools and how to use them effectively.

PMP® Exam Online Practice Test. $39.95.

This 200-question, Web-based practice test precisely follows the PMI® PMP® exam blueprint. You will answer the same number of questions in each of the *PMBOK® Guide* process areas on the actual exam, including the professional responsibility domain. And, the questions are just like the ones that you will see on the real exam. After logging in, you are given exactly four hours to take the exam, and the results are automatically scored, telling you the number of right and wrong answers in each of the process areas tested. Don't use the real exam as your first "practice" test: Rather, reduce your anxiety and let ESI help you succeed. Together with our other proven PMP® exam study tools, this Web-based practice test will greatly increase your chances of passing the PMP® exam.

CAPM® Exam Online Practice Test. $39.95.

This 150-question, Web-based practice test precisely follows the PMI® CAPM® exam blueprint. You will answer the same number of questions in each of the *PMBOK® Guide* process areas as on the actual exam, including the professional responsibility domain. After logging in, you are given exactly three hours to take the exam, and the results are automatically scored, telling you the number of right and wrong answers in each of the process areas tested. Reduce your anxiety and let ESI help you to succeed. This Web-based practice test will greatly increase your chances of passing the CAPM® exam the first time.

Project Management Tools CD, Version 4.3. $125—individual license*.

This practical CD contains more than 100 tools and templates that cover all aspects of project management. These tools and templates will assist the project manager and the team through all the project processes. Each tool was developed by ESI for use in the field.

*For organization-wide use, please contact us at totalsolutions@esi-intl.com.

The Complete Project Management Office Handbook.
Second edition. 2007. 752 pages. $59.99.
Gerard M. Hill, PMP

This handbook offers a structured approach for developing critical project management capabilities through project management office (PMO) functionality. It describes 20 PMO functions that are crucial to defining and developing an effective approach to project oversight, control, and support.

PMessentials: An Online Reference Tool®

PMessentials® provides online, just-in-time access to the information project managers need to solve problems and successfully manage their projects. It is designed to support your organization's ESI training and increase the productivity of your project managers.

With PMessentials®, users can search from a concise, targeted database of hundreds of ESI online learning materials. Users can customize their search by four categories:

1. Key Word or Phrase
2. *PMBOK® Guide* Knowledge Areas
3. ESI Core Project Management Course Content
4. ESI Tools

The comprehensive repository contains a variety of valuable resources, including—

- Expert tips
- Simulated web sites
- Printable ESI tools
- Comprehensive project management glossary of terms
- And much more

For more about PMessentials®, including licensing information, call **(877) 766-3337** or **+1 (703) 558-4445** or e-mail **totalsolutions@esi-intl.com**.

Precedence Diagramming: Successful Scheduling in a Team Environment. **Second edition. 2002. 62 pages. $25.**
Carl Pritchard, PMP

The biggest challenge in project management is bringing order to the sheer volume of competing priorities. By using precedence diagrams, project managers can clearly identify the sequence and interdependence of critical activities, clarify work processes, and solidify team member roles and buy-in.

This concise overview teaches you how to construct and interpret precedence diagrams—the most common model used in software programs—and apply them to strengthen team commitment and project success.

Individual and Organizational Assessments

Whether you're focusing on individual capabilities, or measuring the knowledge and skills of your organization as a whole, ESI has assessment services to help you identify strengths and areas that need improvement.

Individual Assessments

By assessing individual competencies for each employee, you can more effectively target your training efforts, set pre- and post-course benchmarks to measure success, and determine areas in which training reinforcement is necessary.

Our appraisal products provide a snapshot of your team's grasp of best-in-class methods and techniques. This ensures that your employees are receiving the training they need and that you're getting the most from your training dollars.

ESI can also help you assess employee competency beyond technical knowledge. Our 360-degree evaluation measures project managers' hard and soft skills and provides detailed reports of their effectiveness in these key categories:

- Organizational and industry acumen
- Process expertise
- Customer focus
- Team leadership, communications, and effectiveness

Organizational Assessments

ESI's Organizational Maturity Assessments help assess the maturity and capability of your organization and provide recommendations on how to improve efficiency and effectiveness. By assessing organizational performance, you can ensure that you have the systems and processes in place to efficiently complete your projects on time and on budget while also identifying obstacles in the way of success.

With ESI's data-driven assessment models, you can—

- Analyze your project managers' performance within your organization

- Baseline project management capability

- Identify organizational executive-level involvement

- Develop short- and long-term improvement strategies

In addition to conducting organizational maturity assessments, ESI has a proven track record in conducting Level 3 Training Assessments, which can help you gain insight into how much of your employees' new knowledge is being applied back on the job after their training is complete. You'll be able to evaluate the value of your investment and identify the key catalysts for success and the key obstacles that often lead to below-par results.

For more information about ESI's individual and organizational assessments, call **(877) 766-3337** or **+1 (703) 558-4445** or e-mail **totalsolutions@esi-intl.com**.